租船运输实务与法律

PRACTICE & LAW OF CHARTERING SHIPPING

第三版
THIRD EDITION

主编 / 吴书爱 苏同江

大连海事大学出版社

DALIAN MARITIME UNIVERSITY PRESS

图书在版编目(CIP)数据

租船运输实务与法律：英文、汉文 / 吴书爱，苏同
江主编 . — 3 版 . — 大连 ： 大连海事大学出版社，
2025.5 — ISBN 978-7-5632-4690-8

Ⅰ.U695.2；D997.1

中国国家版本馆CIP数据核字第2025HK0875号

大连海事大学出版社出版

地址：大连市黄浦路523号 邮编：116026 电话：0411-84729665(营销部) 84729480(总编室)

http://press.dlmu.edu.cn　E-mail:dmupress@dlmu.edu.cn

大连天骄彩色印刷有限公司印装　　　　　　　大连海事大学出版社发行

2010年5月第1版　　2025年5月第3版　　　2025年5月第1次印刷

幅面尺寸：184 mm×260 mm　　　　　　　　印张：16.75

字数：366千　　　　　　　　　　　　　　　印数：1~1000册

出版人：余锡荣

责任编辑：杨玮璐　　　　　　　　　　　　责任校对：高　颖

封面设计：解瑶瑶　　　　　　　　　　　　版式设计：解瑶瑶

ISBN 978-7-5632-4690-8　　　定价：47.00元

内容摘要

  本书旨在适应我国高等职业教育的教学需要，提高学生英文水平，是为国际航运管理专业和现代物流管理专业学生学习"租船运输业务"课程而编写的一本双语教学专业教材。全书较系统、全面地论述了租船运输基本业务和法律知识，主要内容包括租船运输概述、租船程序和实务、航次租船合同和定期租船合同。为方便读者掌握所学内容，全书以中英对照方式排版。

第三版前言

本教材自2010年首次出版、2015年再版以来，得到了广大读者的支持与厚爱。10年过去了，有关租船运输的法律法规也发生了较大的变化。《中华人民共和国民法典》于2021年1月1日起施行，国际商会（ICC）新公布的2020版《国际贸易术语解释通则》自2020年1月1日起生效，特别是波罗的海国际航运公会（BIMCO）法律文件委员会审议通过了2022年版《统一杂货租船合同》（GENCON 2022），完成了该合同自1922年首次发布后的第3次修订。为此，编者针对国内外法律法规的变化对教材的内容进行了必要的修改和补充。

在体系安排上，本教材做了一定程度的变更，根据工作场景和工作任务设置了4个教学模块，下设教学单元，较好地进行了理论知识和实践技能的结合。除此之外，本教材在内容编写中根据《中华人民共和国民法典》融入了"契约精神"部分内容，较好地完成了思政元素和专业课程的融合。

本教材在修订过程中注重工学结合，邀请山东海运散货运输有限公司李爱新女士参与编写，为本书提供了丰富的教学案例；BIMCO亚太区总经理庄炜先生亦对本书的编写提供了支持，在此一并表示感谢！

由于编者水平有限，书中难免有错误和不足之处，敬请专家与读者批评指正，提出宝贵意见。

编　者

2025年3月

第二版前言

本书是为贯彻落实《教育部关于"十二五"职业教育教材建设的若干意见》精神，提高教材质量，打造精品教材，服务现代职业教育体系建设，开发具有现代国际航运服务业特色的教材，更加有利于培养学生获取和应用知识的能力，培养学生的创新能力，为国际航运业务管理专业以及相关专业学习租船运输理论与实务需要而编写的一本专业性双语教材。

本教材自2010年首次出版发行以来，得到了广大读者的支持和厚爱，在此表示衷心的感谢和敬意。4年过去了，有关租船运输的法律和实务也发生了变化，特别是波罗的海国际航运公会（BIMCO）、国际海事委员会（CMI）、船舶经纪人和代理人协会联合会（FONASBA）、国际干货船船东协会（INTERCARGO）最新推出的《2013租船合同装卸时间定义》，用清晰且标准的术语对装卸时间做出了与时下背景相匹配的定义，给定分止争提供了依据。原教材的部分内容明显落伍，不适应当前教学的需要。为此，编者对教材的内容进行了必要的修改和补充。

在体系安排上，本教材分为四大部分，即租船运输和法律基本知识、租船运输程序和实务、航次租船合同、定期租船合同。全书较系统、全面地论述了租船运输业务、租船合同条款和相关的法律规定、实务操作以及租船案例。在框架结构方面，各章节结构统一，每一章包括：（1）学习目标；（2）学习内容；（3）学习要点；（4）技能要求；（5）学习导图；（6）知识内容；（7）案例实例；（8）目标检测。

本教材适用于全国高等职业院校国际航运业务管理专业教学，可作为相关专业开设"租船运输实务与法律"课程的教学用书。同时，本教材也可以作为航运企业、航运经纪、国际货代、外贸业务、物流管理等企业对员工开展培训的培训教材和参考资料。

本教材由青岛远洋船员职业学院物流与航运管理系苏同汀教授担任主编，高伟老师担任副主编，上海海事大学博士生导师王学锋教授担任主审。参加本书编写工作的有山东国际海运公司李向阳经理，青岛远洋船员职业学院物流与航运管理系王瑞亮、于晓丹、吴书爱、杨晓娜和李莉莉等老师。

由于编者水平有限，书中难免会出现错误和不足之处，敬请专家与读者批评指正，提出宝贵意见。

作　者
2014年12月

第一版前言

　　本书介绍航运租船业务，是为拥有基础航运知识并打算进一步了解和掌握更加广阔的航运业务知识的学生而编写的。直接和简洁是作者的主要目标。作为一本基础教材，本书的某些部分似乎有点肤浅，因为作者没有打算做详细深入的研究。目的是希望通过一种较容易理解的方式便于主修本门课程的学生学习。

　　就分析的目的而言，第一章讲述租船运输概述;第二章为租船的程序和实务;航次租船和定期租船两个主要部分分别为第三章、第四章。每章附有作业供学生练习并根据书中内容进行核对，以把握他们所学到的知识。为了方便学生易于理解英文教材内容，作者在每一章后面均附上中文翻译，希望这将有助于学生和读者学习。

　　本书讲述整个租船运输业务的基本知识，可以作为大学生学习航运业务的教科书，也可以作为对租船运输业务感兴趣的有关人员的参考资料和指南。

　　本书由苏同江教授担任主编，高伟担任副主编，王瑞亮、于晓丹、杨晓娜和冷强参编，上海海事大学王学锋教授担任主审。本书是在参照与租船运输业务有关的各种英文书籍、案例和《中华人民共和国海商法》的规定，以及在青岛远洋船员职业学院校内作为国际航运和物流专业学生的教材使用的基础上编写的。作者欢迎读者的任何建议、评论和意见，以便对本书进行修订，进一步加以完善。

　　对读者和支持者表示万分感谢!

作　者

2010年5月

Content

MODULE | ONE
INTRODUCTION TO CHARTERING SHIPPING

模块一　租船运输概述

◎ LEARNING OBJECTIVES

Through studying this module, students will be required to obtain a basic knowledge of chartering shipping such as the meanings and characteristics of chartering shipping, voyage chartering, time chartering, TCT, COA and bareboat chartering, main parties involved in chartering, charter party forms, charter market, etc.

学习目标

通过学习本模块，学生应获得租船运输的基本知识，诸如租船运输、航次租船、定期租船、航次期租、包运租船和光船租船的概念和特点，租船运输主要当事人，标准租船合同范本，租船市场等。

◎ CONTENTS

1. Chartering Shipping and Participants;
2. Types of Chartering Shipping;
3. Vessels and Cargoes;
4. Standard Charter Party Forms;
5. Charter Market.

学习内容

1. 租船运输及参与方；
2. 租船运输类型；
3. 船舶和货物；
4. 标准租船合同范本；
5. 租船市场。

KEY POINTS

Shipowner; Charterer; Broker; TCT; COA; Voyage Chartering; Time Chartering; Bareboat Chartering; LOA; DWT; GENCON; NYPE; Vessel; Cargo.

学习要点

船舶出租人；船舶承租人；租船经纪人；航次期租；包运租船；航次租船；定期租船；光船租船；船长；载重吨；金康格式；土产格式；船舶；货物。

SKILL REQUIREMENTS

1. Have obtained basic knowledge of chartering shipping;
2. Have the ability to understand voyage chartering;
3. Have the ability to know about description of vessels and cargoes;
4. Have the ability to understand the charter party forms;
5. Have the ability to master and analyze the chartering market.

技能要求

1. 获得租船运输的基本知识；
2. 具备完全知晓航次租船的能力；
3. 具备知晓船舶和货物说明的能力；
4. 具备知晓主要租船合同范本的能力；
5. 具备掌握和分析租船市场的能力。

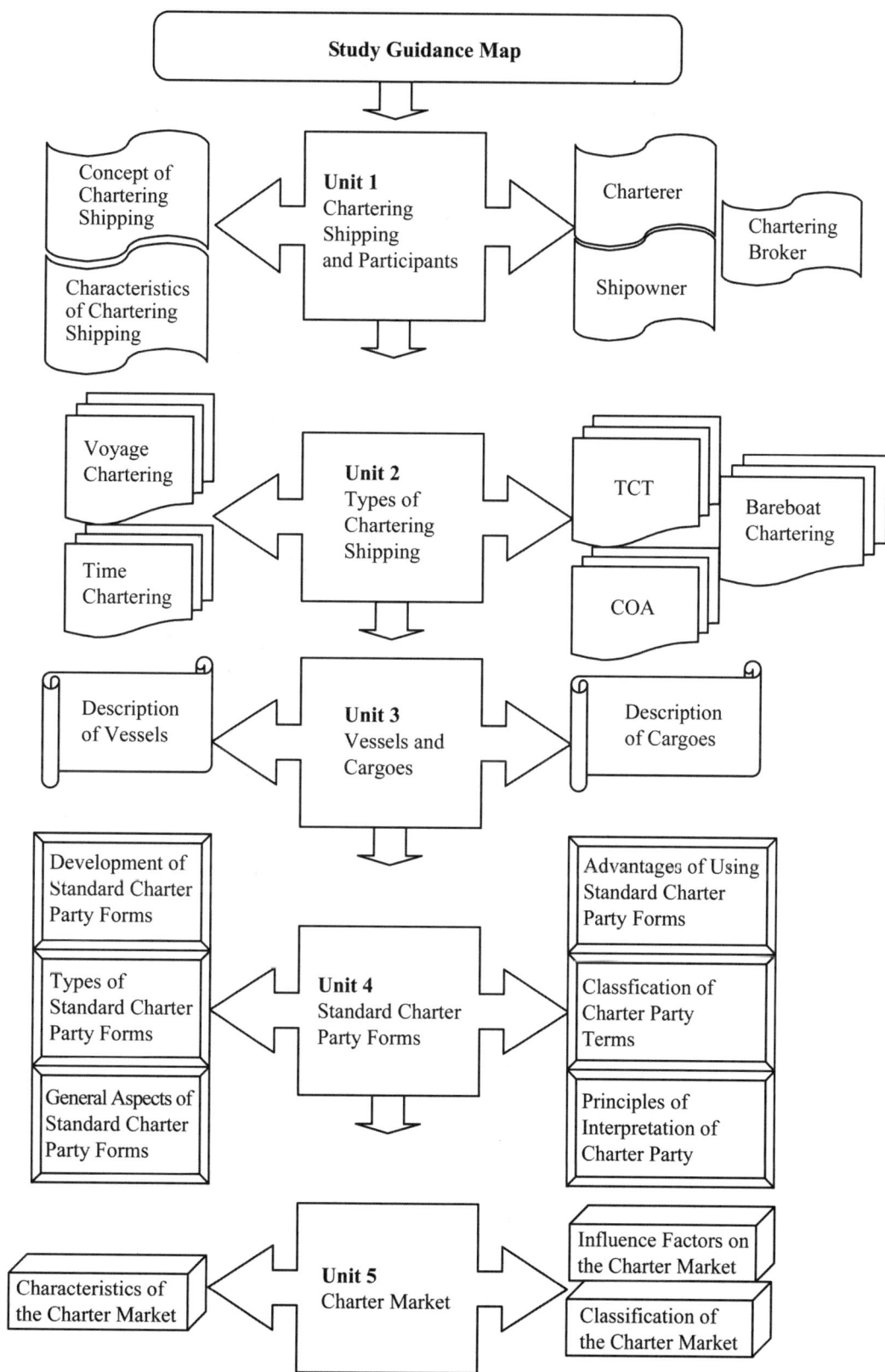

Study Guidance Map

Unit 1
Chartering Shipping and Participants

- Concept of Chartering Shipping
- Characteristics of Chartering Shipping
- Charterer
- Shipowner
- Chartering Broker

Unit 2
Types of Chartering Shipping

- Voyage Chartering
- Time Chartering
- TCT
- Bareboat Chartering
- COA

Unit 3
Vessels and Cargoes

- Description of Vessels
- Description of Cargoes

Unit 4
Standard Charter Party Forms

- Development of Standard Charter Party Forms
- Types of Standard Charter Party Forms
- General Aspects of Standard Charter Party Forms
- Advantages of Using Standard Charter Party Forms
- Classfication of Charter Party Terms
- Principles of Interpretation of Charter Party

Unit 5
Charter Market

- Characteristics of the Charter Market
- Influence Factors on the Charter Market
- Classification of the Charter Market

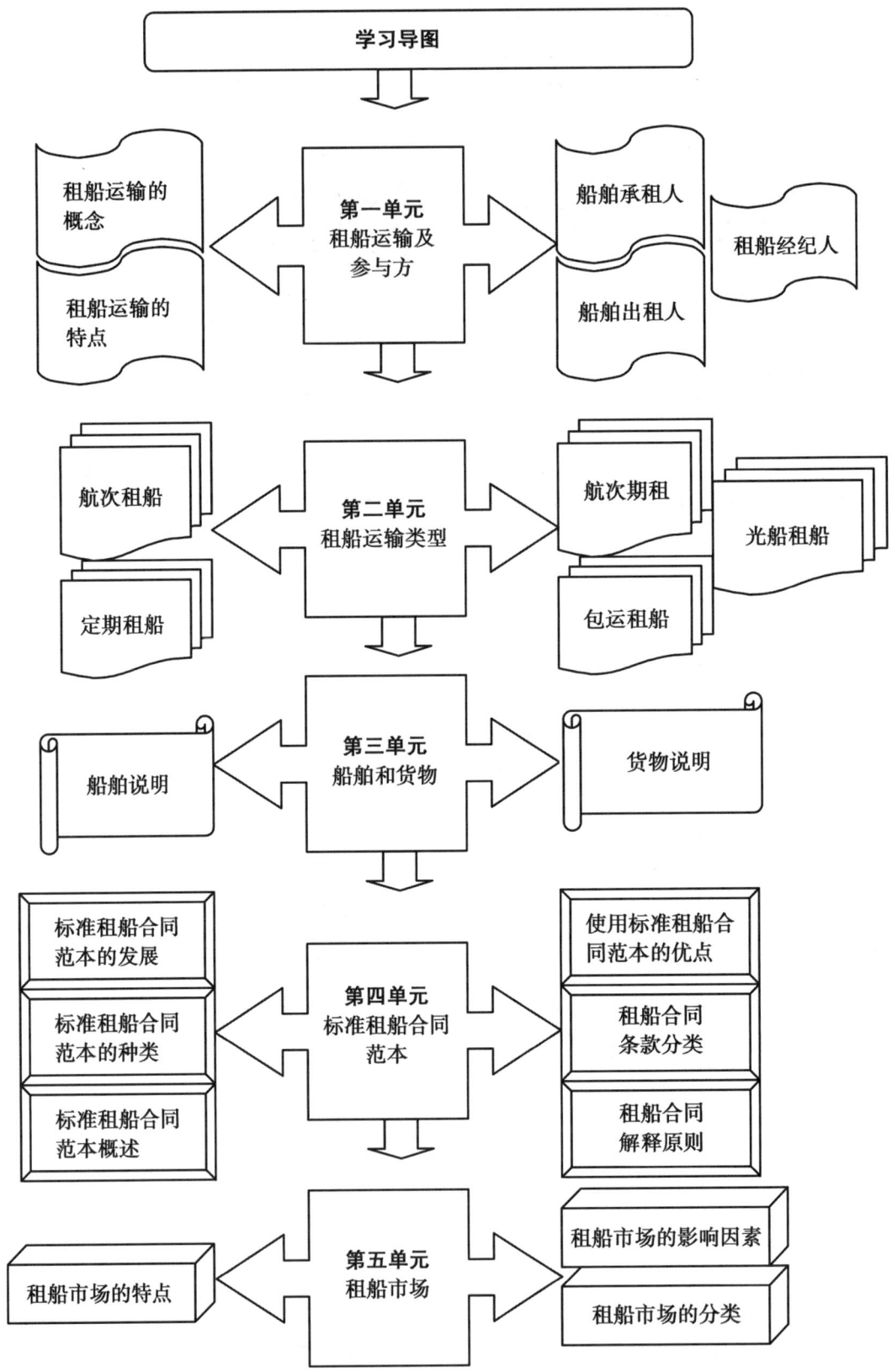

学习导图

第一单元
租船运输及
参与方

租船运输的
概念

租船运输的
特点

船舶承租人

船舶出租人

租船经纪人

第二单元
租船运输类型

航次租船

定期租船

航次期租

包运租船

光船租船

第三单元
船舶和货物

船舶说明

货物说明

第四单元
标准租船合同
范本

标准租船合同
范本的发展

标准租船合同
范本的种类

标准租船合同
范本概述

使用标准租船合
同范本的优点

租船合同
条款分类

租船合同
解释原则

第五单元
租船市场

租船市场的特点

租船市场的影响因素

租船市场的分类

UNIT 1　CHARTERING SHIPPING AND PARTICIPANTS
第一单元　租船运输及参与方

1. Concept of Chartering Shipping
1. 租船运输的概念

Chartering shipping is an activity within the shipping industry. The shipping industry is a service industry that generally provides cargo transportation for international trade. Often, the shipping industry is categorized into two major sectors: one is chartering shipping which provides services mainly in the transportation of raw materials such as crude oil, coal, iron ore, and grains, and the other is liner shipping which provides services in the transportation of final and semi-final products such as computers, manufacturing products and other consumer goods. Chartering shipping is the business of providing employment for the vessels and arranging suitable sea transport for a variety of commodities. It refers to a shipping service performing on waterways without a preset schedule or fixed routes and sailings normally depend on the availability of cargoes entrusted for carriage. So it is also called tramp shipping.

租船运输是航运业中的一种业务经营类型。航运业是提供国际贸易货物运输的一种服务型行业。航运业通常分成两大部分，一部分是提供原材料，如原油、煤炭、铁矿石和谷物的租船运输服务；另一部分是提供成品和半成品，如计算机、制造产品和其他消费品的班轮运输服务。租船运输是提供船舶使用和为各类货物安排适宜海上运输的一种业务。租船运输是一种海上运输经营方式，它没有固定的船舶班期，也没有固定的航线，而是根据货物对运输的要求，安排货物运输，因此又被称为不定期船运输。

2. Characteristics of Chartering Shipping
2. 租船运输的特点

The following are the characteristics of chartering shipping.

租船运输具有以下特点。

(1) Sailings are based on cargo requirements that vary with the vessel's employment, and are usually different for every voyage. The shipowner does not have a fixed schedule of sailings for his vessel and will employ it where and when he can get a cargo. Chartering Shipping is generally not provided on a regularly scheduled basis, but rather as needed, on specialized ships transporting a

specific commodity.

（1）根据货物的要求安排船舶运输航线，通常每个航次都不尽相同。船舶出租人对其船舶没有固定的船期表和航线，而是根据何时何地揽到的货物安排船舶运输。租船运输通常不以定期的船期为基础，而是根据需要，以特定船舶运输特定货物。

(2) The shipowner is a contractual (private) carrier and does not usually hold himself out as a common carrier and his ship is free to operate anywhere on any terms. Freight and hire rates vary from day to day depending upon the supply and demand of the charter market.

（2）船舶出租人是契约承运人而不是公共承运人，他可以任何条款在任何地方自由经营船舶。运费和租金率每日随着租船市场供需关系而变动。

(3) Cargoes carried in tramps generally are those unpackaged either dry, such as grain and ore, or liquid, such as petroleum products, which can be transported in bulk. The value of the cargoes is relatively low, and normally they are carried full shiploads of a single commodity.

（3）不定期船运输的货物通常是未包装的，或者是干货如谷物和矿石，或者是液体货如被散装运输的石油产品。这些货物的价值较低，并且通常整船装的是一种单一货物。

(4) The shipowner must negotiate a separate contract for each employment of his vessel, and the terms of the charter party vary from ship to ship, which is depending upon the bargaining abilities of the shipowner and charterer, and the general trend of the charter market.

（4）船舶出租人对每次其船舶的租用必须洽谈单独的合同，而且租船合同条款内容也不尽相同，这取决于船舶出租人和承租人的洽谈能力和租船市场总的趋势。

(5) Freight and hire rates for tramps vary according to the supply and demand for ships. Rates and services are determined by negotiation between shipowners and charterers, and reflect the specific requirements of the contracting parties.

（5）运费和租金率随着船舶供需关系而变动。费率和船舶营运根据船舶出租人与承租人双方洽谈协商来决定，反映契约当事人的特定需求。

(6) The rights, duties, and responsibilities of shipowners and charterers are governed by the charter parties concluded between them.

（6）船舶出租人与承租人的权利、义务和责任取决于双方当事人之间订立的租船合同。

3. Charterer
3. 船舶承租人

The person entering into the charter party with the shipowner is known as the charterer who is in search of vacant cargo space for transporting his or others' commodities.

船舶承租人是指为运输本人或他人的货物而寻求舱位并与船舶出租人订立租船合同的人。

Many kinds of entities can be charterers, from individuals operating small corporations, to major international trading-houses. The charterer may or may not be the owner of the goods to be carried. In some cases, he may be the seller or the buyer of a commodity. In other cases the charterer may be an intermediary between buyer and seller, that is to say, he is a third party looking to arrange the transport requirements of a seller and/or buyer of a commodity. In almost all carriage cases there are several intermediaries involved in chartering service who can be charterers such as freight forwarders, customs brokers, chartering brokers, and multimodal operators.

从经营小公司的个体到大型的国际贸易商行，各种类型的经济体都可以作为承租人。承租人可能是或不是运输货物的货主。在一些情况下，其可能是货物的卖方或买方。在其他情况下，承运人也可能是介于卖方和买方之间的中间人，也就是说他是第三人，为买卖双方运输需求做安排。在几乎所有运输实例中，有大量的涉及租船业务的中间人可以成为承租人，诸如货运代理人、报关员、经纪人和多式联运经营人。

Some shipowners also can be charterers, this is particularly true in the case of major oil companies, several of whom own large fleets to carry their own cargoes but when necessary, ships will be chartered to meet their additional demands. Many ships under time chartering party are utilized on liner service. Some are used to supplement the insufficiency of the existing ship the liner operators owned,but some liner operators use only chartered ships and own no ships themselves.

一些船东也可以是承租人，特别是大型石油公司，他们拥有大型自有船队运输自己的货物，但当需要时他们也会租船，以应对他们的额外需求。许多定期租船合同下的船舶被用来从事班轮服务。有些船舶是用于补充班轮经营者已有船舶的不足，而有些班轮经营者仅仅使用租船，自己本身没有船舶。

4. Shipowner
4. 船舶出租人

Shipowner means the owner of the merchant vessel, or another organization or person, such as the manager, operator or bareboat charterer, who has assumed the responsibility for the operation of the ship from the owner. In chartering shipping, the person entering into the charter party with the charterer is known as the shipowner.

船舶出租人是指商船拥有者或其他组织或个人，如承担了船东的船舶经营责任的船舶经理、运营人或光船承租人。在租船运输中，船舶出租人是指与船舶承租人订立租船合同的人。

There is a wide variety of shipowners. Some shipowners own a single ship, some have large fleets, and some concentrate on ships of a particular type or size. Many ships are owned, in the legal sense, by financial institutions. This is usually because the ships are being purchased under a hire purchase arrangement. Some shipowners are state-controlled or run their ships under the flag of the country in which they reside, while others operate ships under a "convenient" flag.

船舶出租人有许多类型。有些船舶出租人拥有一条船，有些拥有大型船队，有些专注于某一特定类型和大小的船舶。有些船舶，在法律意义上讲，由金融机构拥有。这通常是因为这些船舶是根据租购协议购买的。有些船舶出租人是国家控股或在本国注册挂旗，而另一些则以"方便"旗形式经营船舶。

From the view of chartering business, shipowners can be divided into actual shipowners and disponent owners. Actual shipowners are the ownership of the vessel, and disponent owners are not the ownership of the vessel. We have seen that from time to time the party acting as the "shipowner" may be the "disponent owner", such as the party who has the ship on time charter.

从租船业务角度上看，船舶出租人分为实际船舶所有人和二船东。实际船舶所有人拥有船舶所有权，二船东未拥有船舶所有权。我们通常看到的作为"船舶出租人"的当事人实际上是"二船东"，诸如使用定期租船租进的船舶承租人。

It is customary to stipulate in voyage, time and bareboat charter parties that the charterer has the right of subletting the whole or part of the ship, subject to the charterer remaining responsible to the shipowner for the due fulfillment of the original charter party.

习惯上，航次租船合同、定期租船合同和光船租船合同规定承租人有转租全部或部分船舶舱位的权利，但承租人仍需对租船合同的履行情况向船舶出租人负责。

This right is of considerable importance to the charterer since it gives him a certain freedom to utilize the vessel in the way that is most economical to him. Subletting frequently occurs in practice. The charterer may have chartered the vessel for the sole purpose of making a profit by rechartering or otherwise subletting it, or he may find that the cargo that he intended to ship is not available or, that he is not in a position to utilize the vessel for the original intended purpose, in which case he will seek other employment for it to be covered for the freight or hire which he is due to pay the shipowner; he may also find, because of a rise in freight market rates, that it is more profitable for him to recharter the vessel than to utilize it in the way originally intended.

这项权利对承租人是相当重要的，因为它给予他通过一定的自由以最经济的方式使用船舶。转租在实务中经常发生。承租人可能仅仅是为了再租船或其他方式转租来获取利润而租用船舶；或者他可能会发现，他打算运输的货物不适宜，或者他无法按照原定用途使用该船舶。在这种情况下，他将寻求其他机会出租船舶以便足够给船舶出租人支付运费或租金；他可能还会发现，由于航运市场运费上升，将船舶转租比原先使用船舶更有利可图。

A vessel may at the same time be involved in several different contracts. The following example illustrates such a chain. A is the registered or real owner of the vessel. Since he is only interested in investing money in shipping, he may have made a bareboat charter with B. B in his turn has time chartered the ship to C. In the relationship between B and C, B acts as a disponent owner, while C is the time charterer. C in his turn has chartered the vessel to D under a voyage charter. In the relationship between C and D, C is the disponent owner, and D is the voyage charterer.

一条船可能同时涉及几个不同的合同。下面的例子说明了这样一个租船链环。A是船舶的登记人或真正的所有人。由于他只对投资于航运感兴趣，他可能与B订立光船租船合同。B将船舶以定期租船形式转租给C。B和C的关系是：B是二船东，而C是定期租船的承租人。C以航次租船形式将船舶租给D。C和D的关系是：C是二船东，而D是航次租船的承租人。

5. Chartering Broker
5. 租船经纪人

Chartering brokers are typically specialists in chartering. The individuals or corporations who are appointed to act on behalf of the shipowners or charterers to secure cargoes for their ships and secure ships for their cargoes are called chartering brokers or shipbrokers. The existence of chartering brokers greatly facilitates the speed and efficiency of the chartering process.

租船经纪人通常为租船领域的专业人士，是指受船舶出租人或者承租人的委托，代表出租人或者承租人专门从事磋商租船业务的航运经纪人。租船经纪人的存在很大程度上提升了租船程序的速度和效率。

5.1 Tasks of Chartering Broker
5.1 租船经纪人的任务

The chartering broker should keep both the shipowner and the charterer continuously informed about the market situation and the market development, available cargo proposals, and shipment possibilities. The chartering broker should in all respects work loyally for his principal and should carry out the task of negotiations and other work connected with the charter scrupulously and skillfully. The chartering broker should act strictly within the given authorities in connection with the negotiations and he has no authority to quote a ship or a cargo, unless duly authorized by his principal.

租船经纪人应该持续向船舶出租人和承租人提供关于市场情况及市场的发展、装运货物的方案和运输可行性的信息。租船经纪人应在各方面忠实地为委托人工作，仔细地进行洽谈以及其他与租约有关的工作。租船经纪人应严格在授权范围内从事洽谈，除非经委托人授权，他无权就船舶或货物询价。

5.2 Number of Brokers Involved in Negociation
5.2 租约洽谈中经纪人的人数

Number of brokers involved in chartering negotiation depends on the intentions of the parties and the market situations. A typical deep-sea dry cargo fixture will normally involve two chartering brokers, one representing the shipowner, and the other representing the charterer; sometimes there will be more brokers in the chain. Whereas it is comparatively unusual for just one chartering broker to be employed in a deep-sea dry cargo fixture, in short-sea and some specialized trades, occasionally only one chartering broker will be engaged between two principals.

租船洽谈中，经纪人的人数取决于各方的意愿和市场情况。一个典型的远洋干散货合同通常涉及两个租船经纪人，一个代表船舶出租人，另一个代表承租人，有时会有更多的经纪人。一份远洋干散货合同仅仅涉及一个租船经纪人的情况比较少见，但在近海和某些特殊交易中，偶尔会出现仅由一名租船经纪人在双方委托人之间促成交易的情况。

5.3 Chartering Broker's Remuneration
5.3 租船经纪人的报酬

The chartering broker's income is in the form of commission or brokerage paid in return for a successful introduction and negotiation between the shipowners and the charterers that lead to a fixture. Even after hard work and expense, a negotiation that does not lead to a fixture will normally result in no payment of any kind to the broker.

租船经纪人的收入以佣金形式存在，该佣金是对其成功促成船舶出租人与承租人之间达成租船交易的介绍及谈判工作的回报。即使付出了辛勤劳动和费用，若谈判未能促成租船交易，经纪人通常无法获得任何形式的报酬。

Unless otherwise expressly agreed, commission is payable only on the freight or hire earned and paid. It is customary in a voyage charter for this to be extended by agreement to allow commission to be payable on dead freight and/or demurrage, if any. Similarly, under a time charter it can be extended to a ballast bonus. In chartering, it is the usual (though not invariable) practice for a commission clause to appear in the contract (the charter party), and the commission is customarily payable by the shipowner to the charterer's broker as well as to the shipowner's broker.

除非另有明确约定，佣金仅按照赚取的运费或租金支付。在航次租船中，惯例是通过协议将佣金支付范围扩大至亏舱费和/或滞期费（如有）。同样，在定期租船中，佣金支付范围可以扩展到空载津贴。在租船业务中，租船合同中通常（虽然不是永恒不变的）会订有佣金条款，且惯例上船舶出租人需向租船经纪人和自身经纪人支付佣金。

UNIT 2 TYPES OF CHARTERING SHIPPING

第二单元　租船运输类型

The worldwide scope of marine trading, the variety of commodities to be shipped and the differences in vessel operations call for several different kinds of chartering, which can currently be divided into the following five main types: voyage chartering, time chartering, time chartering on trip basis (TCT),contract of affreightment (COA), and bareboat chartering.

世界范围的海运贸易、各类货物的运输以及船舶运营方式的不同需要不同的租船形式。目前，这些形式可以分为以下五种：航次租船、定期租船、航次期租（TCT）、包运租船（COA）和光船租船等。

1. Voyage Chartering
1. 航次租船

1.1 General Introduction to Voyage Chartering
1.1 航次租船概述

Voyage chartering means that the shipowner promises to carry a particular cargo on board a specific ship for a single or several voyages from one or more discharging ports. The payment paid by the charterer to the shipowner is called freight, and the contract made by the shipowner and charterer is called a voyage charter party.

航次租船是指船舶出租人承诺使用特定船舶，将特定货物按一个或多个航次从一个或多个装货港运至一个或多个卸货港。承租人向船舶出租人支付的费用称为运费，船舶出租人与承租人签订的合同称为航次租船合同。

A voyage charter party is concluded between the shipowner or disponent owner and the charterer of the ship.

航次租船合同是由船舶出租人或者二船东与船舶承租人订立的。

The person who charters in a ship is known as a voyage charterer. The person who charters out his ship is known as the shipowner or disponent owner. Usually, this form of contract is selected when the charterer has no experience in ship operation or has just one consignment of cargo to be transported .

租进船舶的一方称之为船舶承租人。租出船舶的一方称之为船舶出租人或二船东。通常，当承租人缺乏经营船舶的经验，或者仅有一批货物需要从一个港口运往另一个港口时，选用这种合同方式。

Under a voyage charter, the shipowner retains the operational control of the vessel and is responsible for all the operating expenses such as port charges, bunkers, vessel insurance, taxes, etc. The charterer's costs are usually costs and charges relating to the cargo. Loading and discharging costs are divided between the shipowner and the charterer by the agreement from case to case.

在航次租船合同下，船舶出租人负责船舶的营运调度，负责船舶营运的所有费用诸如港口使费、燃料费、船舶保险费用、税费等。船舶承租人负责有关货物的费用。货物装卸费用根据情况由船舶出租人和承租人依据合同的规定分担。

A voyage charter party shall mainly contain the names of the parties, the name and nationality of the ship, its deadweight and bale or grain capacity, a description of the goods to be loaded, port of loading and discharge, laydays, time for loading and discharge, payment of freight, demurrage, dispatch money, and other relevant matters.

航次租船合同主要包括出租人和承租人的名称、船名、船籍、载重吨、包装或散装容积、货物说明、装货港和目的港、受载期、装卸时间、运费、滞期费、速遣费以及其他有关事项。

There are more standard forms of voyage charter parties than any other form of charter party. The Uniform General Charter, code name GENCON, is the most popular and widely used general-purpose voyage charter party globally for numerous types of cargo. When these forms arc used, they are likely to have several additional clauses to cover eventualities not covered by the printed clauses.

航次租船合同范本要比其他类型的租船合同范本多。统一杂货租船合同，代码"金康"，是全球范围内使用最广泛、适用于多种货物的航次租船合同标准格式。当使用这些范本时，人们往往增加一些附加条款，以弥补标准合同范本未尽到的事宜。

1.2 Manners of Voyage Chartering
1.2 航次租船的形式

1.2.1 Single Voyage Chartering

1.2.1 单航次租船

Single voyage chartering means that both parties reach an agreement in which the shipowner promises to carry a particular cargo on board a specific ship for one voyage. The shipowner will be responsible for the specific goods from the port of loading to the port of discharge. The shipowner's contractual obligations will be completed by the delivery of goods at the port of discharge.

单航次租船是指船舶出租人与承租人双方约定，由船舶出租人承诺使用特定船舶为一个航次运输特定货物。船舶出租人负责将指定的货物从装货港运往目的港。货物运抵目的港卸船交付货物后，船舶出租人的合同义务即告完成。

1.2.2 Return Voyage Chartering

1.2.2 往返航次租船

Return voyage chartering means that both parties reach an agreement in which the shipowner promises to carry a particular cargo on board a specific ship for a round voyage between the loading port and the discharge port. This form of chartering involves two single voyages. The first discharge port may or may not be the loading port of the second voyage. The shipowner's contractual obligations will be completed by the delivery of goods at the port of discharge of the second voyage.

往返航次租船是指船舶出租人与承租人双方约定，由船舶出租人承诺使用特定船舶在装货港与卸货港之间进行往返航次运输特定货物。这种方式包括了两个单航次租船。第一个卸货港可能是也可能不是第二个航次的装货港。在第二个航次卸货港交付货物后，船舶出租人的合同义务即告完成。

1.2.3 Consecutive Single Voyage Chartering

1.2.3 连续单航次租船

Consecutive single voyage chartering means that both parties reach an agreement in which the shipowner provides the vessel to perform a series of consecutive voyages between the loading port and the discharge port instead of only one voyage. Although a consecutive single voyage charter is similar to a single voyage charter, the ship is contracted to undertake a series of cargo-carrying voyages on a defined route. The shipowner's contractual obligations will be completed by the delivery of goods at the port of discharge of the last voyage. This is used when the charterer has a well-defined schedule of cargo to be transported.

连续单航次租船是指船舶出租人与承租人双方约定，由船舶出租人提供船舶在装货港与卸货港之间连续完成几个而不是一个单航次的租船运输方式。连续单航次租船类似于单航次租船，但船舶被约定在指定的航线上连续完成货物运输航次。在最后一个航次卸货港交付货物后，船舶出租人的合同义务即告完成。当承租人有明确的货物运输计划时，会采用这种租船方式。

1.2.4 Consecutive Return Voyage Chartering

1.2.4 连续往返航次租船

Consecutive return voyage chartering means that both parties reach an agreement in which the shipowner provides the vessel to perform several consecutive round voyages between the loading port and the discharge port. The shipowner's contractual obligations will be fulfilled upon the completion of two or more consecutive voyages (round trips). This kind of chartering is seldom used in practice.

连续往返航次租船是指船舶出租人与承租人双方约定，由船舶出租人提供船舶在装货港与卸货港之间连续完成几个往返航次的租船运输方式。被租船舶连续完成两个或多个连续航次（往返航次）后，船舶出租人的合同义务即告完成。这种租船方式在实务中很少使用。

1.3 Characteristics of Voyage Chartering
1.3 航次租船的特点

The following are the characteristics of voyage chartering.

航次租船具有以下特点：

(1) Specific vessels, specific cargoes, specific ports, and specific routes are stipulated in the voyage charter party.

（1）航次租船合同规定了特定船舶、特定货物、特定港口和特定航线。

(2) Rights, duties, and responsibilities of shipowners and charterers are determined by the voyage charter party concluded by them.

（2）船舶出租人与承租人的权利、义务和责任由他们之间订立的航次租船合同来确定。

(3) The charterer should be responsible for the arrangement of the cargo, payment of freight calculated according to the quantity of the cargo loaded or carried, and other expenses concerned.

（3）承租人负责货物的安排，根据装船或载运货物的数量支付运费及相关的费用。

(4) The shipowner possesses and controls the vessel and takes charge of the operation of the vessel and the manning and management of the crew.

（4）船舶由船舶出租人所有和管理，负责船舶的营运以及船员的配备和管理。

(5) The shipowner should bear the operational expenses of the vessel.

（5）船舶出租人负责支付船舶营运费用。

(6) The payment by the charterer to the shipowner for the chartered vessel is usually called freight instead of hire.

（6）承租人向船舶出租人支付的运输费用通常称为运费，而不称为租金。

(7) The shipowner charters out the whole vessel or part of her space to the charterer.

（7）船舶出租人向承租人出租整船或部分舱位。

(8) There are provisions for laytime, demurrage and dispatch money etc., in the voyage charter party.

（8）航次租船合同规定了装卸时间、滞期费和速遣费等。

2. Time Chartering
2. 定期租船

2.1 General Introduction to Time Chartering
2.1 定期租船概述

Time chartering means that the shipowner provides a designated manned ship to the charterer, and the charterer employs the ship during the contractual period for the agreed service against payment of hire. The length of the charter may be the time taken to complete a single voyage (trip charter) or months or years (period charter). A time charter gives the charterer the use of the ship while leaving ownership and management of the vessel in the hands of the shipowner. Under a time charter, the crew is employed by the shipowner, who is also responsible for the nautical operation and maintenance of the vessel and supervision of the cargo.

定期租船是指船舶出租人向承租人提供约定的由出租人配备船员的船舶，由承租人在约定的合同时间内按照约定的用途使用，并支付租金的一种租船方式。定期租船的租期可以是一个航次（程租）或几个月或几年（期租）。船舶出租人将船舶交由承租人使用，船舶的所有权和管理权仍在船舶出租人手上。在定期租船中，出租人配备船员，对驾驶和船舶管理以及货物监督负有责任。

The time charterer may be a shipowner who for a time needs to enlarge his fleet or a cargo owner with a continuous need for transport, and who does not want to invest money in a ship but wants to have control of the commercial operation of the vessel. The charterer may be a speculator taking a position in anticipation of a change in the market. The charterer is liable for costs directly connected with the use of the vessel, for example, bunker costs and port charges, and pays for the loading and discharging costs.

定期承租人可能是那些暂时需要扩大船队的船东，也可能是那些需要持续运输货物但又不想投入资金购买船舶，但又希望对船舶进行经营管理的货主。承租人可能是投机者，根据市场变化采取相应措施。承租人对直接与船舶的使用有关的费用负责，例如，燃料成本和港口费用以及装卸费用。

Although considerably fewer in number than the wide choice available for voyage chartering, there are an adequate number of time forms for use in the time chartering business. The two major forms are NYPE and BALTIME. When used these forms are likely to have several additional clauses attached to cover eventualities not covered by the printed clauses. By far the largest number of time chartering are fixed based on the NYPE Form.

虽然定期租船合同范本数目比航次租船选择适用的范本要少，但也有适宜数目的范本供使用。两个主要范本是土产格式（NYPE）和波尔的姆格式（BALTIME）。当使用这些范本时，往往增加一些附加条款，以弥补标准合同范本未包括的事宜。到目前为止，大多数定期租船合同采用NYPE为蓝本订立。

2.2 Characteristics of Time Chartering
2.2 定期租船的特点

The following are the characteristics of time chartering.

定期租船具有以下特点。

(1) The shipowner should be responsible for the manning of the crew and bear the wages and provisions thereof.

（1）船舶出租人负责配备船员，并负担其工资和伙食。

(2) The master shall be under the orders and directions of the charterer as regards employment and agency. If the charterer shall have reasonable cause to be dissatisfied with the conduct of the master or officers, the shipowner shall on receiving the complaint make a change in the appointments, if necessary.

（2）船长在有关船舶使用和代理方面应服从承租人的指示和命令。如承租人有合理的原因对船长或者高级船员的行为不满意，出租人在收到投诉后，如有必要，予以更换。

(3) The charterer should be responsible for the operation of the vessel and bear the variable operational costs such as bunkers, port charges, handling charges, and canal tolls, etc.

（3）承租人负责船舶的营运调度，并负担船舶营运中的可变费用，如燃料费、港口使费、货物装卸费、运河通行费等。

(4) The shipowner should bear the fixed operational costs such as costs relating to the vessel capital, the ship's maintenance and stores, the ship's insurance premium and so on.

（4）船舶出租人负担船舶营运的固定费用，如船舶资本的有关费用、船舶维修保养费、船用物料费、船舶保险费等。

(5) The ship is chartered as a whole part and the hire is calculated and collected according to the duration of chartering and the agreed hire rate.

（5）船舶以整船出租；租金按租期和约定的租金率计收。

(6) There are provisions for the delivery/redelivery of ship, off-hire, etc., in the time charter party.

（6）定期租船合同中有对交船、还船和停租等事项的规定。

2.3 Distinctive Features of Voyage Chartering and Time Chartering
2.3 航次租船和定期租船的区别

Under a voyage charter party, the shipowner undertakes to provide a vessel for the carriage of certain goods on one or several voyages between named ports. While under a time charter party, the shipowner undertakes to place the use of the vessel at the charterer's disposal for while during which it is agreed that the charterer may freely employ the vessel for his account.

在航次租船合同下，船舶出租人承诺提供一条船舶在指定港口之间进行一个或几个航次运输特定货物。而根据定期租船合同，船舶出租人承诺在一定期间将船舶置于承租人处置之下，在此期间承租人可以自由地使用船舶。

Under a voyage charter party, the actual operation of the vessel is left to the shipowner. While under a time charter party, the time charterer thus takes a substantial part in the operation of the vessel. One result of the time charterer's partaking in the operation of the vessel is that he assumes the costs that are directly incidental to the various voyages on which he directs the vessel. He has, as a rule, to bear the costs for bunkers, port charges, towages, etc. which, under a voyage charter party, are borne by the shipowner.

在航次租船合同下，实际经营权仍在船舶出租人手上。而在定期租船合同下，船舶承租人则会参与到船舶的运营中。定期承租人参与船舶运营的一个结果是，他要负担船舶营运中与航行直接相关的各项事用。他需要承担燃料费、港口使费、拖带费等，这些在航次租船下由船舶出租人负担。

Another point of difference is the basis for calculating the freight or hire. As a rule, the freight, under a voyage charter party, is fixed in proportion to cargo quantity and the agreed rate or in the form of a lump sum for the voyage, while under a time charter party, the hire is fixed in proportion to the time occupied and the agreed hire rate. The risk of loss of time at sea is in principle borne by the shipowner under the voyage charter party, while under the time charter party, the risk of loss of time is normally for the charterer's account.

另外一点的区别是计算运费或租金的依据。通常情况下，在航次租船合同下，运费按货物数量比例和费率或以包干运费确定；而在定期租船合同下，租金按租期以及约定的租金率计收。在航次租船合同下，海上时间损失的风险由船舶出租人承担；在定期租船合同下，通常由船舶承租人承担。

3. Time Charter on a Trip Basis (TCT)
3. 航次期租

Nowadays in international chartering practice, there is another type of chartering frequently used between voyage chartering and time chartering, which is the time charter for a trip basis. Time charter on a trip basis means that the charterers employ vessels on a time charter basis for the duration of a specific voyage to carry cargo. This practice has given rise to the term "time charter on trip basis" (TCT).

目前，国际租船实务中还经常使用一种介于航次租船和定期租船之间的租船方式，即航次期租。航次期租基本上是指由船舶承租人以定期租船形式为一个特定航次运输货物而租用船舶，实务中称之"航次期租"（TCT）。

Time charter on a trip basis is similar to voyage chartering in that the parties intend to employ the vessel for one or two voyages. The period of TCT depends on the voyage and is not fixed as in time chartering. The roles of charterer and shipowner are identical to those in a time charter party. There are no charter party forms designed purely for TCT. It is negotiated based on standard time charter forms and slightly adapted where appropriate. The important feature of the time charter party is still there; the charterer has to pay hire according to the time spent on the voyage, although the period is determined by the duration of the contract voyage.

就双方当事人使用船舶一个或两个航次的意愿而言，航次期租类似于航次租船。航次期租的租期取决于航次，而不像定期租船那样固定。船舶承租人和出租人的角色与定期租船合同中的角色相同。目前没有专门为航次期租标准设计的租船合同范本，而是以定期租船合同范本为蓝本进行洽谈，并做适当修改。航次期租具有定期租船合同的重要特征，尽管租期期限取决于合同航次期间，但承租人仍需根据履行航次所使用的时间支付租金。

A time charter on a trip basis is the simple form of a time chartering. During the time the vessel is on charter the owner is paid an agreed daily rate, for example $20,000 a day. The vessel is directed by the charterer, who tells it where to load cargo, and where to discharge it. The advantage of the TCT to the charterer is that it allows the charterer to provide greater flexibility than a voyage charter under which the contract involves the transport of a specific cargo. The advantage of the TCT to the shipowner is that it may allow the shipowner to avoid risks of loss of time at ports.

航次期租是定期租船的简单形式。在租船期间，船舶出租人按照约定的日租金率收取租金，如每天2万美元。船舶在承租人的指令下驶往装货地以及卸货地。对于承租人来说，采用航次期租的好处是其比航次租船运输指定货物有更大的灵活性。对于船舶出租人来说，采用航次期租的好处是避免船舶在港口因时间损失而承担的风险。

4. Contract of Affreightment (COA)
4. 包运租船（COA）

4.1 General Introduction to Contract of Affreightment
4.1 包运租船概述

Contract of affreightment is a generic term which covers all contracts for the carriage of goods by sea (both charter parties and bills of lading are contracts of affreightment). It is also used in a more limited sense when it means a contract, by which the shipowner promises to satisfy the charterer's need for transport capacity over a certain period of time, often one year or several years. This form of contract is an agreement by a shipowner or operator to transport an agreed quantity of cargoes over a period of time.

包运租船是一个通用术语，涵盖了所有海上货物运输合同（包括租船合同和提单都是运输合同）。它也有更狭义的用法，指船舶出租人承诺在一定时期内（通常为一年或数年）满足租船人运输能力需求的合同。这种合同形式是船东或运营人同意在一段时间内运输约定数量货物的协议。

Under this agreement, the kinds of goods, as well as the period for the contract, are ordinarily clearly defined. The quantity of goods to be carried may be precisely fixed or refer to yearly production. The agreement often fixes a certain minimum quantity to be shipped each time in order that the shipowner shall have a duty to load and carry the goods. The shipowner will agree to carry the cargo for an agreed price per ton and usually specify to deliver a certain tonnage per month, or voyage.

在该协议下，货物种类以及合同的期限通常都有明确的界定。运输货物的数量可以被明确地确定，也可以参照每年运输量。该协议往往规定每次运输的最低数量，以便船舶出租人履行装载和运输货物的责任。船舶出租人同意以每吨货物多少运费运输货物，通常指定为每月或每航次交付一定的吨位。

"Industrial cargoes" such as coal or iron ore are often shipped under contracts of affreightment, with the shipowners agreeing to carry, say 100,000 tons per month, from South Africa to Rotterdam, but leaving the shipowners free to arrange their ships to fulfill this contract. For example, the charterer has a contract to supply ten consignments of 50,000 tons of coal from Colombia to Rotterdam at approximately two-monthly intervals. So he negotiates a contract of affreightment with a shipping company which agrees to undertake the transport at an agreed price per ton. Because details of each voyage and the ship used are left to the shipowner, he can increase his efficiency by planning the operating pattern for his fleet in the most efficient manner.

"工业货物"如煤炭或铁矿石往往是根据包运租船合同运输的，如每月10万吨货物，从南非运输至鹿特丹，船舶出租人自由安排船舶履行这一合同。比如，承租人订立合同提供10批次煤炭货物，每次5万吨，从哥伦比亚到鹿特丹，大约两个月一次。所以承租人与某航运公司洽谈包运租船，后者承诺按照每吨约定运价运输货物。由于每个航次的细节和使用的船舶由船舶出租人确定，因此他可以通过规划船队经营模式以最有效的方式来提高效率。

The advantage of such a contract to the shipowner is that security of employment is obtained for his vessel for the duration of the contract, especially valuable if the shipowner considers that freight rates are about to fall. The advantage of such a contract to the charterer is that security of transportation is obtained. Contract of affreightment is a convenient way of operating for a charterer who has a large quantity of cargo to move over time and that involves many voyages. The charterers may also be able to obtain financial advantage in the event that market freight rates rise once they have committed the shipowner or operator to the contract.

这种合同对船舶出租人而言，优点是在合同期间内能获得货源保证，尤其在船舶出租人认为运费可能下降时更有价值。这种合同对承租人的优点是可以获得运力保证。承租人有大量的货物运输并涉及多个航次时，包运租船是一种操作方便的形式。一旦合同中确认船舶出租人或经营人合同义务时，在航运市场运费率上升的情况下，承租人还可以获得运费优惠。

There are several forms used for contracts of affreightment such as GENCOA and INTERCOA. GENCOA is an updated version of the original BIMCO form and provides users with a set of clearly worded terms and conditions governing the key aspects of any contract of affreightment.

包运租船有不同种类的标准格式，例如 GENCOA 和 INTERCOA。GENCOA 是在原有的 BIMCO 格式基础上制定的范本，为使用方提供了一套措辞清晰的条款，涵盖任何包运租船合同的关键方面。

4.2 Characteristics of Contract of Affreightment
4.2 包运租船的特点

The following are the characteristics of COA.

包运租船具有以下特点。

(1) COA can often be related to voyage charter. Under COA, the individual vessel is less important for the charterer, but the important thing is that the shipowner performs his duty to carry an agreed type of ship, which may very well be a chartered vessel.

（1）包运租船通常与航次租船相关联。在包运租船下，对于承租人而言，单个船舶的重要性相对较低，重要的在于出租人履行其职责，确保提供约定类型的船舶，而这种船舶很可能是租用的船舶。

(2) The length of the chartering period lies on the total quantity of cargo to be transported.

（2）租期的长短取决于运输货物的总运量。

(3) Cargoes carried under COA are usually bulky dry/liquid cargoes large in quantity and the charterers are usually the industrial & mining enterprises, manufacturing & processing groups, etc.

（3）包运租船下的货物主要是运量较大的散装干散货或液体货物，承租人通常是工矿企业和生产加工集团等。

(4) The risk of delay in sailing should be borne by the shipowner like in voyage chartering.

（4）航次中所产生的航行时间延误风险如同航次租船，由船舶出租人承担。

(5) The freight should be calculated based on the quantity of cargo carried and the pre-agreed freight rate.

（5）运费按船舶实际装运货物的数量及约定的运费费率计收。

(6) The partition of the cost of loading and/or discharge is usually as same as that of voyage chartering.

（6）装卸货物费用的划分通常与航次租船相同。

5. Bareboat Chartering
5. 光船租船

5.1 General Introduction to Bareboat Chartering
5.1 光船租船概述

Bareboat chartering is a different type of charter. This contract amounts to a lease of the ship from the shipowner to the charterer. Bareboat chartering ordinarily means that the vessel is put at the disposal of the charterer for a long period of employment without any crew. The charterer thus will take over almost all of the shipowner's functions except for the payment of capital costs. This means that the charterer will have the commercial as well as the technical responsibility for the vessel and will pay for maintenance, crew costs, and vessel insurance, etc.

光船租船是一种不同的租船方式。这种租船方式相当于船舶出租人将船舶以租赁形式租给承租人。光船租船通常意味着船舶由承租人长期使用，其间船舶出租人不给配备船员。除了支付船舶资本外，承租人承担了出租人的所有职能。这意味着承租人负责船舶的经营及技术责任以及承担租期内船舶维修费用、船员费用和船舶保险费用等。

Bareboat chartering is less common than other types of contracts. It is sometimes used where a charterer wishes to operate ships or to supplement his fleet for a while time without incurring the financial commitments of actual ownership, but at the same time requires full control of the chartered vessel, including control of its navigation and management. Further, bareboat chartering is sometimes employed in connection with the financial arrangements for the purchase of the vessel on installment terms. The bareboat charter then serves as a hire purchase contract, by which the shipowner/seller retains formal ownership and thereby security in the vessel until the full purchase price is paid.

光船租船并不像其他租船方式那样常见。有时当船舶承租人在一段时间内欲经营船舶或补充船队，且不产生实际拥有船舶的融资问题，同时需要完全控制租用的船舶，包括航行和管理时，会采用光船租船方式。此外，光船租船还会与分期购买船舶的财务安排有所关联。此时光船租船充当租购合同，据此船舶出租人/卖方保留船舶所有权，从而在全额支付购买价款前拥有船舶担保权益。

There is only one standard form of bareboat charter party nowadays used in bareboat chartering and that is the BARECON Form designed by BIMCO. A close examination of this form will reveal that there are several clauses commonly found in time charter parties. In particular, the clauses relating to delivery, redelivery, cancellation, trading limits, surveys, inspections, hire, general average, war, commission and law and arbitration would be equally effective if used in a time charter party.

目前，光船租船合同标准范本只有一个，即BIMCO设计的贝尔康（BARECON）格式。仔细分析，该范本显示的一些条款通常也与定期租船合同条款相同，尤其是有关交还船条款、解约日、航区限制、检验、检查、租金、共同海损、战争、佣金和法律及仲裁条款，如在定期租船合同中使用，也有相同的效力。

5.2 Characteristics of Bareboat Chartering
5.2 光船租船的特点

The following are the characteristics of bareboat chartering.

光船租船具有以下特点。

(1) The possession of the vessel is transferred to the charterer at the time when the vessel is delivered.

（1）船舶的占有权从船舶交予承租人使用时起，转移至承租人。

(2) The charterer should be responsible for all the operational costs as well as fixed costs.

（2）承租人负担全部固定及运营成本。

(3) Bareboat chartering may often be described as a kind of ship financing rather than as a genuine charter agreement.

（3）光船租船通常被认为是一种船舶融资而不是通常的租船契约。

(4) The charterer manns and equips the vessel and assumes all responsibility for its navigation, management, and operation; he thus acts as the shipowner of the vessel in all important respects during the duration of the charter.

（4）承租人配备全部船员，装备船舶，承担所有船舶航行、管理及营运调度责任；在整个租期内，承租人在所有重要方面均充当该船出租人的角色。

(5) The ship is chartered as a whole part and the hire is calculated and collected according to the duration of chartering and the agreed hire rate.

（5）以整船出租，租金按租期和约定的租金率计收。

5.3 Distinctive Features of Time Chartering and Bareboat Chartering
5.3 定期租船和光船租船的区别

A time chartering is distinguished from a bareboat chartering by the employment of the master and crew. With a time chartering, the master and crew remain the employees of the shipowner, although they will be subject to the directions of the time charterer. The time charterer and therefore does not take possession of the vessel. With a bareboat chartering the master and crew are employed by the charterer, and therefore he takes possession of the vessel.

定期租船和光船租船的区别在于船长和船员的雇佣。在定期租船下，船长和船员虽然听从定期承租人的指示，但他们由船舶出租人雇佣，因此定期承租人并不占有船舶。光船租船下船长和船员由承租人雇佣，因此承租人占有船舶。

5.4 Main Contents of Bareboat Charter Party
5.4 光船租船合同主要内容

A bareboat charter party is a charter party under which the shipowner provides the charterer with an unmanned ship, which the charterer shall possess, employ, and operate within an agreed period, and for that the charterer shall pay the shipowner the hire.

光船租船合同，是指船舶出租人向承租人提供不配备船员的船舶，在约定的期间内由承租人占有、使用和营运，并向出租人支付租金的合同。

A bareboat charter party mainly contains the name of the shipowner and the name of the charterer; the name, nationality, class, tonnage, and capacity of the ship; the trading area, the employment of the ship and the charter period; the time, place and condition of delivery and re-delivery; the survey, maintenance and repair of the ship; the hire and its payment; the insurance of the ship; the time and condition for the termination of the charter and other relevant matters.

光船租船合同的内容，主要包括出租人和承租人的名称、船名、船籍、船级、吨位、容积，航区、用途、租船期间，交船和还船的时间和地点以及条件，船舶检验、船舶的保养维修、租金及其支付，船舶保险，合同解除的时间和条件以及其他有关事项。

UNIT 3　VESSELS AND CARGOES

第三单元　船舶和货物

More than 50,000 merchant ships are trading internationally, transporting every kind of cargo. The world fleet is registered in over 150 nations, and manned by over a million seafarers of different nationalities. The basis of the very existence of maritime transport is the cargo. Over 90% of world trade is carried by the international shipping industry. In this unit，many everyday expressions referring to vessels and cargoes as they are used in connection with the chartering market are explained.

大约有5万艘商船从事国际贸易运输，承运各种不同类型的货物。世界船队在150多个国家注册，有100多万不同国籍的海员。海上运输得以存在的基础是货物。超过90%的国际贸易是通过国际航运业进行的。本单元主要讲解与租船市场有关联的船舶和货物的日常表达。

1. Description of Vessels
1. 船舶说明

The description of the vessel is one of the most important items in the charter party. The need for the description of the vessel in the charter party very much depends on the circumstances. The types of cargo, and the intended ports and sea routes especially determine what details about the vessel must be mentioned during the negotiations, and in the charter party. Normally the vessel's name, dimensions, year of build, flag of nationality, deadweight, gross and net tonnage, cargo capacity, cranes or derricks capacity, number of hatches, type of hatch coverings and length and breadth of hatch openings, and bunker consumption (time chartering and bareboat chartering) are stated in the charter party.

船舶说明是租船合同中最重要的项目之一。在租船合同中，关于船舶的说明需要视情况而定。货物的类别和预定港口以及海上航程特别决定了船舶哪些细节必须在洽谈期间和租船合同中表述。通常情况下，船舶的名称、尺寸、建造年份、国籍、载重吨、总吨及净吨、舱容、吊杆负荷、舱口数、舱盖的种类、舱口的长度和宽度、燃油消耗（定期租船和光船租船）均在租船合同中表述。

1.1 Vessel's Dimensions
1.1 船舶尺寸

For chartering purposes, we need to know the size and dimensions of the ship. The most important dimensions of a vessel are the vessel's length, beam and draught.

对于租船而言，我们需要知道船舶的尺寸。船舶最重要的尺寸是船的长度、宽度和吃水。

The vessel's length is, as the name suggests, measured from the extremes fore and aft, which is expressed in terms of LOA (Length Overall).

船的长度，顾名思义，从船头到船尾的距离，以总长度（LOA）来表示船舶的长度。

The vessel's beam is the breadth of the ship measured at the widest part of the hull, which is expressed in terms of BM (Breadth Molded).

船的宽度是以船舶最宽的部分测量出来的宽度，以型宽（BM）来表示船舶的宽度。

The vessel's draught is the distance from the waterline to the lowest part of the ship (the bottom of the keel) and will be critical to ensure that the ship always has sufficient depth of water to remain afloat. For chartering purposes, it is usual to refer to the draught of the vessel when loaded to her maximum summer deadweight. The draught will determine whether a ship can get into a particular port, or transit a particular channel. The draught, of course, will vary with the amount of cargo, fuel, etc., aboard at any one time. "Air draught" is also important if the ship has to get under bridges, or fit under port loading machinery, so the height of the masts, and often the main deck above the waterline will need to be known.

船舶的吃水是从载重线到船舶最底部（即龙骨底部）的距离，并且确保船舶总是有足够的吃水深度对于维持船舶漂浮是至关重要的。对于租船而言，它通常是指船舶最大的夏季载重吨的吃水。吃水将决定船舶是否可以抵达特定的港口，或通过特定的海峡。当然，吃水将随船舶任何时间的载货量、燃料等的变化而变化。如果船舶通过桥梁，或适宜港口装卸机械，船舶的"空中吃水"也是重要的。因此，经常需要知道桅杆的高度以及船舶水线至主甲板的高度。

1.2 Vessel's Tonnages
1.2 船舶吨位

The specification of the vessel's tonnage is important, and it can be described in several ways such as the deadweight (DWT), summer deadweight (SDWT), deadweight all told (DWAT), deadweight cargo capacity (DWCC), gross tonnage (GT) and net tonnage (NT).

船舶吨位的规定是重要的，它以几个方式来表述，如载重吨（DWT）、夏季载重吨（SDWT）、总载重吨（SWAT）、载货吨（DWCC）、总吨（GT）、净吨（NT）。

The deadweight is the ship's weight of cargo, usually specified in metric ton or long ton. The deadweight of the ship normally includes the vessel's capacity not only for cargo but also for fuel, fresh water, stores, and crew. When describing a ship it is usual to use the vessel's summer deadweight (SDWT). Sometimes the vessel's deadweight is referred to as the deadweight all told (DWAT). Instead of deadweight, the deadweight cargo capacity (DWCC) figure is sometimes used.

载重吨是指船舶载货的重量，通常以公吨或长吨为单位。船舶的载重吨通常不仅包括船舶所装的货物的载重量，还包括燃油、淡水、物料和船员的重量。当描述船舶时，通常使用夏季载重量（SDWT）。有时船舶载重量也被称为总载重吨（DWAT）。有时也会使用载货吨（DWCC）来代替载重吨。

The difference between deadweight and deadweight cargo capacity is that the deadweight cargo capacity does not include the capacity necessary for fuel, fresh water, stores, and constant weights. It must be noted in this connection that when the deadweight cargo capacity is stated in the charter party, the shipowners are not free to bunker the vessel as they wish. Bunker quantity, as well as fresh water and stores, must be adjusted to the intended voyage.

总载重吨和载货吨之间的差异是，载货吨不包括必要的燃料、淡水、物料和船舶常数的重量。在此指出的是，若载货吨在租船合同中已订明，船舶出租人不能任意添加燃油。燃油数量以及淡水和物料的数量，必须根据预定的航程加以调整。

International trading vessels must have an international tonnage certificate which is issued to the shipowner by the government department in case of a ship's gross and net tonnages have been determined by the International Convention of Tonnage Measurement of Ships. The certificate states the gross and net tonnages together with details of the spaces attributed to each. Gross tonnage (GT) is the volume of all the enclosed spaces of the vessel including engine rooms and machinery spaces, crew and passenger accommodation, bridges, and storerooms. Net tonnage (NT) is, as the name suggests, merely the gross tonnage less any spaces not used for the carriage of cargo. The use of a berth when the ship comes into port, and the various services provided while alongside are often charged on the basis of the ship's tonnage. If the ship requires tugs or a pilot, if the ship needs to transit through a canal, it is the tonnage that is used as criterion for charging dues. Port fees are also often reckoned based on GT and NT.

国际航运船舶必须有政府部门颁发给船舶出租人的国际吨位证书，船舶的总吨及净吨根据《国际船舶吨位丈量公约》的规定确定。该证书中记载了船舶的总吨及净吨。总吨（GT）是指船舶所有围蔽处所的总容积，包括机房及机舱、船员和旅客住所、驾驶台和物料舱。净吨（NT），顾名思义，是指总吨减去非供货物使用的任何空间。当船舶抵达港口使用泊位时，各种服务经常按船舶吨位计收。如果船舶需要拖船或引航，或需要过运河，吨位即为收取费用的标准。港口费用也常常将总吨及净吨作为计算的基础。

Both the Suez and Panama Canal authorities each have their unique formulas for calculating the figures. The vessels that regularly trade using the canals will also have certificates of Canal Tonnage denoting the appropriate tonnage to be used by the authorities when calculating canal tolls.

苏伊士运河和巴拿马运河当局都有自己独特的计算标准。定期通过这两条运河的船舶也要持有运河吨位证书——该证书会标明运河当局在计算运河通行费时应采用的相应吨位。

1.3 Vessel's Cubic Capacity
1.3 船舶舱容

The vessel's cubic capacity is usually stated both in grain capacity and in bale capacity. The grain capacity, which is always bigger than the bale capacity, is measured in either cubic feet or cubic meters. The grain capacity is the total volume of cargo space contained inside the hull. The bale capacity is the volume of a vessel's holds to carry packaged dry cargo such as bales, pallets, boxes, cartons, etc. The bale capacity is therefore the grain capacity less any space unusable for such cargoes. The vessel's cubic capacity is a very important figure for vessel-loaded light cargoes.

船舶舱容一般分为散装舱容与包装舱容。散装舱容总是大于包装舱容，以立方英尺或立方米计算。散装舱容是指货舱内实际能够装载散装货物的空间。包装舱容是指舱内实际能够装载包装的干货诸如捆、托盘、箱子、纸箱等的空间。因此，包装舱容是散装舱容减去任何不适用这类货物的空间。船舶舱容对于船舶装载轻泡货而言是十分重要的数据。

1.4 Classification of the Vessel
1.4 船级

Classification of the vessel in the charter party is applied to ensure the seaworthiness of the carrying vessel because the classification of a vessel could serve as the index indicating the technical condition of the vessel recognized by relative departments of inspection e. g. ship's classification societies.

租船合同中对船舶的入级规定旨在确保承运船舶的适航性，因为船舶入级可作为表明船舶技术状况的指标，且该指标为相关检验部门（如船级社）所认可。

1.5 Vessel's Nationality
1.5 船舶国籍

The nationality of a vessel is demonstrated through its flag hoisting. It represents the relation between the vessel and the flag state. All ships must be registered to one of the nations of the world so that responsibility for violations of international laws and conventions may be assigned. These ships then fall under the jurisdiction of their nation of registry. Shipping concerns adopted the practice of shopping around for nations that would give them the best deal on taxes, wages, and legal restrictions. They "conveniently" register their ships with these countries which include Liberia, Panama, Honduras, and the Bahamas, and operate ships under a convenient flag.

船舶国籍是通过船旗来表现的。船舶国籍代表了船舶和船旗国的隶属关系。所有船舶必须在世界上某一国家注册以便对违反国际法和国际公约的行为负责。这些船只受其登记国家的管辖。航运企业选择给予他们最好的税费、船员工资和法律限制优惠的国家进行注册。它们会"便利地"在这些国家（包括利比里亚、巴拿马、洪都拉斯和巴哈马）为船舶办理注册，并悬挂"方便旗"运营船舶。

1.6 Types of Vessels
1.6 船舶种类

Modern cargo vessels range from small coasters to very large tankers but generally fall into several groups such as bulk carriers, general cargo ships, oil tankers, container ships and other ships according to generally used shipping terminology.

现代货船的范围从小型驳船到非常大型的油船，但按照通常使用的航运术语一般分成几种类型，诸如散货船、杂货船、油船、集装箱船和其他船舶。

1.6.1 Bulk Carrier

1.6.1 散货船

A bulk carrier is specifically designed to transport vast amounts of cargo in bulk such as sugar,

grain, ore, coal, steel, etc.

散货船，是专门为运输大宗散装货物设计的，如食糖、粮食、矿石、煤炭、钢铁等。

Bulk carriers are typically categorized into the following types:

散货船通常分为以下几个类型：

（1）Capesize bulk carriers are those with a deadweight tonnage of over 150,000 tons. The largest bulk carrier in the world at present is the Valemax type, with a deadweight tonnage of 400,000 tons, a length of 360 meters, a width of 65 meters, a depth of 30 meters, a full-load draft of 22 meters, and a total of 7 cargo holds.

（1）好望角型散货船（Capesize bulk carrier）指载重量在150 000吨以上的散货船。目前世界最大的散货船为Valemax型，其载重吨位达40万吨，船长360米，船宽65米，型深30米，满载吃水22米，共设有7个货舱。

（2）Panamax bulk carriers refer to those with a deadweight tonnage of 60,000 to 75,000 tons. The maximum dimensions of ships that can pass through the old Panama Canal locks are 294.13 meters in length, 32.31 meters in width, and 12.04 meters in draft; the maximum dimensions for the new locks are 366 meters in length, 49 meters in width, and 15.2 meters in draft, with a deadweight tonnage of around 180,000 tons. In recent years, a new type has emerged: the Kamsarmax bulk carrier, with a deadweight tonnage of over 82,000 tons, a length of 229 meters, a width of 32.36 meters, a depth of 19.9 meters, and a structural draft of 14.35 meters, which can also pass through the Panama Canal.

（2）巴拿马型散货船（Panamax bulk carrier）指载重量在60 000～75 000吨的散货船。能通过巴拿马运河老船闸的船舶最大尺寸为：长294.13米、宽32.31米、吃水12.04米；能通过新船闸的船舶最大尺寸为：长366米、宽49米、吃水15.2米，载重吨位约180 000吨。近年来出现了一种新船型——Kamsarmax型散货船，其载重吨达8.2万吨以上，船长229米，船宽32.36米，型深19.9米，结构吃水14.35米，同样可通过巴拿马运河。

（3）Handysize bulk carriers have a deadweight tonnage of 20,000 to 50,000 tons. Among them, those with a deadweight tonnage of over 40,000 tons are also called Handymax bulk carriers.

（3）轻便型散货船（Handysize bulk carrier）指载重量在20 000～50 000吨的散货船，其中载重量超过40 000吨的船舶又被称为大灵便型散货船（Handymax bulk carrier）。

（4）Lakesize bulk carriers navigate through the St. Lawrence Seaway in the Great Lakes region (on the U.S.-Canada border). These ships generally have a deadweight tonnage of around 30,000 tons and are mostly equipped with cargo handling equipment.

（4）大湖型散货船（Lakesize bulk carrier）指经由圣劳伦斯水道航行于美国与加拿大交界处五大湖区的散货船。该型船载重吨一般在30 000吨左右，大多配备起卸货设备。

1.6.2 General Cargo Ship

1.6.2 杂货船

General cargo ships include refrigerated cargo ships, specialized cargo ships, roll on-roll off (ro-ro) cargo ships, general cargo ships, and general cargo/passenger ships. A general cargo ship is designed to carry pretty well every form of dry cargo. Long iron such as railway lines or construction steel is natural for this type of ship, while rolling stock, agricultural machinery and a whole range of factory plants will need a capable sort of ship to accommodate these large, awkward loads. Steel coils are heavy, difficult cargoes that need special stowage and are ideally suited to the modern general cargo ship.

杂货船包括冷藏货船、特种货船、滚装船、杂货船、杂货/旅客船等。杂货船是专为装运各类干货设计的。长形钢材如铁路铁轨和建筑钢材自然地适用这种船型。而机车车辆、农业机械和广泛的工厂设备需要有一种适宜的船舶类型，以适应这些大型、笨重的货物。螺纹钢是较重、运输较麻烦的货物，需要特殊的积载，较适合现代杂货船。

General cargo ships will invariably have their cargo gear, either cranes or derricks, to enable them to trade into ports where there is little port equipment. They may even have a heavy lift derrick to enable large loads of typically up to 70−80 tonnes to be handled, independently of any shore cranes. More modern general cargo ships tend to have fewer holds so that larger and bulkier cargoes can be handled.

杂货船都有自己的装卸设备，或是起重机或是吊杆，可以挂靠设备不足的港口。杂货船甚至有重型起重机，能够处置重达70~80吨的货物而不依赖任何岸上起重机。更现代的杂货船趋向于较少的货舱，这样可以装卸更大型和更笨重的货物。

1.6.3 Oil Tanker

1.6.3 油船

An oil tanker is a specially designed ship for the transport of crude oils. As with the bulk carriers, several terms are used to describe the size ranges of tankers. HANDYSIZE TANKERS are vessels with deadweight in the region from 10,000 to 40,000 DWT. PANAMAX TANKER is a vessel of between 50,000 and 79,000 DWT. AFRAMAX TANKER is a vessel of 80/124, 999 DWT. SUEZMAX TANKER is a vessel of 125/199,999 DWT which is able to transit the Suez Canal. VERY LARGE CRUDE CARRIER

(VLCC) is a vessel between 200/300,000 DWT. ULTRA LARGE CRUDE CARRIER (ULCC) is a crude oil carrier in excess of 300,000 DWT. PRODUCT CARRIER is also a tanker which is generally below 70,000 DWT and used to carry refined oil products from the refinery to the consumer.

油船是专门为原油运输设计的船舶。如同散货船，有一些术语用来描述油船的尺寸大小。小灵便型油船为 10 000~40 000 载重吨。巴拿马型油船为 50 000~79 000 载重吨。阿芙拉型油船为 80 000~124 999 载重吨。苏伊士型油船为 125 000~199 999 载重吨，能够通过苏伊士运河。超大型油船为 200 000~300 000 载重吨。巨型油船为 300 000 以上载重吨。石油成品船也是油船，一般低于 70 000 载重吨，从炼油厂运输炼油产品至消费者。

1.6.4 Container Ship
1.6.4 集装箱船

Containers are the most obvious elements of international shipping; they are seen everywhere. Container ships carry general cargo including high-value cargo in containers (boxes), some of which may be refrigerated. Capacity is expressed as the equivalent number of TEUs (twenty-foot equivalent units) or FEUs (forty-foot equivalent units). Some container ships are fitted with cells.

集装箱是国际航运的最明显因素，随处可见。集装箱船运输各类货物，包括装在集装箱内的高价值货物，其中一些可能是冷藏货物。载货能力以 TEUs（20 英尺标准箱）或 FEUs（40 英尺标准箱）表示。某些集装箱船配备箱格。

Recent years have seen container ship sizes react to scale economies, with the "1st generation" ships of about 1,200 TEU having now grown to an average over of 5,000 TEU on the deep sea trades. Giants of more than 10,000 TEU container ships are now being used by some large liners.

近年来，集装箱船的大小与规模经济相对应，在远洋运输中，"第一代"集装箱船装载 1 200 标准箱，现在已经发展到平均超过 5 000 标准箱以上。超过 10 000 标准箱的巨型集装箱船正在由大型的班轮公司经营。

1.6.5 Other Ships
1.6.5 其他船舶

There are several types of ships falling into this category which include oil/chemical tankers, other tankers, liquefied gas carriers, passenger ro-ro ship, tank barges, general cargo barges, fishing, offshore supply, and all other types.

属于这一类的船舶有几种类型，包括石油/化学品船、其他油船、液化天然气船、客货船、油驳船、杂货驳船、渔船、供应船和其他船舶等。

2. Description of Cargoes
2. 货物说明

The basis of the very existence of maritime transport is the cargo. Over 90% of world trade is carried by the international shipping industry. The maritime transportation industry is fundamental to international trade. Without shipping the import and export of goods on the scale necessary for the modern world would not be possible.

海上运输存在的基础是货物。世界贸易中的90%以上的货物是由国际航运业运输的。海上运输行业对国际贸易是至关重要的。没有航运，现代世界所必需的货物进口和出口便无从实现。

According to the form in which the cargoes are transported, cargoes may be classified as bulk cargoes and general cargoes. Furthermore, the bulk cargo can be classified dry bulk cargo and wet bulk cargo. The chartering business mainly deals with this kind of cargo.

根据货物的运输方式，货物可分为散货和杂货。散货可进一步分为干散货和湿散货。租船业务主要涉及此类货物。

2.1 Commodities Traded by Sea
2.1 海运货物

The main seaborne commodities are divided into six groups reflecting the area of economic activity to which they are most closely related. These groups can be summarized as follows:

海运货物主要分为六类，反映与经济活动密切相关的区域。这些类别总结如下：

2.1.1 Energy Commodities

2.1.1 能源类货物

Energy commodities dominate bulk shipping. This group of commodities, which accounts for close to half of world seaborne trade, comprises crude oil, oil products, liquefied gas, and thermal coal for use in generating electricity.

能源类货物主宰散货航运。这类货物占了世界海运货物运输的将近一半，包括原油、成品油、液化气体和发电使用的热力煤。

2.1.2 Agricultural Commodities

2.1.2 农业类货物

A total of twelve commodities, accounting for about 13 percent of world sea trade, are the products or raw materials of the agricultural industry. They include cereals such as wheat and barley, animal feedstuffs, sugar, molasses, refrigerated food, oil and fats, and fertilizers, etc.

农业类货物共有12种，约占世界海运货物运输的13%，属于农业产品或农业原产品。它们包括小麦和大麦、动物饲料、糖、糖浆、冷冻食品、油脂和化肥等。

2.1.3 Metal Industry Commodities

2.1.3 金属类货物

This major commodity group, which accounts for about 21 percent of world sea trade, includes raw materials and products of the steel and non-ferrous metal industries, etc.

金属类货物属于主要世界海运货物，约占世界海运货物运输的21%，包括钢铁原材料、钢铁产品和非铁金属工业等。

2.1.4 Forest Products Commodities

2.1.4 林业产品货物

Forest products are primarily industrial materials used for the manufacture of paper, paper board, and in the construction industry. This section, which accounts for about 4 percent of world sea trade, includes timber (logs and lumber), wood pulp, plywood, paper and various wood products, etc. The trade is strongly influenced by the availability of forestry resources.

林业产品主要是用于纸张、纸板制造和建筑业的工业材料。这类货物约占世界海运货物运输的4%，包括木材（原木和木材）、木浆、胶合板、纸张及各种木制品等。这类货物运输受到林业资源的强烈影响。

2.1.5 Other Industrial Materials
2.1.5 其他工业材料

There is a wide range of industrial materials such as cement, salt, gypsum, mineral sands, alumina, chemicals, and many others. The total trade in these commodities accounts for about 9 percent of world sea trade. They cover a whole range of industries.

其他工业材料种类繁多，如水泥、盐、石膏、矿砂、氧化铝、化学品等。这些商品的贸易总量约占世界海上贸易的9%，涵盖各行各业。

2.1.6 Other Manufactures Commodities
2.1.6 其他制造业货物

The final trade group comprises the remaining manufactured goods such as textiles, machinery, vehicles, consumer goods etc. The total tonnage involved in this sector accounts for only about 3 percent of world sea trade, but many of these commodities have a high value, so their share is probably closer to 50 percent.

最后一类贸易商品包括纺织品、机械、车辆、消费品等剩余制成品。该领域的贸易总吨位约占世界海上贸易的3%，但其中许多货物具有很高的价值，所以其价值占比可能接近总量的50%。

2.2 Bulk Shipping Cargoes
2.2 散装货

Bulk cargoes are usually defined as commodities that are neither on pallets nor in containers, and that are not handled as individual pieces. There are two main categories of bulk cargoes. One is the dry bulk cargo, which is further divided into major bulks and minor bulks; the other is liquid bulk cargo, which mainly includes crude oil and petroleum products.

散装货通常定义为既不使用托盘也不装入集装箱，且不作为单件货物装卸的货物。散装货物大致可分为两大类。一类是干散货，进一步细分为大宗散货和小宗散货；另一类是液体散装货物，主要包括原油和石油产品。

2.2.1 Dry Bulk Cargoes
2.2.1 干散货

Dry bulk cargoes are used by many industries such as manufacturing and construction, and are divided into major bulk commodities and minor bulk commodities. Major bulks consist of iron ore, coal, grain, bauxite/alumina, and phosphate. Minor bulks cover a wide variety of commodities, such as forest products, iron and steel products, fertilizers, agricultural products, cement, other construction materials, and salt.

干散货在许多行业如制造业和建筑业使用，分为主要的大宗散货商品和小宗散货商品。

大宗散货主要包括铁矿石、煤炭、谷物、铝土矿、磷酸盐。小宗散货涵盖了许多不同种类的货物，如林业产品、钢铁产品、化肥、农产品、水泥、其他建筑材料以及盐。

Iron ore is shipped in Capesize vessels in the main, the principal trades being from Brazil, Australia, and India.

铁矿石运输以好望角型船为主，铁矿石主要来自巴西、澳大利亚和印度。

The traditional exporting countries for coal are Australia, South Africa, Colombia, the USA, China, and Russia, though in recent years Indonesia has become the biggest supplier. Coal is shipped mainly in Panamax vessels but in the case of the Baltic and the Black Sea, due to draught restrictions in ports, and it is mainly transported in Supramax or Handysize vessels.

传统的煤炭出口国家是澳大利亚、南非、哥伦比亚、美国、中国和俄罗斯，但近年来印度尼西亚已成为最大的供应商。煤炭运输以巴拿马型船为主，但在波罗的海和黑海，由于港口吃水的限制，以超灵便型船和灵便型船为主。

Traditionally the producers of coarse grains and fertilizers are the USA, Latin America, and Australia but there are many smaller suppliers. Seaborne trade is mainly in Panamax and Supramax, and, in smaller ports, Handysize vessels.

传统的粗粮和化肥生产地区是美国、拉丁美洲和澳大利亚，但还有许多较小的供应商。海运贸易以巴拿马型船和超灵便型船为主，在小港口，以灵便型船为主。

Minor bulks are shipped worldwide in Panamax, Supramax and Handysize vessels, depending on the consignments, port limitations, and routes.

小宗散货通过巴拿马型船、超灵便型船和灵便型船在全球范围内运输，具体船型选择取决于货物、港口的限制和航线要求。

2.2.2 Liquid Bulk Cargoes

2.2.2 液体散装货物

Crude oil and petroleum products are major transport commodities, representing approximately one-third of the total world seaborne trade. The group of liquid bulk cargoes also includes a number of other commodities, such as vegetable and animal oils, wine, chemicals etc. Some tankers are employed in the transport of fresh water in the Mediterranean and Arabian Gulf.

原油和石油产品是主要运输商品，大约占世界海运贸易的三分之一。液体散装货物还包括其他货物，如菜籽油和动物油、葡萄酒、化学品等。某些油船在地中海和阿拉伯海湾从事淡水运输。

UNIT 4 STANDARD CHARTER PARTY FORMS
第四单元　标准租船合同范本

The economics of the chartering business do not only depend on the rates, but also on the transport terms and conditions stipulated in the relevant charter parties. To simplify negotiations between the parties, these charter parties are based on standard contract forms designed and published by international bodies. Charter party forms are perhaps one of the most important facilitators of trade and transport. They are an essential tool for sea trading and the avoidance of disputes between the two parties that are involved, and they can be tailored to virtually every kind of trade or ship type.

租船业务的经济性不仅取决于费率，还取决于相关租船合同中规定的运输条款和条件。为了简化各方之间的洽谈，这些租船合同是以国际机构设计和公布的标准合同范本为基础进行的。租船合同范本或许是促进贸易和运输最重要的因素之一。它们是海上贸易的重要工具，可避免相关方之间的纠纷，并且几乎可以针对每种贸易或船舶类型进行定制。

1. Development of Standard Charter Party Forms
1. 标准租船合同范本的发展

It was in the early nineteenth century that shipowners and charterers first became concerned with the draughting of standard charter party forms. Such forms were originally draughted and employed by individual contracting parties, but joint action was later undertaken by groups of shipowners and charterers. An early development began with parties involved in chartering specific trades co-operating on the joint issue of agreed documents.

在19世纪初，船舶出租人和承租人开始着手起草标准租船合同范本。这种范本最初是由个别签约方自行起草并使用，但后来船舶出租人和承租人团体共同采取行动，制定范本。其早期发展于租船业务当事人在特定的货物运输上合作颁布的双方同意的范本。

In the last century, the Baltic and International Maritime Council in Copenhagen (BIMCO), founded in 1905, had played and still plays a significant role in the development of internationally utilized standard forms. BIMCO is a shipping association providing a wide range of services to its global membership of stakeholders with vested interests in the shipping industry, including shipowners, operators, managers, brokers, and agents. The association's main objective is to facilitate the commercial operations of its member by developing standard contracts and clauses, and providing quality information, advice, and education. It has issued or approved a great number of standard charter party forms. Other international bodies are also active in draughting charter parties, and in some trades the charterers themselves have draughted charter parties for their own commodities.

在20世纪，于哥本哈根成立的波罗的海国际航运公会（BIMCO，成立于1905年），对使用国际标准范本的发展发挥了重要作用，并且至今仍在发挥着这一作用。BIMCO是为投资航运业的全球股东会员们包括船舶出租人、经营者、管理者、经纪人和代理人提供广泛服务范围的一个航运协会。该协会的主要目标是通过制定标准合同和条款并提供高质量的信息、咨询、教育，促进成员们的商业运作。它已颁布或批准了许多标准租船合同范本。其他国际机构也积极参与租船合同的起草，在一些货物运输中，承租人自己也为其特定商品草拟了租船合同。

2. Types of Standard Charter Party Forms
2. 标准租船合同范本的种类

Charter party forms used in shipping today are numerous, with many objectives and terms. Some charter party forms can be termed as friendly to the charterers while others can be regarded as favorable from the point of view of the shipowners.

目前航运业使用的租船合同范本种类很多，范本的目的和条件不同。有些租船合同的范本被认为有利于承租人，而其他被视为有利于船舶出租人。

The international bodies have issued or approved a great number of charter party forms many of which are so-called standard charter party forms, as they result from negotiations between charterers' interests, on the one hand, and shipowners' interests, on the other. These are generally referred to as "official" forms because they have been inspected and passed by an authoritative body.

国际机构已签发或批准大量的租船合同范本，其中有许多被称为标准租船合同范本，因为它们是承租人和托运人与船舶出租人之间利益洽谈的结果。这些范本一般被称为"正式"范本，因为它们已经由某个权威机构检查并通过。

A further type of standard charter party form is the so-called "private" form, which is issued and employed by individual firms, usually charterers enjoying more or less of a monopoly in a particular trade and therefore in a position generally to impose their forms on the shipowners.

另外一种类型的标准租船合同范本被称为"私人"范本，是由个别企业签发和使用的。通常此类承租人或多或少垄断某一行业，因此有能力迫使船舶出租人使用他们自己的范本。

3. General Aspects of Standard Charter Party Forms
3. 标准租船合同范本概述

The charter party is the written charter agreement. It contains all the terms and conditions which govern the relationship between the shipowner and charterer. Several charter parties have a code name, often printed at the top of the form. The clauses are numbered and sometimes every line is numbered, this is the case with, e.g., Gencon Form.

租船合同是书面租船协议。它包含所有的条款和条件，制约船舶出租人和承租人之间的关系。有些租船合同有一个代码，常常印在格式的顶部。条款均被编号，有时每行都被编号，例如金康范本。

In the modern charter party forms the box layout system is used, which means that the written agreement is divided into two main parts, the box part is Part 1 with all specifications for the relevant vessel and the voyage, and the text part is the Part 2 with all the printed clauses. In the event of a conflict of conditions, the provisions of Part 1 shall prevail over those of Part 2 to the extent of such conflict.

现代租船合同格式一般使用框栏布局，这意味着书面协议分为两个主要部分，框栏部分是第一部分，规定有关船舶及航程，文本部分为第二部分，包括所有印刷条款。在冲突的情况下，第一部分的规定优先适用于第二部分的规定。

In most cases of chartering business practice, the charter party also has a third section, riders and addenda, where the parties insert additional photocopied standard clauses or typewritten clauses as deemed necessary.

在大多数租船业务中，租船合同还包括第三部分、附加条款和附录，即当事人根据需要插入额外的、复印的或打印的标准条款。

4. Advantages of Using Standard Charter Party Forms
4. 使用标准租船合同范本的优点

The standard charter party form plays a role of considerable importance in present chartering practice. The purpose of using a standard charter party form is to standardize a number of clauses frequently used but varying in different trades, and to help the parties since it will only be necessary to fill in certain items, such as the names of the parties, the vessel, ports, cargoes, laytime, freight payment, notice time, hire, etc.

标准租船合同范本在租船实务中发挥了相当重要的作用。标准租船合同范本的使用规范了许多经常使用但在不同业务中变动的条款，并方便了当事人，因为其只需要填写一些事项，如当事人的姓名、船舶、港口、货物、装卸时间、运费支付方式、通知时间、租金等数据。

As to the advantages to be derived from the use of such a form, it should be pointed out, firstly, that often the parties to a charter contract are domiciled in different countries and that the negotiations, which to a great extent are carried out through the intermediary of one or several brokers, are often performed under considerable time pressure. By basing the negotiations on a standard form, the contents of which are well-known or readily available to both sides, the parties can concentrate their attention on the particular points on which they require individual regulation, leaving all other questions to be regulated by the terms of the standard form. The use of a standard form, moreover, means that the parties run no risk of being caught out by an unusual clause or a clause imposing unreasonable or unexpected burdens on them. This, in turn, means cheaper freight rates since the shipowner does not have to reckon on the freight to cover him for such risks. Generally speaking, it reduces the risk of misunderstanding and ensuing disputes arising in respect of the matters covered by the contract.

使用这种范本的优点，应被指出的是，第一，通常情况下，租船合同的当事方居住在不同的国家，双方的洽谈在很大程度上是通过一个或几个经纪人进行，且要在时间紧迫的情况下完成。立足一个标准范本的洽谈，其内容是众所周知或可随时提供给双方的，双方可以把精力放在他们需要单独注意的地方，让所有其他问题由标准范本解决。标准范本的使用，意味着对各方来说没有一个不寻常的条款或对他们施加不合理的或意外的风险，反之又意味着运费更便宜，因为船舶出租人的运费计算可以不考虑这种风险。一般来说，它能降低就合同所涉事项产生误解及随之引发争议的风险。

The employment of standard forms in international chartering has an important effect also from a general legal standpoint, in that they contribute to international uniformity. The fact is that standard forms are very largely draughted in the English language and are based on English legal thinking supports this tendency toward international uniformity. Selected major charter party forms are shown in Table 1.

从一般的法律角度上看，使用国际租船标准范本有重要作用，因为它们有助于国际一致性。事实上，标准范本在很大程度上是以英语起草的，并以英语为基础的法律思想支持这一国际统一的趋势。主要精选租船合同标准范本清单如表1所示。

Table 1 List of Selected Major Charter Party Forms

VOYAGE FORMS			
Name	Date	Code Name	Publisher
Uniform General	1922, 1976, 1994, 2022	GENCON	BIMCO
North American Grain	1973(amended 1989)	NORGRAIN 89	ASBA
Australian Wheat	1990	AUSTWHEAT	Australian Wheat Board
Australian Barley	1975(revised 1980)	AUSTBAR	Australian Barley Board
Fertilizer Charter	1942 (amended 1974)	FERTICON	UK Chamber of Shipping
North American Fertilizer	1978 (revised 1988)	FERTIVOY 88	Canpotex Shipping Services
Americanized Welsh Coal	1953 (revised 1993)	AMWELSH	ASBA
Australian Coal Charter		AUSCOAL	
Standard Ore	1980	OREVOY	BIMCO
Voyage charter party for the transportation of bulk cement	1990 (revised 2006)	CEMENTVOY 2006	BIMCO
Iron Ore	1973	NIPPONORE	The Japan Shipping Ex. Inc.
Mediterranean Iron Ore		C (ORE) 7	
Sugar C/P	1999		
Cuban Sugar	1973	CUBASUGAR	
Baltic Wood	1964 (revised 1997)	NUBLTWOOD	UK Chamber of Shipping
Russian Wood	1995	RUSWOOD	BIMCO

VOYAGE FORMS			
Name	Date	Code Name	Publisher
C/P for Logs	1967	NANYOZAI	The Japan Shipping Exchange Inc.
Tanker Voyage C/P	1994	TEXACOVOY 94	TEXACO
Tanker Voyage C/P	1990	EXXONVOY 90	Exxon International
Tanker Voyage C/P	1994	VELAVOY 94	Vela International Marine Ltd.
Tanker Voyage C/P	1987	TANKERVOY 87	INTERTANKO
Gas Voyage Charter Party	2005	GASVOY 2005	BIMCO
TIME CHARTER FORMS			
Uniform Time Charter	1939 (amended 1974, revised 2001)	BALTIME	BIMCO
New York Produce Exchange T/C	1913 (amended 1921, 1931, 1946, 1993)	NYPE 1993	ASBA
Uniform Time Charter for Container Vessels	1990 (revised 2004)	BOXTIME	BIMCO
Tanker Time Charter	2001	BPTIME	BP Shipping Limited
BAREBOAT CHARTER FORM			
Standard Bareboat	1989 (amended 2001)	BARECON	BIMCO

5. Classification of Charter Party Terms
5. 租船合同条款分类

In determining whether the innocent party has the right to treat the contract as discharged it seems that regard must first be had to the nature of the contractual term that has been breached. For this purpose, the contractual terms may be placed in one of three categories, namely condition, warranty, and intermediate terms.

为了明确受害方是否有权解除合同，首先要看被违反的租船合同条款的性质。就此目的而言，租船合同中的条款基本上可分为三类，即条件条款、保证条款和中间性条款。

5.1 Condition Terms
5.1 条件条款

A condition in this context is a term of such important that any breach of it entitles the innocent party to treat the contract as discharged and claim damages.

条件条款是指合同中那些重要条款，违反这些条款，受害方有权取消合同，并可提出赔偿要求。

Condition terms will be so classified, it seems, in the following cases:

条件条款归纳如下：

(1) Where the obligation is designated as a condition in a statute;

（1）成文法中明文规定作为条件的义务责任条款；

(2) Where the obligation is specifically designated in the contract as a condition;

（2）合同中明确指出作为条件的义务责任；

(3) Where the obligation has been held to be a condition in another case;

（3）判例中被视为条件的条款；

(4) Where the supposed intention of the parties, as indicated from the terms and general background of the contract, so indicate.

（4）根据合同条款、合同背景所表示出的双方意图，确定为条件的条款。

5.2 Warranty Terms
5.2 保证条款

A warranty in this context is a term of the contract of such minor importance that any breach of it does not entitle the innocent party to treat the contract as discharged. For breach of such a term, the innocent party can make only a claim for damages.

保证条款是指合同中次要的条款，违反这种条款，受害方不能取消合同，但可提出赔偿要求。

5.3 Intermediate Terms
5.3 中间性条款

Any term of the contract that cannot be classified as a condition or a warranty will be classified as an intermediate term. Whether a breach of such a term does or does not entitle the innocent party to treat the contract as discharged depends on the nature and consequences of the particular breach that has occurred.

中间性条款是指介于条件条款和保证条款之间的合同条款。合同当事人一方违反这种条款时，受害方究竟是按违反条件条款处理，还是按违反保证条款处理，要视违约程度和后果而定。

The court will inquire whether the resulting event has the effect of depriving the other party of substantially all the benefit which it was the intention of the parties that he should obtain from the contract. If the event has this effect, the innocent party may treat the contract as discharged; otherwise, he can make only a claim for damages.

法院将审查由此产生的事件是否具有这样的效果，即剥夺了另一方当事人本应从合同中获得的，双方当事人意图使其得到的实质上的全部利益。如果有这种影响，受害的一方可以将合同解除，否则他只能要求损害赔偿。

6. Principles of Interpretation of Charter Party
6. 租船合同解释原则

The relationship between shipowner and charterer is determined by the charter party and the basis will then normally be a standard charter party form which is modified and amended by riders and addenda by the individual agreement. Several legal problems may arise when the individual terms and conditions are entered into the standard charter party form.

船舶出租人和承租人之间的关系取决于租船合同，其通常是以一个标准的租船合同范本为蓝本并根据各自协议通过附加条款和附录的形式加以修改或变更。当单独的条款和条件纳入标准租船合同范本时，一些法律问题可能会出现。

Courts and arbitrators may apply various principles or methods in their interpretation. The primary consideration in construing any contract is the intention of the contracting parties.

法院和仲裁员在加以解释时可能采用不同的原则和方法。解释任何合同时主要考虑缔约各方的意愿。

One interpretation principles is generally considered to be that clauses stamped or typed into the charter party will prevail over the original printed text. In this case, the written, stamped on or typed clause should usually prevail, as it clearly expresses the intention of the parties.

解释的原则之一是通常认为盖章或打印条款将优于印就的原始文本。在这种情况下，书面的、盖章或打印的条款通常应该优先适用，因为其清楚地表达了各方的意愿。

Where both clauses are printed or both typewritten, a clause specifically designed to deal with a limited range of circumstances will, so far as concerns matter falling within that range, prevail over a clause of general application.

如果两个条款都是印就的或打印的，则针对特定情形专门设计的条款，就该情形范围内的事项而言，应优先于普遍适用的条款。

Another principle that may be applied is that imprecise and ambiguous wording will be construed against the party who furnished the provision.

另一种可能采用的原则是对于不确切和模棱两可的条款，应做出对提供该条款一方不利的解释。

The rule of interpretation known as the "ejusdem generis" rule is often applied. That is to say, general words that are tacked on to specific words are to be construed as referring only to things or circumstances of the same kind as those described by the specific words. The ejusdem generis rule may be excluded by apt words in the document.

"同类规则"也经常作为解释原则来使用。也就是说，对附随于确定性文字之后的总括性词语的含义，应当根据确定性文字所涉及的同类或者同级事项予以确定。文本中适当的文字可能会排除适用同类规则。

The words must be construed in their ordinary meaning, but technical words must be given their technical meaning. Where the words are capable of two constructions, the reasonable construction is to be preferred as representing the presumed intention of the parties.

条款用语必须根据其通常含义来解释，而专业术语必须赋予其专业含义。当条款用语可作两种解释时，则应优先采用合理解译，以此体现双方当事人的推定意图。

UNIT 5　CHARTER MARKET
第五单元　租船市场

The charter market is a specific geographical area where the demand and supply of tramp services interact and transport prices are established.

租船市场是一个特定的地理区域，在此区域内，不定期船运输服务的供需相互作用，运输价格得以确定。

1. Characteristics of the Charter Market
1. 租船市场的特点

The charter market is highly competitive, and exhibits many of the characteristics of the perfect competition model. The commodities is homogeneous, entry costs are very low, many companies are competing for business (arguably each ship is a separate competitive unit), and information flows make the market very transparent. The freight rates achievable in the market are highly volatile, depending on market circumstances.

租船市场极具竞争性，展现出完全竞争模型的许多特征。货物是均质的；进入成本很低；许多企业进行商业竞争（每艘船可以说是一个单独的竞争单位）；信息的流动使市场非常透明。市场上可达成的运费率波动幅度极大，具体取决于市场形势。

The charter market is complex and often volatile, in which large sums can sometimes be gained or lost. Therein lies one of the fascinations of the shipping industry. Tramp shipping revenues are determined competitively in the international marketplace, generally through the well-developed network of shipbrokers and agents that facilitate these transactions. However, the precise nature of the process differs for bulk and specialized segments.

租船市场复杂且通常波动剧烈，在那里会赚取或损失大量的资金，航运业的魅力之一就在于此。不定期船的运费收入在国际市场中通过竞争确定，通常借助成熟的船舶经纪人和代理人网络促成交易。然而，这一过程的具体特征在散货运输板块和专业运输板块中存在差异。

Tramp shipping has relatively few barriers to entry. New investors require equity, but commercial shipping banks will provide loans to creditworthy applicants against a first mortgage on the ship. There is a comprehensive network of support services to which new investors can subcontract most business functions (subject to sound management controls). Ship management companies will manage the ships for a fee. Chartering brokers arrange employment for the vessels, collect revenues, and handle claims. Sale and purchase brokers will buy and sell ships. Maritime lawyers and accountants undertake legal and administrative functions. Classification societies and technical consultants provide technical support.

不定期船运输的准入门槛相对较低。新投资者需要自有资金，但商业航运银行会向信誉良好的申请人提供贷款，以船舶的首次抵押作为担保。新投资者可将大部分业务职能分包给完善的支持服务网络（需符合健全的管理控制要求）。船舶管理公司会收取费用为船舶提供管理服务。租船经纪人负责为船舶安排营运任务、收取运费并处理索赔事宜。船舶买卖经纪人负责船舶的买卖交易。海事律师和会计师承担法律及行政职能。船级社和技术咨询机构提供技术支持。

Information systems in the bulk shipping business are very open, providing buyers and sellers of ships, operators, and charterers with a timely flow of commercial data. Information about revenues and asset prices is published daily and widely circulated within the industry to both shipowners and charterers by shipbrokers business and information publishers. These information services ensure a high degree of transparency. In addition, the operating costs of different ships types are well known, making it easy for potential investors to estimate prevailing profit levels and enter the market quickly. Up-to-the-minute knowledge of developing in the charter market is the key to successful chartering, as in other businesses. A constant flow of information is exchanged via telex, radio and phone, e-mail, or internet between the world's major shipping centers, covering the latest rates, available commodities for shipment, ship schedules, tonnage offered, etc.

不定期航运业务的信息系统非常开放，给船舶的买家和卖方、经营者和承租人提供实时的商业数据。收入和资产价格信息由船舶经纪人和信息出版商每日发布并广泛散发给船舶出租人和承租人。这些信息服务确保了高透明度。另外，经营不同类型的船舶成本是众所周知的，这使潜在的投资者易于估算当前的利润水平并快速投入市场。获取航运市场的最新信息是租船业务取得成功的关键，如同其他业务一样。持续不断的信息流通过电传、电报、无线电话、电子邮件或互联网在世界主要航运中心之间交换，内容包括最新的费率、可装运的货物、船期、可提供的吨位等。

2. Influence Factors on the Charter Market
2. 租船市场的影响因素

The charter market is huge and complex with shipowners, operators, and charterers at the mercy of fluctuating freight rates. Thousands of events can have an impact on the cost of sea transport and anyone moving bulk commodities operates in an extremely volatile environment. The charter market is subject to a wide range of external variables, but it is fundamentally driven by the following factors.

租船市场是巨大的、复杂的，船舶出租人、经营者和承租人在波动的运费中随波逐流。数以千计的事件可能对海上运输成本产生影响，任何运输散货的人都是在一个非常动荡的环境中经营。租船市场受到众多外部因素的影响，但主要是受以下因素影响。

2.1 Fleet Supply
2.1 船队供给

If, for instance, more vessels are available in a given area of the world than commodities for shipment, the shipowner would most probably be forced to accept a lower rate to secure employment for the ship. This is determined by the number of available ships, their capacity, and the utilization rates. Additionally, the average age of the fleets will determine where they are in the life cycle. The average ship lasts 25 years. If the average is closer to that number, supply will be decreasing in the short term. Also, supply is greatly determined by the delivery of new vessels.

如果，在世界某一特定地区船舶数量比货物需求多，船舶出租人很可能会被迫接受较低的运价，以确保船舶货载。这是由现有的船舶数目、载货量和利用率所决定的。此外，船队的平均船龄将决定它们的营运周期。船舶的平均船龄为25年。如果平均值接近这一数字，在短期内供给将会减少。同样，新船交付在很大程度上决定了供给。

2.2 Commodity Demand
2.2 货物需求

What are the levels of industrial production? Has the grain harvest been successful? Are the power stations importing more coal? How is the steel industry performing? If there are more cargoes for shipment than available vessels, the charterer will be compelled to pay more than he originally anticipated when scanning the market for empty cargo space for his commodity.

工业生产的水平如何？粮食产量是否理想？发电厂是否在进口更多的煤炭？钢铁行业的表现如何？如果货物数量比船舶供给多的话，当承租人在租船市场上寻求舱位时，他将不得不付出超过他最初预期的运费。

2.3 Seasonal Pressure
2.3 季节性压力

The weather has a big impact on the shipping markets from the size of harvests to ice in ports and river levels. For demand, cold weather may increase the demand for coal and other energy-creating raw materials.

气候对航运市场有很大影响，其影响范围涵盖农作物收成规模、港口结冰情况及河流水位高低。从需求来看，寒冷天气可能会增加对煤炭等能源原材料的需求。

2.4 Bunker Fuel Prices
2.4 燃油价格

Bunker fuel is a type of fuel oil a ship uses for propulsion. With bunker fuel accounting for between one-quarter and one-third of the cost of running a vessel, oil price movements directly affect shipowners. Higher crude oil prices also mean higher bunker fuel prices which will be reflected in higher charter market prices.

船用燃油是一种船舶航行使用的燃油。由于船用燃油占船舶营运费用的四分之一或三分之一，石油价格变动直接影响着船舶出租人。较高的原油价格也意味着较高的船用燃油价格，反映在租船市场则是更高的运费价格。

2.5 Choke Points
2.5 咽喉要道

This factor can particularly affect tankers with almost half of the world's oil passing through a handful of relatively narrow shipping lanes. These points include the Straits of Hormuz and the Straits of Malacca, the Suez Canal and Panama Canal, and other important channels. Their closure, whether due to conflict, terrorist attack, or collision in overcrowded shipping lanes, would change the entire world's supply patterns.

这一因素尤其会对油船产生影响，因为全球近一半的石油会经过少数几条相对狭窄的航道运输。这些航道包括霍尔木兹海峡、马六甲海峡、苏伊士运河和巴拿马运河及其他重要航道。这些航道的关闭，无论是因为冲突、恐怖袭击或在拥挤航道中发生碰撞，都将改变整个世界的供给格局。

These geographic choke points cause natural caps in the number of ships that can pass through each day, month, or year and therefore also limit the bulk tonnage capacity of certain shipping routes. If anything disrupts the flow of ships through the choke points, the charter market rates will increase.

这些地理上的咽喉要道造成了船舶每天、每月和每年通过数量的自然瓶颈，因此也限制了某些航线的运输总吨位。如果有任何事情中断船舶在咽喉要道的通过，租船市场运价就会上涨。

2.6 Port Congestion
2.6 港口拥挤

This acts as another great buffer against supply increases that would lower market prices. The infrastructure of these ports prevents more ships from entering the market. The ports simply cannot handle more traffic. Until major changes are made to these vital terminals, there will be upward pressure on dry bulk prices.

这构成了另一个重要缓冲，可抵御供应增加可能导致的市场价格下跌。这些港口的基础设施限制了更多船舶进入市场。港口根本无法承载更多的运输量。除非对这些关键码头进行重大改造，否则干散货价格将面临上涨压力。

3. Classification of the Charter Market
3. 租船市场的分类

The charter market cannot be rigidly divided into separate segments but it is possible to identify its rough divisions. Basedon ship type, size and particular commodities, it can be divided into categories such as the dry cargo market, heavy-lift market, reefer market, tanker market, etc. The charter market is divided by the length of the charter: the short-term "spot" market and the longer-term "period" market. Short-term chartering may take the form of voyage charters or TCTs. The period market includes longer-term time charters, COA, and long-term bareboat charters. Long ago, several important charter markets developed, such as the Baltic Mercantile and Shipping Exchange in London (recognized as the market with the longest history and the most chartering activity), the N.Y. Shipping Exchange, the North Europe Market, and Asian Markets including Tokyo, Hong Kong, Shanghai, and Singapore.

　　租船市场不能被死板地划分为不同的细分市场，但可以区分其主要分类。根据船舶种类、尺寸及特定货物，租船市场可以分为干散货市场、重件货市场、冷藏货市场、油船市场等。根据租约的期限可分为短期"即期"市场和长期"定期"市场。即期租船形式包括航次租船或航次期租形式。定期市场包括长期定期租船、包运租船和长期的光船租船。在很久之前，几个重要的租船市场即已经形成，如伦敦的波罗的海商业和航运交易所（被公认为拥有最长历史和租船业务最活跃的市场），纽约航运交易所、北欧市场以及包括日本东京、中国香港、中国上海和新加坡在内的亚洲市场。

【ASSIGNMENT】

Ⅰ. **Answer the following questions and check your answers from the text.**

1. What does voyage chartering mean?

2. What does time chartering mean?

3. What does bareboat chartering mean?

4. What does COA mean?

5. What does TCT mean?

Ⅱ. **Choice questions.** (Choose the one you think is correct from the following.)

1. The person who enters into a voyage charter with the shipowner is called (　　).

　　A. shipowner　　　　　　　　B. charterer

　　C. broker　　　　　　　　　　D. agent

2. Which of following charters is used in a voyage chartering? (　　)

　　A. GENCON.　　　　　　　　B. NYPE.

　　C. BALTIME.　　　　　　　　D. BARECON.

3. Which of following charters is used in a time chartering? (　　)

　　A. GENCON.　　　　　　　　B. NYPE.

　　C. MULTFORM.　　　　　　　D. BARECON.

4. The bunker is payable by (　　) during the period of time chartering.

　　A. shipowner　　　　　　　　B. charterer

　　C. shipper　　　　　　　　　　D. broker

5. Consecutive voyage chartering is a special type of (　　).

　　A. voyage charter　　　　　　B. time charter

　　C. bareboat charter　　　　　　D. TCT

Ⅲ. **True or false questions.**

1. The risk of loss of time at sea is in principle borne by the shipowner under the time charter party, while under a voyage charter party, the risk of loss of time is normally for the charterer's account. (　　)

2. Gross tonnage is the ship's weight of cargo. (　　)

3. The vessel's cubic capacity is a very important figure for loading heavy cargo. (　　)

4. A condition is a term of the contract that is of such importance that any breach of it will entitle the innocent party to treat the whole contract as discharged. (　　)

5. The charter market is a definite geographical area where the demand and supply of tramp services are confront each other and the price of transport is established. (　　)

MODULE |TWO
CHARTERING PROCEDURE AND PRACTICE

模块二　租船程序和实务

LEARNING OBJECTIVES

Through studying this module, students will be required to obtain a basic knowledge of chartering procedures and practices such as chartering quotes, chartering offers, counter offers, and chartering acceptances, and familiarize themselves with the terms and conditions in fixture notes.

学习目标

通过学习本模块，学生应获得租船程序和实务的基本知识，诸如租船询价、租船要约、租船还价、租船承诺以及熟悉租船确认书中的条款和条件。

CONTENTS

1. Chartering Procedure;
2. Chartering Practice

学习内容

1. 租船程序；
2. 租船实务。

⊙ KEY POINTS

Chartering Quote; Chartering Offer; Subject to Details; Subject to Open; Subject to Stem; Voyage Chartering Fixture Notes; TCT Fixture Notes; Chartering Practice.

学习要点

租船询价；租船要约；以细节内容为条件；以船舶未出租为条件；以发货人同意受载期为准；航次租船确认书；航次期租确认书；租船实务。

⊙ SKILL REQUIREMENTS

1. Have obtained basic knowledge of chartering procedures;

2. Have the ability to make out a quote of voyage chartering;

3. Have the ability to make out an offer of voyage chartering;

4. Have the ability to understand charter fixture notes;

5. Have the ability to master chartering practice.

技能要求

1. 获得租船程序的基本知识；

2. 具备编制航次租船询价的能力；

3. 具备编制航次租船要约的能力；

4. 具备理解租船确认书的能力；

5. 具备掌握租船实务的能力。

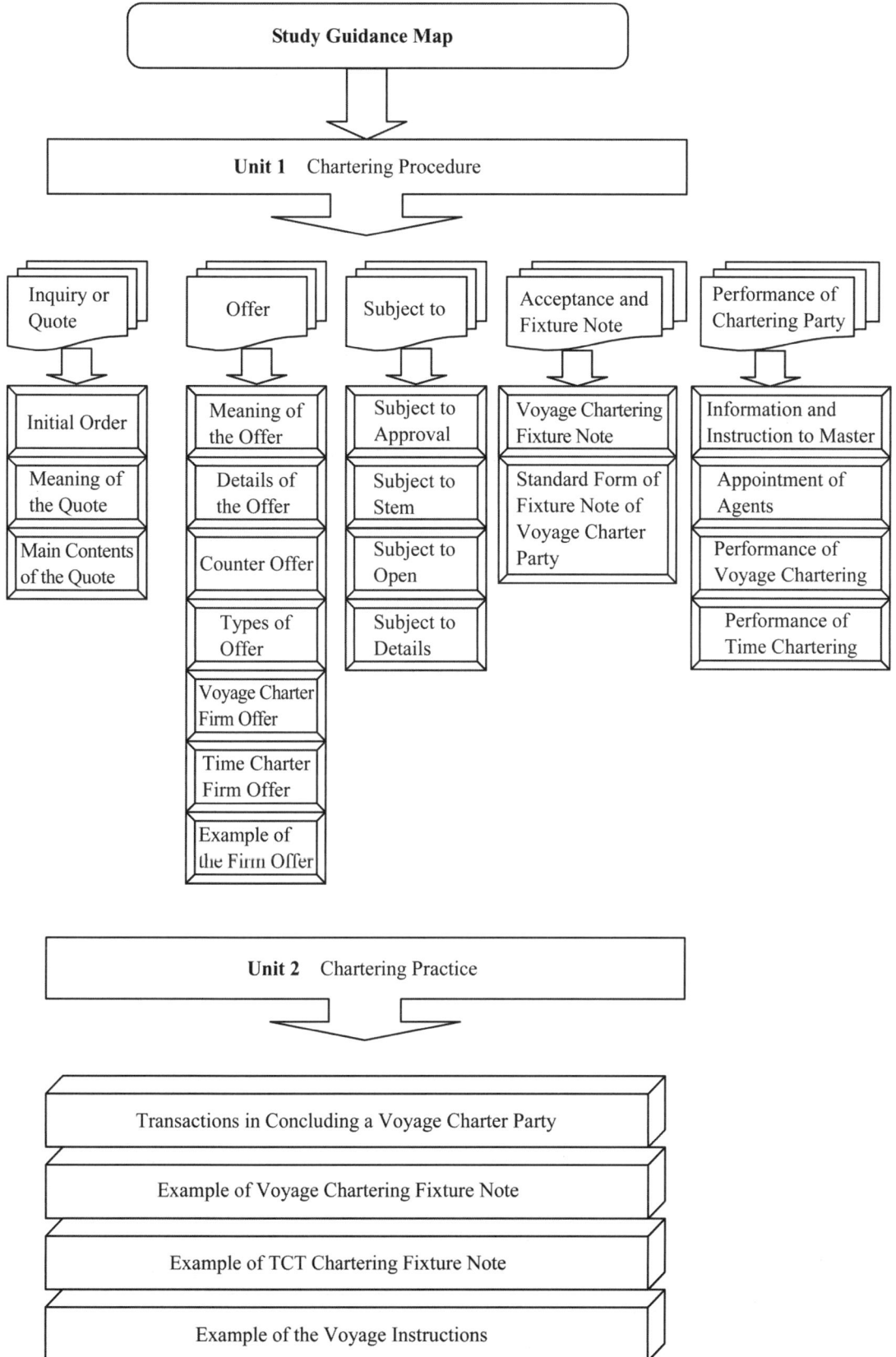

Study Guidance Map

Unit 1 Chartering Procedure

Inquiry or Quote

Offer

Subject to

Acceptance and Fixture Note

Performance of Chartering Party

Initial Order

Meaning of the Quote

Main Contents of the Quote

Meaning of the Offer

Details of the Offer

Counter Offer

Types of Offer

Voyage Charter Firm Offer

Time Charter Firm Offer

Example of the Firm Offer

Subject to Approval

Subject to Stem

Subject to Open

Subject to Details

Voyage Chartering Fixture Note

Standard Form of Fixture Note of Voyage Charter Party

Information and Instruction to Master

Appointment of Agents

Performance of Voyage Chartering

Performance of Time Chartering

Unit 2 Chartering Practice

Transactions in Concluding a Voyage Charter Party

Example of Voyage Chartering Fixture Note

Example of TCT Chartering Fixture Note

Example of the Voyage Instructions

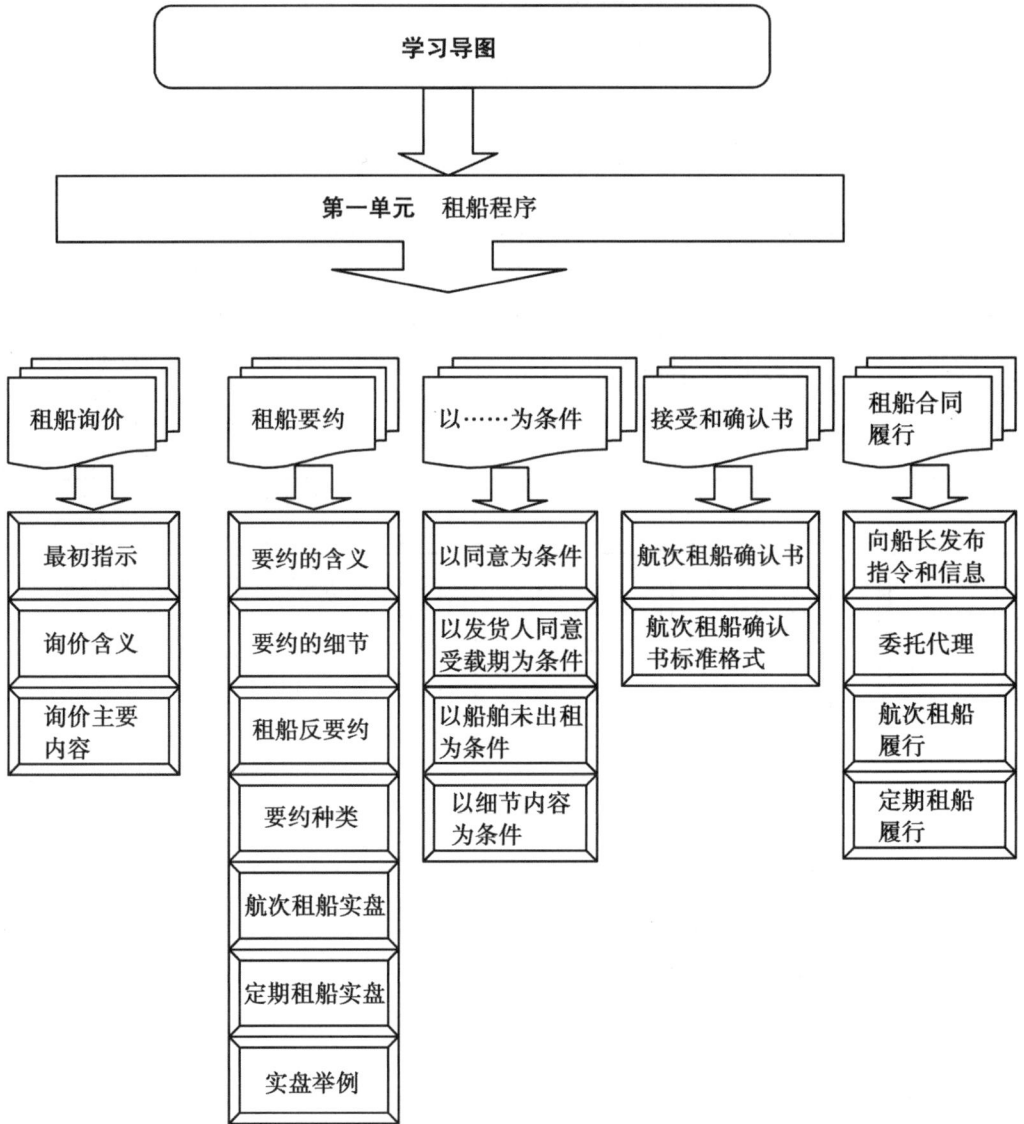

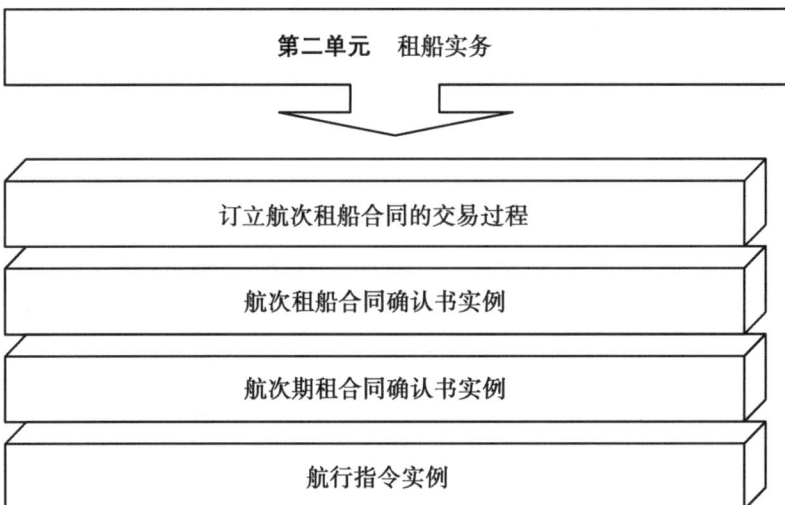

UNIT 1　CHARTERING PROCEDURE
第一单元　租船程序

The essential elements to all charters, indeed to all contracts, are offers and acceptance. In chartering negotiations, steps such as offers and counter offers are exchanged between brokers or parties until the business is either concluded by one party accepting the other's last offer or by one or the other party withdrawing from negotiations if their last offer is rejected. If both parties agree to the terms by signing a fixture note, the charter party is finally and formally concluded between the shipowner and the charterer.

所有租船合同，乃至所有合同的基本要素都是要约和承诺。在租船洽谈中，租船要约、租船反要约等步骤在经纪人和委托人之间传递，直到一方接受另一方的最后要约或者一方或另一方的最后要约被拒绝而停止。如果双方同意签署租船确认书就条款达成一致，船舶出租人和承租人之间的租船合同即正式订立。

1. Inquiry or Quote
1. 租船询价

1.1 Initial Order
1.1 最初指示

It is usual to consider the initial order to come from the charterer, since the movement of cargo is the core element of the shipping industry. The following is an example of the initial order from the charterer to the broker for time chartering: "Please find a ship of about ten thousand tons that we could charter for 12 months to carry consignments of wheat from ports of North America to various ports along China's coast. The issue of speed is important, as the ship we need must be able to achieve a fast turnaround. Please advise us if you can secure a suitable ship and let us know the relevant terms and conditions."

通常认为，最初指示来自承租人，因为货物运输是航运业的核心要素。下面是承租人向租船经纪人就定期租船发出的指示示例："请寻找一艘载重吨大约为 10 000 吨的船舶，我们将租用 12 个月，从北美港口运输小麦到中国沿海各口岸。航速的问题很重要，因为我们需要船舶必须能够尽快地往返航行。如果你能找到一艘合适的船舶，请告知我们并让我们知晓相关条款和条件。"

1.2 Meaning of the Quote
1.2 询价含义

Once a charterer has passed their order to their brokers, the brokers will be galvanized into action to request quotes from all shipowners they contact who have a ship in position. The party requesting chartering service is said to place a quote on the market and will then await responses from shipowners who may be interested in the quote.

一旦承租人向他的经纪人发出指示，将促使经纪人采取行动，向所有有该类船舶的船舶出租人发出询价。请求租船服务的一方当事人将询价发至市场，然后等待可能对询价感兴趣的船舶出租人的回应。

Quotes are the common term for all requests for transportation a specific cargo from one port to another. Quotes are made by the broker when he receive an order from the charterer, then sent to the shipowners or their brokers through e-mail or fax. On the other hand, quotes can also be made by the broker on behalf of the shipowner when the broker receives an order from the shipowner requesting cargo for their ship to transport.

询价是对所有从一个港口运输特定货物到另一个港口的请求的通用术语。询价是由经纪人发出的，当他收到承租人的指示后，他将通过电子邮件或传真将询价传给船舶出租人或其经纪人。另一方面，询价也可以由船舶出租人为承揽货载而首先通过租船经纪人向租船市场发出。

From a legal perspective, a quote is not binding on the party making it. Under the *Civil Code of the People's Republic of China*, a quote is not an offer; it is merely an invitation for offer. An invitation for offer is a proposal to request other parties to make offers to the principal.

从法律的角度来看，一项询价对于发出询价的人来说是没有法律约束力的。根据《中华人民共和国民法典》的规定，询价不是要约，它只是一个要约邀请。要约邀请是希望他方向自己发出要约的意思表示。

1.3 Main Contents of the Quote
1.3 询价主要内容

1.3.1 Quote Made by Charterer/Broker under Voyage Chartering

1.3.1 承租人/经纪人的航次租船询价

—The charterer's name and address.

—Quantity and description of the commodity.

—Loading and discharging ports.

—Laydays and canceling date.

—Loading and discharging rates and terms.

—Any restrictions or preferences regarding the type or size of the ship.

—The charter party form on which the charterer wishes to base the terms and conditions.

—Commissions to be paid by the shipowner.

——承租人的名称及营业地点；

——货物数量和说明；

——装卸港口名称；

——受载期和解约日；

——装卸率和装卸条款；

——船舶类型需求；

——承租人希望采用的租船合同范本；

——船舶出租人需支付的佣金。

1.3.2 Quote Made by Shipowner/Broker under Voyage Chartering

1.3.2 出租人/经纪人的航次租船询价

—The shipowner's name and address.

—Description of the vessel.

—Loading and discharging ports.

—Laydays and canceling date.

—Loading and discharging rates and terms.

—Freight rate and payment terms.

—The charter party form on which the shipowner wishes to base the terms and conditions.

—Commissions to be paid by the shipowner.

——船舶出租人的名称及营业地点；

——船舶概况；

——装卸港口；

——受载期和解约日；

——装卸率和装卸条款；

——运费率及运费支付条款；

——船舶出租人希望采用的租船合同范本；

——船舶出租人需支付的佣金。

1.3.3 Quote Made by Charterer/Broker under Time Chartering

1.3.3 承租人/经纪人的定期租船询价

—The charterer's name and address.

—The tonnage and type of the ship.

—The duration of the charter.

—The place of delivery/redelivery.

—The delivery date and canceling date.

—The hire rate and payment terms for hire.

—The charter party form on which the charterer wishes to base the terms and conditions.

—Commissions to be paid by the shipowner.

——承租人的名称及营业地点；

——船舶载重吨、类型；

——租期；

——交/还船地点；

——交船日期和解约日；

——租金率及租金支付条款；

——承租人希望采用的租船合同范本；

——船舶出租人需支付的佣金。

1.3.4 Quote Made by Shipowner/Broker under Time Chartering

1.3.4 出租人/经纪人定期租船询价主要内容

—The shipowner's name and address.

—The ship's name, tonnage, nationality, and other particulars.

—The duration of the charter.

—The place and date of delivery/redelivery.

—The hire rate and payment terms for hire.

—The charter party form on which the shipowner wishes to base the terms and conditions.

—Commissions to be paid by the shipowner.

——出租人的名称及营业地点；

——船舶名称、载重吨、船籍和其他概述；

——租期；

——交/还船的地点和日期；

——租金率及租金支付条款；

——船舶出租人希望采用的租船合同范本；

——船舶出租人需支付的佣金。

1.3.5 An Example of a Quote

1.3.5 询价实例

—ABC GRAIN CORPORATION

—30,000 MT WHEAT IN BAGS, 10 PCT MOLOO

—1/2 SB, 1/2 SP, US GULF

—1/2 SB, 1/2 SP, CHINA

—5 WWDSHEXE IU

—LAYCAN 30 SEPT/10 OCT

—USUAL TERMS, BASIS NORGRAIN CP

—WITH 1.5 PCT ADDRESS COMMISSION

—BEST OFFER INVITED

——ABC谷物有限公司；

——30 000公吨袋装小麦，10%增减由船舶出租人选择；

——1/2安全泊位，1/2安全港口，美国海岸；

——1/2安全泊位，1/2安全港口，中国；

——5个晴天工作日，星期天节假日除外，即使已使用；

——受载期和解约日为9月30日至10月10日；

——通常条件依照北美谷物租船合同；

——1.5%洽租佣金；

——邀请最好的要约。

2. Offer
2. 租船要约

2.1 Meaning of the Offer
2.1 要约的含义

When a shipowner is informed that a charterer needs a type of tonnage that the shipowner may provide, he will make a calculation based on the actual vessel. The shipowner needs to obtain necessary information concerning costs of operating the vessel, e. g., costs of handling cargo in ports, port charges and dues associated with the ship's call, costs of canal passages, notes about bunker prices, etc. If the calculation seems reasonable, the shipowner may make an offer.

当船舶出租人获悉，船舶出租人可以提供承租人需要的船舶类型时，他会根据实际船舶进行计算。船舶出租人需要获取有关船舶经营成本的相关信息，例如，货物在港口的装卸费用、船舶挂靠港口的费用、运河通行费、燃料价格等。如果核算看起来是合理的，船舶出租人可发出要约。

According to the *Civil Code of the People's Republic of China*, an offer is a proposal expressing the intention to enter into a charter party with other parties. The general contract principle is that an offer is binding on the party making it.

根据《中华人民共和国民法典》的规定，要约是一个希望与其他人订立租船合同的意思表示。总的合同原则是要约约束发出要约的人。

However, no one in shipping expects an offer to remain open forever so it is usual to place a time limit on the validity of the offer. If the offer prescribes a certain time before which it must be accepted, the expiration of this time means that the offeror is no longer bound. This allows either party to begin negotiations with the other if no acceptance has been made within the time limit. This does not mean that after the expiry of the time the parties cannot continue negotiating provided they both wish to do so and neither party has begun negotiating with a third party.

航运中没有人期望要约永远有效，因此通常把有效期限定在要约中。如果要约规定了必须在某个特定时间之前作出接受的承诺，那么超过这个时限就意味着要约人不再受约束。如果在有效期内没有收到接受方的回复，任何一方当事人都可以与另一方开始洽谈。这并不意味着双方不能继续洽谈，只要他们都希望这样做，并且任何一方未与第三方进行洽谈。

If no time has been expressly stated the basis is that the offeree shall have reasonable or customary time at their disposal to reply. This time is determined with regard to the importance of the business, the circumstances under which the offer has been given, the speed of the transactions in the trade, etc.

如果没有明确期限，准则是被要约人应在合理的或习惯的时间内答复。这个期限取决于业务的重要性、要约发出的情形、交易的速度等。

2.2 Details of the Offer
2.2 要约的细节

In voyage chartering, the first offer that starts the negotiations will contain the following details:
在航次租船中，开始洽谈的首份要约包括下列项目：

—The shipowner's business name and address.

—The ship's name and particulars.

—Quantity and description of the commodity.

—Loading and discharging ports and berths.

—Laydays/canceling date.

—Loading and discharging rates and terms.

—Demurrage and dispatch rates.

—Freight amount and freight payment conditions.

—Charter party form.

—Commissions.

——船舶出租人的名称及营业地点；

——船舶名称和概况；

——货物数量和说明；

——装卸港口和泊位；

——受载期/解约日；

——装卸率和装卸条款；

——滞期费和速遣费率；

——运费金额和运费支付条件；

——租船合同范本；

——佣金。

The details of the vessel that are included in the particulars given in the negotiations are the vessel's name, year built, flag, deadweight, GT/NT, cubic capacity, number of hatches and holds, cargo gear, LOA, and BM, etc.

洽谈过程中提供的船舶详情清单所包含的船舶的具体信息包括船名、建造年份、船旗、载重吨、总吨/净吨、舱容、货舱和舱口数量、船舶吊具、船舶总长和型宽等。

2.3 Counter Offer
2.3 租船反要约

In practice it never happens that one party replies to the first offer with a clean acceptance; instead, the reply contains some points that differ from the offer made by the shipowners. Counter offers refer to the process where the offeree puts forward his new conditions or the amendments to the offer. In the procedure of chartering, many offers are met with counter offers. When one makes a counter offer, it means that "I decline your offer and I now make you the following new offer". Then a counter offer will be regarded as a rejection of the original offer and a new offer binding upon the person who has given the counter offer.

在租船实务中，一方直接接受对方首次提出的要约是不会发生的，而是就船舶出租人提供的要约做出修改的答复。反要约是指受要约的一方提出了新的条件或修改要约。在租船过程中，许多要约被还价。当一方发出还价时，实际上意味着"我拒绝你的要约，我现在给你新的报价"。反要约将被视为对原要约的拒绝，是一个新的要约，对发出人具有约束力。

2.4 Types of Offer
2.4 要约种类

Current offers can be grouped into absolute offers and conditional offers, customarily known as firm offers and offers without engagement. A firm offer, when accepted within its validity period, binds the offeror and thereby concludes the negotiations; acceptance after the expiration of the time limit is considered a counter offer. A conditional offer means the offer contains collateral conditions affecting its validity and the contract is concluded only when such conditions are fulfilled.

租船要约可分为绝对发盘（实盘）和条件发盘（虚盘）两种情形。实盘若在有效期内被接受，对发盘人具有约束力且意味着谈判达成；超过有效期的接受视为反要约。条件发盘是指要约生效附加条件，只有条件达成时，合同才成立。

2.5 Voyage Charter Firm Offer
2.5 航次租船实盘

A firm offer for a voyage charter from a shipowner generally includes the following details:
船舶出租人发出的航次租船实盘一般包括以下细节：

—The ship's name.

—Cargo quantity and description.

—Rate of freight: Where and how paid to.

—FIOS/FIOT/FIOST.

—Loading port(s)/Discharging port(s).

—Laydays/Canceling date.

—Loading rate/Discharging rate or permitted days.

—Demurrage/Dispatch money.

—Dues/taxes (for account of whom).

—Shipowners/Charterers to appoint/nominate agents at both ends.

—Extra Insurance (for the account of whom).

—Total commission including address commission.

—Form of charter party: Gencon, Norgrain, etc.

—Subject to further terms and conditions and any other required subjects.

——船名；

——货物数量和说明；

——运费率：地点以及如何支付；

——船舶出租人不负责装卸、积载费/不负责装卸、平舱费/不负责装卸、积载费、平舱费；

——装货港/卸货港；

——受载期/解约日；

——装卸率或允许装卸天数；

——滞期费/速遣费；

——规费/税费（由谁支付）；

——船舶出租人/承租人委托或指定代理人；

——额外保险费（由谁承担）；

——包括洽租佣金在内的总佣金；

——租船合同范本：金康、北美谷物等；

——要求的其他条件和条款。

2.6 Time Charter Firm Offer

2.6 定期租船实盘

—Description of the vessel.

—Delivery port/area.

—Redelivery port/area.

—Laydays/Canceling date.

—Position and expected readiness date for delivery.

—Duration of the time charter.

—Permitted trading limits.

—Cargo exclusions/permitted cargoes.

—Rate of hire (per day).

—When/how payable.

—Bunker quantities; prices on delivery/redelivery.

—Total commission including address commission.

—Form of charter party: BALTIME, NYPE, etc.

—Subject to further terms and conditions and any other required subjects.

——船舶说明；

——交船港口/地区；

——还船港口/地区；

——受载期/解约日；

——船舶位置和准备预计交船的日期；

——合同期限；

——航区限制；

——除外货物/允许货物；

——租金率（每日）；

——何时/如何支付租金；

——燃油数量；交船/还船的价格；

——包括洽租佣金在内的总佣金；

——租船合同范本：波尔的姆格式、土产格式等；

——要求的其他条件和条款。

2.7 Example of the Firm Offer

2.7 实盘举例

Following is an example of the firm offer made by the charterer.

以下实例是承租人发布的实盘。

TKS FOR YOUR FAX THIS MORNING AND CHRTS FIRM OFFER ASF FOR YOUR REPLY W/I 30 MINS:

FULL N COMPLET CGO MAINLY INCL PIG IRON IN BULK, STEEL, ETC. AT CHRTS

OPTION.

LAYCAN 08TH–13TH MAY 2001.

1 SB 1 SP QINGDAO, CHINA.

1 SB 1 SP ASIA, BANGKOK, THAILAND.

FRT USD 100,000 IN LUMP SUM, FIOST, BSS 1/1.

FULL FRT TO BE PAID W/I 5 BKG DAYS AFT COMPLETION OF LOAD.

OWRS TO APPOINT AGENTS WHO ARE TO BE NOMINATED BY CHRTS BENDS.

L/DISRATE CQD/CQD.

SHIPSIDE TALLY OWRS ACCT SHORESIDE TALLY CHRTS ACCT.

MASTER TO GIVE 7/5/3/2/1 DAYS ETA NOTICE BENDS.

ANY TAXES/DUES ON CGO CHRTS ACCT SAME ON FRT/VSL OWRS ACCT.

L/S/D IF ANY TB FOR CHRTS ACCT.

SHORE CRANES IF USED TO BE FOR CHRTS ACCT, BUT IF VSL'S GEARS BE OUT OF ORDER OR BREAK DOWN AT LD/DISPORT, THEN SHORE CRANES TO BE FOR OWRS ACCT.

ALL HATCHES/HOLDS TO BE DRY AND CLEAN TO CHRTS/SHIPRS SATISFACTION BEFORE LOADING COMMENCEMENT.

OTHERS AS PER GENCON CP.

COMM TTL 3.75%.

MV AAA PRC FLAG BLT 1988 GT/NT 6,500/3,500 DWT 7,500 MT ON 7.50M LOA/BM 120/18 TWEEN-DECK 3HA/3HO BALE 12,000 CBM.

PLS CNFM BY RTN W/I 30 MINS.

B.RGDS

感谢今早的传真，承租人报实盘如下，请在30分钟内答复：

满载货物包括散装生铁、钢材等，承租人选择。

受载期/解约日为2001年5月8日至13日。

一个安全泊位，一个安全港口，中国青岛。

一个安全泊位，一个安全港口，亚洲泰国曼谷。

包干运费100 000美元，船舶出租人不负责装卸、积载、平舱费，一港装一港卸。

全部运费在装完货后的5个银行工作日内支付。

船舶出租人在装卸港口委托承租人指定的人作为船舶出租人的代理人。

装卸率按港口习惯尽快装卸。

船舶出租人负责船边理货，承租人负责岸上理货。

船长应于预计抵港7/5/3/2/1天发出通知。

承租人负责对货物征收的税费，船舶出租人负责运费和对船舶征收的税费。

绑扎/固定/垫舱，如有的话由承租人负责。

如果使用岸上吊具，由承租人负责费用，但如果在装卸港口船上吊具损坏，使用岸上吊具则由船舶出租人负责费用。

所有舱口和货舱在装货前应干燥和清洁并使承租人/托运人满意。

其他见金康租船合同范本。

佣金总额3.75%。

船舶：AAA，中国船旗，1988年建造，总吨/净吨 6 500/3 500，载重吨 7 500公吨，吃水 7.50米，总长/型宽 120/18米，双层甲板 3 个舱口/3 个货舱，包装舱容 12 000立方米。

请确认并在30分钟内答复。

祝好

3. Subject to
3. 以……为条件

Often an offer or counter offer is forwarded or accepted subject to special conditions. The shipowner and the charterers can almost always make provisions on "subjects" in their offers or counter offers, i.e., "Subject to charterers' board's approval", "Subject to receiver's approval", "Subject to stem", "Subject to details". It is important to note that no fixture has been concluded until all "subjects" have been lifted.

通常一份要约或反要约以特定条件发出或接受。船舶出租人和承租人几乎总是在要约或反要约中规定"以……为条件"，例如"以承租人董事会同意为条件"，"以收货人同意为条件"，"以发货人同意受载期为条件"，"以细节内容为条件"等。重要的是，租船确认书必须等所有条件满足时才能成立。

3.1 Subject to Approval
3.1 以同意为条件

When the parties have in their negotiations used such phrases as "Subject to approval", it is a matter of construction of all the exchanges in context to decide whether there is (a) no binding contract at all; or (b) a contract which binds immediately but whose main obligations come into operation only if and when the approval has been given. There is an obligation upon one or both of the parties not to prevent the fulfillment of the requirement.

当双方当事人在洽谈中使用类似"以同意为条件"术语时，通过他们之间交谈的所有文件来解释是否：(a)完全无约束力；或者(b)当同意的话，合同立即有效。任何一方当事人有义务不能妨碍这种同意的达成。

"Subject to shipper's or receiver's approval" is used when the shippers or receivers of the cargo have to give their approval of the vessel.

在货物的托运人或收货人对船舶予以认可的情况下使用"以托运人或收货人同意为准"的术语。

"Subject to head charterer's approval" will normally indicate that the cargo in question is a relet or sublet and charterers have to get approval of the vessel from their head charterers. Most voyage charter parties have a relet or sublet clause therein.

"以上一个承租人同意为准"通常表明该货物是在转租情况下，承租人必须得到上一个承租人同意才能签订合同。大多数航次租船合同载有转租条款。

"Subject to board's approval" is used when the board of directors of either principal has to approve the final fixture but should be viewed with caution as such approval can be refused without a specific reason being given.

"以董事会同意为条件"用在任何一方董事会必须同意确认书的情况下，必须要注意的是，在没有特别理由的情况下也可能不同意。

3.2 Subject to Stem
3.2 以发货人同意受载期为条件

"Subject to stem" is used to give charterers time to put the vessel at their shippers' disposal to confirm that they can accept the vessel to load the agreed quantity of cargo on the agreed laydays. "Subject to stem" is only to be used to determine the availability of cargo. The restriction "Subject to stem" shall only apply to shippers' and/or suppliers' agreement to make cargo available for specified dates.

"以发货人同意受载期为条件"是指给承租人时间由发货人确认他们能够接受在约定的船舶受载期装运约定的货物。"以发货人同意受载期为条件"仅用来确定货物的适合性。该术语仅限制用于发货人同意在特定日期备妥货物。

A typical example may be that of a merchant who wants to secure shipping space for goods he is about to buy or sell. He may find it practical to have tonnage at hand and negotiate all arrangements for shipment before buying or selling the goods. In such a case the charter offer is made "Subject to stem", meaning that he is in no way committed if the purchase or sale of the goods should not materialize. It is an expression used to qualify an agreement to load under a charter party by making the obligation subject to the agreement of suppliers to make cargo available at the relevant time.

典型的例子可能是贸易商想要为他打算出售或买入的货物获得舱位。他可能会觉得，在出售或买入货物前先就货运安排进行洽谈以拿到舱位是较为实际的方法。在这种情况下，要约中会使用"以发货人同意受载期为条件"，意味着如果买卖合同没有达成，他没有合同义务。它是用来限定一项根据租船合同装货义务的协议，以托运人同意在相关时间内配妥货物为条件。

3.3 Subject to Open
3.3 以船舶未出租为条件

Another example is that of the shipowner who makes a firm offer "Subject to open", meaning that he retains the right to withdraw his offer in case the vessel should be fixed for other business before the acceptance of the offer in question. In general, such an offer is no more than an indication or quote.

另一个例子是"以船舶未出租为条件"，指假如该要约被接受前船舶已经出租给他人，船舶出租人保留撤回要约的权利。一般来说，该要约只不过是一个询价。

The restriction "Subject to open" shall only apply when a ship is already under offer, and the "Subject to open" offer shall be made within the same time limit. No extension shall be granted and no further negotiation shall take place until the time limit has expired or until both offers have been answered.

"以船舶未出租为条件"仅适用于船舶已处于要约情况下，并且该条件受同样的时间限制。不需要任何延期以及进一步洽谈，直到时限已过或直至两个要约给予答复。

3.4 Subject to Details
3.4 以细节内容为条件

The expression "Subject to details" commonly used in charter party negotiations, will usually prevent the formation of a binding contract. This term is a well-known expression in chartering practice and is intended to entitle either party to resile from the contract if in good faith either party is not satisfied with any of the details as discussed between them. English authority supports the view that the use of the qualification "Subject to details" indicates that the parties do not yet intend to be bound.

租船合同谈判中常用的"以细节内容为条件"通常是防止形成有约束力合同的术语表示。该术语是租船实务中一项众所周知的表示方法，基本含义是如果有诚意的任何一方对他们之间任何细节的讨论表示不满意，任何一方有权终止合同。英国判例明确支持这种观点，使用"以细节内容为条件"表明当事人还没有打算受其约束。

【Case】In *The Junior K* ［1988］2 Lloyd's Rep. 583, a case on a voyage charter party of *The Junior K*, it was held by the court that the stipulation "Subject to details of the Gencon charter party" conveys that the fixture is conditional upon agreement reached on the details of the Gencon form, which had not yet been discussed. Gencon form charter party contained many blanks and optional provisions such that the reference merely to the Gencon form imported too many uncertainties to enable anyone to say what terms had or had not been agreed.

【案例】在 The Junior K 航次租船合同一案（1988年，劳氏报告第593号）中，法院判决，以"金康租船合同的细节内容为条件"的规定表明确认书是"以金康租船合同的细节内容达成为条件"，但这些细节内容尚未被讨论。金康租船合同范本有很多空白和可选择的规定，仅涉及金康范本导致太多的不确定因素，使得任何人很难说哪些条件已经或尚未商定。

It is important to note that no fixture has been concluded until all "subjects" have been lifted. If a fixture is confirmed, or an offer is accepted "Subject to approval of details" or "Subject to details" such negotiations shall only be suspended if one party cannot agree and the other party maintains one or more of such "details". The above provision cannot be taken as an excuse to break off negotiations for some other reason.

非常重要的是，除非所有的"条件"达成，否则确认书不成立。如果一份确认书被确认，或一份要约被接受，取决于"以细节通过为条件"或者"以细节内容为条件"，如果一方不同意以及另一方保持一个或多个"细节"，这种洽谈应暂停。因某些其他原因，上述限制性条款不能被作为借口断绝洽谈。

It should also be noted that there are American cases to the contrary effect. The widespread practice of fixing "Subject to details" ordinarily will not be construed as requiring agreement on each and every charter term before a binding contract is created. Once there has been agreement on essential terms, a contract is deemed to exist and the negotiation of remaining details becomes a minor task.

还应指出的是，有一些美国案例给出了相反的结果。普遍使用的"以细节内容为条件"通常不会被解释为具有约束力的合同达成之前的条件要求。一旦主要条款达成协议，合同即被认为是存在的，剩余的细节洽谈是一项次要的工作。

4. Acceptance and Fixture Note
4. 接受和确认书

The contract is concluded on the acceptance of a firm offer or an absolute counter offer. An acceptance is a statement made by the offeree indicating assent to an offer. An acceptance shall reach the offeror within the time limit fixed in the offer. According the *Civil Code of the People's Republic of China*, a contract is established when the acceptance becomes effective. An acceptance becomes effective when its notice reaches the offeror. The contents of an acceptance shall comply with those of the offer. If the offeree substantially modifies the contents of the offer, it shall constitute a new offer.

合同在一份实盘或者一份完全的反要约被接受后成立。接受是受要约人表示同意的意思表示。接受应在要约规定的期限内到达要约人。根据《中华人民共和国民法典》的规定，承诺生效时合同成立。承诺通知到达要约人时生效。承诺的内容应当与要约的内容一致，受要约人对要约的内容做出实质性变更的，为新要约。

Then both parties will reach a fixture for signature. The charter agreement is called a fixture. A fixture is arrived at by the exchange of firm offers between brokers acting on behalf of their principals, a shipowner and a charterer, and when concluded, that is, when all terms and details agreed upon and subjects (if any) lifted, it is an enforceable contract.

随后，双方将签署一份租船确认书。租船协议被称为租船确认书。租船确认书是经纪人代表他们的委托人，即船舶出租人和承租人，通过交换意见达成的，当确认书成立时，意味着所有的条件和细节双方已同意，它即是有法律效力的合同。

4.1 Voyage Chartering Fixture Note
4.1 航次租船确认书

It is mutually agreed between the shipowner and the charterer that:

船舶出租人和承租人双方同意如下：

—Cargo 15,000 MT Rice in bags 5% more or less at shipowner's option (shipowner to declare quantity to be shipped 2 days before vessel arriving at loading port).

—Loading at one safe port in Bangkok, Thailand.

—Discharging at one safe port in Qingdao, China.

—Laydays and Canceling Date: 20th/30th Oct. 2005.

—Freight rate USD 20.00 per Metric ton FIOST, CQD both ends.

—100% freight prepaid by T/T to the shipowner's account in US dollars in Singapore after completion of loading before releasing the bill of lading.

—Any dues/taxes on the vessel, on freight to be for the shipowner's account. Any dues/taxes on cargo are to be for charterer's account.

—If the charterer fails to ship as agreed quantity, he is liable to pay the dead freight at the freight rate as agreed.

—Otherwise details as per Gencon C/P.

For and on behalf of   For and on behalf of

(shipowner)   (charterer)

　　——15 000公吨袋装大米，5%增减由船舶出租人选择（船舶出租人在船舶抵达装货港前2天宣布装船数量）。

　　——装货港为泰国曼谷的一个安全港口。

　　——卸货港为中国青岛的一个安全港口。

　　——受载期/解约日为2005年10月20—30日。

　　——每公吨运费20美元，船舶出租人不负责货物装卸、积载、平舱费，在装卸港口按港口习惯尽快装卸。

　　——在装完货后签发提单前100%预付运费，以美元电汇至船舶出租人在新加坡的银行账户。

　　——船舶出租人负责运费和对船舶征收的任何税费。承租人负责对货物征收的任何税费。

　　——如果承租人不能提供规定的货物数量，其可按照约定的运费率支付亏舱费。

　　——其他细节见金康合同范本。

船舶出租人代表签字　　　　　　　　　　承租人代表签字

4.2 Standard Form of Fixture Note of Voyage Charter Party

4.2 航次租船确认书标准格式

The following is a standard form of fixture note of the voyage charter party made by China Chamber of International Commerce.

以下是中国国际商会制定的标准航次租船合同确认书。

China Chamber of International Commerce

Fixture Note of Voyage Charter Party

（2000 Standard Form）

day_____/month_____/year_____

It is mutually agreed between_____ as Owners (address:_____ fax:_____ telephone: _____) and_____ as Charterers (address:_____ fax:_____ telephone: _____)

that this Fixture Note shall be performed subject to the following terms and conditions:

1. Particulars of Performing Vessel:

MV:_____ Flag:_____ Built:_____ Classification:_____ Registered Shipowners:_____

GT/NT/DWT:_____/_____/_____ TS SSW:_____ LOA/BM:_____/_____ MS

Grain/BaleCapa:_____/_____ CBMS Ho/Ha:_____/_____

Derr:_____ Tweendeck:_____

[add other items when necessary]_____

2. Cargo and Quantity: [Indicate Alternative(A)or(B)with√]

[ ] (A)_____m/ts of _____in_____[bag or bulk],_____% more or less at _____ option [Owners' option or Charterers' option].

[ ] (B) _____cbms of_____% more or less at _____ option [Charterers' option or Owners' option].

3. Laycan：_____ / _____.

4. Loading /Discharging Port(s): [Indicate Alternative (A) or (B) with√]

[ ] (A) _____ safe port(s) at_____ / _____ .

[ ] (B) _____ safe berth(s) at port(s) of _____ / _____.

5. Loading/Discharging Rate: [Indicate Alternative (A) or (B) or (C) with√]

[ ] (A) _____ / _____ m/ts per weather working day, Sundays, and holidays excepted unless used (PWWD SHEX UU).

[ ] (B) _____ / _____ m/ts per weather working day, Sundays, and holidays excepted even if used (PWWD SHEX EIU).

[ ] (C) Customary quick dispatch at port(s) of _____ [loading or discharging](CQD).

6. Laytime Calculation: [Indicate Alternative (A) or (B) with√]

[ ] (A) Separate laytime for loading and discharging.

[ ] (B) Total laytime for loading and discharging.

7. Freight Rate: [Indicate Alternative (A) or (B) or (C) or (D) with√]

[ ] (A) Lumpsum _____ fiost.

[ ] (B) _____ per_____ [net or gross] m/t fiost.

[ ] (C) _____ per_____ [net or gross] m/t on free in and liner out.

[ ] (D) _____ per_____ [net or gross] cbm fiost.

8. Freight Payment: [Indicate Alternative (A) or (B) or (C) with√]

[ ] (A) Freight to be paid within _____ banking days after completion of loading.

[ ] (B) Freight to be paid within _____ banking days after completion of loading, but always before breaking bulk.

Freight collected or to be collected as per aforesaid (A) or (B) shall be deemed earned by Owners upon cargo loading on board, and such freight must be paid by Charterers non-returnable and non-discountable whether vessel/cargo lost or not.

[ ] (C) Freight to be paid within _____ banking days after completion of discharging.

9. Demmurage/Dispatch:

_____ / _____ per day or pro rata to be settled within_____ days after completion of discharging provided that the Owner's lien, if any, on the cargo shall not be affected by this provision.

10. Taxes/Dues/Fee:

Taxes/dues/fees if any on vessel/freight to be for Owners' account, howsoever the amount thereof may be assessed. Same on cargo if any to be for Charterers' account, howsoever the amount thereof may be assessed.

11. Agency: [Indicate Alternative (A) or (B) with√]

[ ] (A) Owners' agents on both ends.

[ ] (B) Owners' agent at loading port and Charterers' agent at discharging port.

12. Commission: [Indicate Alternative (A) or (B) with√]

[ ] (A) Commission on freight, dead-freight and demurrage totals_____ percent including address commission.

[ ] (B) Commission on freight, dead-freight and demurrage totals_____ percent, plus_____ percent to be for _____.

13. Law and Arbitration：

This Fixture Note shall be governed by and construed by Chinese law, and the Charter Party shall be established when this Fixture Note is signed. Any dispute arising out of or in connection with this Fixture Note shall be submitted to China Maritime Arbitration Commission for arbitration in Beijing. The arbitration award shall be final and binding upon the parties.

14. Gencon Charter: [Indicate Alternative (A) or (B) with√]

[ ] (A) Other terms and conditions are as per Gencon Charter 1994, except Clause 2.

[ ] (B) Other terms and conditions are as per Gencon Charter 1976, except Clause(s).

15. Special Provisions:

_____

_____

_____

_____　　　　　　　_____
Owners' signature　　　　　　　　　　　　　　Charterers' signature

航次租船合同确认书（2000年标准版本）

_____年_____月_____日

出租人_____

（地址：传真：_____电话：_____）

与承租人_____

（地址：_____传真：_____电话：_____）

双方同意按下列条款和条件履行本确认书：

第一条　承运船舶的规范：

船名：_____船旗国：_____建造时间：_____船级：_____登记船东：_____

总吨/净吨/载重吨：_____/_____/_____吨　夏季干舷：_____米

总长/型宽：_____米/_____米　散装舱容/包装舱容：_____立方米/_____立方米

舱/舱口：_____/_____吊杆：_____二层甲板：_____

[可根据需要增加项目]_____

_____

第二条　货物和数量：[使用√标明选择（A）或（B）]

[ ]（A）_____公吨_____[袋装或散装]货物_____，增加或减少_____%，由_____[出租人或承租人]选择。

[ ]（B）_____立方米货物_____，增加或减少_____%，由_____[承租人或出租人]选择。

第三条　受载期：

_____年_____月_____日/_____年_____月_____日。

第四条　装货/卸货港：[使用√标明选择（A）或（B）]

[ ]（A）在_____/_____的_____个安全港口。

[ ]（B）在_____港/_____港的_____个安全泊位。

第五条　装货/卸货率：[使用√标明选择（A）或（B）或（C）]

[ ]（A）每晴天工作日_____公吨/_____公吨，星期日、节假日除外，除非已经使用。

[ ]（B）每晴天工作日_____公吨/_____公吨，星期日、节假日除外，即使已经使用。

［　］（C）在＿＿＿＿＿＿＿［装货港或卸货港］ 按港口习惯快速装/卸货。

第六条　装卸时间的计算：［使用√标明选择（A）或（B）］

［　］（A）装货时间与卸货时间分别计算。

［　］（B）装货时间与卸货时间合并计算。

第七条　运费率：［使用√标明选择（A）或（B）或（C）或（D）］

［　］（A）包干运费＿＿＿＿＿＿＿＿＿＿，出租人不负担装卸、堆舱及平舱费。

［　］（B）每＿＿＿＿＿＿＿［净或毛］公吨＿＿＿＿＿＿，出租人不负担装卸、堆舱及平舱费。

［　］（C）每＿＿＿＿＿＿＿［净或毛］公吨 ＿＿＿＿＿＿，出租人不负担装货费，负担卸货费。

［　］（D）每＿＿＿＿＿＿＿［净或毛］立方米＿＿＿＿＿＿，出租人不负担装卸、堆舱及平舱费。

第八条　运费的支付：［使用√标明选择（A）或（B）或（C）］

［　］（A）运费应于装货结束后＿＿＿＿＿＿＿个银行工作日内支付。

［　］（B）运费应于装货结束后＿＿＿＿＿＿＿个银行工作日内支付，但至迟应在开舱卸货以前。

按照以上（A）或（B）已收取或应收取的运费，在货物装上船后即为出租人所赚取；不论船舶/货物灭失与否，承租人必须支付，无须返还，不得扣减。

［　］（C）运费应于卸货结束后＿＿＿＿＿＿＿个银行工作日内支付。

第九条　滞期费/速遣费：

滞期费/速遣费为每天＿＿＿＿＿＿/＿＿＿＿＿＿，不足一天按比例计算，于卸货结束后＿＿＿＿＿＿天内结算，但出租人如有留置货物的权利，不受本条规定的影响。

第十条　税费/规费/费用：

船舶运费的税费/规费/费用由出租人负担，不论其计算方法如何。货物的税费/规费/费用由承租人负担，不论其计算方法如何。

第十一条　代理：［使用√标明选择（A）或（B）］

［　］（A）装卸港均为出租人的代理。

［　］（B）装货港为出租人的代理，卸货港为承租人的代理。

第十二条 佣金：［使用√标明选择（A）或（B）］

［　］（A）运费、亏舱费和滞期费的佣金包括洽租佣金合计＿＿＿＿＿＿＿%。

［　］（B）运费、亏舱费和滞期费佣金合计＿＿＿＿＿＿＿%，另加 ＿＿＿＿＿＿%付给＿＿＿＿＿＿＿。

第十三条　法律和仲裁：

本确认书适用中国法律并根据中国法律解释，自签订之日起租船合同成立。本确认书产生的或与本确认书有关的任何争议均应提交中国海事仲裁委员会在北京仲裁。仲裁裁决是终局的，对当事人均有约束力。

第十四条 金康租船合同：［使用√标明选择（A）或（B）］

［　］（A）其他条款和条件按1994年金康租船合同，但第2条除外。

［　］（B）其他条款和条件按1976年金康租船合同，但第__条除外。

第十五条　特别规定：

_____

_____

_____

_____　　　　　　　　_____
出 租 人 签 字　　　　　　　　　　　　承 租 人 签 字

5. Performance of Chartering Party
5. 租船合同履行

After signing the fixture notes there remain some additional matters to be done which form part of the chartering work. The charterers, or the brokers who have negotiated on their behalf, have to draw up, copy, and distribute the charter party and see to it that the documents are duly signed. Thereafter, it is also necessary for all parties involved to follow up on notices, payments of freight and hire and all other matters that contribute to good performance from both sides. We will explain some general operating tasks that need to be done after a fixture note is signed and the charter party is made from the viewpoint of the shipowner.

签订租船确认书后还有其他事项要做，这些工作属于租船工作的一部分。承租人或代表他们洽谈的经纪人应起草、复制和分发租船合同，并督促该文件正式签字。然后，还需要有关各方遵循通知、运费和租金支付以及双方为较好履约所做出的其他事项。我们将从船舶出租人的角度解释签订租船合同后应做的一般性工作。

5.1 Information and Instruction to Master
5.1 向船长发布指令和信息

Based on the fixture note and the charter party, the shipowner can compose his instructions to the ship, stating the most important points of the employment agreement and attaching relevant notices to which the master should adhere. The master should know the ports at which he is going to call, the agent who is going to assist him when in port, and details of the commodity his ship is going to carry.

根据租船确认书和租船合同，船舶出租人向船舶发布他的指示，说明协议的最重要事宜，并附上船长应遵循的通知。船长应当知道要挂靠的港口、港口代理、船舶要装载货物的细节。

The voyage instructions in general contain the following items:

在航行指令中通常包括以下内容：

—Names of the ports of call.

—Name of the commodity.

—Names of the agents at the calling port.

—Quantities to be loaded/discharged at each port.

—Loading/unloading conditions and terms.

—Where and how much bunkers are to be supplied.

—Where and how many crew members are to embark/disembark.

—Where supplies for the ship can be lifted, etc.

——挂靠港名称；

——货物名称；

——挂靠港代理名称；

——各港装卸货物数量；

——装卸条件和装卸条款；

——何处及多少燃油要加；

——何处及多少船员要下船和上船；

——何处提供供应品等。

The list may contain a lot more information of which the master should be made aware and instructions for him to carry out depending on the trade in which his ship is engaged as well as on the size of his ship.

该清单可能包含更多需告知船长的信息，以及需船长执行的指令——具体内容取决于其船舶所从事的贸易类型及船舶规模。

5.2 Appointment of Agents
5.2 委托代理

5.2.1 Introduction to Ship's Agent
5.2.1 船舶代理概述

The ship's agent is the local expert who will represent the shipowner in every port the ship visits. A ship's agent is a person or firm that transacts all business of a ship in a port on behalf of shipowners or charterers. In a voyage charter, the port agent is appointed by the shipowner. In a time charter, the port agent is appointed by the charterer. However, the shipowner has to appoint his protective agent in his interest. The services and assistance tendered by an agent to the ship are important. The performance of an agent will also greatly influence the overall results of the ship's deployment, and affect the results achieved by the shipowner.

船舶代理是当地的专家，代表挂靠各个港口船舶的出租人。船舶代理是一个人或公司，代表船舶出租人或承租人处理挂靠港口的船舶的所有业务。通常在航次租船下，港口代理是由船舶出租人委托的。在定期租船下，港口代理是由承租人委托的。但船舶出租人不得不任命保护代理来保护他的利益。代理提供的服务和协助对船舶是非常重要的。代理的服务也将极大地影响使用船舶的整体结果，并影响船舶出租人所要达到的结果。

Agency assistance and services extended to a ship require proper and detailed instructions issued by the shipowner before the vessel's arrival and during its stay in port. The shipowner should see to it that brief instructions are dispatched to the agent as soon as he gets enough information from the agent on various issues that might arise with the expected call for his ship at a port in question.

对于船舶所获得的代理协助和服务，需要船舶出租人在船舶抵达前以及在港口停留期间下达详尽准确的指示。船舶出租人应确保：一旦从代理处获取足够信息（涉及船舶预计停靠该港口可能出现的各类问题），便向代理发送简要指示。

5.2.2 Appointment of an Agent
5.2.2 代理委托

To the shipowner of an international trading ship, which rarely calls at her "home" port, the appointment of an agent in every foreign port is essential, ensuring that the visit to the port will go smoothly. The following is an example of the appointment of an agent made by the shipowner under voyage charter:

对于一艘从事国际贸易的船舶的船舶出租人而言，该船很少会停靠其"母港"，所以在每一个外国港口任命代理是至关重要的，这样可以确保船舶顺利挂靠港口。以下是由船舶出租人根据航次租船委托与代理人的来往函电示例：

TO: AAA AGENCY CO.

FM: BBB SHIPPING CO., LTD.

MV CCC

PLS BE ADVD THAT THE SUBJ VSL IS SCHEDULED TO CALL QINGDAO PORT FOR DISCHG ABT 150,000 MT IRON ORE. WE ARE PLEASED TO APPT YOU AS PORT AGENT TO EFFECT SMOOTH OPERATION. DETAILS/INSTRUCTIONS WL BE GIVEN AFTER CONFIRMATION OF OUR APPOINTMENT.

B. REGARDS

至：AAA 代理公司

来自：BBB 航运有限公司

船舶：CCC

请注意，该船舶计划挂靠青岛港卸载大约 150 000 公吨铁矿石。我们很高兴地委托你们为港口代理人以便使货物作业顺利进行。详情和指示将在你们确认我们的委托后发出。

祝好

TO: BBB SHIPPING CO., LTD.

FM: AAA AGENCY CO.

MV CCC

THANKS A LOT FOR YOUR AGENCY APPOINMENT, WE HEREBY CONFIRM THAT WE'LL ATTEND TO THE SUBJ VSL ON YOUR BEHALF AND ACT UPON YOUR INSTRUCTIONS CLOSELY WITHOUT FAIL. EVERY EFFORT WILL BE MADE TO ENSURE THE VSL HAS A SAFE SMOOTH DISCHG OPERATION DURING HER STAY AT QINGDAO.

B. REGARDS

至：BBB 航运有限公司

来自：AAA 代理公司

船舶：CCC

非常感谢你们的代理委托，我们确认将代表你们照料该船舶并按你们的指示办理。我们将努力确保船舶在青岛的安全卸载。

祝好

5.2.3 Agency Services

5.2.3 代理服务

The ship's agents are to protect the ship's interests at all times. This includes ensuring a fast turnaround of the ship at the lowest possible expense. Agency services for shipowners include the following matters:

船舶代理的职责是始终维护船舶的利益。这包括确保船舶以尽可能低的费用快速周转。为船舶出租人提供的代理服务包括下列事项：

——Attending to the procedures for the ship's entry into and departure from the ports and sea areas; and arranging pilotage, berth, loading and unloading, etc.

——Attending to marine survey, ship's repair; supplies of fresh water, provisions, and stores;

purchasing and/or forwarding the ship's spare parts, sea charts, etc.

—Attending to the matters of the ship's tenancy, sales, and delivery.

—Attending to the business of chartering ships and providing consultation and information.

—Arranging for passports, visas, medical treatment, repatriation, and sightseeing for crew members.

—Attending to the maritime affairs.

——办理船舶进出港口的手续，安排引航、靠泊、装卸货等；

——办理海事检验、船舶修理，淡水提供、供应品和物料供给，采购和/或转发船舶备件、海图等；

——办理船舶租赁、买卖和交付事项；

——办理船舶租船业务并提供咨询和信息服务；

——安排船员护照、签证、医疗、遣返和观光；

——办理海事事务。

One of the prime functions of a port agent is to produce a written record of events occurring during a vessel's port visit—known as a "port operations log". Thus are recorded a ship's arrival date and time: including when berthed or shifted to another berth, when worked cargo, when bunkered and when departed, the time "notice of readiness" was tendered and accepted, weather conditions and whatever else is relevant.

港口代理的主要功能之一是书面记载船舶在港口时的相关事项，即众所周知的"船舶港口日志"。它记录船舶的抵达日期和时间：包括何时停泊或转移到另一个泊位的时间；装卸货时间；加油和驶离时间；"装卸准备就绪通知书"的递交和接收时间；天气情况以及其他相关事宜。

No matter what the reason for a vessel's visit to port is, whether it is for dry docking or repairing, bunkering, cargo-working, whether on a voyage or time charter, a port agent should produce a Statement of Facts form to forward to his principal upon the vessel's departure. Many port agents use their in-house designed forms for this purpose but standard documents which can be used at any port, worldwide, are available from BIMCO and can be used if the agent or his principal so wishes.

无论船舶挂靠港口的原因为何，无论是入船坞或修理、燃料补给、货物作业，还是航次租船或期租状态，港口代理应该填制事实记录，并在该船离开时提交给他的委托人。许多港口代理使用自己的格式，如果代理人或其委托人愿意的话，可以使用BIMCO制定的标准格式。

To avoid unnecessary disputes, interested parties to a vessel's visit to the port, e.g. the ship's master, port agents, charterers or shipper/receivers should sign the completed statement of facts form. If, however, one or other of the parties has an objection to the contents of a statement of facts form, it should be signed "under protest", a statement being added, clarifying the reason(s) for the objection.

为避免不必要的纠纷，与船舶进港口相关的各方如船舶的船长、港口代理、承租人或托运人/收货人应该在事实记录上签字。然而，如果任何一方对此有争议的话，应当签署"抗议下签字"，并附加表述，阐明反对的原因。

5.3 Performance of Voyage Chartering
5.3 航次租船履行

The vessel must be directed to the port of loading. Often a canceling date has been determined for the latest arrival of the ship at the port of loading, and if she has not arrived at that time the charterer may cancel the charter party. The charterer may also be entitled to claim damages when the arrival of the vessel is delayed. The shipowner then has a duty to carry out the agreed voyage without delay and without deviating from the agreed or customary route.

　　船舶必须直接驶向装货港。通常合同中会约定解约日，如果船舶没有在解约日抵达，承租人可以解除合同。承租人也可就船舶延误要求赔偿。船舶出租人也有义务履行约定的航程，不能偏离约定的或习惯的航线。

In the port of loading the charterer must deliver the agreed cargo. Without a particular agreement to the contrary, the cargo must not be dangerous. The charterer usually has a duty to deliver a full cargo within the ship's capacity. If too little cargo is delivered or the cargo is delivered in such a state that the ship's capacity cannot be utilized, a freight compensation, the so-called dead freight, can be claimed by the shipowner. This compensation is based on the difference between the full freight to which the shipowner would have been entitled if all cargo were delivered and the freight to be paid according to the intake quantity less any expenses saved for short-delivered cargo. If, on the other hand, the vessel cannot load the agreed quantity, a corresponding freight reduction will be made. In addition, the charterer may eventually claim compensation for additional costs, for example, for another vessel that has been chartered.

　　在装货港，承租人必须履行交付约定的货物。如果没有特别相反的协议，货物不得具有危险性。承租人通常有责任交付满载货物。如果交付货物较少，或交付货物使得船舶的运力不能被利用，运费损失补偿即所谓的空舱费，可以由船舶出租人索赔。这个赔偿是基于全部运费和实际运费之间的差额，减去少交货物节省的费用。另一方面，该船无法装载约定的数量，则相应减少运费。除此之外，承租人甚至可能要求赔偿额外费用，例如，租用另外的船舶来运输未装的货物。

The freight will be paid for cargo discharged after the voyage. If the ship is lost or does not reach her destination, no freight will be paid at all. To protect the shipowner's right to freight, the freight prepaid clause is often added or amended with "freight shall be considered as fully earned upon shipment and nonreturnable in any event whether or not the voyage shall be performed and whether or not the vessel and/or cargo shall be lost".

　　运费将在航程卸货后支付。如果该船灭失或没有到达目的地，不支付运费。为了保护船舶出租人对运费的权利，预付运费条款"运费视为在装运时赚取，任何情况下不退还，不论航行是否履行，不论船舶和/或货物灭失与否"通常载入合同。

On arrival at the port of destination, the master will, provided that the freight has been paid, deliver the cargo to the consignee named in the bill of lading or to the first person who presents a properly endorsed bill of lading.

　　抵达目的港，在运费付清的情况下，船长将货物交付提单上标明的收货人或第一个出示提单上适当背书的收货人。

5.4 Performance of Time Chartering
5.4 定期租船履行

The ship must be delivered to the time charterer not later than a certain date, and any delay beyond the canceling date entitles the charterer to cancel the charter. The voyages also have to be carried out without delay. If the vessel is delayed due to a breakdown of machinery or for other specified reasons, she may be off-hire, and then a reduction of the time may be made so that no hire will be paid during the off-hire period. However, under a time charter party, the shipowner is not liable for delays not caused by the ship.

船舶必须交付承租人的时间不得迟于某一特定日期，任何超过解约日的延误使得承租人有权解除合同。航程还必须毫不延误。如果船舶延误的原因是机械故障或其他特定原因，它将可能停租并在时间上给予扣减，停租期间不支付租金。不过，根据定期租船合同，船舶出租人基本上是不承担非船舶原因造成延误的责任。

The hire is payable in advance for a month or other period. If the hire is not paid promptly the shipowner may be entitled to cancel the charter. The liability for the cargo may be determined in different ways and may rest with the shipowner or with the charterer or may be divided between them in one way or another.

租金一般提前一个月或在其他期限内支付。如果租金支付不及时，船舶出租人可能有权解除租约。货物的赔偿责任可能会以不同的方式确定，可能由船舶出租人承担或承租人承担或者在他们之间分配。

When giving orders to the vessel the charterer must keep within the trading restrictions prescribed by the contract, concerning geographical areas as well as cargoes to be carried. Unless the parties have reached an agreement to the contrary, the charterer may only order the vessel to safe ports and berths. He must follow the terms and conditions of the charter party as to excepted cargoes and, as in a voyage charter, he must not ordinarily have goods carried that may cause damage to the ship, the personnel, or other cargo.

当承租人给船舶下达指令时，承租人必须保证船舶航行在合同规定的航区限制内的地理区域，同样所装运的货物也要符合合同规定。除非当事各方已达成协议，否则承租人只能指令船舶挂靠安全的港口和泊位。他必须遵守租船合同中关于除外货物的条款，且与航次租船相同，通常不得装运可能对船舶、人员或其他货物造成损害的货物。

At the end of the charter period, the charterer has to redeliver the vessel at the agreed place. It would often be hard for the charterer to use the ship effectively during the last part of the charter period if he had to redeliver her on a particular day. The charter party therefore ordinarily contains provisions on the overlap, entitling the charterer to use the vessel for a reasonable time after the expiration of the charter against an agreed hire; or on the underlap, entitling the charterer to redeliver her somewhat earlier than the basic charter provides for.

在租期结束时，承租人必须在规定的地点还船。其既要在租船期间的最后部分有效使用船舶，又要在特定日期还船，这通常对于承租人较难。因此，租船合同通常包括对于超期的规定，在期满后的合理时间内承租人有权使用船舶、支付规定的租金或者提前还船，承租人有权比合同规定的日期提早还船。

UNIT 2　CHARTERING PRACTICE
第二单元　租船实务

1. Transactions in Concluding a Voyage Charter Party
1. 订立航次租船合同的交易过程

In this unit, the example of chartering practice, from the very beginning of the sale contract made by sellers and buyers to the conclusion of the charter party signed by the charterer (seller or buyer) and shipowner, will be described in detail.

本单元就从买卖双方订立货物买卖合同开始，到承租人（卖方或买方）与船舶出租人签订租船合同的细节过程举一实例。

1.1 A Sales Contract
1.1 买卖合同

The following is the abstract from the sales contract made by the seller and buyer.

以下是由卖方和买方订立的货物买卖合同摘要。

—Contract No.: 003.

—Date: 14/3/2005.

—The sellers: China AAA Import and Export Co.

—The buyers: Thailand BBB Trading Co., Ltd.

——合同号码：003。

——合同日期：2005年3月14日。

——卖方：中国AAA进出口公司。

——买方：泰国BBB贸易有限公司。

The buyers agree to buy and the sellers agree to sell the following goods on terms and conditions as set forth below:

买方同意购买及卖方同意出售下列货物并按下列所述的条款和条件：

—Coke 7,000 MT in bulk FOBT QINHUANGDAO USD70/MT. Total amount. USD 490,000.00

—Payment: L/C at sight to be issued to CNAAAIEC.

—Advising bank: bank of China, Qinhuangdao Branch.

—Shipment quantity: 10% more or less allowed seller's option.

—Time of shipment: To be shipped on or before May 5th, 2005.

—Port of loading: Qinhuangdao.

—Port of discharging: Bangkok.

—Insurance: To be affected by buyers.

——7 000公吨散装焦炭FOBT秦皇岛，每吨70美元，总额490 000美元。

——付款方式：即期信用证给中国AAA进出口公司。

——通知银行：中国银行秦皇岛分行。

——装运量：卖方选择10%增减。

——装运时间：2005年5月5日或之前。

——起运港：秦皇岛。

——卸货港：曼谷。

——保险：买方负责。

1.2 Steps of Concluding a Voyage Charter Party
1.2 订立航次租船合同的步骤

The buyer: Thailand BBB Trading Co., Ltd.

买方：泰国BBB贸易有限公司。

The shipowner: CCC Shipping Co., Ltd. Hong Kong.

出租人：香港CCC航运有限公司。

* *

1.2.1 Quote Made by the Charterer
1.2.1 承租人发出询价
TO: CCC HKG   2/4/2005
FM: BBB BKK
RE: 7,000 MT COKE IN BULK QINHUANGDAO/BANGKOK
7,000 MT COKE IN BULK SF ABT 1 8 M³ 5 PCT MOLCO
QINHUANGDAO/BANGKOK FIOST BSS 1/1
LYCN 25/4 − 3/5 2005
ADCOM 2.5 PCT
PLS ADV ANY SUTBL VSL AVLBL N YR REST OFFER
TKS/BRGDS

发至：香港CCC航运有限公司　2005年4月2日
来自：泰国BBB贸易有限公司
关于：7 000公吨散装焦炭秦皇岛/曼谷
7 000公吨散装焦炭积载因数大约1.8立方米，承租人选择5%增减
秦皇岛/曼谷 船舶出租人不负责装卸、积载、平舱费用，一港装一港卸
受载期与解约日为2005年4月25日至5月3日
洽租佣金为2.5%
请告知任何适宜船舶以及你方报价

谢谢/祝好

1.2.2 Offer Made by the Shipowner

1.2.2 出租人发出要约

TO: BBB BKK　3/4/2005

FM: CCC HKG

RE: 7,000 MT COKE IN BULK QINHUANGDAO/BANGKOK

RYFAX 2/4/05 ON THE CPTND SUBJ N OFFER AS FLWS:

1 SBP QINHUANGDAO /1 SBP BANGKOK

7,000 MT COKE IN BULK 5 PCT MOLOO SF ABT 1.8 M^3

LYCN 20/30 APR 2005

LOAD/DISCH 2,500/2,500 MT WWDSHEXUU

USD20.00 PMT FIOST l/l BSS

FULL FRT BE PAID W/I 3 BANKING DAYS AFT COMPLTN OF LOADING

DEM/DES USD 5,000/DHD,

OWS AGENTS BENDS

AP ON CGO DUE TO VSLS AGE IF ANY TB FOR CHTR'S ACCT

ADCOM 2.5 PCT

SUBJ DTLS OWISE PER GENCON

FYI VSL'S MAIN PARTL ASFLWS

MV DDD-PAN-85 BLT-SDBC-4HOLDS-LOA l20-DWT 8,700-7.6MSSW

G/B 12,600/l1,500 M^3,4×20T DERS, l3 K

YR EARLIEST CFM THE ABV APRECD

BRGDS

发至：泰国BBB贸易有限公司　2005年4月3日

来自：香港CCC航运有限公司

关于：7 000公吨散装焦炭秦皇岛/曼谷

参照贵方2005年4月2日传真，报价如下：

1个安全泊位和港口秦皇岛/1个安全泊位和港口曼谷

7 000公吨散装焦炭，船舶出租人选择5%增减，积载因数大约1.8立方米

受载期与解约日为2005年4月20—30日

装卸率为2 500/2 500公吨，晴天工作日、周日、节假日除外，除非使用

每公吨运费20美元，船舶出租人不负责装卸、积载、平舱费用，一港装一港卸

装货后3个银行工作日支付全部运费

滞期费5 000美元，速遣费2 500美元

装卸两港船舶出租人代理

由于船龄加收的额外货物保险费由承租人负责

洽租佣金为2.5%

以金康范本细节为准

船舶明细如下：

船舶名称DDD，巴拿马旗，1985年建造，单层甲板散货船，4个舱，船长120米，载重量8 700吨，吃水7.6米，散装容积12 600立方米，包装容积11 500立方米，吊杆4个，负荷各20吨，航速13节。

敬请尽快确认

祝好

1.2.3 Counter offer Made by the Charterer

1.2.3 承租人反要约

TO: CCC HKG　　4/4/2005

FM: BBB BKK

MV DDD 7,000 MT COKE IN BULK QINHUANGDAO/BANGKOK

TKS FOR YR OFFER 3/4/2005 WE COUNTER AS FLWS

LOAD/DISCH 1,500/2,000 MT WWDSHEEIU

USD 18.00 PMT FIOST 1/1 BSS

DEM/DES USD4,000/DHD

AP IF ANY LPSM USD 1,000 OWS ACCT

OTHERS AS PER YRFAX 3/4/05

PLS URG CFM THE ABV

TKS BRGDS

TO: BBB BKK　　5/4/2005

FM: CCC HKG

TKS FOR YR COUNTER 4/4/05 WE FIRM OFFER AS FLWS

LOAD /DISCH 2,000/2,500 MT WWDSHEXUU

USD 19.50 PMT FIOST 1/1 BSS

ADCOM 1.25PCT

OTHERS AS PER OUR PREVIOUS FAXES

SUBJ OWRS BOD APRVL W/1 24HRS

BRGDS

TO: CCC HKG　　6/4/2005

FM: BBB BKK

MV DDD 7,000 MT COKE IN BULK QINHUANGDAO/BANGKOK

TKS FOR YR FIRM OFFER AS GOOD RELATION BTWN US YR FIRM OFFER ACPTD

PLS ADJST FRT SUGST USD 19.00 PMT

PLS URG CFM THE ABV

BRGDS

发至：香港 CCC 航运有限公司　2005 年 4 月 4 日

来自：泰国 BBB 贸易有限公司

<u>船舶 DDD 7 000 公吨散装焦炭秦皇岛/曼谷</u>

感谢贵方 2005 年 4 月 3 日的要约，我们还价如下：

装卸率为 1 500/2 000 公吨，晴天工作日、周日、节假日除外，即使使用

每公吨运费 18 美元，船舶出租人不负责装卸、积载、平舱费用，一港装一港卸

滞期费 4 000 美元，速遣费 2 000 美元

额外货物保险费包干 1 000 美元由船舶出租人负责

其他见贵方 2005 年 4 月 3 日的传真

敬请尽快确认上述信息

祝好

发至：泰国 BBB 贸易有限公司　2005 年 4 月 5 日

来自：香港 CCC 航运有限公司

感谢贵方 2005 年 4 月 4 日的还价，我们报实盘如下：

装卸率为 2 000/2 500 公吨，晴天工作日、周日、节假日除外，除非使用

每公吨运费 19.50 美元，船舶出租人不负责装卸、积载、平舱费用，一港装一港卸

洽租佣金为 1.25%

其他见我们以前的传真

以我们董事会 24 小时同意为准

祝好

发至：香港 CCC 航运有限公司　2005 年 4 月 6 日

来自：泰国 BBB 贸易有限公司

<u>船舶 DDD 7 000 公吨散装焦炭秦皇岛/曼谷</u>

感谢贵方实盘，介于双方友好关系，我们接受。

请将运费调整到每公吨 19 美元

敬请尽快确认上述信息

祝好

1.2.4 Firm Offer Made by the Shipowner

1.2.4 出租人发实盘

TO: BBB BKK　6/4/2005

FM: CCC HKG

<u>MV DDD 7,000 MT COKE IN BULK QINHUANGDAO/BANGKOK</u>

TK U FOR UR FAX 6/4/05 N PREVIOUS FAXES WE RECAP FIXTURE AS FLWS

7,000 MT COKE IN BULK 5 PCT MOLOO SF ABT 1.8 M^3

LYCN 20/30 APR 2005

LOAD /DISCH 2,000/2,500 MF WWDSHEXUU

USD 19.00 PMT FIOST 1/1 BSS

FULL FRT BE PAID W/I 3 BANKING DAYS AFT COMPLTN OF LOADING

DEM/DES USD 4,000/DHD

OWRS AGTS BENDS

AP IF ANY LPSM USD 1,000 OWRS ACCT TB DEDUCTED FM FRT PAYMT

ADCOM 1.25 PCT

C/P DTLS TB REF TO OWRS PROFORMA WHICH WL FAXU PROFORMA IN MINUTES (GENCON FORM)

PLS ACK RCPT THE ABV N YOU COMMENTS

BRGDS

发至：泰国BBB贸易有限公司　2005年4月6日

来自：香港CCC航运有限公司

船舶DDD 7 000公吨散装焦炭秦皇岛/曼谷

感谢贵方2005年4月6日及以前的传真，我们概括确认书如下：

7 000公吨散装焦炭，船舶出租人选择5%增减，积载因数大约为1.8立方米

受载期与解约日为2005年4月20—30日

装卸率为2 000/2 500公吨，晴天工作日、周日、节假日除外，除非使用

每公吨运费19美元，船舶出租人不负责装卸、积载、平舱费用，一港装一港卸

装货后3个银行工作日支付全部运费

滞期费4 000美元，速遣费2 000美元

装卸两港由船舶出租人代理

额外货物保险费包干1 000美元，由船舶出租人承担，从运费中扣除

洽租佣金为1.25%

租船合同细节参照出租人范本，马上传真给贵方（金康范本）

请确认收到上述和贵方意见

祝好

1.2.5 Acceptance Made by the Charterer

1.2.5 承租人接受

TO: CCC HKG　　7/4/2005

FM: BBB BKK

TKS FOR YR FIRM OFFER AND YR FIRM OFFER ACPTD

PLS GO AHEAD TO PREPARE C/P FOR EARLIER SIGNATURE

TK YOU VERY MUCH

BRGDS

发至:香港CCC航运有限公司　2005年4月7日

来自:泰国BBB贸易有限公司

感谢贵方实盘,我们接受

请进一步准备租船合同以便尽快签约

非常感谢

祝好

8th April, 2005

Messrs Thailand BBB Trading Co. Bangkok

Dear Sirs,

Please find enclosed herewith two sets of the Charter Party dated. Hong Kong 7th April, 2005 as per our faxes exchange from 2nd to 7th April, 2005 covering a shipment of 7,000.00 metric tons of coke in bulk from Qinhuangdao to Bangkok.

Please check and sign them and return us one set which is duly signed by your good selves.

We thank you very much for prompt fixture of the Charter Party based on your support and our board appreciates cooperation between our two parties and looking forward to developing our good relation.

For your information, MV "DDD" is now sailing to Pusan to discharge there a full cargo of gypsum in bulk and we expect she can depart from Pusan around the 22nd instant and arrive at Qinhuangdao on the 23rd.

Vice President
CCC Shipping Co., Ltd.

2005年4月8日

泰国BBB贸易有限公司

先生们：

随信附上两套日期为2005年4月7日、签约地为香港的租船合同，关于2005年4月2—7日我们来往传真所涉及的7 000公吨散装焦炭从秦皇岛运至曼谷。

请核对、签署并寄回一份贵公司签字的合同。

我们非常感谢贵方的支持使得租船合同确认书及时签署，我们董事会非常赞赏我们之间的合作，期待进一步发展双方关系。

船舶"DDD"号正在驶往釜山并在那里卸货，我们预计该船大约于本月22日离开釜山，23日抵达秦皇岛，供贵方参考。

副总裁
香港CCC航运有限公司

1.2.6 Outline of the First Part of This Charter Party
1.2.6 租船合同第一部分（范本见英文部分）概述

1. Shipbroker	RECOMMENDED THE BALTIC AND INTERNATIONAL MARITIME COUNCIL UNIFORM GENERAL CHARTER (AS REVISED 1922,1976) INCLUDING "FIO", ALTERNATIVE ETC. (To be used for trades for which no specially approved form is in force) CODE NAME: "GENCON" Part 1

	2. Place and date **Hong Kong 7th April, 2005**
3. Owners/Place of business (Cl.1) **CCC Shipping Co., Ltd. Hong Kong**	4. Charterers/Place of business (Cl.1) **Thailand BBB Trading Co., Ltd. Bangkok**
5. Vessel's name (Cl.1) **"DDD"**	6. GT/NT (Cl.1) **6,500/3,800**
7.Deadweight cargo carrying capacity in tons (abt)(Cl.1) **8,700 metric tons**	8. Present position (Cl.1) **Now trading**
9. Expected ready to load (abt) (Cl.1) **20th April, 2005**	
10. Loading port or place(Cl.1) **One safe berth one safe port, Qinhuangdao**	11.Discharging port or place(Cl.1) **One safe berth one safe port, Bangkok**

12. Cargo (also state quantity and margin in Owners' option, if agreed; if full and complete cargo not agreed state "part cargo"(Cl.1) **7,000 metric tons of coke in bulk 5% more or less owner's option**	

13. Freight rate (also state if payable on delivered or intaken quantity (Cl.1) **USD 19 per metric ton against Bill of Lading quantity basis one/one**	14.Freight payment (state currency and method of payment; also beneficiary and bank account)(Cl.4) **See Clause No. 18**
15. Loading and discharging costs [state alternative (a) or (b) of Cl. 5 also indicate if the vessel is gearless] **Free/in/out/stowed/trimmed**	16. Laytime [if separate laytime for load and discharge is agreed, fill in (a) and (b). if total laytime for load and discharge, fill in (c) only (cl.6)] (a)Laytime for loading **2,000 MT PWWDSHEXUU**
17. Shippers/Place of business (Cl.6) **China AAA Import and Export Co.**	(b)Laytime for discharging **2,500 MT PWWDSHEXUU** (c)Total laytime for loading and discharging **Laytime to be reversible**
18. Demurrage rate and manner payable (loading and discharging)(Cl.7) **USD4,000/DHD PDPR BOTH ENDS**	19. Canceling date(Cl.10) **30th April, 2005**

20. Brokerage commission and to whom payable (Cl.14) **Total 1.25% commission on freight/demurrage to be deducted from freight**	
21. Additional clauses covering special provisions, if agreed **Rider Clauses Nos. 18 to 41 as attached hereto to fully incorporated in this charter party**	

It is mutually agreed that this contract shall be performed subject to the conditions contained in this charter party which shall include Part 1 as well as Part 2. In the event of a conflict of conditions, the provisions of Part 1 shall prevail over those of Part 2 to the extent of such conflict.

兹相互同意应按本租船合同的第一部分和第二部分中所定条件履行本合同。当条件间发生抵触时,第一部分的规定优先于第二部分适用,但以所抵触的范围为限。

2. Example of Voyage Chartering Fixture Note
2. 航次租船合同确认书实例

IT IS ON THIS DATE OF MAY 26TH, 2009 MUTUALLY AGREED BETWEEN AAA SHIPPING CO.,LTD. AS SHIPOWNER AND BBB TRADE CO.,LTD. AS CHARTERER ON THE FOLLOWING TERMS AND CONDITIONS.

CHTR: BBB TRADE CO., LTD.

OWNER: AAA SHIPPING CO.,LTD.

1. PERFORMING VSL: MV. CCC, SDBC, 1985 BLT, 25,000 DWT / 10.00 M, HA/HO 4/4, G/B 32,000 / 31,000 M³, CRANE 4×25 MT.

2. COMMODITY: THAILAND RICE IN BAGS.

3. QTTY: 18,000 MT RICE IN BAGS 5% MOLOO (ABT S.F 1.3 CBM WOG).

4. LAYCAN : 1ST JUN.—05TH JUN. 2009.

5. LOADPORT: 1SBP BANGKOK, THAILAND.

6. LOAD RATE: 6,000 MTS PER WWD SHEX.

7. DISCHARGING PORT: 1SBP QINGDAO, CHINA.

8. DISCHARGE RATE: 5,000 MT PER WWD SHEX.

9. DEM/DES: USD 5,000 PDPR / DHD.

10. DEM/DES IF ANY AT THE LOADING PORT TO BE SETTLED TOGETHER WITH FREIGHT, AT DISCH. PORT TO BE SETTLED WITHIN 7 DAYS AFTER COMPLETION OF DISCH. AND AGAINST THE SHIPOWNER'S SUPPORTING DOCUMENTS SUCH AS NOTICE OF READINESS/TIMESHEET/STATEMENT OF FACT WHICH WERE SIGNED AND CONFIRMED BY THE SHIPPING AGENCY AT THE LOADING/DISCHARGING PORT.

11. FREIGHT RATE: USD 20.00 PMT ON FIOST BSS 1/1.

12. PAYMENT: 100 PCT FREIGHT LESS COMM TO BE PAID TO SHIPOWNER NOMINATED A/C WITHIN 03 BANKING DAYS AFTER COMPLETION OF LOADING. FREIGHT IS TO BE DEEMED EARNED AS CARGO TAKEN ON BOARD, DISCOUNTLESS, AND NON-RETURNABLE WHETHER VSL AND/OR CGO LOST OR NOT. IF CHTRS REQUEST "FREIGHT PREPAID" BS/L, THE SHIPOWNER WILL S/R "FREIGHT PREPAID" BS/L AGAINST COPY OF BANK SLIPS.

13. OAP IF ANY TO BE FOR CHTR'S A/C.

14. LOAD/DISCH. PORT AGENT: SHIPOWNER TO NOMI NATE AGENTS BENDS.

15. N.O.R. TENDER AND LAYTIME COMMENCE AS PER GENCON 94, N.O.R. TO BE TENDERED AT OFFICE HOUR 0800−1700HRS ON MON TO FRI AND 0800−1200HRS ON SAT. LAYTIME FOR LOADING/DISCHARGING SHALL COMMENCE AT 1300LT WHEN NOR TB TENDERED BEFORE NOON AND 0800LT THE NEXT WORKING DAY IF NOR IS

TENDERED AFTERNOON. IF LOADING/DISCHARGING IS MADE BEFORE THE COMMENCEMENT OF LAYTIME, ONLY THE TIME USED TO BE COUNTED AS LAYTIME.

16. FUMIGATION TO BE FOR CHTR'S ACCOUNT, ARRANGEMENT AND RISK. SHIPOWNER TO GRANT FREE 12HRS FOR FUMIGATION EACH AT LOADING AND/OR DISCHARGING PORT.

17. VSL FULL COMPLY WZ ISM CODE N ISPS CODE N HOLD THE CERTIFICATES.

18. TAXES/DUES ON CGO TO BE FOR CHTR'S ACCT. THE SAME ON FRT/VSL IS TO BE FOR SHIPOWNER'S ACCT.

19. LIGHTERAGE IF ANY TO BE FOR CHTR'S ACCT.

20. ARBITRATION/GA IF ANY TO BE SETTLED IN HONG KONG, ENGLISH LAW TO APPLY.

21. CGO RELEASE TO BE AGAINST O/BILL, CGO TO BE ENTIRELY DISCHARGED AGAINST EITHER ORIGINAL BS/L OR CHTR'S SINGLE L. O. I. IN SHIPOWNER'S PNI WORDING W/O BANK ENDORSEMENT.

22. SHORE'S CRANE/FLOATING CRANE IF ANY TO BE FOR CHTR'S ACCT AT BENDS. SHIPS CRANE CANNOT BE USED FOR LOADING AND DISCHARGING.

23. COMM 3.75 TTL AS BROKERAGE FOR DISTRIBUTION.

24. OWNERS/MASTER/AGENT TO KEEP CHARTERERS/SHIPPERS/CONSIGNEE INFMD OF VESSEL'S ETA AT LOADING/DISCHARGING PORT PRIOR TO 7/5/3/2/1 DAY(S).

25. AT LDPORT N DISPORT, THE DRAFT SURVEY TO BE CARRIED OUT BY THE INDEPENDENT SURVEYOR JOINED WITH THE SHIP'S MASTER. B/L FIGURES ARE AS DRAFT SURVEY FIGURES.

26. THE VESSEL IS TO BE DRIED AND CLEANED BEFORE LOADING AND ARRANGE VENTILATION FOR THIS VOYAGE.

27. COMBINED CARGO NOT ALLOWED.

28. OTHERS AS PER GENCON CP REVISED 1994.

END

ON BEHALF OF SHIPOWNER:　　　　　ON BEHALF OF CHARTERER:

船舶出租人AAA航运有限公司与承租人BBB贸易公司，双方于2009年5月26日达成下列条款和条件：

承租人：BBB贸易公司

船舶出租人：AAA航运有限公司

1.承运船舶："CCC"轮，1985年建造，载重量25 000吨，吃水10.00米，船舱/舱口4/4，散装/包装舱容分别为32 000/31 000立方米，船吊负荷为4×25公吨。

2.货物：泰国袋装大米。

3.货物数量：18 000吨袋装大米，5%增减由船舶出租人选择（货物积载因数大约为1.3立方米，不保证）。

4.受载期和解约日：2009年6月1—5日。

5.装货港口：1个安全港口1个安全泊位，泰国曼谷港。

6.装货效率：每个晴天工作日6 000公吨，周日、节假日不包括在内。

7.卸货港口：1个安全港口1个安全泊位，中国青岛港。

8.卸货效率：每个晴天工作日5 000公吨，周日、节假日不包括在内。

9.滞期费/速遣费：每天5 000美元/每天2 500美元，不足一天按比例计算。

10.装港滞期费或者速遣费应跟运费一并结算，卸港滞期费/速遣费应于卸货完毕后7天内结算。船舶出租人凭相关单据结算，如船舶代理人签字并确认的装卸事实记录和装卸就绪通知书。

11.运费率：每公吨20.00美元，船舶出租人不负责装卸、积载和平舱，一港装一港卸。

12.运费支付：扣除经纪人佣金后的所有运费应于装货完毕后的3个银行工作日内付到船舶出租人账户。运费在货物装船时被认为已赚取，无论船舶或者货物灭失与否，运费没有折扣且不能退还。如果承租人要求签发"运费预付"提单，那么船舶出租人将凭银行水单副本签发 并开具"运费预付"提单。

13.如果有老龄船货物保险费，承租人负担。

14.装/卸港口船舶代理：船舶出租人指定装卸港代理。

15.装卸就绪通知书的递交和装卸时间的起算遵照金康合同1994年版本执行，装卸就绪通知书在周一到周五的工作时间0800~1700递交，在周六的0800~1200递交。如果在上午递交装卸就绪通知书，装卸时间的起算从下午1300开始，如果在下午递交，则装卸时间从下一个工作日0800点起算。如果装卸货在装卸时间起算之前已经开始，那么实际作业的时间计入装卸时间。

16.货物熏蒸应由承租人安排并负担费用和风险。船舶出租人同意两港共24小时的免费熏蒸时间。

17.船舶完全遵循《国际安全管理规则》和《国际船舶与港口设施保安规则》并持有证书。

18.货物的税费由承租人负担，相应的有关运费和船舶的税费由船舶出租人负担。

19.如果发生驳船费用，由承租人负担。

20.如果需要仲裁/共同海损，在香港解决，适用英国法律。

21.卸港放货应凭借正本提单。全部货物卸货应凭借正本提单或者由承租人出具的按照船东保赔协会格式的单方面保函，不须银行担保。

22.如果两港使用岸吊或者浮吊作业，由承租人方面安排并负担费用，不使用船吊装卸货物。

23.租船佣金总额的3.75%由租船经纪人分配。

24.船舶出租人/船长/代理人应于船舶抵达两港前7/5/3/2/1天通知承租人/发货人/收货人预计抵达时间。

25.在装卸港，水尺的检验应该在船长的参与下由独立检验机构执行。提单的货物数量应该与水尺报告一致。

26.船舶在装货前应保持干燥清洁，并且在航行过程中保持通风。

27.船舶不应搭配其他货物。

28.其他未尽条款按照金康合同1994年版本。

结束

船舶出租人代表：　　　　　　　　　　船舶承租人代表：

3. Example of TCT Chartering Fixture Note
3. 航次期租合同确认书实例

It is this day mutually agreed through friendly consultation between shipowner and charterer on chartering of MV "ABC" with terms and conditions as follows:

(1) Delivery place: port of Yantai, China.

(2) Delivery time: around 12/15 July, 2000. Delivery time begins with the moment that the inward document is completed or the pilot is onboard the vessel whichever occurs last, whether on Sunday, Holiday or not, when in day or night.

(3) Redelivery place: the last discharging port in Japan of the voyage.

(4) Redelivery time: when the outward pilot is dropped at the place of clause 3.

(5) Daily hire: USD 5,000 per day or pro rata including crew's overtime.

(6) Hire payment: first 15 days hire will be paid in advance before the vessel is delivered, the rest shall be paid within 3 banking days after the vessel is redelivered.

(7) Stevedores damage to the vessel: charterers are to be fully responsible for damage to the vessel caused by stevedores or other employees of the charterers.

(8) Agents: charterers are to appoint agents at both ends and pay agency fees.

(9) Commission: 2.5 percent total.

(10) Other terms and conditions are subject to NYPE.

船舶出租人与承租人双方通过友好协商就"ABC"号船的租用于本日达成下列条款和条件：

（1）交船地点：中国烟台港。

（2）交船时间：大约在2000年7月12—15日。交船时间自进口手续办妥或者引航员登船之日起算，以后发生者为准，无论是否为星期日、节假日，昼夜均适用。

（3）还船地点：最后航程的卸货港（日本）。

（4）还船时间：同第3条，引航员下船止。

（5）日租金：每天5 000美元或按比例，包括船员加班费。

（6）租金支付：交付船前预付15天租金，其余租金在还船后3个银行工作日内支付。

（7）装卸工人对船舶造成的损坏：承租人将完全负责装卸工人或其他雇员造成的船舶损坏。

（8）代理人：承租人任命装卸港代理人并支付代理费。

（9）佣金：总租金的2.5%。

（10）其他条款及条件以土产格式合同为准。

4. Example of the Voyage Instructions
4. 航行指令实例

Following is an example of the voyage instructions made by the charterer to the master under time charter party:

下列是定期租船合同下，承租人向船长发布的航行指令实例。

GENERAL INSTRUCTION TO MASTER BY TIME CHARTERER

PLSD TO INFO YOU TT "ABC" IS YR NEXT CHRTS.

很高兴通知你，"ABC"是你的下一个承租人。

UNLESS YOU GET INSTRUCTED OTHERWISE, YOU ARE REQUESTED TO PROCEED WITH MAX C/P SPEED AT ALL TIMES AT SEA, EXCEPT ONLY WHEN NAVIGATING IN RESTRICTED WATERS N HV ALL HATCHES REQUIRED FR LOADING/DISCHARGING OPENED BEFORE BERTHING TO AVOID DELAYS TO CGO OPERATIONS.

除非得到另外指示，要求你在海上的所有时间内以合同规定的最大速度航行，限制海域除外，在靠泊前应打开所有舱盖，以避免延误货物装卸作业。

ARVL N DEPARTURE REPORTS TB SENT FM EVERY PORT OF CALL STATING THE FLW:

每一个挂靠港口都要发送抵港和离港报告表明下列内容：

ON ARVL P/S N ON BERTHING

DATE N TIME OF ARVL, BUNKERS N FW ON BOARD, DRAFT ON ARVL, BERTHING PROSPECTS N ANY SIGNIFICANT DELAY OF ETS.

抵达引航站和靠泊时：

抵达日期和时间，船上燃油和淡水，抵达吃水，预计靠泊以及任何延误开航的重要事项。

ON SAILING

DATE AND TIME OF SAILING, QTY OF CGO LOADED, BUNKERS AND FW ON BOARD, BUNKERS TAKEN IF ANY, DRAFT ON DEPARTURE , KIND AND QTY OF CGO LOADED/DISCHARGED, ESTIMATED ARVL DRAFT AT NEXT PORT AND ETS.

开航时：

离港日期和时间，装货数量，船上燃油和淡水，加油情况，离港吃水，装上及卸下货物的种类和数量，下一港口预计抵达吃水和预计开航时间。

NOR TB TENDERED IMMEDIATELY UPON ARVL AND REPEATED W/I THE HRS DURING WHICH N.O.R CAN BE TENDERED, IN CASE THE VESSEL DID NOT ARRIVE W/I OFFICE HOURS. NOR TB TENDERED BY CABLE ON ARRIVAL AT ALL/BOTH LOADING AND DISCHARGING PORT(S).

抵达后应立即递交装卸准备就绪通知书，如果船舶不能在办公时间内抵达，应在装卸准备就绪通知书能够递交的时间内再次递交。在所有装货港和卸货港，船舶抵达即以电报形式递交装卸准备就绪通知书。

FREE PRATIQUE BY RADIO

SOMETIMES IN OUR CARGO FIXTURES, FREE PRATIQUE IS CONSIDERED A PRE-CONDITION FOR TENDERING OF N. O. R AND COMMENCEMENT OF LAYTIME. THEREFORE PLEASE APPLY TIMELY TO THE LOCAL HEALTH AUTHORITY SO THAT THE FREE PRATIQUE CAN BE GRANTED PROMPTLY.

电报检疫：

我们订立的货物买卖合同确认书中，有时会规定检疫是递交装卸准备就绪通知书和装卸时间开始的先决条件。因此请及时向当地卫生当局申请，以便能够通过检疫。

BUNKERS

IF BUNKERS ARE SUPPLIED TO YOUR VESSEL, PLS ALWAYS CFM TO US THE EXACT QTY RCVD AS PER RECEIPT, TIME BUNKERING COMMENCED AND TIME COMPLETED. PLS PROTEST EVENTUALLY IF THE QTY RCVD DOES NOT MATCH THE FIGURES ON THE BUNKER RECEIPT. UPON COMPLETION OF BUNKERING YOU ARE REQUESTED TO ADVISE: A) IN WHICH TANKS NEW BUNKERS HAVE BEEN FILLED B) WHETHER NEW BUNKERS HAVE BEEN MIXED WITH OLD BUNKERS ROB.

燃油：

如果你船加油，请向我们确认按收据收到的确切数量、加油开始和完毕时间。如果数量与收据不一致，请提出异议。加完油后，请告之：A）加在何舱；B）新油是否与船上旧油混用。

BS/L

PLS DO NOT SIGN OR RELEASE ANY ORI BSL WITHOUT OUR WRITTEN CFM AND WHEN A LETTER OF AUTHORIZATION IS GIVEN TO AGENTS, SAME MUST STATE VERY CLEARLY THAT THEY ARE NOT TO RELEASE ORI BSL WITHOUT WRITTEN CFM FM US.

提单：

在没有我们书面确认的情况下，不能签发任何正本提单。当授权书赋予代理人时也应清楚，在没有我们书面确认的情况下，不能签发任何正本提单。

CGO WORK

货物作业：

(1) TO PROPERLY RIG UP CARGO GEAR N GET THE VESSEL ALWAYS READY FOR CARGO WORK TO AVOID WASTING TIME IN ANY CASE.

（1）将船舶吊具准备就绪以避免任何延误。

(2) DURING LOADING N DISCHARGING OPERATIONS, OFFICERS N CREWS ON DUTY SHOULD ATTEND CARGO OPERATIONS. ANY PROBLEM ARISES, PLEASE IMMEDIATELY INFO US/OUR AGENT OF THE DETAILS WITH A STATEMENT OF FACTS.

（2）在装卸作业期间，值班船员应当照料货物作业。任何问题出现，请立即将详细事实告知我们和代理人。

(3) TRY YOUR BEST TO AVOID ANY STANDBY CAUSED BY THE VESSEL AND IT IS BETTER NOT TO SIGN ANY STAND-BY SHEET REQUEST BY THE STEVEDORE COMPANY.

（3）尽最大努力避免由船舶引发的停工，最好不要签署任何码头公司要求的停工单据。

REPORTS

报告

A)REPORTS ON VSL TROUBLE

A）船舶问题报告

IF YOU ANTICIPATE ANY DELAY DUE TO A REPAIR, WHICH MAY HINDER THE

VESSEL FM CONTINUING ON ITS NORMAL VOYAGE, PLEASE INFO US.

如果由于修理而影响正常航行，请告知我们。

B)REPORTS ON CGO CONDITION

B）货物情况报告

TO AVOID POSSIBLE CARGO CLAIMS AND TO SETTLE ANY CARGO CLAIMS ISSUED, SMOOTHLY N QUICKLY, IT IS ESSENTIAL TO INFORM US IMMEDIATELY.

为避免可能的货物索赔以及尽快顺利解决货物索赔，请立即告知我们。

C)STEVEDORE DAMAGES

C）码头工人损坏

IN THE EVENT OF STEVEDORE DAMAGE, YOU ARE TO NOTIFY THE PARTY CAUSED THAT SUCH DAMAGE IMMEDIATELY IF FEASIBLE, BUT IN NO CASE LATER THAN 24 HOURS AFTER ITS OCCURRENCE IN WRITING, INDICATING THE CAUSE AND THE EXTENT/FULL DESCRIPTION OF THE DAMAGE AND TO OBTAIN STEVEDORES ACCEPTANCE. PLEASE EXERCISE YOUR INFLUENCE TO OBTAIN REPAIRS WITHOUT DELAY TO LOADING/DISCHARGING OPERATIONS AND/OR DELAY TO VESSEL'S DEPARTURE. PLEASE INFO US IMMEDIATELY OF ANY SUCH DAMAGES THAT OCCUR SO THAT WE CAN SUPPORT YOU IN OBTAINING RECTIFICATION/SETTLEMENT. YOU ARE ALSO REQUESTED TO INFORM US W/I 24 HOURS, IN CASE YOU DISCOVER HIDDEN DAMAGES.

若发生码头工人造成的损坏，如有可能应立即向其指明。但无论如何，不能迟于24小时用书面清楚地表明原因、范围、详情并取得码头工人的确认。请尽力施加影响，促使船舶修理以便不影响装卸货作业和延误船舶离港。请将发生的损坏情况立即告知我们，使我们能够支持你以便问题获得解决。如果发现隐藏损坏，请在24小时内通知我们。

D)SEA PROTEST

D)海事报告

A SEA PROTEST IS A MASTER'S REPORT ON ANY SEA CASUALTIES ENCOUNTERED DURING A VOYAGE, SUCH AS VERY BAD WEATHER OR A MARINE ACCIDENT. PLEASE SEND IT TO US TO SETTLE WITH THE CARGO DAMAGE CLAIM LOADED BY THE SHIPPER'S CONSIGNEES AND/OR INSURANCE COMPANY.

海事报告是船长就海上航行中遭遇的货物损坏所作的报告，如恶劣气候、海上事故。请发给我们以便与货主及保险公司处理货物损失问题。

C/P MAIN TERMS:

租船合同主要条款：

DEL:1 SP SINGAPORE.

交船：1个安全港口，新加坡。

REDLY:DLOSP 1SP SPORE/JAPAN RGE PICO ATDNSHINC.

还船：最后一个引航员下船，一个安全港口新加坡/日本，区域由承租人选择，包括周日、节假日，白天和夜晚。

LYCN: 0000HR LT 01ST JUNE-2400HRS LT 05TH JUNE 2006.

受载期和解约日：当地时间2006年6月1日0点到当地时间6月5日24点。

SPEED & CONSUMPTION:

航速和燃油消耗：

ABT 15.0 KN ON ABT 35 MT(B) IFO 180 CST /ABT 15.0 KN ABT 37 MT(L) IFO 180 CST+ABT 2.5 MT MDO AT SEA IN PORT ABT 3.5 MT MDO.

空载消耗大约35公吨180型号重油，航速约15节。满载消耗大约37公吨180型号重油，航速约15海里。加上2.5公吨轻油在航，在港约3.5公吨轻油。

APPRECIATE YR CORDIAL COOPERATION TO ACCOMPLISH THIS VOY SUCCESSFULLY AND WISH U AND YR CREW GOOD HEALTH.

感谢你的合作，顺利完成本航次，祝你和船员身体健康。

BRGDS

祝好

TIME CHARTERER

定期承租人

〔ASSIGNMENT〕

Ⅰ. **Answer the following questions and check your answers from the text.**

1. What is the meaning of an offer?

2. What is the meaning of subject?

3. What does ETA mean?

4. What does MOLOO mean?

5. What does SHEX mean?

Ⅱ. **Choice questions.** (Choose the one you think is correct from the following.)

1. From a legal point of view, a quote is (　　) on the party making it.

　　A. not binding　　　　　　　　　B. binding

　　C. an offer　　　　　　　　　　　D. a fixture

2. The general contract principle is that an offer is (　　) on the party making it.

　　A. binding　　　　　　　　　　　B. binding for any length of time

　　C. a fixture　　　　　　　　　　　D. invitations for offer

3. (　　) signifies the time a ship will be expected to depart from the loading port.

　　A. ETA　　　　　　　　　　　　　B. ETD

　　C. ATA　　　　　　　　　　　　　D. ATD

4. Which of the following terms does not appear in the Quote of time chartering? (　　)

　　A. Delivery.　　　　　　　　　　B. Redelivery.

　　C. Laytime.　　　　　　　　　　　D. Off-hire.

5. Which of the following terms does not appear in the Quote of voyage chartering? (　　)

　　A. Freight payment.　　　　　　　B. Laytime.

　　C. Hire payment.　　　　　　　　　D. Loading port.

Ⅲ. True or false questions.

1. Referring to the construction of the expression "subject to details", both English and American law give the same meaning of it. (　　)

2. The general contract principle is that an offer is binding for any length of time. (　　)

3. Both ends refer to the loading and discharge ports. (　　)

4. For the charterer's account signifies that the charterer is liable for payment. (　　)

5. A ship's agent is a person or firm who transacts all business of a ship in a port on behalf of shipowners or charterers. (　　)

MODULE | THREE
VOYAGE CHARTER PARTY

模块三　航次租船合同

LEARNING OBJECTIVES

Through studying this module, students will be required to obtain a basic knowledge of voyage charter parties such as the owner's responsibility clause, payment of freight clause, loading and discharging clause, laytime clause, demurrage clause, lien clause, canceling date clause, deviation clause, bill of lading clause, taxes and dues clause, agency clause, brokerage clause, law and arbitration clause, etc.

学习目标

通过学习本模块，学生应获得航次租船合同的基本知识，诸如：船舶出租人责任条款、运费支付条款、装卸货物费用条款、装卸时间条款、滞期费条款、留置权条款、解约日条款、绕航条款、提单条款、规税条款、代理人条款、佣金条款、法律适用和仲裁条款等。

CONTENTS

1. Description of Vessel, Port and Cargo;
2. Shipowner's Responsibility;
3. Freight and Freight Index;
4. Loading and Discharging Costs;
5. Laytime;
6. Demurrage and Dispatch Money;
7. Other Clauses.

学习内容

1. 船舶、港口和货物说明；
2. 船舶出租人的责任；

3. 运费和运价指数；

4. 装卸费用；

5. 装卸时间；

6. 滞期费和速遣费；

7. 其他条款。

KEY POINTS

Shipowner's Responsibility; Payment of Freight; Loading and Discharging Costs Clause; Laytime and Demurrage Clause; Lien Clause, Canceling Date Clause; Deviation Clause; Bill of Lading Clause; Brokerage Clause; Law and Arbitration Clause.

学习要点

船舶出租人的责任；运费支付；装卸货物费用条款；装卸时间和滞期费条款；留置权条款；解约日条款；绕航条款；提单条款；佣金条款；法律适用和仲裁条款。

SKILL REQUIREMENTS

1. Have obtained basic knowledge of voyage charter party;

2. Have the ability to calculate the amount of freight;

3. Have the ability to calculate the amount of deadfreight;

4. Have the ability to calculate the laytime;

5. Have the ability to calculate the demurrage and dispatch money.

技能要求

1. 获得航次租船合同的基本知识；

2. 具备计算运费的能力；

3. 具备计算亏舱费的能力；

4. 具备计算装卸时间的能力；

5. 具备计算滞期费和速遣费的能力。

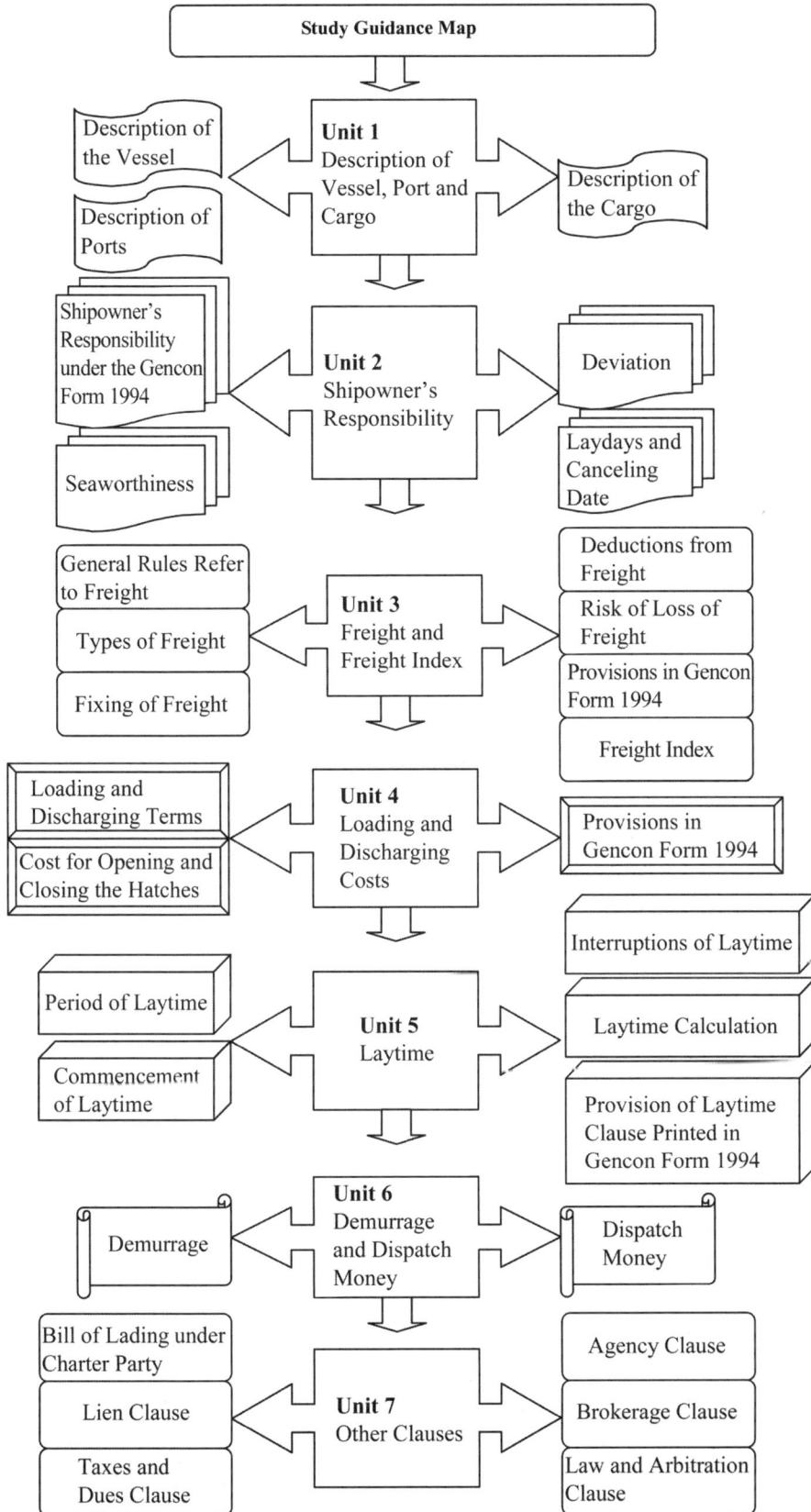

Study Guidance Map

Unit 1
Description of Vessel, Port and Cargo

- Description of the Vessel
- Description of Ports
- Description of the Cargo

Unit 2
Shipowner's Responsibility

- Shipowner's Responsibility under the Gencon Form 1994
- Seaworthiness
- Deviation
- Laydays and Canceling Date

Unit 3
Freight and Freight Index

- General Rules Refer to Freight
- Types of Freight
- Fixing of Freight
- Deductions from Freight
- Risk of Loss of Freight
- Provisions in Gencon Form 1994
- Freight Index

Unit 4
Loading and Discharging Costs

- Loading and Discharging Terms
- Cost for Opening and Closing the Hatches
- Provisions in Gencon Form 1994

Unit 5
Laytime

- Period of Laytime
- Commencement of Laytime
- Interruptions of Laytime
- Laytime Calculation
- Provision of Laytime Clause Printed in Gencon Form 1994

Unit 6
Demurrage and Dispatch Money

- Demurrage
- Dispatch Money

Unit 7
Other Clauses

- Bill of Lading under Charter Party
- Lien Clause
- Taxes and Dues Clause
- Agency Clause
- Brokerage Clause
- Law and Arbitration Clause

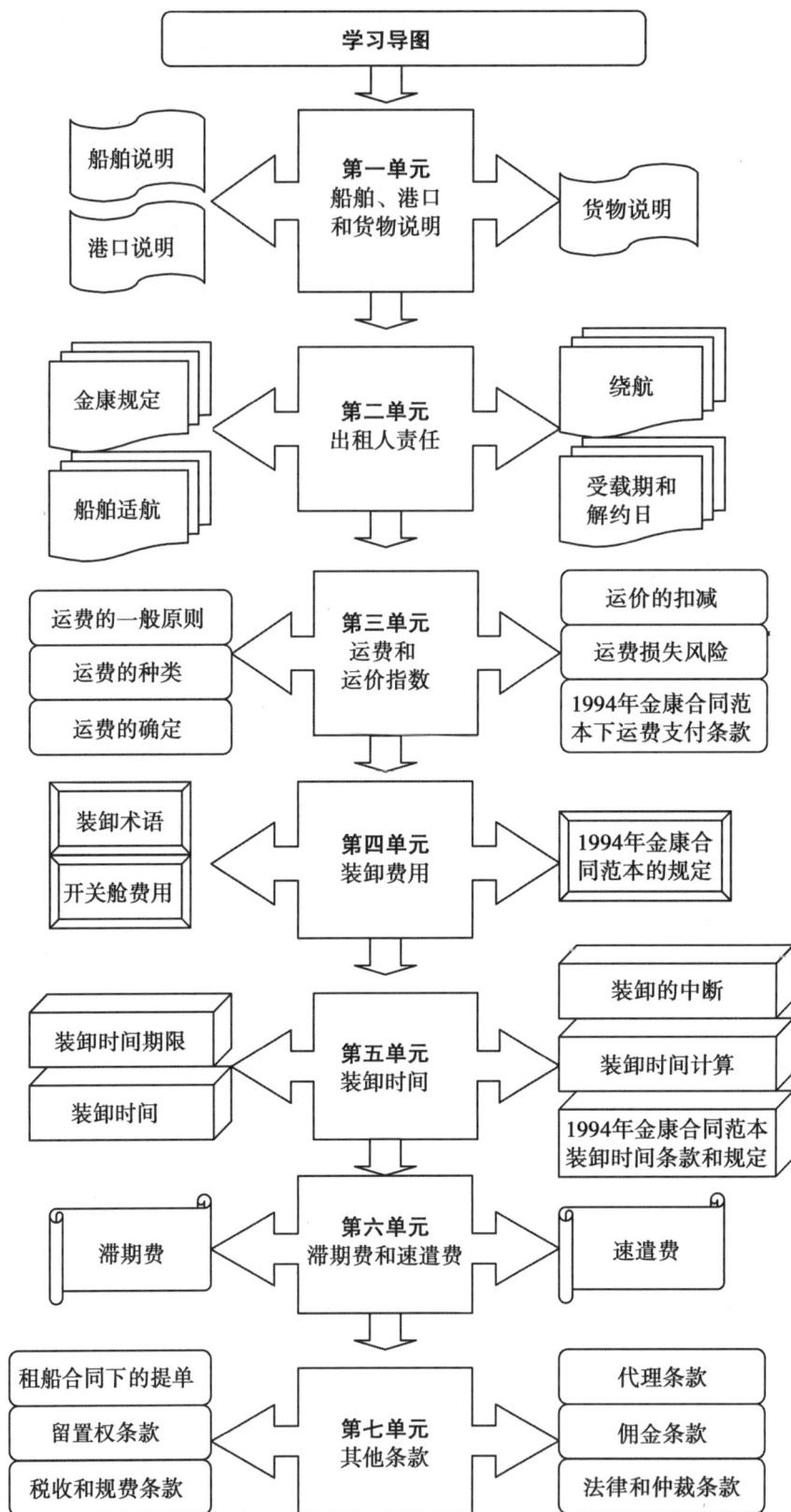

学习导图

第一单元
船舶、港口
和货物说明

船舶说明

港口说明

货物说明

第二单元
出租人责任

金康规定

船舶适航

绕航

受载期和
解约日

第三单元
运费和
运价指数

运费的一般原则

运费的种类

运费的确定

运价的扣减

运费损失风险

1994年金康合同范
本下运费支付条款

第四单元
装卸费用

装卸术语

开关舱费用

1994年金康合
同范本的规定

第五单元
装卸时间

装卸时间期限

装卸时间

装卸的中断

装卸时间计算

1994年金康合同范本
装卸时间条款和规定

第六单元
滞期费和速遣费

滞期费

速遣费

第七单元
其他条款

租船合同下的提单

留置权条款

税收和规费条款

代理条款

佣金条款

法律和仲裁条款

UNIT 1　DESCRIPTION OF VESSEL, PORT AND CARGO

第一单元　船舶、港口和货物说明

A voyage charter party is a charter party under which the shipowner charters to the charterer the whole or part of the ship's space for the carriage by sea of the intended goods from one port to another and the charterer pays the agreed amount of freight. The rights and obligations of the shipowner and charterer are governed by the voyage charter party. The shipowner and charterer are quite free to make their contract in any form that they choose. But usually, they use charter parties in a standard form such as the Gencon Form.

　航次租船合同是指船舶出租人向承租人提供船舶或者船舶的部分舱位，装运约定的货物，从一港运至另一港，由承租人支付约定运费的合同。船舶出租人和承租人的权利和义务根据航次租船合同确定。船舶出租人和承租人可以自由选用任何范本来订立他们的合同，但通常他们选用标准范本，如金康范本。

In general, the following provisions are found in most voyage charter parties: preamble; shipowner's responsibility clause, deviation clause, payment of freight clause, loading and discharging clause, laytime clause, demurrage clause, lien clause, canceling date clause, bill of lading clause, both to blame collision clause, general average and new Jason clause, taxes and dues clause, agency clause, brokerage clause, general strike clause, war risks clause, general ice clause, law and arbitration clause, etc.

一般来说，大多数租船合同都包括下列条款：序言、船舶出租人的责任条款、绕航条款、运费支付条款、装货和卸货条款、装卸时间条款、滞期费条款、留置权条款、解约日条款、提单条款、双方碰撞责任条款、共同海损和新杰森条款、税费条款、代理条款、佣金条款、罢工条款、战争险条款、冰冻条款、法律和仲裁条款等。

In this module, the interpretation and effect of the main printed clauses are discussed with reference to the text of the Gencon Form 1994 which is widely used in voyage chartering.

本模块参照航次租船中广泛使用的1994年金康合同范本就上述印刷条款的效力和释义进行讲述。

1. Description of the Vessel
1. 船舶说明

The description of the vessel is one of the most important items in the voyage charter party. Charters often commence with a description of the ship, stating the vessel's name, class, capacity, location, and date on which she will be ready to load. The name of the vessel is one of the most important items in the description of the vessel. There are three methods that could be employed to nominate a carrying vessel. They are named vessel, substituted vessel, and vessel to be named.

船舶说明是航次租船合同中最重要的事项之一。合同开头通常为船舶的说明，表述船舶名称、船级、载重量、船舶位置和预计装货的日期。船舶名称是船舶说明中最重要的事项之一。有三种表明履约船舶的方式，即指定船舶、代替船舶和船舶待指定。

1.1 Named Vessel
1.1 指定船舶

Named vessel means that the shipowner nominates a specific vessel to perform the voyage stipulated in the charter party. A basic feature of the charter is that the nominated vessel shall be put at the disposal of the charterer. When a certain ship is fixed for a charter, the existence of the agreement is also dependent on the existence of the vessel. If the vessel is lost or declares a constructive total loss, the charter is frustrated, which means that it is terminated automatically and no longer exists. The charter is for the named ship alone and the charterers cannot be required to accept another ship, even of identical characteristics. Also, the shipowner has no obligation to supply another vessel to perform the voyage.

指定船舶，就是指船舶出租人在航次租船合同中明确地指定一艘船舶来履行合同航次。此类租船的基本特点是，指定的船舶应处于承租人使用之下。当合同指定船舶，合同的存在取决于船舶的存在。如果原来指定的船舶灭失或者宣布推定全损，则合同受阻，这意味着合同自动解除不再存在。合同仅为指定的船舶，不能要求承租人接受其他船舶，即使船舶类型相同也不行。同样，船舶出租人也没有义务提供另外一艘船舶履行合同。

1.2 Substituted Vessel
1.2 代替船舶

In practice, it is often agreed that the vessel may be substituted by another vessel. It means that the shipowner with the right of option nominates a substituted vessel to perform the voyage instead of a specific vessel. It is essential to specify how far this right to substitute goes. The parties may also agree that the substitution be made at any time, whether before the start of the charter period, during it, or after the loss of the named or any substituted ship.

在实务中，通常同意用另一条船舶代替既定船舶，这表明船舶出租人有权选择一条代替船来履行航次。其中，明确船舶出租人选择权的范围是非常重要的。双方当事人也可以同意在任何时间行使替代权，不论是合同开始前、合同期间或者指定船舶或者任何替代船灭失后。

1.3 Vessel to Be Named
1.3 船舶待指定

It is unusually agreed by parties that conclude "the vessel to be nominated" in the charter party before it is unknown what vessel will be used. A vessel to be named means that the shipowner would nominate a certain vessel after the commencement of implementation of the charter party within a reasonable period and notify the charterer of the ship's name. If the vessel is named by the shipowner later in due time, she becomes the named vessel and the shipowner could not make an exchange.

在租船合同中约定"待指定船舶"的各方通常一致认为，在约定之时，具体将使用哪艘船舶尚不确定。"待命名船舶"是指，船舶出租人需在租船合同履行开始后的合理期限内指定某一特定船舶，并将船名通知承租人。若船舶出租人后续在约定期限内完成船舶命名，则该船舶即成为"指定船舶"，此后船舶出租人不得擅自更换。

1.4 *Maritime Law of the People's Republic of China* (CMC) Regulation
1.4 《中华人民共和国海商法》(CMC) 规定

Article 96 of CMC stipulates that "The shipowner shall provide the intended ship. The intended ship may be substituted with the consent of the charterer. However, if the ship substituted does not meet the requirements of the charter party, the charterer may reject the ship or cancel the charter. Should any damage or loss occur to the charterer as a result of the shipowner's failure in providing the intended ship due to his fault, the shipowner shall be liable for compensation".

《中华人民共和国海商法》第 96 条规定："出租人应当提供约定的船舶；经承租人同意，可以更换船舶。但是提供的船舶或者更换的船舶不符合合同约定的，承租人有权拒绝或者解除合同。因出租人过失未提供约定的船舶致使承租人遭受损失的，出租人应当负赔偿责任。"

1.5 Vessel's Particulars
1.5 船舶细节

Where the ship is nominated, the vessel's name and often also the year of build, flag of nationality, deadweight, gross and net tonnage are stated in the charter party. The need for the description of the vessel in the voyage charter party very much depends on the circumstances. The type of cargo and the intended ports and sea route especially determine what details about the vessel must be mentioned during the negotiations and in the charter party.

当船舶被指定时，船舶的名称和建造年份、船旗、载重吨、总吨和净吨也应在合同中表明。航次租船合同下是否需要进行船舶说明取决于不同情形。在洽谈期间，货物种类、预挂靠港口和航线决定着在合同中需要表明哪些船舶细节。

Also, the equipment for cargo handling (winches, cranes, pumps, etc.) and the condition of the cargo compartment are often important for the vessel's fitness for the intended cargo. The number of hatches, type of hatch covering, and length and breadth of hatch openings are important details when the charterers and the shipowners estimate the speed and cost of loading and discharging.

此外，船舶装卸设备（绞车、起重机、水泵等）和货舱的条件往往对船舶是否适合承运预定货物是重要的。舱口的数量、类型、长度和宽度是船舶出租人和承租人估计装卸速度和成本的重要细节。

2. Description of Ports
2. 港口说明

Ports are the places for loading and discharging the goods, therefore the description of loading and discharging ports are very important matters in the voyage charter party.

港口是装卸货物的地点，因此在航次租船合同下，装货港和卸货港的说明是很重要的事情。

2.1 Nomination of Ports
2.1 装卸港口的约定

The places for loading or discharging can be agreed in several ways, for instance: "a fixed berth, e.g. berth 2 at Kobe", or "a fixed port, e.g. 1 safe port Sydney" or "a fixed area, e.g. 1 safe port and 1 safe berth Japan".

约定装卸港的方法有几种："一个确定泊位，如神户港2号泊位"；或"一个明确的装卸港，如悉尼的一个安全港口"；或"一个明确的区域，如日本的一个安全泊位和港口"。

It is normal to nominate the port or ports when concluding the charter. If a port is to be nominated later, and thus is not in the charter party, it is advisable to state the latest time at which the charterer can nominate the port.

通常在订立租约时指定港口。如果随后指定港口，也就是说合同没有规定时，应当规定承租人最迟指定港口的时间。

Also, when no such clause is inserted into the charter party the charterers should nominate the port or ports in such a good time in advance that no extra cost for waiting time and deviation is caused to the vessel. When the charter party contains several loading ports or discharging ports, it is common that the shipowners try to introduce a clause saying that the ports shall be called "in geographical rotation". The intention is to avoid extra steaming time.

同样，如果合同中没有规定，承租人应当提前指定港口以避免因等待和绕航而产生额外的费用。当租船合同中列有几个装货港或卸货港时，船舶出租人应在合同中规定以"地理顺序"挂靠，以避免额外绕航。

Article 101 of CMC stipulates: "The shipowner shall discharge the goods at the port of discharge specified in the charter party. Where the charter party contains a clause allowing the choice of the port of discharge by the charterer, the master may choose one from among the agreed ports to discharge the goods, in case the charterer did not, as agreed in the charter, instruct in time as to the port chosen for discharging the goods. Where the charterer did not instruct in time as to the chosen port of discharge, as agreed in the charter, and the shipowner suffered losses thereby, the charterer shall be liable for compensation; where the charterer has suffered losses as a result of the shipowner's arbitrary choice of a port to discharge the goods, in disregard of the provisions in the relevant charter, the shipowner shall be liable for compensation."

《中华人民共和国海商法》第101条规定："出租人应当在合同约定的卸货港卸货。合同订有承租人选择卸货港条款的，在承租人未按照合同约定及时通知确定的卸货港时，船长可以从约定的选卸港中自行选定一港卸货。承租人未按照合同约定及时通知确定的卸货港，致使出租人遭受损失的，应当负赔偿责任。出租人未按照合同约定，擅自选定港口卸货致使承租人遭受损失的，应当负赔偿责任。"

2.2 Safe Ports
2.2 安全港口

Most charter parties state that the ports and berths nominated by the charterers shall be safe. A safe port means a port to which a vessel can get laden as she is and at which she can lie and discharge, always afloat. The safety of the port should be viewed in relation to a vessel properly manned and equipped, and navigated and handled without negligence and with good seamanship. The port must be safe for the particular vessel carrying the cargo she has on board. It must be politically as well as physically safe.

大多数航次租船合同中都规定承租人指定的港口和泊位必须是安全的。安全港是指一个港口能使船舶在满载时停靠和卸载，并始终漂浮。安全港口应理解为在没有疏忽下，船舶不会处于运用了良好的航海技术和船艺仍不能避免的危险中。港口必须对于一条装载货物的特定船舶是安全的。安全港必须具备政治局势方面以及实质条件方面的安全。

【Case】The *Houston City* was ordered under a voyage charter to proceed to one or two safe ports in Western Australia and to load there at a safe wharf as ordered. She was ordered to a berth at Geraldton which was exposed to northerly winds but which would ordinarily have been safe for a ship of the *Houston City*'s size. To reduce the danger from northerly winds there were two hauling-off buoys and a fender on the wharf. However, one of the buoys had been removed for repair, although the master was told that its return was imminent. A 50-ft section of the fender on the wharf was also missing. The ship was damaged in a northerly gale as a result of the absence of the hauling-off buoy and the missing section of the fender. It was held that Geraldton was unsafe for the ship because of these deficiencies and that the master of the vessel had acted reasonably in going there.

【案例】在航次租船合同下，"休斯敦城"号船被指令驶往澳大利亚西部一至两个安全港口，根据指示在一个安全码头装货。船舶被指令到杰拉尔顿的一个泊位装货，该泊位暴露于北风之下，但这通常对于类似"休斯敦城"号的船舶是安全的。为了降低来自北风的风险，码头上设有两个浮动浮筒和一块防护栏。然而，其中一个浮筒被送去修理，虽然船长被告知浮筒会立即返回。防护栏上有一块50英尺的部分缺失。由于缺少浮筒和部分防护栏，船舶因遭遇北风而受损。判决：因为这些缺陷，杰拉尔顿对船舶来说是不安全的，而船长抵达那里的行为是合理的。

As a general rule it can be said that the earlier the shipowners are informed about intended ports and berths, the more liability rests on them as regards investigation of the safety. This means that when the shipowners, during the negotiations, and in the charter party, have accepted a certain port or a certain berth they have little chance of getting damages from the charterers if the port or the berth turns out to be unsafe. On the other hand, the charterers have little chance of escaping liability for damage to the ship when the port or berth has been nominated after the negotiations and the fixture. In the latter case, the shipowners have little or no possibility of influencing the choice of port or berth.

就一般规则而言，可以说船舶出租人越早获悉预定的港口及泊位，其在安全调查方面承担的责任就越多。这意味着在洽谈过程中以及在租船合同中，当船舶出租人接受一个特定港口或泊位，如果该港口或泊位后来被证实不安全，他们从承租人处获得赔偿的可能性不大。反之，港口或泊位在洽谈和订立合同之后确定，承租人在船舶受损逃避赔偿责任的可能性不大。在后一种的情况下，船舶出租人几乎没有或完全没有能力影响港口或泊位的选择。

2.3 Near Clause
2.3 附近港口条款

There is an obligation on the shipowner to take the vessel to the agreed loading or discharging place. To protect the shipowner's interests against unforeseeable difficulties, a so-called near clause is often inserted in the voyage charter party. The clause "or so near thereto as she may safely get and lie always afloat" is often added after the name of the ports of loading and discharge.

船舶出租人的义务是将船舶驶往指定的装货港或卸货港。为了保护船舶出租人应对不可预见的障碍，一条所谓附近港口条款经常被引入航次租船合同中。该条款"或船舶能安全抵达并始终浮泊的附近地点"经常附加在指定装卸货港口条款后面。

The clause intends to protect the shipowner's interests against such hindrances that arise after the negotiations and the fixture. The clause relates only to obstacles that are regarded as permanent, not to such as ordinary incidents of the voyage. A temporary obstacle, such as an unfavorable state of the tide or insufficient water to enable the ship to get into the dock, will not make the place unsafe to relieve the shipowner from liability to unload there. If a ship is prevented on her arrival from reaching the place of loading or unloading, she is bound to wait a reasonable time before adopting the alternative place of loading or discharge, if by so waiting she can get to the port or dock or berth named for loading or unloading. This reasonable time will be fixed by the commercial considerations and by the nature of the voyage in which the ship is engaged. The interests of both parties have to be considered in determining what, from a commercial point of view, would be reasonable.

这种条款的目的是保护船舶出租人应对洽谈和订约后出现的障碍。该条款仅针对被认为的持久性障碍，而不是航次中的通常事件。暂时的障碍，如潮水问题，使得船舶不能进入泊位，不能被认定为港口不安全以免除船舶出租人在那里卸货的责任。如果船舶到达时受阻，不能抵达装卸地点，在采用替换的装卸地点前要等待一个合理的时间，即如果等待使船舶能够到达指定的港口或码头或泊位装卸。合理的时间应依据商业因素和船舶涉及航次的性质来确定。在判断何为商业上合理的时间时，必须同时考虑双方的利益。

Article 91 of CMC stipulates that "If, due to force majeure or any other causes not attributable to the fault of the carrier or the shipper, the ship could not discharge its goods at the port of destination as provided for in the contract of carriage, unless the contract provides otherwise, the master shall be entitled to discharge the goods at a safe port or place near the port of destination and the contract of carriage shall be deemed to have been fulfilled. The master shall, in deciding the discharge of the goods, inform the shipper or the consignee concerned and shall take the interests of the shipper or the consignee into consideration".

《中华人民共和国海商法》第91条规定："因不可抗力或者其他不能归责于承运人和托运人的原因致使船舶不能在合同约定的目的港卸货的，除合同另有约定外，船长有权将货物在目的港邻近的安全港口或者地点卸载，视为已经履行合同。船长决定将货物卸载的，应当及时通知托运人或者收货人，并考虑托运人或者收货人的利益。"

3. Description of the Cargo
3. 货物说明

The description of the cargo for transportation is important. Shipowners, who during the negotiations and in the fixture accept certain goods are also obliged to carry out the transportation of the cargo. The shipowners have to get all necessary details of the cargo from the charterer or from someone else, in order to be able to find out whether the cargo is suitable for the vessel and to be able to estimate the costs of handling and transportation.

货物运输的说明是非常重要的。船舶出租人在经过洽谈和订约后接受特定货物时就有履行运输该货物的义务。船舶出租人需要从承租人或其他人那儿获得货物的所有详细资料，以确保船舶适货，并且能够计算运输货物的成本。

3.1 Contracted Cargo
3.1 契约货物

In the absence of express stipulations, it is the absolute duty of the charterer, if he can legally do so, to furnish a cargo according to the charter. If the cargo delivered to the vessel is not in accordance with the description, the shipowners might be entitled to compensation and, in some cases, when the cargo delivered differs in essential points from the previous description, the shipowners may also be entitled to cancel the contract and to claim compensation for loss of freight.

在合同没有明文规定的情况下，如果法律许可，承租人有绝对义务提供合同指定的货物。如果承租人提供的货物与合同规定不一致，船舶出租人有权要求赔偿损失，在某些情况下，交付货物与指定货物有很大不同，船舶出租人有权解除合同并且要求赔偿运费损失。

Article 100 of CMC stipulates: "The charterer shall provide the intended goods, but he may replace the goods with the consent of the shipowner. However, if the goods replaced are detrimental to the interests of shipowners, the shipowners shall be entitled to reject such goods and cancel the charter. Where the shipowner has suffered losses as a result of the failure of the charterer in providing the intended goods, the charterer shall be liable for compensation."

《中华人民共和国海商法》第100条规定："承租人应当提供约定的货物；经出租人同意，可以更换货物。但是，更换的货物对出租人不利的，出租人有权拒绝或者解除合同。因未提供约定的货物致使出租人遭受损失的，承租人应当负赔偿责任。"

The charterer may be relieved from such obligations in cases where events have rendered the performance of the contract illegal by the law of the country in which the performance was to have taken place; where the shipowner has broken a condition precedent; where there are express provisions in the contract which relieve the charterer; where the whole adventure has been frustrated; where the failure to load a cargo is due to the shipowner's default provided that he has no legal excuse for such default.

承租人在下列情况下可以免除责任：在根据合同履约地法律为非法的情况下；当船舶出租人违反前提条件时；当合同明文中规定免除承租人责任时；当整个航程受阻时；由于船舶出租人过失而没有合法理由使承租人无法供货时。

3.2 Quantity of the Cargo
3.2 货物数量

It is important both for the charterers and for the shipowners that the cargo quantity is specified. The freight is often calculated on the cargo quantity and the shipowners must therefore be certain that at least a minimum quantity is stated in the charter party. For the charterers, the specification of a cargo quantity in the charter party is important as the shipowners' acceptance of the quantity also means that the charterers have a chance to claim damages if the shipowners fail to load the accepted quantity.

货物数量的规定对于承租人和出租人都是非常重要的。运费通常根据货物数量计收，船舶出租人必须确定合同中规定的最少数量。对于承租人来说，在合同中规定货物数量是重要的，出租人接受货物数量也就意味着如果出租人不能装运所接受的数量，承租人有权索赔。

The cargo quantity can be fixed in several ways. Many charter parties state that the charterers shall furnish the ship with "a full and complete cargo". This means that the charterers are obliged to load as much cargo as the vessel can carry, i.e., the vessel's deadweight capacity is fully used when it is a heavy cargo and the cubic capacity is used when it is a light cargo. If a full and complete cargo is not loaded, the charterer must pay not only freight on the goods shipped but also dead freight.

有几种方法来规定货物数量。许多租船合同中规定了承租人有义务对船舶提供"满载货物"。这意味着承租人有义务提供达到船舶的货物装载能力的货物数量，也就是说，当装运重货时要达到船舶载重量，当装载轻货时要达到船舶的舱容。如果承租人不能提供满载货物，他不但要付运费，还要付亏舱费。

Other ways to state the cargo quantity are "10,000 tons", "about 10,000 tons", "between 9,000 and 10,000 tons", "between about 9,000 and 10,000 tons", "not less than 10,000 tons", etc. The word "about" gives a flexibility that varies depending on the type and quantity of the cargo and the trade (5% is often regarded as a recognized variation figure). If the charter party prescribes a certain variation, it should also state in whose interest there is such flexibility, for instance "in owners' option", "in charterers' option", etc. The charter party usually states that the amount of cargo to be loaded is to be decided by the shipowners, e.g., "10,000 MT wheat in bulk 5% more or less at shipowners' option".

其他表示货物数量的方式是"10 000 吨""大约 10 000 吨""9 000~10 000 吨""约 9 000~10 000 吨""不少于 10 000 吨"等。"大约"一词给了一个灵活幅度，它取决于货物种类、数量和贸易性质情况（5% 通常被认定为可接受的幅度）。如果租船合同规定了一定的增减幅度，还应规定谁有选择权，如"出租人选择""承租人选择"等。租船合同中通常规定货物数量由出租人选择，如"10 000公吨散装小麦，5%增减由出租人选择"。

When quantities are stated, the type of ton referred to should always be mentioned explicitly. It is thus not sufficient to say, for instance, 5,000 tons. It must also be stated what kind of tons are meant (metric tons, long tons, etc.). This can also be important when the stowage factor is used, as the stowage factor sometimes is based on long tons and sometimes on metric tons.

当表示货物数量时，所涉及的重量吨也必须明确规定。单说 5 000 吨是不够的，还必须标明是何种吨（公吨、长吨等）。当使用积载因数时，它也是非常重要的，因为积载因数有时按照长吨计算，有时按照公吨计算。

The stowage factor is a figure usually expressed in cubic feet or cubic meters, indicating the amount of space one ton of cargo will occupy. It is then a simple matter of dividing the available space by the stowage factor of the cargo to determine the weight of cargo the ship can accommodate.

积载因数通常以立方英尺或立方米为单位来表示，它表明1吨货物所占用的空间。用空间除以货物的积载因数可得出船舶所能装载的货物重量。

3.3 Deck Cargo
3.3 甲板货

If shipment of deck cargo has been agreed between the shipowners and the charterers, liability for loss of or damage to such cargo should always rest with the charterers, at the charterers' risk and responsibility.

如果船舶出租人和承租人双方同意装运甲板货，则这种货物灭失或损坏的责任始终落在承租人身上，风险和责任也由承租人自负。

UNIT 2　SHIPOWNER'S RESPONSIBILITY
第二单元　船舶出租人的责任

The liability for the cargo, in the voyage charter party, is allocated as the shipowners and charterers agreed. There is no minimum liability for shipowners as there is in the *Hague Rules*, *Hague-Visby Rules*, and *Hamburg Rules*. These Rules do not apply to charter parties. Remember that in China the shipowners under the voyage charter party must make the ship seaworthy before, and at the beginning of the voyage and carry the goods to the port of discharge on the agreed or customary or geographically direct route. That is a compulsory obligation for shipowners under a voyage charter party in China according to CMC.

在航次租船合同中，货物的赔偿责任应根据船舶出租人与承租人的约定进行分配。与《海牙规则》、《海牙-维斯比规则》和《汉堡规则》不同，船舶出租人在这些规则中并不具有最低赔偿责任的限制。这些规则不适用租船合同。请注意，在中国，船舶出租人在航次租船中必须履行在开航前和开航当时使船舶处于适航状态，并按照约定的、习惯的或地理上的直接航线将货物运输至卸货港的义务，这是《中华人民共和国海商法》对航次租船合同下船舶出租人规定的强制性义务。

1. Shipowner's Responsibility under the Gencon Form 1994
1. 1994年金康合同范本下船舶出租人的责任

The shipowner's responsibility for cargo is under many standard forms, for instance under the Gencon Form, very limited as follows:

在许多标准范本中船舶出租人对货物的责任非常有限，例如金康范本规定：

"The Owners are to be responsible for loss of or damage to the goods or for delay in delivery of the goods only in case the loss, damage or delay has been caused by personal want of due diligence on the part of the Owners or their Manager to make the Vessel in all respects seaworthy and to secure that she is properly manned, equipped and supplied, or by the personal act or default of the Owners or their Manager.

"船舶出租人仅在下列情况下对货物灭失、损坏或延迟交付承担责任：该灭失、损坏或延迟等是因船舶出租人或其经理人未恪尽职守使船舶在各方面适航，未确保船舶配备适当船员、设备及补给，或因船舶出租人或其经理人的个人行为或过失所致。

And the Owners are not responsible for loss, damage, or delay arising from any other cause whatsoever, even from the neglect or default of the Master or crew or some other person employed by the Owners on board or ashore for whose acts they would, but for this clause, be responsible, or from unseaworthiness of the Vessel on loading or commencement of the voyage or at any time whatsoever."

因其他任何原因造成的货物灭失、损坏或延迟，即使该损失源于船长或船员或船舶出租人雇佣的船上或岸上人员的疏忽或不履行职责，或源于船舶在装货时、开航当时或其他任何时候的不适航所造成的，船舶出租人均不负责（无本条规定，船舶出租人应对他们的行为负责）。"

The shipowners are only liable under the clause for personal want of due diligence to make the ship seaworthy on their part or the part of their managers and personal act or default of the owners or their managers.

在该条款下，船舶出租人只有在其本人或经理人本人的行为或错误引起以及自身未恪尽职责使船舶适航的情况下才会对货物的损坏、缺少及延误交货负责。

In chartering practice, this clause is often deleted and a paramount clause is inserted that makes the *Hague Rules* or *Hague-Visby Rules* applicable to the liability for cargo under the charter party. This clause takes its wording from BIMCO's Standard General Clause Paramount, which was issued in October 1997, and which makes the *Hague Rules* or the *Hague-Visby Rules* as the case may be, also applicable to the charter party. Applying the *Hague Rules* or *Hague-Visby Rules* in the charter party means that as far as the owners' responsibilities and immunities are concerned they shall be the same under the charter party and the bills of lading.

租船实务中比较常见的是将该条款删除，然后并入一条首要条款使《海牙规则》《海牙–维斯比规则》对货物责任的规定也适用于租船合同。该条款采用1997年10月BIMCO颁布的标准首要条款，使《海牙规则》《海牙–维斯比规则》也适用于租船合同。租船合同适用《海牙规则》或《海牙–维斯比规则》意味着船舶出租人的责任和免责在租船合同下与提单一致。

2. Seaworthiness
2. 船舶适航

It is usually stated in the charter party that the shipowner shall keep the vessel in a seaworthy condition. Also, when no such clauses are inserted, the shipowners must usually, by law or by an implied warranty, keep the vessel in a seaworthy condition.

租船合同通常规定船舶出租人要使船舶处于适航状态。同样，当没有此类条款时，船舶出租人通常根据法律或一项默示保证使船舶处于适航状态。

2.1 Concept of Seaworthiness
2.1 适航的概念

The concept of seaworthiness can be described as having three aspects: seaworthiness from the technical point of view, cargoworthiness, and seaworthiness concerning the intended voyage.

适航概念可以分为三个方面：技术角度上适航；适货；适合特定航线。

Technical seaworthiness includes the ship's design and condition in hull and machinery and also her stability. Cargoworthiness means that the vessel shall be suitable for the intended cargo and seaworthiness concerning the intended voyage means that she will be satisfactorily equipped, bunkered, etc., for the intended voyage.

技术角度上适航包括船舶设计和船壳及机器条件以及船舶稳性；适货指船舶适合所装的货物；适合特定航线指的是船舶为特定航线配备满意的设备和足够的燃油等。

2.2 Effect of Unseaworthiness
2.2 不适航的后果

If the charterer discovers that the ship is unseaworthy before the voyage begins, and the defect cannot be remedied within a reasonable time, he may throw up the contract. After the voyage has begun, the charterer is no longer in a position to rescind the contract, but can claim damages for any loss caused by initial unseaworthiness.

如果承租人发现船舶在航程开始之前不适航，并且缺陷不能在合理时间内修正时，他可以解除合同。在开航后，承租人不能再解除合同，但可就不适航所造成的任何损失要求赔偿。

Further, although the vessel is unseaworthy, the shipowner can still rely on the exception clauses in the charter party, if the loss has not been caused by unseaworthiness.

此外，尽管船舶是不适航的，但如果损失并非是不适航造成的，船舶出租人仍然可以援引租船合同的除外责任条款。

Examples of unseaworthiness include: insufficient bunkers, inefficient crew, defective or inadequate equipment, improperly cleaned or prepared holds, maps and charts not on board or out of date, and/or poor stowage that endangers the safety of the ship.

不适航的例子包括：燃油不足；不能胜任的船员；设备有缺陷或不足；货舱清洗不当或准备不足；船上没有地图和海图或已过时；积载不当危及船舶的安全。

2.3 Seaworthiness by Statute
2.3 适航的法律规定

The charter parties usually contain a paramount clause that makes the *Hague Rules* or *Hague-Visby Rules* applicable to the liability for cargo under the charter party or to the whole charter party as the case may be. Therefore the express obligation for the shipowners regarding seaworthiness is that: "the carrier shall, before and at the beginning of the voyage, exercise due diligence to make the ship seaworthy, properly man, equip and supply the ship and to make the holds, refrigerating and cooling chambers and all other parts of the ship in which goods are carried, fit and safe for their reception, carriage and preservation."

在租船合同中通常包含首要条款，使《海牙规则》或《海牙-维斯比规则》适用于租船合同下货物的赔偿责任，或适用于整个租船合同（视具体情况而言）。因此，船舶出租人在适航方面的明确义务是："承运人在船舶开航前和开航当时，应当谨慎处理，使船舶处于适航状态，妥善配备船员、装备船舶和配备供应品，并使货舱、冷藏舱、冷气舱和其他载货处所适于并能安全收受、载运和保管货物。"

3. Deviation
3. 绕航

Most voyage charter party forms contain a printed deviation clause. Sometimes this clause is a frequent expression used in bills of lading. The deviation clause in Gencon Form 1994 has the following wording:

大多数航次租船合同范本都包含一条印就的绕航条款。有时候，该条款在提单中经常使用。1994年金康合同范本中绕航条款措辞如下：

"The vessel has the liberty to call any port or ports in any order, for any purpose, to sail without pilots, to tow and/or assist vessels in all situations, and also to deviate to save life and/or property."

"船舶有权为任何目的以任何顺序挂靠任何港口，有无引航员在船均可航行，在任何情况下拖带和/或救助他船，亦可为拯救人命和/或财产而绕航。"

The deviation clauses are usually interpreted to the benefit of the charterers and if a shipowner wishes to safeguard his rights to deviate for a certain reason he must specify this, as far as possible, during the negotiations and in the charter party. In practice, most countries make restrictive explanations on this clause that vessels can only call at ports agreed upon in charter parties or ports along the customary ocean routes in geographical order and that only lawful deviation is allowed.

绕航条款通常做出对承租人有利的解释，如果船舶出租人真的要保障自己绕航的权利，他必须尽可能地在洽谈期间和租船合同中明确规定。在实务中，多数国家就这一条款做出限制性解释：船舶只能挂靠合同中约定的港口，或者按地理顺序停靠习惯航线上的港口，且仅允许合法的绕航。

The distinction between lawful deviation and unlawful deviation is important. The borderline between these two concepts is not always so easy to find. Generally, it can be said that deviation to avoid danger to crew, vessel, and cargo and deviation to save life or property, are lawful deviations. Naturally, the deviation must be reasonable and when judging whether the deviation is reasonable, not only the interests of the shipowners, but also the interests of the charterers, must be considered. Unlawful deviation is a breach of contract and the charterers are entitled to damages as well as, in some cases, to cancel the charter agreement.

区分合法和非法绕航是重要的。这两个概念之间的界限并不总是那么容易找到。一般来说，为避免对船员、船舶和货物构成危险以及以拯救生命或财产为目的的绕航，都是合法的绕航。当然，绕航必须是合理的，并且当判断绕航是否合理时，不仅要考虑船舶出租人的利益，承租人的利益也必须予以考虑。非法绕航是违反合同的，承租人有权要求赔偿，并可以在某些情况下解除租船合同。

4. Laydays and Canceling Date
4. 受载期和解约日

Laydays refer to the period when the chartered vessel shall arrive at the port of loading and shall be ready for the loading of cargo. Laydays could also be comprehended as the period during which the chartered vessel could arrive at the port of loading, either on the first day or on the final day of it, and she should also be ready for the loading of the cargo.

受载期是指船舶在租船合同规定的日期内到达约定的装货港，并做好装货准备的期限。受载期可以概括为船舶应到达装货港的一个期限，无论是在此期限中的第一天还是最后一天，船舶抵达装货港并做好装货准备即可。

Canceling date refers to a date at which if the chartered vessel has not arrived at the loading port and is ready to receive the cargo, it gives the charterer an absolute right to cancel the contract. The ordinary canceling clauses are also applicable when the ship has been delayed for reasons which cannot be controlled by the shipowner and when the shipowner and the master have done their utmost to speed up the vessel.

解约日是指定的一个日期，如果船舶在此日期之前不能抵达装货港，承租人有解除合同的绝对权利。通常的解约日条款也适用于非船舶出租人所能控制的原因引起的延误，尽管船舶出租人和船长已尽最大努力加速航行。

When it is obvious to the shipowner that the vessel has no chance of arriving at the first loading port before the canceling date, he needs to get the charterer's declaration of whether or not he will cancel. Under English law, the charterer is not obliged to give such a declaration unless it is expressly stated in the charter party. To protect the shipowner's interest, the "interpellation" clause is often added to the voyage charter party. The purpose of the interpellation provisions is that the vessel should not have to proceed on a long ballast voyage towards the loading port not knowing whether or not the charterers will accept the vessel once it arrives.

如船舶已经不可能在解约日之前或当天抵达第一个装货港，对于船舶出租人重要的是获得承租人是否解约的通知。根据英国法，承租人无义务给予通知，除非合同另外有明确规定。为了保护船舶出租人的利益，船舶出租人往往会在合同中订有"询问"条款。该条款设定的目的是，在不知道承租人是否在船舶抵达时接受船舶的情况下，船舶无须空载驶往装货港。

According to the Gencon Form 1994, the charterer must, on demand, declare his option to cancel at least 48 hours after the receipt of the owners' notice, not as in the old form before the vessel's expected arrival at the port of loading. The following is the provision of the canceling clause printed in Gencon Form 1994:

根据1994年金康合同范本，承租人必须在收到船舶出租人通知后的48小时内宣布选择解除。而旧的范本规定为在船舶预期抵达装货港前48小时宣布。以下是1994年金康合同范本印就的解约日条款规定：

"(a) Should the vessel not be ready to load (whether in berth or not) on the canceling date indicated in Box 21, the charterers shall have the option of canceling this charter party.

"（a）如船舶未能在第21栏规定的解约日做好装货准备（不论靠泊与否），承租人有权解除本合同。

(b) Should the owners anticipate that, despite the exercise of due diligence, the vessel will not be ready to load by the canceling date, they shall notify the charterers thereof without delay stating the expected date of the vessel's readiness to load and asking whether the charterers will exercise their option of canceling the charter party, or agree to a new canceling date.

（b）如船舶出租人预计虽谨慎处理仍无法在解约日前做好装货准备，则应立即通知承租人其预计准备好的日期，并询问是否解约或同意新的解约日。

Such an option must be declared by the charterers within 48 running hours after the receipt of the owners' notice. If the charterers do not exercise their option of canceling, then this charter party shall be deemed to be amended such that the seventh day after the new readiness date stated in the owners' notification to the charterers shall be the new canceling date.

承租人应在收到该通知后48小时内宣布合同解除。如承租人未行使其解约权，则视为本租约被修改为船舶出租人在通知中宣布的准备完毕日期后的第七天为新的解约日。

(c) The provisions of sub-clause (b) of this clause shall operate only once, and in case of the vessel's further delay, the charterers shall have the option of canceling the charter party as per sub-clause (a) of this clause."

（c）本条（b）款规定只能适用一次，如船舶再次延误，则承租人可选择按本条（a）款解除本租约。"

The provision of CMC has the same effect which stipulates that: "If the shipowner has failed to provide the ship within the laydays fixed in the charter, the charterer is entitled to cancel the charter party. However, if the shipowner has notified the charterer of the delay of the ship and the expected date of its arrival at the port of loading, the charterer shall notify the shipowner whether to cancel the charter within 48 hours of the receipt of the shipowner's notification. Where the charterer has suffered losses as a result of the delay in providing the vessel due to the fault of the shipowner, the shipowner shall be liable for compensation."

《中华人民共和国海商法》也做出同样的规定："出租人在约定的受载期限内未能提供船舶的，承租人有权解除合同。但是，出租人将船舶延误情况和船舶预期抵达装货港的日期通知承租人的，承租人应当自收到通知时起四十八小时内，将是否解除合同的决定通知出租人。因出租人过失延误提供船舶致使承租人遭受损失的，出租人应当负赔偿责任。"

【Case】The Plaintiff and Defendant had entered into a charter party in the Gencon Form. Defendant was not able to meet the agreed-upon loading date and, as a consequence, Plaintiff exercised its right to cancel the charter party and found another vessel to carry the cargo. The Plaintiff claimed the difference in the freight payable under the two charter parties. Defendant argued that under the charter party, Plaintiff's remedy was to cancel the charter party and that it had no right to claim damages. The Court reviewed the authorities and held that the charterer who cancels a charter party has a claim for damages if the failure of the ship to arrive by the canceling date was a result of a breach on the part of the shipowner of his obligation to load by a particular date.

【案例】原告与被告以金康合同范本为蓝本签订了租船合同。被告未能在约定的受载期抵达，结果原告行使其权利，取消了租船合同，并寻找另一艘船运输货物。原告要求赔偿两份租船合同下运费支付的差价。被告辩称，根据租船合同，原告的补救办法是取消合同，他无权要求赔偿。法院判决，如果船舶未能在解约日到达是船舶出租人未尽到在特定日期装货的义务造成的，取消租船合同的承租人有权要求损害赔偿。

UNIT 3 FREIGHT AND FREIGHT INDEX
第三单元 运费和运价指数

Freight is the consideration paid to the shipowner for performing his part in the carriage of cargo by sea under the voyage charter party. Typically this means that freight is payable according to the weight or volume of cargo carried to and delivered at its destination. In general, it is open to the parties to make whatever agreement they wish about how freight shall be calculated, earned, and paid.

运费是船舶出租人根据航次租船合同完成海上货物运输后收取的对价。这通常意味着按运送到目的地货物的重量或体积支付约定的运费。一般来说，各方可以按照意愿自由做出运费如何计算、赚取和支付的任何协议。

1. General Rules Refer to Freight
1. 运费的一般原则

Unless a special agreement is made, e.g. for payment in advance, or of a lump sum, the general rules referring to freight are that:

除非做出特别协议，例如预付运费或包干运费，运费的一般基本原则是：

Payment of freight and delivery of the cargo at the port of discharge are concurrent conditions. The principle rule is that the freight is earned when the shipowners have fulfilled their obligations to carry the cargo and are ready to deliver it to the receiver. This means that if, for some reason, the shipowners cannot deliver the cargo they are not entitled to freight. The freight risk lies with the shipowners.

运费支付和在目的港交付货物是并存的条件。运费的基本原则是只有船舶出租人将货物运抵目的地，准备交货时才能赚取。这意味着，若船舶出租人由于某些原因不能交付货物，也就无权要求运费。运费的风险由船舶出租人承担。

Nevertheless, the shipowner is entitled to freight if either he is ready, willing, and able to deliver the cargo in accordance with the charter party or if he is only prevented from delivering by some act or omission of the cargo owner.

然而，如果船舶出租人根据运输租船合同准备、想要并能够交付货物，或由于货主的过失而无法交付货物，则有权要求承租人支付运费。

No freight is payable if the shipowner cannot deliver the cargo because it has been lost or destroyed. It does not matter how or why the cargo is lost or destroyed, or even if it destroy themselves through inherent vice. No freight is payable even where the loss occurs without fault on the part of the shipowner and even if the cause of the loss is an excepted peril. Excepted perils may prevent the shipowner from being sued for losing or damaging the cargo, but they do not normally give a right to freight.

如果在运输途中货物灭失或损毁，船舶出租人不能交付货物，则无权要求承租人支付运费，不管货物是如何或为何灭失或损毁，甚至由于自身缺陷所致。船舶出租人无权要求运费，即便不是他们的过失原因，甚至过失原因属于可免责风险。免责风险只能保护船舶出租人免受货物损失或灭失索赔，但通常不会赋予船舶出租人要求运费的权利。

Freight is payable in full on cargo which is delivered damaged. No deductions can be made from or setoff against freight that is payable on goods delivered, for the value of other goods which are lost or damaged; but a separate action may be brought to recover damage for which the shipowner is responsible, provided liability is not excluded by excepted perils.

货物虽受损交付，但运费仍需全额支付。对于已交付货物应支付的运费，不得因其他货物的灭失或损坏价值而从中扣除或进行抵销；但船舶出租人责任未被除外风险排除的前提下，货方可另行提起诉讼，要求赔偿船舶出租人应承担货损责任。

If lump sum freight is agreed the shipowners are entitled to full freight if some part of the cargo reaches the port or place of destination. If all cargo is lost the shipowners are not, according to the above-described principle, entitled to freight.

如果约定为包干运费，只要部分货物运到目的地，船舶出租人即有权要求全额运费。根据上述原则，如果全部货物灭失，船舶出租人无权要求承租人支付运费。

The rules about when the freight is earned and payable are often modified by the parties in the charter party. A clause like "freight earned and payable upon shipment, ship and/or cargo lost or not lost" is frequently found in voyage charter parties. The clause means that the shipowners are entitled to freight at the loading port and the freight is not repayable if part of the cargo, or the whole cargo and the vessel, do not reach the destination.

关于运费何时赚取和支付的原则经常被双方当事人在租船合同中加以修改。像航次租船合同中一般都会写明"运费在装运时被认为已赚取和支付，不论船货是否灭失"。该条款的含义是船舶出租人有权在装货港要求全额运费，即使部分货物、全部货物乃至船舶未能抵达目的地，已收取的运费也无须退还。

2. Types of Freight
2. 运费的种类

Freight is the remuneration payable to the shipowner for the carriage of cargo by sea. There are different types of freight. A frequent provision is that freight is to be paid in advance. When there is no provision to the contrary, freight is payable on the delivery of the cargo. Sometimes the parties agree that a lump sum freight shall be paid irrespective of the amount of cargo carried. In certain cases a pro rata freight is payable. If the receiver does not take delivery of the cargo, the shipowner may be entitled to a back freight. If the charterer does not load a full cargo, damages for deadfreight may be claimed.

运费是支付给船舶出租人海上货物运输的报酬。运费分为不同种类。常见的规定是运费预付。如果没有相反的规定，运费到付。有时，双方同意包干运费，不论其载货量。在特定情况下，运费可以按比例支付。如果收货方不接收货物，船舶出租人有权要求回程运费。如果承租人未提供满载货物，要支付亏舱费。

2.1 Advanced Freight or Freight Prepaid
2.1 预付运费

Voyage freight may be payable in advance which means that freight is payable on or around the date of shipment of the cargo. It is acknowledged that freight can either be fully paid on the release of signed bills of lading or paid in part within a certain number of days after signing bills of lading. Voyage freight is also frequently paid in stages. It is commonplace for a majority of the freight—say 90%—to be paid during a voyage, with the balance within a set period after discharge has been completed, together with adjustment for demurrage or dispatch owed by one party or the other. For example: "Ninety percent of freight to be paid within five banking days of signing and releasing bills of lading marked 'freight payable as per charter party'; balance to be paid within one month of completion of discharge, duly adjusted for laytime used during loading and discharging operations."

航次运费可预先支付，这意味着运费是在航次装运日期前后支付的。事实上运费可以在签发提单时全部支付或者在签发提单后的一定日期内部分支付。航次租船运费还经常按阶段支付。多数情况下90%的运费预付，余额留待卸货完毕后的一段时间内支付，以调节滞期费或速遣费。例如："90%的运费在签发注明按照租约支付的提单后五个银行工作日支付；余额留待卸货完毕后一个月内支付，并需根据装卸货作业期间实际使用的装卸时间进行适当调整。"

2.2 Freight Payable on Delivery
2.2 到付运费

Freight payable on delivery means that freight is payable on the delivery of cargo or at the destination but before discharge. Payment of freight and delivery of the cargo at the port of discharge are unless otherwise agreed, concurrent conditions. The principal rule is that the freight is earned when the shipowners have fulfilled their obligation to carry the cargo and are ready to deliver it to the receiver. This means that if, for some reason, the shipowners cannot deliver the cargo they are not entitled to freight. The freight risk lies with the shipowners.

到付运费是指交付货物或在目的地卸货前支付。除非另有约定，运费支付和在目的港交付货物是并存的条件。基本原则是运费只有在船舶出租人将货物运抵目的地并准备交货时才能赚取。这意味着，由于某些原因船舶出租人不能交付货物，则无权要求运费。运费的风险由船舶出租人承担。

But freight will not be payable by the charterer unless the cargo is delivered in such a condition that it is substantially and in a mercantile sense the same cargo as that shipped.

但是，除非货物在交付时在商业角度上与实际装运时的货物保持相同的状态，否则，承租人不必支付运费。

【Case】One ship carrying dates was sunk in the Thames. The dates were recovered but in a state that rendered them unfit for human food. They were sold for distilling purposes. Held, no freight was payable because the goods delivered were, for business purposes, something different from those shipped.

【案例】一艘载有大枣的船舶沉没在泰晤士河。大枣被捞回，但已不适合人类食用。大枣被出售用作蒸馏。法院判决：承租人无须支付运费，因为交付的货物，从商业角度看与装运时已完全不同。

2.3 Lump Sum Freight
2.3 包干运费

A lump sum freight is not directly related to the quantity of cargo carried. It is a definite sum agreed to be paid for the hire of a ship for a specified voyage. This may be the easiest way to define the freight obligation when the charterer does not know the exact quantity of cargo that will be loaded or when it is difficult to measure the quantity loaded.

包干运费与实际装船货物的数量没有直接的关系。它是双方同意为特定航次雇佣船舶支付的一笔明确的运费。当承租人不知道装载多少货物或很难衡量实际装载的准确数量时，这可能是确定支付运费义务的最简单的方法。

2.4 Pro Rata Freight
2.4 比例运费

Sometimes pro rata freight is payable, i.e. a payment proportionate to the part of the voyage accomplished or to the part of the cargo delivered.

实务中，有时会支付比例运费，也就是说根据部分航程履行或者在部分货物交付的情况下按比例支付的运费。

2.5 Deadfreight
2.5 亏舱费

All the major charter parties make provision for the payment of deadfreight if the agreed quantity of cargo is not supplied. When the charterers fail to deliver the agreed quantity of cargo to the vessel, the shipowners will normally be entitled to compensation for their loss of freight. This compensation is called deadfreight and is calculated by deducting what is saved in costs from the freight that should be paid for that part of the cargo which has not been delivered.

所有主要的租船合同都规定，如果承租人没有提供约定数量的货物，应支付亏舱费。当承租人没有提供约定数量的货物装船时，船舶出租人通常有权要求其赔偿运费损失。这种赔偿就是亏舱费，其计算方式是：从本应就未支付货物部分收取的运费中，扣除因此节省的费用。

2.6 Back Freight
2.6 回程运费

The shipowners are entitled to payment as freight for merchandise returned through the fault of either the consignees or the consignors. Such payment is called back freight.

船舶出租人有权要求由于收货人或托运人过失导致的回程货物的运费。这种被支付的运费被称为回程运费。

3. Fixing of Freight
3. 运费的确定

The freight can be fixed in several ways.

有几种确定运费的方法。

One way is to base it on the cargo quantity or volume. It is important to specify how the cargo quantity is to be established. Sometimes there are disputes about the question of whether the freight shall be based on intake or delivered quantity and if it shall be based on the gross or the net weight of a cargo. Concerning the latter problem, it is usually said that the freight will be based on the gross weight unless otherwise agreed or customary in the trade. As regards the first question, the basic rule under English law is that the freight is payable only on so much cargo as has been both shipped and delivered and this means that the smallest of the two quantities is the base for the calculation of freight. Both these questions are often expressly dealt with in the charter party.

一种方法是依据货物数量或体积。其中，重要的是要明确货物的数量如何确认。有时引发的纠纷问题是，运费是按照装船还是交付数量计收，是根据货物毛重还是货物净重计收。关于后一个问题，除非另有约定或行业习惯，运费通常按货物毛重计算。至于第一个问题，按照英国法的基本规则是，运费按照装船和交付货物数量支付，这意味着按照这两个数量之间最小的来计收。这些问题常常都要在租船合同中明确规定。

Another way is to fix the freight at a certain amount independent of the cargo quantity. This is usually called lump sum freight.

另一种方法是以一定数额来确定运费而不考虑货物的数量，通常称之为包干运费。

4. Deductions from Freight
4. 运费的扣减

Other than the right, when applicable, to pay pro rata freight, the charterer does not have any right to make stoppages from freight for amounts he believes may be due to him.

除了按比例支付运费外，承租人没有任何权利停付应当支付的运费。

The reason why deductions from freight are not permitted without a clause to the contrary would seem to come from the fact that the amount due for freight is an amount that is easily determined whereas a deduction in support of a claim is not easily ascertained and may or may not be legally due.

在没有相反条款的规定下，不允许扣除运费的原因似乎来自这样的事实，即运费金额是很容易确认的，而支持索赔所做的扣除则是不容易确定的，可能或不能获得法律上的支持。

5. Risk of Loss of Freight
5. 运费灭失风险

Unless otherwise specifically agreed, the risk of losing the freight before the safe delivery of the cargo falls upon the shipowner. Frequently shipowners negotiate that freight "deemed earned upon loading" or "freight payable on shipment", in which case the risk of losing the cargo and of being liable to pay freight becomes that of the charterer.

除非另有明确约定，运费灭失风险在货物安全交付前由船舶出租人承担。船舶出租人在洽谈时经常采用运费"在装载时赚取"或"装运时支付运费"方式，在这种情况下货物灭失和支付运费的风险由承租人承担。

The risk of loss of freight is independent of when freight is physically paid. Thus, even if freight is paid by a charter party term stating that "freight to be paid within seven days after signing and releasing bills of lading", in the event of a total loss of ship and cargo, say fifteen days into the voyage, freight might have to be returned to charterers if the risk of loss was deemed to be the shipowners'. As a result of this, some shipowners will put the issue beyond doubt by including in their contract words such as: "freight deemed earned upon loading, non-returnable and without discounts , cargo and/or vessel lost or not lost."

运费灭失的风险独立于运费实际上的支付。因此，即使支付运费按照租船合同术语"运费将在签署和交付提单七天内支付"，在开航十五天后，当船舶及货物全部损失时，如果船舶出租人承担运费损失的风险，运费可能要归还承租人。由于这一结果，一些船舶出租人会毫无疑问地在合同中订有诸如"运费在装运货物时被认为赚取，不退还，没有折扣，无论货物和/或船舶灭失与否"的规定。

6. Provisions in Gencon Form 1994
6. 1994年金康合同范本下运费支付条款

The followings are the provisions of the Payment of Freight clause printed in Gencon Form 1994:

下列是1994年金康合同范本下运费支付条款的规定：

"(a)The freight at the rate stated in Box 13 shall be paid in cash calculated on the intake quantity of cargo.

"（a）第13栏规定的运费费率，应按所装货物的数量计算并以现金支付。

(b) Prepaid. If according to Box 13, freight is to be paid on shipment, it shall be deemed earned and non-returnable, vessel and/or cargo lost or not lost. Neither the Owners nor their agents shall be required to sign or endorse bills of lading showing freight prepaid unless the freight due to the Owners has been paid.

（b）运费预付。如按第13栏规定，运费应预付，运费在装运货物时应赚取已被确认，无论船舶/货物是否灭失，不得返还。除非运费已支付给船舶出租人，否则船舶出租人或其代理无须签发运费预付提单。

(c) On delivery. If according to Box 13 freight, or part thereof, is payable at the destination it shall not be deemed earned until the cargo is thus delivered. Notwithstanding the provisions under (a), if freight or part thereof is payable on delivery of the cargo the Charterers shall have the option of paying the freight on delivered weight/quantity provided such option is declared before breaking bulk and the weight/quantity can be ascertained by official weighing machine, joint draught survey or tally.

（c）运费到付。如按第13栏规定运费或部分运费为到付，则运费直到货物卸完才视为赚取。不论（a）款如何规定，如运费或部分运费为到付，承租人有权在开舱前选择按卸货重量/数量支付运费，且该重量/数量可由官方计量器、联检或理货确定。

Cash for the vessel's ordinary disbursements at the port of loading to be advanced by the Charterers, if required, at the highest current rate of exchange, subject to two (2) percent to cover insurance and other expenses."

如经要求，承租人应现金垫付船舶在装货港的日常费用，按最高兑换率折合并附加2%以抵偿保险费和其他费用。"

7. Freight Index
7. 运价指数

Index refers to a number used to measure change in price, wages, markets, production, etc. The freight index is used to reflect the variation in freight rate. The freight indexes, which serve as barometers for the shipping market, are such that it can be justifiably asserted that no shipping operators or brokers aiming at long-term development can afford to neglect the relevant freight indexes. It quickly won worldwide acceptance as the most reliable general measure of the dry cargo freight market.

指数是指用来衡量价格、工资、市场和生产等变化的数字。运价指数是用来反映运费率的变化的。运价指数作为航运市场的晴雨表，无可非议，以长期发展为目标的航运经营者或经纪人非常重视运价指数。作为干散货运费市场最可靠的衡量指标，运价指数迅速赢得了世界认可。

7.1 The Baltic Dry Index
7.1 波罗的海干散货运价指数

On 4 January 1985, the Baltic Exchange commenced publication of a daily freight index the Baltic Freight Index (BFI). It quickly won worldwide acceptance as the most reliable general measure of the dry cargo freight market. On 1 November 1999, the Baltic Exchange Dry Index (BDI), replacing the Baltic Freight Index (BFI), was introduced to provide a good general indicator of movements in the dry bulk market. The Baltic Dry Index is composed of BCI, BPI and BHI.

1985年1月4日，波罗的海交易所开始颁布每日运价指数——波罗的海运价指数（BFI）。作为干散货运市场最可靠的衡量指标，波罗的海运价指数迅速赢得世界认可。1999年11月1日，波罗的海干散货运价指数（BDI）取代了波罗的海运价指数（BFI），旨在为干散货市场动态提供良好的综合指标。波罗的海干散货运价指数是由波罗的海好望角型船运价指数（BCI）、波罗的海巴拿马型船运价指数（BPI）和波罗的海灵便型船运价指数（BHI）构成的。

In a move designed to help boost derivative trading, the Baltic Exchange implemented changes to the way in which the Baltic Exchange Dry Index (BDI) is calculated. As of 1 July 2009, the BDI is calculated by taking the time charter components of the Baltic's capesize, panamax, supramax, and handysize indexes. Each type of vessels' routes make up 25% of the BDI.

为了帮助推动衍生金融工具交易，波罗的海交易所改变了波罗的海交易所干散货运价指数（BDI）的计算方法。自2009年7月1日起，BDI改以波罗的海好望角型船、巴拿马型船、超灵便型船和灵便型船指数的期租数据相加计算。每种船舶类型的航线各占BDI的25%。

7.2 Baltic Capesize Index
7.2 波罗的海好望角型船运价指数

On 1 March 1999, trials began for the Baltic Capesize Index (BCI). This comprises four time charter and seven voyage routes. The Index began at 1,000 points. On 26 April 1999, the BCI was published as assessed by a panel of brokers.

1999年3月1日，波罗的海好望角型船运价指数（BCI）开始试算。它包括4个期租航线和7个航次航线。该指数从1 000点开始。1999年4月26日，由经纪人小组计算的BCI开始发布。

7.3 Baltic Panamax Index
7.3 波罗的海巴拿马型船运价指数

On 23 November 1998, the Baltic Panamax Index (BPI) was first calculated on a trial basis consisting of four time charter and three voyage routes. On 21 December 1998, the BPI was first published as assessed by a panel of brokers, having successfully undergone a trial period.

1998年11月23日，波罗的海巴拿马型船运价指数（BPI）第一次试算，包括4个期租航线和3个航次航线。1998年12月21日，经过成功运作，由经纪人小组计算的BPI开始发布。

7.4 Baltic Supramax and Handysize Index
7.4 波罗的海超灵便型船和灵便型船运价指数

On 4 September 2000, trials of the new Baltic Handymax Index (BHMI) began. The index comprises six time charter routes, which are calculated on a dollar basis. Initially, this was published together with the BHI, which was calculated on an index basis. On 2 January 2001, the BHMI superseded the BHI. The new BHMI replaced the BHI in the calculation of the BDI.

2000年9月4日，新的波罗的海大灵便型船运价指数（BHMI）开始试算。该指数由6个期租航线组成，以美元计算。最初，它与BHI一起颁布。2001年1月2日，BHMI取代BHI。在计算BDI时，新BHMI取代BIII。

On 1 June 2005, trials of the new Baltic Exchange Supramax Index (BSI) began. On 3 January 2006, BSI replaced BHMI, which was no longer published. The BSI commenced contributing to BDI.

2005年6月1日，新的波罗的海交易所超灵便型船运价指数（BSI）的试算开始。2006年1月3日，BSI取代BHMI，不再发布。BSI加入BDI的计算中。

On 23 May 2006, trials of the Baltic Exchange Handysize Index (BHSI) were first published. Following a four-week blind trial period, the Trial BHSI was first published on 23 May 2006. The index was realigned to start from 1,000 points. On 2 January 2007, the trial status of the Handysize index and routes was lifted, and the BHSI started contributing towards the calculation of the BDI.

2006年5月23日，新波罗的海灵便型船运价指数（BHSI）试算首次发布。经过4周的试验期，新BHSI首次公布于2006年5月23日。该指数进行了调整，从1 000点起计算。2007年1月2日，灵便型船运价指数和航线的试算测试结束，BHSI开始加入到BDI的计算中。

7.5 Baltic International Tanker Routes
7.5 波罗的海国际油船运价指数

The Baltic International Tanker Routes (BITR) was the average rate, expressed on a scale, on major oil routes, both dirty and clean, as assessed by a panel of brokers. On 1 August 2001, a Baltic International Tanker Routes (BITR) Index was officially launched comprising nine dirty routes (T1–T9) and three clean routes (T10–T12), with all routes having equal weighting.

波罗的海国际油船运价指数（BITR）是由经纪人小组评估的主要油船航线（包括原油和成品油航线）的平均费率，以等级表示。2001年8月1日，波罗的海国际油船运价指数（BITR）正式推出，包括9条原油航线（T1~T9）和3条成品油航线（T10~T12），所有航线的比重相同。

On 1 October 2001, BITR was divided into dirty and clean routes to form the Baltic Dirty Tanker Index and the Baltic Clean Tanker Index. The Baltic Dirty Tanker Index (BDTI) is the average of the rates on the dirty routes. The Baltic Clean Tanker Index (BCTI) is the average of the rates on the clean routes.

2001年10月1日，BITR分为波罗的海原油油船运价指数和波罗的海成品油油船运价指数。波罗的海原油油船运价指数（BDTI）公布的是原油航线的平均运价。波罗的海成品油油船运价指数（BCTI）公布的是成品油航线的平均运价。

7.6 China Coastal Bulk Freight Index
7.6 中国沿海散货运价指数

The China Coastal Bulk Freight Index (CCBFI), under the guidance of the Ministry of Communications of China and compiled by the Shanghai Shipping Exchange began to be published in November 2001. The CCBFI provides a good general indicator of coastal bulk cargo movement in China.

在中华人民共和国交通部的指导下，上海航运交易所编制了中国沿海散货运价指数（CCBFI），于2001年11月开始发布。该指数为中国沿海散货运输提供了一个非常好的通用指标。

UNIT 4　LOADING AND DISCHARGING COSTS
第四单元　装卸费用

As the costs for handling the cargo at loading and discharging ports are often an important part of the total costs for the voyage, both parties should, during the negotiation, carefully investigate what costs will be involved in the intended voyage. It is, of course, also important that the clauses dealing with loading and discharging make sufficiently clear the allocation of costs, duties and liabilities.

货物在装卸港口的费用往往是航次总成本的一个重要组成部分，双方当事人应在洽谈中，仔细地调查预定航次涉及哪些费用。当然，同样重要的是在合同中要充分明确有关装卸货物的费用、义务和责任的分配。

1. Loading and Discharging Terms
1. 装卸术语

Detailed below is a list of some of the most frequently used abbreviations and their definitions that you may come across from time to time.

下面是一些经常使用的装卸货物费用术语的缩写及其定义。

1.1 Free In (FI)
1.1 舱内收货（FI）

FI means that cargo is to be loaded free of expense to the shipowners. The word "Free" as used in the charter shipping terms means not including. It is most important to remember that the "Free" reference is viewed from the shipowner's point of view, not the charterer's. Some charterers get caught out when they read the word "Free" as they incorrectly believe that it refers to them. FI is a pricing term indicating that the charterer of a vessel is responsible for the cost of loading goods onto the vessel.

舱内收货是指船舶出租人不负责货物装船费用。在租船航运界使用"Free"一词的字眼是指不包括。最重要的是要记住，"Free"一词，是从船舶出租人的角度看而不是从承租人的角度。有些承租人在读到"Free"一词时，错误地领会认为其是有利于他们的。舱内收货是一个价格术语，表明该船承租人负责货物装船的费用。

1.2 Free Out (FO)

1.2 舱内交货（FO）

FO means that the cargo is to be discharged free of expense to the shipowners. FO is a pricing term indicating that the charterer of a vessel is responsible for the cost of unloading goods from the vessel.

舱内交货是指船舶出租人不负责货物卸船费用。舱内交货是一个价格术语，表明该船承租人负责从船上卸下货物的费用。

1.3 Free In and Out (FIO)

1.3 舱内收交货（FIO）

FIO means that the cargo is to be loaded and discharged free of expense to the shipowners. FIO is a pricing term indicating that the charterer of a vessel is responsible for the costs of loading goods onto the vessel and unloading goods from the vessel.

舱内收交货是指船舶出租人不负责货物装船和卸船费用。舱内收交货是一个价格术语，表明该船承租人负责将货物装上船和从船上卸下货物的费用。

1.4 Free In, Out, Stowed (FIOS)

1.4 舱内收交货和积载（FIOS）

FIOS means that the cargo is to be loaded, stowed, and discharged free of expense to the shipowners. The shipowner is only responsible for expenses arising as a result of the ship calling into the port, i.e. tugs, pilots, light dues, etc. Another very important consideration when booking cargo on FIOS terms is that the shipowner does not bear any responsibility for the speed of loading or discharging.

舱内收交货和积载是指船舶出租人不负责货物装船、积载和卸船费用。船舶出租人仅对船舶在挂靠港时产生的费用负责，如拖船费、引航费、灯塔费等。订立舱内收交货和积载条款还要考虑的是，船舶出租人对装卸货物的速度不承担责任。

1.5 Free In, Out, Stowed and Trimming (FIOST)

1.5 舱内收交货和积载、平舱（FIOST）

FIOST means that none of the loading, discharging, stowing, or trimming expenses will be for the account of the shipowner. On the other hand, the charterer will bear the costs of loading, unloading, stowing, or trimming. Nowadays FIOST is frequently used in voyage chartering practice.

舱内收交货和积载、平舱是指船舶出租人不负责货物装船、积载、平舱和卸船费用。从另一个方面来说，这些费用由承租人承担。目前航次租船实务中经常使用该术语。

1.6 Free Alongside Ship (FAS)

1.6 船边交货（FAS）

FAS means that the cargo is to be brought alongside the carrying vessel at the port of loading by the charterer and the shipowner is responsible for the costs of loading and unloading.

船边交货是指承租人负责将货物送至装货港船边，船舶出租人负责货物装卸费用。

1.7 Gross Terms
1.7 总承兑条款

Gross Terms mean that the shipowner has to arrange and pay for cargo handling. According to the Gencon Form 1976, Gross Terms mean the cargo is to be brought alongside in such a manner as to enable the vessel to take the cargo with her tackle. Charterers procure and pay the necessary men on shore or on board the lighters to do the work there, and the vessel only heaving the cargo on board. If the loading takes place by elevator, the cargo is to be put free in the vessel's holds. Owners only pay trimming expenses. Any piece and/or packages of cargo over two tons weight shall be loaded, stowed and discharged by charterers at their risk and expense. The cargo is to be received by merchants at their risk and expense alongside the vessel and not beyond the reach of her tackle.

总承兑条款是指船舶出租人负责安排并支付货物装卸费用。根据1976年金康合同范本，总承兑条款是指货物应运至船边，使船舶能用自己的吊钩起吊货物。承租人应安排岸上和驳船上装船作业所需人员并负担其费用，船舶仅负责起吊货物装船。如果使用岸上起重机进行装船，则应将货物送至舱内，船舶出租人仅付平舱费用。任何每件和/或每包货物超过两吨者，由承租人负责装载、积载和卸载，并承担一切风险和费用。收货人应在船边不超过船舶吊钩所及范围之处收取货物，并承担一切风险和费用。

1.8 Liner Terms
1.8 班轮条款

Liner Terms mean that the responsibility and cost of loading, carrying, and discharging cargo is that of the shipowners from the moment the cargo is placed alongside the carrying vessel in readiness for loading, until discharged alongside at their destination. Time spent on cargo handling is also at the shipowner's risk.

班轮条款是指船舶出租人从货物被送至船边准备装货时起到目的港卸完货止，负责货物装卸和运输费用。货物装卸所用的时间也是由出租人承担风险。

1.9 Liner In and Free Out (LIFO)
1.9 船舶出租人负责装货费，不负责卸货费 (LIFO)

LIFO means that the shipowner pays for the loading of the cargo but is free of discharging and on the other hand, the charterer pays for the discharging of the cargo but free of loading.

该术语表示船舶出租人负责装货费，但不负责卸货费。从另一个方面来说，承租人负责卸货费，但不负责装货费。

1.10 Free In and Liner Out (FILO)
1.10 船舶出租人不负责装货费，但负责卸货费(FILO)

FILO means that the shipowner pays for the discharging of the cargo but is free of loading and on the other hand, the charterer pays for the loading of the cargo but is free of discharging.

该术语表示船舶出租人负责卸货费，但不负责装货费。从另一个方面来说，承租人负责装货费，但不负责卸货费。

2. Cost for Opening and Closing the Hatches
2. 开关舱费用

Whether the shipowner or the charterer is to bear the cost of opening and closing the hatches depends on the terms of the charter party.

船舶出租人或承租人是否承担货舱的开启和关闭费用取决于租船合同条款的规定。

A clause in the charter party stated: "Charterers' stevedores to be employed by the vessel at discharge port and discharge to be free of expense to the vessel." The stevedores at the port of discharge opened and closed the hatches during discharge. The shipowner alleged that the cost (other than the first opening and last closing) was part of the cost of discharging the vessel, whilst the charterers contended that the cost was part of the cost of the ship fulfilling her duty to take proper care of the cargo during discharge. Held, that the opening and closing of the hatch were part of the operating of discharge, and that therefore the charterer was liable.

租船合同条款规定："船舶出租人在卸货港雇佣承租人的装卸工人，船舶出租人不承担卸货费用。"在卸货港卸货过程中，装卸工人开启和关闭舱口。船舶出租人声称该费用（除了第一次开启和最后一次关闭）是履行该船卸货的一部分费用。而承租人争辩说，费用是船舶出租人在卸货过程中履行其适当的管理货物义务费用的一部分。判决：舱盖的开和关是卸货作业的一部分，因此由承租人承担费用。

3. Provisions in Gencon Form 1994
3. 1994年金康合同范本的规定

According to the Gencon Form 1994, the main part of the costs and risks lie on the charterers. They should not only deliver the cargo to the vessel but also load and sometimes stow and trim it. At the discharging port all arrangements are similarly the responsibility of the charterers. The following are the main contents of Gencon Form 1994.

根据1994年金康合同范本，费用和风险的主要部分由承租人承担。承租人不仅要交付货物装船，而且要负责积载和平舱。在卸货港，其同样由承租人承担责任。以下是1994年金康合同范本的主要内容。

3.1 Costs/Risks
3.1 费用/风险

The cargo shall be brought into the holds, loaded, stowed and/or trimmed, lashed and/or secured and taken from the holds and discharged by the charterers, free of any risk, liability, and expense whatsoever to the shipowners. The charterers shall provide and lay all dunnage material as required for the proper stowage and protection of the cargo on board, the shipowners allowing the use of dunnage available on board. The charterers shall be responsible for and pay the cost of removing their dunnage after discharge of the cargo under this charter party and time to count until the dunnage has been removed.

承租人负责把货物送至舱内，装船、积载和/或平舱，绑扎和/或加固，并从舱内提货和卸货，船舶出租人不承担任何风险、责任和费用。如要求适宜积载并为保护所装货物，承租人应提供并放置所有垫舱物料，船舶出租人允许在船上使用所有现有的垫料。承租人应负责并支付本租船合同项下卸货后移走所有垫料的费用，且该移除时间应计入装卸时间或滞期时间。

3.2 Cargo Handling Gear
3.2 船吊

Unless the vessel is gearless or unless it has been agreed between the parties that the vessel's gear shall not be used and stated as such in Box 15, the shipowners shall throughout loading or discharging give free use of the vessel's cargo handling gear and of sufficient motive power to operate all such cargo handling gear. All such equipment must be in good working order. Unless caused by negligence of the stevedores, time lost by breakdown of the vessel's cargo handling gear or motive power—pro rata the total number of cranes/winches required at that time for the loading/discharging of cargo under this charter party—shall not count as laytime or time on demurrage.

除非船舶无船吊或双方同意并在第15栏中记载不使用船舶装卸设备，否则船舶出租人应在整个装卸货物的过程中免费提供该装卸设备，并提供足够的动力来操作此类装卸设备。所有此类设备应处于良好工作状态。除非因装卸工人的过失导致，否则所有因船舶装卸设备或故障动力不足引起的时间损失——根据本租约规定的船吊/吊车数量按比例计算——不计入装卸时间或滞期时间。

On request, the shipowners shall provide free-of-charge cranemen/winch men from the crew to operate the vessel's cargo handling gear, unless local regulations prohibit this. In the latter event shore laborers shall be for the account of the charterers. Cranemen/winchmen shall be under the charterers' risk and responsibility and as stevedores to be deemed as their servants but shall always be under the supervision of the master.

应要求，船舶出租人应提供船员充当船吊/吊车司机，以操作船舶的货物装卸设备，除非当地法律禁止。若属后一种情况（即当地法律禁止），则承租人应负责岸上的劳工费用。船吊/吊车司机的风险和责任由承租人承担，装卸工人应被视为其雇佣人员，由船长监督其工作。

3.3 Stevedore Damage
3.3 装卸工人损害

The charterers shall be responsible for damage (beyond ordinary wear and tear) to any part of the vessel caused by stevedores. Such damage shall be notified as soon as reasonably possible by the master to the charterers or their agents and their stevedores, failing which the charterers shall not be held responsible. The master shall endeavor to obtain the stevedores' written acknowledgment of liability.

承租人承担由装卸工人造成的对船舶的损坏（除正常的损耗）。该损害应由船长尽可能快地通知承租人或其代理和装卸工人，否则承租人不负责任。船长应尽力取得装卸工人的书面确认责任证据。

The charterers are obliged to repair any stevedore damage before completion of the voyage, but must repair stevedore damage affecting the vessel's seaworthiness or class before the vessel sails from the port where such damage was caused or found. All additional expenses incurred shall be for the account of the charterers and time lost shall be for the account of and shall be paid to the owners by the charterers at the demurrage rate.

承租人必须在航次结束前修复装卸工人造成的损坏，但如果该损坏有损船舶的适航或船级，则应于起航前在造成或发现损坏的港口修复。所有额外费用由承租人负责，时间损失按滞期费率由承租人支付给船舶出租人。

3.4 Stevedore Damage Clause for FIO Voyage Charter Parties 2008
3.4 2008年航次租船合同FIO术语下装卸工人损害条款

The BIMCO Stevedore Damage Clauses have been revised and updated to reflect current commercial practice and to provide a balanced solution to this often contentious issue. The clauses were adopted by the Documentary Committee at its meeting in London in May 2008.

BIMCO装卸工人损害条款已进行修订和更新，以反映当前的航运习惯做法，并就经常引起争议的问题提供一个均衡的解决方法。该条款于2008年5月在伦敦由波罗的海国际航运公会单证委员会通过。

(a) The charterers shall be responsible for damage (fair wear and tear excepted) to any part of the vessel caused by stevedores. The charterers shall be liable for all costs for repairing such damage and for any time lost, which shall be paid in an amount equivalent to the demurrage rate.

（a）承租人应当对装卸工人造成的船舶任何部分的损害负责（正常损耗除外）。承租人应承担修复这种损害的费用和任何的时间损失，按滞期费率由承租人支付给船舶出租人。

(b) The master or the owners shall notify the charterers or their agents and the stevedores of any damage as soon as reasonably possible, failing which the charterers shall not be responsible.

（b）船长或船舶出租人应将装卸工人对船舶造成的任何损害尽快通知承租人或其代理人以及装卸工人，否则承租人不负责任。

(c) Stevedore damage affecting seaworthiness shall be repaired without any delay before the vessel sails from the port where such damage was caused or discovered. Stevedore damage affecting the vessel's trading capabilities shall be repaired before leaving the last port of discharge, failing which the charterers shall be liable for resulting losses. All other damage that is not repaired before leaving the last port of discharge shall be repaired by the owners and settled by the charterers on receipt of the owners' supported invoice.

（c）在装卸工人的损害影响适航的情况下，应于起航前在造成或发现损害的港口立即进行修复。装卸工人的损害影响了船舶的营运能力，应在离开最后卸货港前修理，否则该承租人应当对造成的损失承担责任。所有其他未修理的损害应在船舶离开最后卸货港前由船舶出租人修复，承租人按修理发票结算。

UNIT 5　LAYTIME
第五单元　装卸时间

According to *Laytime Definitions for Charter Parties 2013*, laytime shall mean the period agreed between the parties during which the shipowner will make and keep the vessel available for loading or discharging without additional payment to the freight.

根据《2013 租船合同装卸时间定义》，装卸时间是指合同当事人双方约定的船舶出租人使船舶并且保证船舶适于装卸货物，无须在运费之外支付附加费的时间。

Laytime is invariably regulated in standard voyage charter party forms. A great many of all the discussions and disputes that arise out of the voyage charter party are connected with the calculation of laytime.

装卸时间总是在标准航次租船合同范本中加以规定。航次租船合同引起的许多讨论和争议与装卸时间计算有关系。

1. Period of Laytime
1. 装卸时间期限

Period of laytime can be divided into three categories: fixed laytime, calculable laytime and indefinite laytime.

装卸时间期限可以分为三种：确定的装卸时间、计算的装卸时间和非确定的装卸时间。

1.1 Fixed Laytime
1.1 确定的装卸时间

Fixed laytime is the simplest of the three categories and specifies how many days/hours are allowed, whether for loading or for discharging, or for both activities, the latter sometimes being known as for "all purposes". Terms might be: "Cargo to be loaded within 5 weather working days of 24 consecutive hours" or "7 working days of 24 consecutive hours, weather permitting, for all purposes".

确定的装卸时间是三种分类中最简单的, 规定允许多少天/小时装货、卸货或者装卸货, 后者通常被称为"装卸共用时间"。术语可以为："合同规定装货时间为 5 个连续 24 小时良好天气工作日"或者"装卸时间共为 7 个连续 24 小时工作日, 天气许可"。

The use of fixed laytime is the standard practice in the tanker trades and is almost always fixed at 72 hours being allowed for the combined loading and discharging, regardless of the size of the vessel.

油船运输中使用确定的装卸时间是行业的标准做法，不论船舶大小，几乎总是确定装卸共用时间为72小时。

In a voyage charter party, which provides for more than one loading port or discharge port, should the laytime allowed be calculated separately for each port? For example, six days of total laytime is allowed, but there are two loading ports stipulated in the charter party. Should the six days run continuously from the commencement of laytime at the first load port until used up, or three days at each loading port?

当在航次租船合同中规定了几个装货港或卸货港时，是否允许分别计算每个港口的装卸时间？例如装卸时间总共为6天，租船合同规定了2个装货港口。这6天是从第一个装货港装卸时间开始时持续计算直到期满，还是每一个装货港为3天装卸时间？

Under English law (although it is always a question of construction of the charter and the language used will be examined in detail) there is effectively a presumption that the correct answer is the laytime runs continuously from the commencement of laytime at the first load port until used up rather than running separately at every load port. If charterers wish to ensure that a period of laytime runs separately at every load port or discharge port, they should ensure that the charter party states this in clear terms.

根据英国法（尽管这始终是合同解释以及语言使用细节探讨的问题）有效推定的正确答案是从第一个装货港的装卸时间开始连续计算直到期满，而不是每一个港口分别计算。如果承租人希望确保每个装货港或卸货港装卸时间单独计算，承租人应当在租船合同中明确规定。

1.2 Calculable Laytime
1.2 计算的装卸时间

Calculable laytime means that the periods of definite laytime as described above can only be established once a calculation has first been carried out. Based on factors contained in the contract and in the statement of facts form, calculable laytime can be sub-divided into two further sub-sections.

计算的装卸时间是指装卸时间首先需要进行计算才能明确具体的时间。根据合同规定的要素和事实记录表格，计算的装卸时间可进一步分为两个方面。

1.2.1 Tonnage Calculations
1.2.1 吨位计算

Tonnage calculations are the most common type of calculable laytime. A contract will state that a vessel is to load and/or discharge at a set rate of tons per day/hour. Thus, for a ship loading 40,000 metric tons of cargo, at a rate of 10,000 metric tons daily, there will be 4 days of laytime available to her charterers.

吨位计算是装卸时间计算中最常见的类型。合同表述为船舶每天/小时装载率和/或卸载率多少吨。因此，对于装船40 000吨货物，装卸率每天10 000吨，承租人总共有4天的装卸时间。

However, it might be that the ship's master has a margin within which to load, e.g. 40,000 tons (5% more or less). Thus, if the ship eventually loaded 41,258 tons of cargo, available laytime can be assessed as follows:

然而，船长对于装船货物数量有一定幅度的权力，例如40 000吨货物（上下浮动5%）。因此，如果该船舶最终装载41 258吨货物，装卸时间的计算过程为：

41,258 tons ÷ 10,000 tons per day = 4.1258 days.

41 258 吨 ÷ 10 000 吨/天 = 4.1258 天

There are times however when for whatever reason the charterer cannot provide the full amount of cargo. You have already learned that the shipowner can claim "dead freight" in such cases but should the lack of cargo affect the laytime calculation? Under English law, laytime is applied only to the portion of cargo loaded. However, a shipowner/operator claiming dead freight must return to the charterer any benefit received. American law is more straightforward in cases of dead freight, calculating laytime on what has been loaded, plus tonnage equivalent to the dead freight paid by charterers.

不过有时因某些原因，承租人不能提供全部数额的货物。在这种情况下，船舶出租人可以要求"亏舱费"，但货物短缺是否影响货物装卸时间的计算呢？根据英国法，装卸时间仅针对货物的实际装载部分计算。不过，船舶出租人或经营者必须将由此获得的额外利益返还给承租人。美国法下则更直接，根据实际装载货物数量加上由承租人支付的亏舱费所对应的吨位计算装卸时间。

1.2.2 Hatch Calculations

1.2.2 舱口计算

Hatch calculations are more complicated than tonnage calculations but occasionally need to be performed; nonetheless, there are well-established methods to assist.

实务中有时会出现舱口计算问题，舱口计算比吨位计算更复杂，但可以引用一些确定的方法来解决。

1.2.2.1 Per Hatch per Day

1.2.2.1 每日每舱装卸

Per hatch per day shall mean that the laytime is to be calculated by dividing (A), the quantity of cargo, by (B), the result of multiplying the agreed daily rate per hatch by the number of the vessel's hatches. Thus:

每日每舱装卸是指用船舶具体装卸的货物数量除以每舱日装卸率乘以船舶舱口数的积而得出装卸日数。即：

Laytime = (Quantity of cargo)/(Daily Rate × Number of Hatches)= Days

装卸时间 = （货物数量）/（每舱日装卸率×船舶舱口数）=天数

Let us assume that a general cargo vessel "AAA" is discharging bagged wheat flour based on: "A discharge rate of 175 tons per hatch day, total cargo of 7,000 tons, 1,575 tons cargo in the largest cargo compartment and vessel has five (5) hatches."

让我们假设杂货船"AAA"按以下条件卸载袋装面粉："卸货率为每天每舱175吨，总共7 000吨货物，最大的货舱装载1 575吨货物，船舶共有5个舱口。"

Thus 5 (hatches) × 175 tons per day = 875 tons daily

所以：5（舱）×175 吨/天 =875 吨/天

Thus 7,000 tons ÷ 875 tons per day = 8 days permitted laytime

所以：7 000 吨÷875 吨/天=8 天允许卸货时间

1.2.2.2 Per Workable Hatch Per Day

1.2.2.2 每日每工作舱装卸

"Per working hatch per day" or "per workable hatch per day" shall mean that the laytime is to be calculated by dividing (A), the quantity of cargo in the hold with the largest quantity, by (B), the result of multiplying the agreed daily rate per working or workable hatch by the number of hatches serving that hold. Thus:

"每日每工作舱装卸"是指以船舶最大货舱载货量除以每舱日装卸率乘以该舱口数的积而得出装卸时间。即：

Laytime = (Largest Quantity in One Hold)/(Daily Rate per Hatch × Number of Hatches Serving That Hold) = Days

装卸时间 =（最大货舱载货量）/（每舱日装卸率×该舱口数）= 天数

Taking the above example of the "AAA", first, it is necessary to establish the "largest" unit of cargo in the vessel. Reference to the "stowage plan" shows that No.1 holds contained 1,200 tons; No.2 holds 1,500 tons; No.3 holds 1,575 tons; No.4 holds 1,400 tons and No.5 holds 1,325 tons. Therefore 1,575 tons contained in No.3 hold constitutes the "largest" unit.

以上例为例，首先要确认船舶"最大"的货舱载货量。根据"积载图"表明1号舱装载 1 200 吨货，2号舱装载 1 500 吨货，3号舱装载 1 575 吨货，4号舱装载 1 400 吨货，5号舱装载 1 325 吨货。因此，3号舱装载量 1 575 吨为"最大"的货舱。

Thus 1,575 tons ÷ 175 tons per day = 9 days laytime overall.

所以：1 575 吨÷175 吨/天= 总共9天卸货时间。

However, where two or more hatches serve the largest unit of cargo, the unit tonnage must be sub-divided. Assuming two hatches served No. 3 hold and tween deck, for example, 1,575 tons would first be divided by 2 before applying the factor of 175 tons per day. In that case, the largest indivisible cargo unit would become the 1,500 tons contained in the No. 2 hold and the laytime duration calculation would then be:

但是，如果最大的舱有两个或更多的舱口，该单位吨位必须细分。假设两个舱口服务于 3号舱和二层甲板，例如，在除以每天装卸率175吨前，1 575 吨应首先除以2。在这种情况下，最大的货舱为2号，装有 1 500 吨货物，装卸时间为：

1,500 tons ÷ 175 tons per day = 8.571428 days laytime.

1 500 吨 ÷175 吨/天=8.571428 天卸货时间

1.3 Indefinite Laytime

1.3 非确定的装卸时间

Occasionally, a shipowner or operator will agree for his ship to be loaded or discharged as per "custom of the port" (COP), "customary dispatch" (CD), "customary quick dispatch" (CQD) or "fast as can" (FAC) terms. Nowadays the most frequently used term in indefinite laytime is CQD.

偶然情况下，船舶出租人或经营人同意以"港口习惯"(COP)、"按习惯尽快装卸"(CD)、"按港口习惯尽快装卸"(CQD)或"尽可能快"(FAC)等术语进行装卸货物。目前非确定的装卸时间中经常使用的术语是CQD。

The term "CQD" implies an agreement on the part of the charterer to load or discharge within a reasonable time and by the settled and established practice of the port. If he fails to do so, the shipowner will at the outset be entitled to damages for detention. It should be noted that the charterer's obligation extends not only to the actual cargo operation, but also to facilitate the commencement and completion of these operations. To advance a claim for damages for detention successfully, the shipowner will have to establish that the delay was attributable to acts or omissions on the part of the charterer. Consequently, the onus of proving that the charterer was in fact in breach rests with the shipowner rather than the charterer.

CQD术语意味着承租人的部分义务是在合理时间内并且按照港口已经形成的习惯装卸货物。如果承租人未履行的话，船舶出租人首先有权获得滞留损失的赔偿。应当注意的是，承租人的义务不仅包括实际的货物作业，而且要促进这些作业事实上的动工和完成。船舶出租人为了能够成功地获得滞留损失的赔偿，他必须确认延误是由于承租人的行为或疏忽造成的。因此，证明承租人事实上违约的责任在出租人身上而不在承租人身上。

It is unreasonable, for example, for cargo not to be available upon a vessel's arrival within agreed laydays, and in such a case, the shipowner would normally become entitled to reimbursement by damages for detention. But the risks of bad weather, port congestion, and such like are all for the shipowner to bear. Following is the case referring to the charterer's liability in quick dispatch at the discharging port.

不合理的情况有船舶按期抵达后货物没有备好，在这种情况下，船舶出租人通常有权要求滞留损失。但恶劣天气、港口拥堵等类似风险都由船舶出租人承担。下例是有关承租人承担在卸货港尽快速遣责任的案例。

【Case】The charter party provides in Article 7(2) that "the charterer is responsible for cargo storing at loading port, loading/discharging port Tianjin/Shekou, one berth one port", and it further provides in Article 10(1) "CQD at discharging port, but if buyer cannot take delivery of goods timely and has caused detention of ship, charterers shall pay shipowner RMB 30,000 per day". During discharging at Shekou, the vessel was ordered by the port authority to stop and move to anchorage; 2 days later the vessel moved to another berth to continue discharging. The shipowner sued the charterer for time loss due to disruption during discharging.

【案例】租船合同第7条第（2）款规定："承租人负责装货港货物的储存，装货/卸货港为天津/蛇口，一个泊位一个港口。"第10条第（1）款进一步规定："在卸货港按港口习惯尽快装卸，但如果买方不能及时提货，造成了船舶滞留，承租人应支付船舶出租人每天3万元人民币。"在蛇口卸货过程中，该船被港口当局指令停工，移至锚地；2天后船舶转移到另一个泊位继续卸货。船舶出租人就卸货中断的时间损失起诉承租人。

Held by the Court: Article 7(2) is a printed clause in the charter party; it is only a provision regarding the charterer's responsibility at the loading port; Article 10(1) is a typed clause of the contract and is a provision relating to responsibility at discharging port. CQD applies to the discharging port, i.e. the shipowner is to be liable for time loss at the discharging port. Although the vessel used 2 berths at the discharging port contrary to the agreement of "one berth one port", there is no evidence to prove that it is caused by the charterer's breach of contract. The charterer is not liable for time loss at the discharging port and the case is dismissed accordingly.

法院认为：第7条第（2）款是租船合同的印刷条款，它只是涉及承租人在装货港的责任；第10条第（1）款是合同的手写条款，是关于在卸货港责任的条文。CQD适用于卸货港，即船舶出租人对在卸货港的时间损失承担责任。虽然该船使用了卸货港的2个泊位，违反了"一港一泊位"的协议，但也没有证据证明它是由承租人违约造成的。承租人不承担在卸货港的时间损失，案件被驳回。

2. Commencement of Laytime
2. 装卸时间起算

Unless a different agreement has been made, in general, three conditions must be satisfied before laytime will start: (1) the vessel must have "arrived" at the place where cargo operations are to be performed; (2) the vessel must in all respects be ready to load or discharge the relevant cargo; (3) the notice of readiness must be tendered by the master or agent on behalf of the master.

除非另有规定，通常情况下船舶需要满足以下三个条件才能起算装卸时间：（1）船舶"抵达"租船合同规定的装卸地点；（2）船舶在各个方面做好装卸货物的准备；（3）船长或其代理人递交装卸准备就绪通知书。

2.1 Arrived Ship
2.1 到达船舶

In general, laytime commences when a vessel is an "arrived ship". Simply put, it could be considered the time that the vessel arrives at the agreed place. Therefore, the more detailed the description of that place the more careful the shipowner must be to reach that place.

通常情况下，当船舶成为"到达船舶"时，装卸时间开始起算。简单地说，起算时间即认定为船舶抵达指定地点的时间。因此，指定地点的表述越详细，船舶出租人越要小心并必须抵达那个地点。

Whether a ship is an arrived ship will depend on whether the charter party is a port charter party or a berth charter party. "The vessel shall proceed to Bergen" is less onerous than "The vessel shall proceed to No. 2 berth Bergen". The former is known as a "port charter" and the latter a "berth charter".

船舶是否成为到达船舶取决于租船合同是港口租船合同还是泊位租船合同。"船舶驶往卑尔根"不如"船舶驶往卑尔根2号泊位"清晰。前者称之为"港口租船合同"，后者称之为"泊位租船合同"。

2.1.1 Port Charter Parties
2.1.1 港口租船合同

According to *Laytime Definitions for Charter Parties 2013*, "PORT" shall mean any area where vessels load or discharge cargo and shall include, but not be limited to, berths, wharves, anchorages, buoys, and offshore facilities as well as places outside the legal, fiscal or administrative area where vessels are ordered to wait for their turn no matter the distance from that area.

根据《2013 租船合同装卸时间定义》，港口是指船舶装货或者卸货的任何区域，包括但不限于泊位、码头、锚地、浮筒和近海设施；也包括船舶被指令等待依次进港的区域，而不论该区域与港口的法定、税收或行政管辖区域的距离远近。

Nowadays it is more common to find port charter parties and that means a particular port or ports, have been stipulated in the charter party.

当今，更常见的是港口租船合同，即在租船合同中已明确约定某一特定港口或若干特定港口。

The English courts once held that the vessel must be within the commercial area of the port and this has been amended to mean the "normal waiting area for a port". The rule is that the charter party names a port simply, without further particularity or qualification, the ship is an arrived ship when, if she cannot proceed immediately to a berth, she has reached a position within the port where she is at the immediate and effective disposition of the charterer. If she is at the place where waiting ships usually lie, she is in such a position unless there are some extraordinary circumstances, proof of which lies on the charterer. Following is the case referring to an arrived ship under a port charter party.

英国法院曾经裁定，船舶必须抵达港口的商业区，现已改为"港口通常等待区域"。法律原则是，在租船合同中仅简单提及一个港口，没有进一步规定的情况下，当船舶不能即刻驶往泊位时，只要它已抵达港口内可由承租人直接和有效支配的位置，船舶即构成到达船舶。如果船舶处于等候泊位的船只通常停泊的位置，那么它就处于这种可被承租人直接和有效支配的位置，除非存在某些特殊情况，而特殊情况的举证责任在于承租人。以下是一个与港口租船合同下已到船相关的案例。

【Case】A vessel carrying grain under a port charter party anchored at the BAR anchorage at Liverpool, waiting for a berth for 17 days. The anchorage was about 17 miles from the usual discharging berth, but was the usual place where grain vessels lay while awaiting a berth. The anchorage was within the legal and administrative limit of the port of Liverpool. Held by the House of Lords that she was an arrived ship when she reached the anchorage, for she was then at the immediate and effective disposition of the charterer.

【案例】一艘装载谷物的船舶在利物浦的"BAR"锚地停泊，等待泊位共17天。锚地距离通常卸货的泊位约17英里，但它是通常等待泊位的地方。该锚地位于利物浦港的法律和行政管辖之内。英国最高法院上议院判决，当船舶到达锚地，即为到达船舶，因为它在承租人立即和有效的处置之下。

Where a vessel is directed to go to the port, she does not become an arrived ship by anchoring at a place that is outside the legal and administrative limits of the port.

当船舶抵达港口，如果它锚泊在港口法律和行政管辖之外的地点，则船舶不构成到达船舶。

【Case】The Maratha Envoy was bound for the port of Brake on the Weser River, the berth was full and she was told to wait at the Weser Lightship where ships for grain discharging usually lie. Indeed there is no waiting area within the port of Brake other than the Weser Lightship anchorage. But this anchorage is outside the legal port limit. This case is quite different from the above case where the anchorage was technically within the legal port limit of Liverpool.

【案例】"Maratha Envoy"号船驶往威悉河上的布雷克港口，泊位爆满，该船被告知在威悉河灯船锚地等候，那里是通常等待的地点。除了在威悉河灯船锚地等待，布雷克港口内确实没有等待区域。但该锚地不属于港口法律管辖范围。该案与上一个案子不同，上一个案子锚地位于利物浦港的法定和行政管辖之内。

When the case reached the Court of Appeal, it held that it did not matter whether the waiting area lay outside or inside the legal limit of the port. In the House of Lords, it was reversed. The House of Lords refused to deviate from their earlier decision in *The Johanna Oldendorff* and the Reid Test had been reasserted strongly by Lord Diplock. Therefore an arrived ship must come within the port limits to have the laytime clock started.

当案件诉至上诉法院，法院判决未考虑等候区是否在港口的法定管辖内。然而，在上议院，该判决被推翻。英国上议院拒绝偏离其早些时候在"The Johanna Oldendorff"一案中作出的判决，迪普洛克法官强烈重申"里德标准"的适用效力。因此，到达船舶必须处于港口管辖范围内才能开始计算装卸时间。

2.1.2 Berth Charter Parties

2.1.2 泊位租船合同

According to *Laytime Definitions for Charter Parties 2013*, "BERTH" shall mean the specific place where the vessel is to load or discharge and should include, but not be limited to, any wharf, anchorage, offshore facility or other location used for that purpose. Berth charter parties mean that a particular dock or berth has been stipulated in the charter party.

根据《2013租船合同装卸时间定义》，"泊位"是指船舶准备装货或卸货的特定区域，包括但不限于泊位、锚地、近海设施或其他以装卸货为目的的地点。泊位租船合同意味着租船合同对某一个特定的码头或泊位做出规定。

Where the charter parties expressly reserve to the charterer the right to name a particular dock or berth, the laytime does not begin until the ship has arrived at that dock or berth. If the vessel berths on arrival without delay there can be no disagreement as to when the vessel is ready and the "clock starts" but if there is a delay the situation is less clear. The duty to reach this agreed point or place for loading or discharging is very tough on the shipowners. Even if the vessel has to wait in the immediate vicinity for the particular berth agreed upon by the charter party, the vessel is not considered to have arrived. Therefore any loss of time in waiting for the berth to become vacant will fall on the shipowners.

如果租船合同明确保留承租人有权指定一个特定的码头或泊位，装卸时间直至船舶已抵达该码头或泊位才开始。如果船舶抵达泊位时没有延误，船舶准备就绪，"时钟开始起算"没有问题；但如果有延迟，情况则不是很清楚。驶往规定的装货或卸货地点或地方对于船舶出租人来说是较难的。即使船舶在租船合同规定的特定的泊位附近等候，船舶也不被认为已经抵达。因此，任何等待泊位空闲的时间损失都由船舶出租人承担。

【Case】A charter party required a vessel to proceed to one or two safe ports in East Canada, place or places as ordered by charterers. She entered the port of Miramichi, and on arrival was told that she would be required to load at Millbank, a place within the port. As there was not then a berth for her, she had to wait for six days, in respect of which the shipowners claimed demurrage. Held that the charter party gave the charterers an express right to nominate a place, meaning a berth within the port. Therefore the vessel did not become an arrived ship until arriving at the berth, and demurrage was not payable.

【案例】租船合同要求船舶在承租人指令下驶往加拿大东部一个或两个安全港口。该船进入米罗米奇港口，抵达时获悉，需要在港内米尔班克地点装货。由于当时没有泊位，该船等待了6天，船舶出租人索赔滞期费。判决：租船合同给予承租人明确权利指定一个地点，即港内的一个泊位，因此该船直至到达泊位才能作为一艘到达船舶，承租人无须支付滞期费。

In order to protect shipowners' interests, there is the usual provision of "whether in berth or not" inserted in the charter parties, and that will effectively expand a berth charter party into a port charter party.

为了保护船舶出租人的利益，通常将"无论靠泊与否"的规定写入租船合同中，这将把泊位租船合同有效地扩展为港口租船合同。

According to *Laytime Definitions for Charter Parties 2013*, "Whether in berth or not" (WIBON) shall mean that if the designated loading or discharging berth is not available on arrival, the vessel on reaching any usual waiting place at the port, shall be entitled to tender notice of readiness from it and laytime shall commence in accordance with the charter party.

根据《2013租船合同装卸时间定义》，"无论靠泊与否"(WIBON)是指船舶抵达后，指定的装货或卸货泊位没有空闲时，船舶抵达港口的任何通常等候地点即有权递交装卸准备就绪通知书，装卸时间应按租船合同规定开始起算。

WIBON was designed to convert a berth charter party into a port charter party, and to ensure that under a berth charter party, the notice of readiness could be given as soon as the ship had arrived within the port concerned, so that the laytime could start to run on its expiry. But English law has restricted the meaning of WIBON somewhat. That is in *the Kyzikos*.

WIBON的目的是将泊位租船合同转换成港口租船合同，并确保在泊位租船合同下，只要船舶抵达港口内，装卸准备就绪通知书就可以递交，可以起算装卸时间。但是英国法在"Kyzikos"一案中对此做出了限制性解释。

【Case】The Kyzikos was fixed to load a cargo of steel products in Italy for Houston. In the charter party in the Gencon form, the discharge port or place was stated as "1/2 safe always afloat, always accessible berth(s) each port..." So it was a berth charter party. But Clause 5 stated: "Time to commence at 2 pm if notice of readiness is given before noon, at 8 am next working day if notice of readiness is given during office hours after noon. WWWW."

【案例】"Kyzikos"号船洽租在意大利，装载钢铁产品到休斯敦卸货。在金康合同格式中的卸货港或地方定为"1/2安全港口，始终漂浮，一经抵港即可靠泊"。所以这是一个泊位租船合同。但第5条规定："如果装卸准备就绪通知书在中午前递交，装卸时间从下午2点开始起算；如果装卸准备就绪通知书在中午后工作时间递交，装卸时间从次一工作日上午8点开始起算，无论靠泊与否，无论靠港与否，无论清关与否，无论检疫通过与否。"

The Kyzikos arrived at Houston, the discharge port, at 0645H on December 17, 1984. Notice of readiness was tendered by the master soon enough. The berth she was supposed to proceed to was available at all times. However, as fog had closed the pilot station, she could not proceed until December 20, 1984, on which date she was berthed at 1450H.

1984年12月17日6点45分，"Kyzikos"号船抵达卸货港休斯敦，船长很快递交装卸准备就绪通知书。该船预计靠泊的泊位在任何时候都空闲。然而，由于大雾，引航站关闭了，该船直到1984年12月20号14点50分才靠泊。

The shipowner claimed that laytime commenced at 1400H on December 17. However, the charterer maintained that WIBON was no protection for the shipowners if the berth was available and the vessel was prevented from berthing due to other reasons beyond the control of the charterers. Thus, the charterer would only accept laytime commencing after the vessel became an "arrived" ship when she berthed on December 20. Only a little over three days of demurrage (USD 30,435.72) was in dispute but the case was taken to the House of Lords.

船舶出租人称，装卸时间从12月17日14点开始。但是，承租人认为如果泊位空闲出来了，由于超出承租人控制的其他原因致使该船无法靠泊，"无论靠泊与否"并不保护船舶出租人。因此，承租人只接受当船舶构成到达船舶时，即12月20日靠泊时，装卸时间才开始计算。虽然引起争议的仅是三天多一点的滞期费（30 435.72美元），但该案件被诉至英国最高法院上议院。

In arbitration, it was decided that the shipowner's claim succeeded in full on the ground that "on well-established authority, the words had the effect of making a berth charter into a port charter."

在仲裁中，裁决船舶出租人索赔成功的理由是："根据公认的判例，该术语已将泊位租船合同变为港口租船合同。"

On appeal in the High Court, the award was reversed. It was held that there was no previous decision of any court which was binding on the court on the point. The Lord said, "When a vessel is unable to come alongside because no berth is available, the WIBON provision in the ordinary case has, in practice, that effect; but in my view, it cannot be said without doubt that the authorities which I have considered, read as a whole, support the proposition that it has that effect in law, still less that it converts a berth charter into a port charter."

该案上诉到高等法院后，裁决被推翻。法官认为：不存在任何法院之前的判决对此问题有约束力。法官认为："在实践中，当因为没有泊位可用，船舶不能靠泊时，虽然'无论靠泊与否'有这种效力；但我认为，以前的主张引用本案不能说没有疑问，更不用说它实际上已转换成一个港口租船合同。"

In the Court of Appeal, however, the arbitration award was restored and it was held that WIBON turned a berth charter into a port charter so that time commenced to run when the vessel was waiting in the named port of destination to proceed to berth.

在上诉法院，仲裁裁决再次被认可，判决"无论靠泊与否"将泊位租船合同变为港口租船合同，因此装卸时间从船舶等待时起算。

In the House of Lords, finally, the Court of Appeal's decision was unanimously reversed. Lord Brandon gave the only reasoned speech. It appeared the main reason for the House of Lords' decision was based on the absence of any reported case that applied the WIBON to any cause of delay other than the non-availability of a berth, thus justifying the inference that the purpose of WIBON was only for the limited application of non-availability of berth/congestion. Lord Brandon said that "whether in berth or not" was the shorthand for "whether in berth (a berth being available) or not in berth (a berth not being available)".

英国上议院最终一致推翻了上诉法院的判决。布兰登法官是唯一给出理由的法官。上议院作出这一判决的主要依据是：目前尚没有已报道案件适用WIBON下空闲泊位的情况，因此有理由推论WIBON的适用范围仅限于"泊位不可用/港口拥堵"这一特定情况。布兰登法官认为，"无论靠泊与否"，是"无论已靠泊（泊位正在可用）或未靠泊（泊位不可用的）"的简略表述。

It is clear that WIBON will still protect the shipowners in the event of port congestion, hence preventing the vessel in a berth charter from becoming an arrived ship. WIBON would be even better in protecting the shipowners if the waiting for the nominated berth to be free is not within the port limit.

很明显，"WIBON在港口拥挤情况下仍将保护船舶出租人，从而防止泊位租船合同下船舶不能成为抵达船舶。如果等待指定泊位的地点不属于港区范围，WIBON将更好地保护船舶出租人。

2.1.3 Time Lost in Waiting for Berth to Count as Laytime

2.1.3 等泊损失时间计入装卸时间

"Time lost in waiting for berth to count as laytime" is a well-known printed clause that can be found in the Gencon form of charter party and is freely incorporated by many shipowners in the rider clauses of other forms of voyage charter parties. It is a further important provision aimed at relieving shipowners of the hardship caused by the narrow interpretation of the "arrived ship" under English law. The purpose of the clause is to make charterers assume the financial burden of the risk of waiting for a berth due to congestion whether it is a port charter or a berth charter party.

"等泊损失时间计入装卸时间"是一个众所周知的印刷条款，金康合同范本也有此规定，许多船舶出租人以附加条款或其他形式自由地将其订立在航次租船合同中。这是一个重要的规定，目的在于缓解英国法对到达船舶的狭义解释所使船舶出租人面临的困境。该条款的目的是使承租人承担由于港口拥挤带来的等待泊位的风险，无论是港口租船合同还是泊位租船合同。

According to the *Laytime Definitions for Charter Parties 2013*, the "time lost" provision shall mean that if no loading or discharging berth is available and the vessel is unable to tender a notice of readiness at the waiting place then any time lost to the vessel is counted as if laytime were running, or as time on demurrage if laytime has expired. Such time ceases to count once the berth becomes available. When the vessel reaches a place where she can tender notice of readiness, laytime or time on demurrage resumes after such tender and, in respect of laytime, on expiry of any notice time provided in the charter party.

根据《2013租船合同装卸时间定义》，"时间损失"的规定是指，如果没有装卸泊位可用，并且该船无法在等待地点递交装卸准备就绪通知书时，船舶任何损失时间应计入已开始计算的装卸时间或装卸时间届满时计入滞期时间。当泊位可用时，时间应停止计算。当船舶到达一个地点并能够递交装卸准备就绪通知书时，装卸时间或滞期时间根据合同规定恢复起算。

【Case】The Darrah was chartered to carry a cargo of cement from Novorossisk in the Black Sea to Tripoli. The charter party was a port charter based on the Gencon form. The Darrah duly completed her carrying voyage and reached a usual waiting place for her turn within the limits of the port of Tripoli. The Darrah rightly gave notice of readiness to discharge on January 2, 1973, laytime being triggered shortly after the notice time. The Darrah had to wait for an available discharge berth for over seven days. That seven days and six hours, included two non-working days, a Friday (non-working day in Tripoli) and a legal holiday, and a period from noon on the day before each. If this seven days and six hours waiting time counted as proper laytime, the non-working period would have to be disallowed under the charter party. The shipowners claimed that the whole of the seven days and six hours would have to be counted continuously under the "time lost" provision, because it took priority over the "laytime" provision. This would effectively exhaust all the laytime (eight days and seven hours) and leave only 25 hours. These 25 hours were promptly used after berthing and so, the shipowner argued, the vessel was thereafter on demurrage counting continuously without applying any excepted periods for the benefit of the charterers. The shipowners ended up with 10 more days on demurrage than the charterers would admit.

【案例】"Darrah"号船从黑海的新罗西斯克港装载水泥货物到黎波里港。租船合同是以金康合同范本为蓝本的港口租船合同。"Darrah"号船完成航行，并抵达了黎波里港口管辖内的通常等候地点等待靠泊。"Darrah"号船于1973年1月2日递交了卸货准备就绪通知书，装卸时间不久起算。该船等泊共7天多。这7天6小时，包括两天非工作日、星期五（在黎波里为非工作日）和一个法定节假日，以及这两天的前一天中午之后的一段时间。如果这7天6小时等候时间计入的话，按照装卸时间规定，则非工作时间不能计入。船舶出租人声称根据"等泊损失时间计入装卸时间"的规定，7天6小时都应计算在内，因为它比装卸时间的规定优先适用。这样计算的话几乎有效地用尽所有的装卸时间（8天7小时），只剩余25小时。靠泊后这25个小时会很快使用完，因此，船舶出租人认为应持续计算滞期费，且不得适用有利于承租人的除外时间。最终，船舶出租人主张的滞期天数比承租人认可的天数还多10天。

In the High Court, it was held that where time was lost waiting for a berth, all the time so lost was to count whenever and wherever the waiting took place, and the special exceptions about laytime calculation would only operate until the berth was ready. When it came to the Court of Appeal, it was held that the ship was an arrived ship, and the laytime provisions would apply, with all the exceptions to be applied. In the House of Lords, justice was further expanded. The House of Lords now had the chance to correct the earlier decisions and held that the "time lost" provision would have to be computed exactly like the permissible laytime calculation, as if the vessel had been berthed. So in the case of an arrived ship under a port charter, there is no conflict between the laytime clauses and the "time lost" provision, because both calculations are the same and neither need prevail over the other. But even a berth outside the port would still be counted as the laytime with all the exceptions like Sundays and holidays being excluded.

高等法院判决：等泊损失的时间，无论何时何地发生的所有等待时间都计入，装卸时间的除外规定仅在泊位就绪时适用。案子上诉至上诉法院，法院判决：该船是到达船舶，适用装卸时间的规定，所有的除外规定也适用。最终案件提交至上议院，其裁判规则被进一步细化，上议院借此机会纠正了此前的裁判规定。法院判定："时间损失"规定的计算方式和装卸时间规定的计算方式一样，仿佛船舶已实际靠泊。因此，在港口租船合同下的船舶抵达情况中，两个条款没有冲突，因为这两者的计算逻辑都是相同的，不需要判定谁比谁优先适用。即便船舶等待的泊位位于港口界限之外，相应时间仍应计入装卸时间，但需扣除所有法定或约定的除外期间（例如星期日及法定节假日）。

2.2 Readiness
2.2 准备就绪

Not only must a ship have arrived at named places under the charter party but she must also be ready in order to tender an effective notice of readiness so as to trigger off the laytime clock. Readiness means that the vessel must be in all respects ready to load or discharge in both the legal and physical sense.

根据租船合同，船舶不但要抵达指定的地点，它还必须准备就绪以便递交有效的装卸准备就绪通知书来起算装卸时间。准备就绪意味着从法律和实质的意义上讲，该船必须在各方面准备好装载或卸货。

2.2.1 Legal Readiness
2.2.1 法律上准备就绪
2.2.1.1 Free Pratique
2.2.1.1 检疫

The requirement for free pratique is a legal readiness that a vessel has to fulfill. It used to be harsh on the shipowners. In normal circumstances, free pratique is a mere formality. However, the time for its granting depends entirely on the custom of the particular port which the vessel is calling at. Some ports make it very simple by radio if the vessel's last port of call is a healthy place. Some ports are the other extreme where free pratique could not be obtained from the authority by the port regulations in force until the vessel had berthed.

检疫要求是一个船舶在法律上必须履行准备就绪的义务。它曾经对于船舶出租人来说是苛刻的。通常情况下，检疫只是例行公事。然而，检疫通过时间完全取决于特定港口的习惯规定。一些港口办理流程很简单，如果船舶最后停靠的港口是一个健康的地方，通过电报即可通过。一些港口则相反，根据港口规定，直到船舶停泊后才能从当局获得检疫通过。

【Case】A vessel reached the commercial area of Tuapse at 0100 hours on 19 February. Her master gave notice of readiness to load. She was directed to her berth on 24 February and arrived there at 1320 hours. Free pratique was granted at 1600 hours. Loading began at 2150 hours. It was held that the mere fact that free pratique had not been obtained did not prevent the vessel from being able to commence the laytime counting, as long as the free pratique could be obtained at any time and without the possibility of delaying the loading or discharging.

【案例】一艘船舶在2月19日01点抵达图普塞港商业区。船长递交装卸准备就绪通知书。2月24日其被指示靠泊并在13时20分抵达。16时检疫通过，21时50分开始装货。判决：未获得检疫通过并不妨碍船舶开始装卸时间的计算，只要可在任何时候获得检疫通过并且没有拖延装卸就行。

【Case】The vessel was chartered on the Gencon form for the carriage of a cargo of soya beans.

The relevant charter party clauses were as follows:

【案例】一艘以金康合同格式出租的船舶装载大豆进行货物运输。有关租船合同条款如下：

Clause 22 provided that: "IMMEDIATELY AFTER ARRIVAL OF THE SHIP AT THE PILOT STATION BOTH AT LOADING AND DISCHARGING PORTS, WHETHER IN PORT OR NOT, WHETHER CUSTOMS CLEARED OR NOT, BUT ALWAYS IN FREE PRATIQUE, WRITTEN OR WIRELESS NOTICE OF READINESS IS TO BE TENDERED BY THE MASTER AND/OR OWNER'S AGENT TO SHIPPERS/CHARTERERS/AGENTS AND TO RECEIVERS/CHARTERERS/AGENTS RESPECTIVELY. LAYTIME FOR LOADING AND DISCHARGING PORT SHALL COMMENCE AT 1300 HRS IF NOTICE OF READINESS TENDERED UP TO AND INCLUDING 1200 HRS SAME DAY OR 0800 HRS NEXT WORKING DAY IF NOTICE OF READINESS TENDERED DURING OFFICE HOURS AFTER 1200 HRS. LOCAL AND LEGAL HOLIDAYS ARE EXCLUDED UNLESS USED. TIME USED FOR SHIFTING FROM WAITING AREA TO LOADING BERTH NOT TO COUNT AS LAYTIME."

第22条规定："无论在装货港和卸货港，船舶到达引航站后，无论是否已进入港口，是否已完成清关，但始终需在检疫通过的前提下，船长及/或船舶出租人的代理人应立即向托运人/承租人/代理人以及收货人/承租人/代理人分别以书面或无线递交装卸准备就绪通知书。如装卸准备就绪通知书在中午12时之前（包括12时）递交，装卸时间从当日13时起算；如通知书在当日12时以后的工作时间递交，装卸时间从下一个工作日上午8时起算。当地法定节假日不计入装卸时间，除非该节假日期间实际用于装卸作业（则需计入）。船舶从候泊区移至装货泊位所耗费的时间，不计入装卸时间。"

Notice of readiness was given at 0906 on 18 March. On that basis, the shipowners submitted that laytime began at 1300 on 18 March. The charterers contended that since the vessel did not obtain free pratique until 1900 on 20 March, laytime did not commence until 1300 on 21 March. The shipowners responded that the fact that free pratique was only granted on 20 March did not mean that the ship was not in "free pratique" under clause 22 of the charter on giving notice of readiness on 18 March. The ship had a free bill of health. She was on 18 March in a fit state to obtain free pratique on first inspection. It was a pure formality, they said, that the ship could not be inspected for free pratique until she arrived at the inner anchorage, which she did on 20 March. The shipowners relied on *The Delian Spirit* [1971] 1 Lloyd's Rep 506.

装卸准备就绪通知书于3月18日0906时递交。据此，船舶出租人提出，装卸时间于3月18日1300时开始计算。承租人争辩说，由于该船直到3月20日1900时才通过检疫，装卸时间应从3月21日1300时起算。船舶出租人回答，3月20日获得检疫通过的事实并不意味着根据合同第22条的含义该船在3月18日未检疫通过。事实上，船舶有健康单证。它在3月18日处于适航的状态，第一次检查便可获得检疫通过。这是一个纯粹的例行公事，该船直到在内锚地才能检查，也就是3月20日。船舶出租人引用了 The Delian Spirit 一案的判决。

Held, that *The Delian Spirit* was concerned with a different issue, namely whether a ship could be regarded as an "arrived ship" if she was not in free pratique. The point in the present case was not whether the ship was an "arrived ship" but whether she complied with the explicit requirement of clause 22, that the ship should be in "free pratique". The ship did not comply until 1900 on 20

March, when she was given free pratique. Laytime could not therefore commence until 1300 on 21 March. London Arbitration 1/00.

判决：The Delian Spirit 案涉及的是另外一个问题，即如果船舶没有获得免检通过，船舶是否可以作为"到达船舶"。在本案中，问题不是"到达船舶"的问题，而是它是否符合第22条的明确规定，即船舶应是"检疫通过"。该船直到3月20日1900时才获得检疫通过。装卸时间直到3月21日1300时起算。伦敦仲裁2000年第一号。

2.2.1.2 Customs Clearance

2.2.1.2 清关

Normally this is again an idle formality. If the vessel supplies copies of cargo manifest and other necessary documents customs clearance will be almost automatic. But if shipowners voluntarily or negligently permit the customs clearance as a condition precedent in the charter party before the ability to tender notice of readiness they can be caught badly.

通常又是一个例行公事的形式。如果船舶提供货物舱单的副本和其他必要的文件，清关流程几乎可自动完成。但是，如果船舶出租人自愿或因疏忽而允许清关作为合同中递交装卸准备就绪通知书的前提条件，那么船舶出租人可能会陷入极为被动的境地。

【Case】The vessel, Puerto Rocca, arrived at the Mersey Bar anchorage and gave notice of readiness to the charterers. The charterers rejected it on the ground that the vessel was not customs cleared by the clause. A vessel couldn't obtain customs clearance at Mersey Bar. So the shipowners, whilst maintaining the validity of the notice of readiness tendered upon arrival at the anchorage, made efforts and expense to procure a lay-by berth in Seaforth Dock for the vessel, to obtain customs clearance and then served a second notice of readiness four days later than the first one, but without prejudice to it.

【案例】"Puerto Rocca"号船抵达 Mersey Bar 锚地并递交装卸准备就绪通知书给承租人。承租人拒绝接受，理由是该船并没有按照条款规定取得清关手续。而船舶在 Mersey Bar 锚地是不可能取得清关的。因此，船舶出租人维持在锚地递交有效的装卸准备通知书的情况下，尽力并花费一定费用驶往在西福斯码头的一搁置泊位，以便获得通关，然后送达第二份装卸准备就绪通知书，这一次送达比第一份迟了4天但不影响第一份的效力。

It was held by the High Court that the first notice of readiness was valid and the clause entitled them to do so if she was unable to berth immediately on arrival.

高级法院判决：第一份装卸准备就绪通知书有效，如果它到达时无法立即靠泊，有权递交。

2.2.2 Physical Readiness

2.2.2 实质上准备就绪

A ship must be physically capable of performing cargo operations e.g. at a loading port, holds must be cleaned and prepared for receiving cargo and, if the contract so specifies, holds must be inspected and declared suitable by an appropriate authority before notice of readiness will be accepted.

船舶必须在实质上能够进行货物作业，例如在装货港，货舱必须进行清洗和做好接收货物的准备，如果合同规定，货舱在递交装卸准备就绪通知书前必须经过有关当局的检验和认可。

2.2.2.1 Seaworthiness

2.2.2.1 适航

The vessel must of course be seaworthy. But it seems she need not be seaworthy in the sense of being ready and able to sail to the open sea, unless of course, she cannot even shift to the loading or discharging berth designated and/or safely to load or to discharge cargo. Therefore the vessel is perfectly entitled to tender notice of readiness, and have laytime commenced while simultaneously effecting repairs to the main or auxiliary engines, or having bunker supplied in preparation for sailing after cargo work.

船舶当然必须适航。但似乎不需要与能够航行于公海所要求的适航的意义相同，当然，除非它甚至不能移泊到指定的装卸泊位安全地装货或卸货。因此，该船完全有权递交装卸准备就绪通知书，在装卸时间开始的同时进行主机或辅机维修，或者在货物作业后添加燃油、做好航行准备。

2.2.2.2 Cargo Hold's Inspection

2.2.2.2 货舱检查

The ship must be completely ready in all her holds to afford the charterers complete control of every portion of the ship available for cargo. Unless there is an express provision in the charter party that notice of readiness may not be tendered until after inspection by the charterer's inspector or other relevant authority, then if the vessel is in all respects ready to load and all that is required is a routine inspection of holds in which nothing is found to cause delay for the loading, such inspection is a mere idle formality and not a condition precedent to the ability to tender notice of readiness and commencement of laytime.

船舶货舱必须完全准备就绪，使租船人能够对船舶所有可用于装载货物的区域行使完全控制权。除非租船合同中存在明确条款，规定"需经租船人检验员或其他相关机构检验后，方可递交装卸准备就绪通知书"，否则，若船舶在各方面均已具备装货条件，仅剩租船人对货舱的常规检验（且该检验未发现任何可能导致装货延误的问题），则此类检验仅属无实际意义的形式，而非"递交装卸准备就绪通知书"及"起算装卸时间"的前提条件。

2.2.2.3 Cargo Gears

2.2.2.3 货物吊具

It appears that the rule for readiness to load or to discharge applicable to cargo gear is not as stringent as the rule for cargo space. The vessel is ready to tender the notice of readiness if the facts reveal that the loading or discharging method does not require the use of the ship's gears or shore cranes could be readily employed.

准备就绪的规则对船舶装卸设备的要求不像对货舱那样严格。如果事实表明，装卸方法不需要使用船上吊具或岸上起重机可随时使用时，则船舶被认为处于就绪状态，可以递交装卸准备就绪通知书。

【Case】The vessel, Demosthenes, arrived at Alexandria on May 26, 1983, and tendered notice of readiness. It was rejected on the ground that the vessel did not have the necessary vacuators for the discharging according to Clause 18 which stated that the shipowner had to supply sufficient vacuators and consequently the vessel was not considered ready for discharge. To the shipowner, it looked like the charterer was finding any excuse to decline the notice of readiness to avoid laytime from commencing, when it was known there would be a prolonged delay in berthing. So the shipowner was forced to take precautions to make the notice of readiness mature just in case. Three vacuators were arranged to be put on board two days later on May 29, and another three were put on board on June 15, enabling the master to re-tender a second notice of readiness on June 17, without prejudice to the earlier one. The vessel eventually berthed on July 12. The shipowner claimed demurrage. The charterer resisted, contending the vessel was not ready without vacuators. The Judge held that the vacuators were essential equipment that was to emerge from the shore when the operation of discharge was to commence; the vessel as a vessel was ready. Therefore the notice of readiness on arrival in Alexandria was a valid notice of readiness.

【案例】"Demosthenes" 号船在1983年5月26日抵达亚历山大港并递交装卸准备就绪通知书，但被拒绝，理由是根据第18条的规定该船没有卸货所必需的吸粮机，因此，该船被认为没有做好卸货的准备。对于船舶出租人来说，看上去似乎承租人知道靠泊会拖延，所以寻找借口拒绝接收通知书以避免开始计算装卸时间。因此，为了以防万一，船舶出租人被迫采取预防措施使通知书有效。两天后，5月29日，3个吸粮机被安排放在船上，6月15日另外3个吸粮机被安排放在船上，船长于6月17日递交第二份通知书并表明不影响较早的通知书。7月12日该船最终靠泊。船舶出租人索赔滞期费。承租人坚持船舶没有吸粮机就是没有准备就绪。法官认为，当卸货作业开始时，作为主要卸货设备的吸粮机出现在岸上时，该船作为一个船舶是准备就绪的。因此，抵达亚历山大港的通知书是一个有效的通知书。

2.3 Notice of Readiness
2.3 装卸准备就绪通知书

Notice of Readiness (NOR) shall mean the notice to the charterer, shipper, receiver or other person as required by the charter party that the vessel has arrived at the port or berth, as the case may be, and is ready to load or discharge.

递交装卸准备就绪通知书（NOR）是船舶抵达合同规定的港口或泊位后，船长或其代理人向承租人、托运人、收货人或租船合同规定的其他人发出本船已在各个方面准备就绪等待装卸货物的通知。

2.3.1 Valid Notice of Readiness

2.3.1 有效的装卸准备就绪通知书

Notice of Readiness can be given orally but usually, a written form is used. It is an important function of a port agent to assist a ship's master in tendering notice of a ship's arrival and also to ensure that shippers/receivers officially "accept" the vessel's notice of readiness, usually accomplished usually by signing and timing acceptance on the notice form, although many shippers/receivers or charterers' nominated port agents, will "accept subject to charter party terms and conditions".

装卸准备就绪通知书可以以口头形式但通常采用书面形式递交。当船舶抵达时，协助船长递交通知书并确保托运人/收货人正式"接收"装卸准备就绪通知书是船舶港口代理的一个重要的职能，通常，托运人/收货人会在通知书上签字并注明接收的时间，尽管许多托运人/

收货人或承租人指定的港口代理人会"在租船合同条款范围内接收"。

It should be noted that the giving of a notice of readiness is an essential element in the laytime process. Furthermore, a ship's master or agent must have tendered a notice of readiness, in accordance with the contract requirements (e.g. within office hours, Mondays to Fridays). It is not however conclusive proof that the ship is ready. Since the master gives the notice of readiness it is in truth only his opinion that the ship is ready. On final inspection, the charterer may not agree and refuse to accept the notice of readiness.

应该注意的是，装卸准备就绪通知书的递交是装卸时间进程的重要因素。此外，船长或代理人必须按照合同的要求递交装卸准备就绪通知书（如在办公时间，星期一至星期五）。这不能作为船舶已准备就绪最终证明。船长递交装卸准备就绪通知书，只是他认为该船已经准备就绪。在最后检查时，承租人可能不同意并拒绝接受装卸准备就绪通知书。

A notice of readiness is not valid unless it indicates that the vessel is ready to load or discharge as the case may be, at the time at which it is given. It is insufficient if the notice merely indicates that she will be ready at a future time. Also if a notice of readiness is invalid when the ship is not ready, the shipowner needs to tender a second notice of readiness when the ship is ready.

除非船舶在递交装卸准备就绪通知书时已准备就绪，否则递交的通知书是无效的。如果通知书只是表明它将在未来的时间做好准备是不够的。另外，如果该船还没有准备好，准备就绪通知书无效，当船准备好了，船舶出租人需要递交第二份装卸准备就绪通知书。

【Case】The Mexico I had been chartered to carry 5,000 tons of bagged maize from Argentina to Angola. It was a part cargo and the shipowner was expressly given the right to complete the cargo with other lawful merchandise. The vessel did load other cargo at Santos after loading the 5,000 tons of bagged maize at Necochea. The vessel arrived at Luanda, Angola, and gave notice of readiness on January 20, 1985. However, it was not until February 6, 1985, that the over stowed cargo was cleared and the maize cargo became accessible. It was even later February 19, 1985, before a start was made on unloading the bagged maize.

【案例】"Mexico I"号船舶被租用装运5 000吨袋装玉米从阿根廷到安哥拉。这是部分货物，船舶出租人被赋予装载其他合法货物的权利以达到船舶的满载。船舶在内科切阿港装载5 000吨袋装玉米后又在桑托斯港装载其他货物。船舶抵达安哥拉的罗安达港后，于1985年1月20日递交了装卸准备就绪通知书。然而，直到1985年2月6日，压在玉米货物上面的货物才清理完毕。直到1985年2月19日玉米货物才开始卸载。

The arbitration was in favor of the shipowner for the "bad" notice of readiness tendered on January 20 became "effective" or "revived" when the maize cargo was fully accessible on February 6. The charterer appealed to the court. In upholding the award in the shipowner's favor, the court said that the facts of the particular case show that the charterer no longer has the right to insist upon a further notice of readiness being given. The correct conclusion in law is that the notice became effective at 1025 on February 6. The charterer took the matter further to the Court of Appeal. It was held to be wrong insofar as it suggested that when a notice of readiness was given before the vessel was ready, no further notice of readiness was required. The notion that the invalid notice of readiness became inchoate and automatically became effective without further notice at the moment when the ship was ready, was rejected. As a result, the charterer's appeal was allowed and the laytime started to count, not from the moment of the invalid notice of readiness on January 20, 1985, not from the time the vessel was ready physically and cleared of overstowed cargo on February 6, 1985, but from the moment of actual discharge given later, at 1130 on February 19, 1985.

仲裁庭作出了有利于船舶出租人的裁决，认为当2月6日玉米货物可以卸货时，1月20日递交的"不成熟"装卸准备就绪通知书"有效"或"复活"。承租人上诉至法院。在支持有利于船舶出租人的裁决中，法院认为，这个案子的事实表明，承租人不再有权利坚持要第二份准备就绪通知书。法律上的正确结论是，通知书在2月6日10点25分变为有效。承租人将此案诉至上诉法院。上诉法院判决：到目前为止，认为船舶在事实准备就绪前递交装卸准备就绪通知书而无须再递交另一份通知书是错误的。法院拒绝了当船舶实际上准备就绪而无须递交第二份通知书，无效的通知书自动生效的观点。结论为，接受承租人的上诉，装卸时间既不是从1月20日递交无效装卸准备就绪通知书时起算，也不是从2月6日压在玉米货物上面的货物清理完毕准备就绪时起算，而是从2月19日11点30分实际卸货时开始起算。

In January 2002, the High Court of London decided a case, *The Mass Glory*, which dealt with the commencement of laytime and invalid notices with reference to *The Happy Day*, and previous judgments. It was held that it should now have been reaffirmed that an invalid notice of readiness cannot and will not start the laytime clock ticking unless in the event of an express agreement between shipowners and charterers to the contrary, or waiver/estoppel.

2002年1月，伦敦高等法院就The Mass Glory一案中涉及装卸时间开始和无效的通知书问题，参照The Happy Day和先前的案例作出判决。现在应该再次确认无效的通知书是不能够起算装卸时间的，除非船舶出租人和承租人有明确的规定或放弃/禁止翻供。

2.3.2 Arrival Before Laydays

2.3.2 受载期前抵达

Laydays refer to the period when the chartered vessel shall arrive at the port of loading and be ready for the loading of cargo. Laydays could also be comprehended as the period during which the chartered vessel could arrive in the port of loading, either on the first day or on the final day of it, and she should also be ready for the loading of the cargo.

受载期是指租船合同约定的船舶应到达约定的装货港，并做好装货准备的期限。受载期可以概括为一段时间，即已租船舶应到达装货港并做好装货准备，无论是受载期的第一天还是最后一天。

There is nothing to prevent a vessel that arrives before her laydays are due to start from giving notice of readiness. From a legal viewpoint, laytime will start to count in accordance with the relevant terms of the charter party. However, the period between then and the point at which the agreed laydays commence will be excluded time under the charter party terms.

船舶在受载期开始前抵达，仍可提交装卸准备就绪通知书。从法律角度看，装卸时间将按合同相关条款规定起算，但从提交通知书至受载期开始的期间，属于合同约定的除外时间。

There are advantages for the shipowners when giving notice before laydays, particularly in the dry cargo trades. This is because dry cargo charters usually require notice to be given during office hours with laytime starting to commence at the beginning of the next work period following. By giving notice before laydays it is likely that the time allowed to the charterer will have passed and that therefore time will start to count at the start of hours on the first layday. Had the notice been given during office hours on the first layday time would only have started to count at 1300 or 1400 on that day.

船舶出租人在受载期之前递交通知书是有好处的，特别是在干散货运输中。这是因为在干散货运输中通常通知书被要求在办公时间内递交，装卸时间在下一个工作日开始起算。在受载期之前递交通知书，允许承租人扣除的时间已过去，因此时间将从受载期的第一天凌晨开始。如果该通知书在受载期的第一天办公时间递交，装卸时间要等到当天13点或14点起算。

In order to avoid such situations charterers will try to include clauses expressly prohibiting the presentation of the notice of readiness before the commencement of laydays.

为了避免这种情况，承租人尝试将明确禁止在受载期前递交装卸准备就绪通知书加入条文。

3. Interruptions of Laytime
3. 装卸时间中断

Once laytime has commenced, unless a vessel's cargo-handling equipment breaks down or it is due to the shipowner's fault, it will continue unhindered until the completion of cargo operations or until laytime expires or demurrage commences. Nevertheless, contracts frequently include express clauses interrupting laytime in the event of Sundays and holidays, shifts to and between anchorages/berths, strikes, bad weather, breakdowns, etc.

一旦装卸时间开始起算，除非船舶货物装卸设备发生故障或因船舶出租人的过错，它将持续不受阻碍直至货物装卸作业完成，或直至装卸时间届满或滞期开始。然而，合同常常有明示规定的条款来中断装卸时间，如星期日和节假日、于锚地/泊位之间移泊、罢工、不良天气、故障等。

3.1 Sundays and Holidays
3.1 星期日和节假日

If Sundays and holidays are to interrupt laytime, the contract can be said to be on "SHEX" terms (Sundays and Holidays Excepted). Should Sundays and holidays count as laytime, the contract can be said to be based on "SHINC" (Sundays and Holidays Included). In these more enlightened times many workers are allowed two full days off on Saturdays and Sundays and so the terms "SHEX" and "SHINC" are sometimes amended to "SSHEX" and "SSHINC" indicating that Saturday also is to be included in the relevant term.

如果星期日及节假日中断装卸时间，则合同使用"星期日和节假日除外"术语。星期日和节假日如计算在装卸时间中，合同可以订立"星期日和节假日包括在内"术语。现今，许多工人允许在星期六及星期日两天休息，所以"星期日和节假日除外"术语和"星期日和节假日包括在内"术语有时修订为"星期六、星期日和节假日除外"和"星期六、星期日和节假日包括在内"，表明周六也将包括在相关术语内。

Normally a charter party will specify the actual time before a holiday or a Sunday that laytime is to be suspended—e.g. "from 1800 hours on the day preceding a Holiday". If no such time is specified, laytime is usually suspended from midnight on the day preceding a holiday.

租船合同通常规定，节假日或星期日前一天的一段时间不计入装卸时间，例如："节假日前一天的18点之后"。如果没有这样的时间规定，装卸时间通常是从节假日前一天午夜中断。

A charter party will normally specify the actual time of resumption of laytime following a holiday or Sunday—e. g. 0700 hours Monday. If no such time is specified, laytime will usually recommence at 0001 hours on the day following a holiday or Sunday.

租船合同通常规定，节假日或星期日后一天的一段时间不计入装卸时间，例如："星期一7点之前"。如果没有这样的时间规定，装卸时间通常会在节假日或星期日后一天的凌晨重新起算。

If cargo work is performed during an excepted period, laytime will not normally count, unless the contract allows it to—e. g. "time not to count during holidays and Sundays, unless used". Alternatively, a contract may emphasize that "time used during holidays and Sundays is not to count, even if used. Occasionally, an agreement is reached that 'used to count'". It may also be agreed that the period between the tender of the notice of readiness and the commencement of laytime may count as laytime if "used".

如果货物作业是在除外时间内进行的，除非合同允许，通常不会计入装卸时间，例如："节假日及星期日不计入装卸时间，除非已使用"。另外，合同可能会强调"即使在节假日及星期日进行了作业，该时间也不计入"。有时，也会约定"按实际使用的时间计入"。双方还可能约定，若"已使用"，则从装卸准备就绪通知书提交至装卸时间开始的期间可计入装卸时间。

3.2 Shifting Between Anchorages/Berths
3.2 于锚地/泊位之间移泊

It is common practice for contract wording to permit loading/discharging at more than one berth or anchorage at each port. Consequently, time spent shifting between berths/anchorages is normally taken to be for the shipowner's account. However, should the agreed number of berths/anchorages be exceeded, it becomes reasonable that the shifting time involved should count as laytime and that the expenses involved—e.g. towage and pilotage—should also be for the account of the charterers. In almost all trades if the vessel has anchored off upon arrival either to wait for suitable tides or a free berth the time taken to shift to the berth is excluded from laytime.

合同通常规定允许每个港口在一个以上的泊位或锚地装载。因此，于锚地/泊位之间移泊的时间通常由船舶出租人承担。但是，如果超出规定的泊位或锚地数量，则移泊时间应合理地计算为装卸时间，而且所涉及的开支，例如拖船和引航费也应该由承租人承担。几乎在所有航运业务中，如果船舶到达时在外锚泊或是等待潮水或泊位，移泊时间是排除在装卸时间以外的。

3.3 Strikes
3.3 罢工

Strikes shall mean concerted industrial action by workmen causing a complete stoppage of their work which directly interferes with the working of the vessel. Refusal to work overtime, go-slow, or work to rule and comparable actions not causing a complete stoppage shall not be considered a strike. A strike shall be understood to exclude its consequences when it has ended, such as congestion in the port or effects upon the means of transportation bringing or taking the cargo to or from the port. There is nearly always an express clause in a contract to the effect that delays due to shore strikes are not to count as laytime.

罢工是指行业工人的联合行为导致全面停工，直接影响船舶作业。拒绝加班、怠工或变相怠工以及类似未导致全面停工的行动，不视为罢工。罢工应被理解为排除罢工结束的后果，例如港口的拥挤，或影响向港口里或外运送货物的运送方式。合同几乎总是有一个明确条款，即岸上罢工不计为装卸时间。

3.4 Bad Weather
3.4 不良天气

Clauses in a shipping contract referring to bad weather interruptions of laytime could be divided into four types—weather working day, weather working day of 24 hours, weather working day of 24 consecutive hours; weather permitting.

运输合同条款中关于不良天气中断装卸时间的计算可分为四类，即"晴天工作日"、"24小时晴天工作日"、"连续24小时晴天工作日"和"天气许可工作日"。

3.4.1 Weather Working Day
3.4.1 晴天工作日

According to the *Laytime Definitions for Charter Parties 2013*, "Weather Working Day" shall mean a working day or part of a working day during which it is, or if the vessel is still waiting for her turn, it would be possible to load/discharge the cargo without interruption due to the weather. If such interruption occurs (or would have occurred if work had been in progress), there shall be excluded from the laytime a period calculated by reference to the ratio which the duration of the interruption bears to the time which would have or could have been worked but for the interruption.

根据《2013租船合同装卸时间定义》，晴天工作日是指一个工作日或工作日的一部分，在这段时间内船舶可以在（船舶可能在等待靠泊时）没有天气妨碍的情况下进行装卸货作业。如果天气妨碍发生，或者装卸货作业已经进行而天气妨碍了作业，则装卸时间应参照妨碍持续时间与无妨碍时的正常工作时间之比例扣减。

In cases of "weather working day", laytime does not count during periods of bad weather that interrupt loading or discharging nor does laytime count when bad weather occurs during a working day even if, had the weather been fine, no attempt would have been made to work. "Weather working day" describes a type of working day. It does not matter whether the vessel was working or not.

在"晴天工作日"下，影响装卸的不良天气时间不计入装卸时间，而且即使工作日中出现不良天气（即便当时天气状况是良好的，也不会尝试进行装卸作业时），该不良天气导致的停歇时间也不计入装卸时间。"晴天工作日"描述的是工作日的类型，不论船舶实际工作与否。

It follows, therefore, that even if a ship is not actually on the loading or discharging berth, for example, because it is occupied by another ship, if time has started to run and bad weather occurs during a working day, that time will not count against charterers as laytime.

因此，即使船舶未在装货或卸货泊位上，如由于泊位被另外一条船舶占用，若装卸时间已开始起算，天气不良的工作日仍可以不计入装卸时间。

The term "weather working day" on its own without qualification is indeed affected by the number of hours worked in a port. Should bad weather occur outside working periods in normal, non-working, and otherwise idle time, laytime will not be affected. However, if bad weather occurs during normal working time, even if the vessel was idle at the time, laytime will be interrupted and the degree of interruption has to be determined by apportioning working time in a port against a 24-hour day.

"晴天工作日"一词本身未加任何修饰的话，会受到港口实际工作小时数的影响。如果不良天气是在正常工作时间以外的非工作日和其他空闲时间发生的，装卸时间不会受到影响。但是，如果在正常工作时间内出现不良天气，即使该船在此期间空闲，装卸时间仍将中断，中断的时间以港口工作时间与24小时之比例计算。

Thus assuming port labor works a 12-hour day, from 0700 hours until 1900 hours: the laytime used is calculated in Table 2.

因此，假设港口工作时间每天12个小时，从上午7时至19时，装卸时间为表2所示。

Table 2　Laytime Expression

Day	Work Status	Time Interval (Start/End)	Equivalent Working Days	Daily Hours
Day 1	Worked	0700/1900	1.00 day	24 hours
Day 2	Worked Rain	0700/1900 2200/2400	1.00 day	24 hours
Day 3	Rain	0001/2400	0.00 day	00 hours
Day 4	Rain	0700/1900	0.00 day	00 hours
Day 5	Worked Rain	0700/1300 1300/1900	0.50 day	12 hours
Day 6	Worked Rain	0700/1000 1000/1900	0.25 day	06 hours
Day 7	Rain Worked	0700/1000 1000/1900	0.75 day	18 hours

表2　装卸时间表述

天数	工作状态	时间区间（起止）	折算工作天数	当日小时数
第1天	工作	0700/1900	1.00天	24小时
第2天	工作 下雨	0700/1900 2200/2400	1.00天	24小时
第3天	下雨	0001/2400	0.00天	00小时
第4天	下雨	0700/1900	0.00天	00小时
第5天	工作 下雨	0700/1300 1300/1900	0.50天	12小时

天数	工作状态	时间区间（起止）	折算工作天数	当日小时数
第6天	工作 下雨	0700/1000 1000/1900	0.25天	06小时
第7天	下雨 工作	0700/1000 1000/1900	0.75天	18小时

3.4.2 Weather Working Day of 24 Hours

3.4.2 24小时晴天工作日

According to the *Laytime Definitions for Charter Parties 2013*, "Weather Working Day of 24 Hours" shall mean 24 hours made up of one or more working days during which it is or, if the vessel is still waiting for her turn, it would be possible to load/discharge the cargo without interruption due to the weather. If such interruption occurs (or would have occurred if work had been in progress), it shall be excluded from laytime for the actual period of such interruption.

根据《2013租船合同装卸时间定义》，24小时晴天工作日是指在由一个或多个工作日的工作时间加起来构成的24小时中，船舶可以在（船舶可能在等待靠泊时）没有天气妨碍的情况下进行装卸货作业。如果发生天气妨碍，或者装卸货作业已经进行而天气妨碍了作业，则实际妨碍的时间要从装卸时间中扣除。

This is an artificial day made up of twenty-four working hours. An eight-hour working day is equal to three calendar days' laytime but with laytime suspended for stoppages due to bad weather in working hours or in working hours when work was contemplated.

这是由24个工作小时构成的一个假设日。一个8小时工作的工作日相当于三个日历日装卸时间。如果在工作小时中出现不良天气妨碍工作，则实际妨碍的时间要从装卸时间中扣除。

3.4.3 Weather Working Day of 24 Consecutive Hours

3.4.3 连续24小时晴天工作日

According to the *Laytime Definitions for Charter Parties 2013*, "Weather Working Day of 24 Consecutive Hours" shall mean a working day or part of a working day of 24 consecutive hours during which it is or, if the vessel is still waiting for her turn, it would be possible to load/discharge the cargo without interruption due to the weather. If such interruption occurs (or would have occurred if work had been in progress), there shall be excluded from the laytime the period during which the weather interrupted or would have interrupted work.

根据《2013租船合同装卸时间定义》，连续24小时晴天工作日是指在一个连续24小时的工作日或工作日的一部分中，船舶可以在（船舶可能在等待靠泊时）没有天气妨碍的情况下进行装卸货作业。如果发生天气妨碍，或者装卸货作业已经进行而天气妨碍了作业，则实际妨碍的时间要从装卸时间中扣除。

3.4.4 Weather Permitting (Working Day)

3.4.4 天气许可工作日

According to the *Laytime Definitions for Charter Parties 2013*, "Weather Permitting (Working

Day)" has the same meaning and interpretation as "Weather Working Day of 24 Consecutive Hours".

根据《2013租船合同装卸时间定义》，"天气许可工作日"和"连续24小时晴天工作日"意思相同。

3.5 Breakdown
3.5 故障

It is reasonable that if a vessel's gear is being used and it breaks down, laytime should not continue during the period of breakdown. It may be that, for example, one crane out of four has broken down, and, in such a case, apportionment of the degree of loss must be carried out. In that relatively simple example, laytime would continue at a rate of 75% until the crane is repaired.

如果正在使用的船舶吊具发生故障，装卸时间不应在故障期继续计算，这是合理的。它可能是，例如，4个起重机有1个发生故障，在这种情况下，装卸时间按比例给予扣除。在这个相对简单的例子中，装卸时间将以75%的比例继续计算，直到起重机修复完毕。

4. Laytime Calculation
4. 装卸时间的计算

The method for laytime calculation should in reality be divided into separate laytime and total laytime. The latter could further be subdivided into reversible laytime and average laytime.

装卸时间的计算方法在实际中可分成装卸时间分别计算和装卸时间统算。装卸时间统算又可进一步分为可调节装卸时间和平均计算装卸时间。

4.1 Separate Laytime
4.1 装卸时间分别计算

If nothing is specifically mentioned in the contract and where loading and discharging port laytime allowances are separately assessed, it can be taken that laytime is "normal" or "non-reversible".

如果航次租船合同没有特别规定，对装货港和卸货港的装卸时间是分别给予单独核算的，则可以认为装卸时间为"正常装卸时间"或"不可调节装卸时间"。

Laytime for loading port(s) and for discharging port(s) is assessed entirely separately and it is possible even to calculate, claim, negotiate, and settle the load port(s) dispatch/demurrage sums before even a vessel has reached her discharge port(s).

装货港和卸货港的装卸时间是完全分别计算的，甚至在船舶抵达卸货港前，都有可能计算、索赔、洽谈和结算装货港的速遣费或滞期费数额。

4.2 Reversible Laytime
4.2 可调节装卸时间

"Reversible laytime" shall mean an option given to the charterer to add together the time allowed for loading and discharging. Where the option is exercised the effect is the same as the total time being specified to cover both operations.

可调节装卸时间是指给承租人选择将约定的装货时间和卸货时间加在一起计算的权利。行使这种权利如同规定装卸时间合并计算。

Where allowance for both the loading and discharging ports is added and calculated together, either the contract may openly be on "reversible" terms without actually stating so—e.g. 7 days, "all purposes" or "16 total days"—or there may be an express clause giving the charterers the right or the option to apply reversible conditions if they so wish. In other words, if they calculate it to be in their favor to do so. Thus any laytime saved from the loading ports can be carried forward and added to the laytime allowed at the port(s) of discharge.

凡允许装货港和卸货港时间加在一起并且合并计算，租船合同可以订立可调节装卸时间而不用表述如共用7天或总共16天；或者如果他们愿意的话，明确给予承租人权利来选择适用。也就是说，如果他们认为此种计算方法对他们有利，他们就可以这么做。因此，任何从装货港节省的装卸时间可添加到卸货港的装卸时间中。

4.3 Average Laytime
4.3 平均计算装卸时间

"Average laytime" shall mean that separate calculations are to be made for loading and discharging and that any time saved in one operation is to be set off against any excess time used in the other.

"平均计算装卸时间"是指分别计算装货时间和卸货时间，用一个作业中节省的时间抵消另一作业中超出的时间。

This arises where separate calculations are performed for the loading and the discharging ports, with the final results for each being combined to assess what is finally due—e.g. 2 days' demurrage at the load port would be canceled out by 2 days, dispatch at the discharge port, even though the daily value of demurrage may be twice that of dispatch money.

装卸港口分别计算，最终结果相互抵销，例如2天在装货港滞期将被2天在卸货港的速遣抵消，即使滞期费是速遣费的两倍。

At first sight, it may appear there is no difference between the application of reversible and average laytime. Differences can arise and, with the same basic facts, it is possible to reach three different results by applying each of the above alternatives.

乍看，可调节装卸时间与平均计算装卸时间之间可能会没有区别。但事实上两者会出现不同，在相同的基本事实下，选择三种不同的计算方法可能得到三种不同的结果。

4.4 Example of Laytime Calculation
4.4 装卸时间计算举例

The charter party stipulated "5WWDSHEX for loading and 5WWDSHEX for discharging, once on demurrage, always on demurrage, demurrage rate USD 5000." Assumed that the statement of facts is as shown in Table 3:

租船合同规定："装卸港口各为'5个晴天工作日，星期日、节假日除外'，一旦滞期永远滞期，滞期费5 000美元"。假定事实记录如表3所示：

Table 3 Statement of Facts

Load port 5WWDSHEX		Discharge port 5WWDSHEX	
Date (Day/Weekday)	Operation status	Date (Day/Weekday)	Operation status
1/4Mon.	loading	17/4Wed.	discharge
2/4Tue.	loading	18/4Thu.	discharge
3/4Wed.	loading	19/4Fri.	discharge
4/4Thu.	loading	20/4Sat.	raining
5/4Fri.	loading	21/4Sun.	stoppage
6/4Sat.	raining	22/4Mon.	raining
7/4Sun.	stoppage	23/4Tue.	raining
8/4Mon.	loading	24/4Wed.	discharge completed
9/4Tue.	loading completed		

表3 装卸记录

装货港5个晴天工作日，星期日、节假日除外		卸货港5个晴天工作日，星期日、节假日除外	
日期（日/星期）	作业状态	日期（日/星期）	作业状态
1/4周一	装货	17/4周三	卸货
2/4周二	装货	18/4周四	卸货
3/4周三	装货	19/4周五	卸货
4/4周四	装货	20/4周六	下雨
5/4周五	装货	21/4周日	停工
6/4周六	下雨	22/4周一	下雨
7/4周日	停工	23/4周二	下雨
8/4周一	装货	24/4周三	卸货完毕
9/4周二	装货完毕		

Based on the separate laytime calculation, there were 4 days of demurrage at the loading port and 1 day of dispatch at the discharging port. The total demurrage should be USD 17,500 (4 days × 5,000−1 day×2,500). Based on the reversible laytime calculation, there were total 5 days of demurrage. Therefore the total demurrage should be USD 25,000. If under the average laytime, the total demurrage time would be 3 days (4 days demurrage−1 day dispatch), so the demurrage should be USD 15,000 (3 days ×5,000).

按照装卸时间分别计算，装货港为4天滞期，卸货港为1天速遣。滞期费总额为17 500美元（4天×5 000 − 1天×2 500）。按照可调节装卸时间计算，共滞期5天。因此，滞期费总额为25 000美元。如果采用平均计算装卸时间，滞期总时间为3天（4天-1天），所以滞期费应该是15 000美元（3天×5 000）。

If we suppose that the vessel finished loading just one day before the above example, the result would also be different. As shown in Table 4.

如果假设船舶在装货港提前1天完成装货，结果又不同。如表4所示。

Table 4   Statement of Facts

Load port 5WWDSHEX		Discharge port 5WWDSHEX	
Date (Day/Weekday)	Operation status	Date (Day/Weekday)	Operation status
1/4Mon.	loading	17/4Wed.	discharge
2/4Tue.	loading	18/4Thu.	discharge
3/4Wed.	loading	19/4Fri.	discharge
4/4Thu.	loading	20/4Sat.	raining
5/4Fri.	loading	21/4Sun.	stoppage
6/4Sat.	raining	22/4Mon.	raining
7/4Sun.	stoppage	23/4Tue.	raining
8/4Mon.	loading completed	24/4Wed.	discharge completed

表4   装卸记录

装货港5个晴天工作日，星期日、节假日除外		卸货港5个晴天工作日，星期日、节假日除外	
日期（日/星期）	作业状态	日期（日/星期）	作业状态
1/4周一	装货	17/4周三	卸货
2/4周二	装货	18/4周四	卸货
3/4周三	装货	19/4周五	卸货
4/4周四	装货	20/4周六	下雨
5/4周五	装货	21/4周日	停工
6/4周六	装货	22/4周一	下雨
7/4周日	停工	23/4周二	下雨
8/4周一	装货完毕	24/4周三	卸货完毕

Based on the separate laytime calculation, there were 3 days of demurrage at the loading port and 1 day of dispatch at the discharging port. The total demurrage should be USD 12,500 (3 days × 5,000−1 day×2,500). Based on the reversible laytime calculation, there was a total of zero days on demurrage. If under the average laytime, the total demurrage time would be 2 days (3 days demurrage−1 day dispatch), so the demurrage should be USD 10,000 (2 days×5,000).

按照装卸时间分别计算，装货港为3天滞期和卸货港为1天速遣。滞期费总额为12 500美元（3天×5 000−1天×2 500）。按照可调节装卸时间计算，没有滞期。如果采用平均计算装卸时间，滞期总时间为2天（3天−1天），所以滞期费应该是10 000美元（2天×5 000）。

5. Provision of Laytime Clause Printed in Gencon Form 1994
5. 1994年金康合同范本装卸时间条款的规定

5.1 Separate Laytime for Loading and Discharging
5.1 装货和卸货分别计算时间

The cargo shall be loaded within the number of running days/hours as indicated in Box 16, weather permitting, Sundays and holidays excepted, unless used, in which event time used shall count.

如果天气许可，货物应在第16栏规定的连续天/小时数内装完，星期日和节假日除外，除非已使用，只计算实际使用的时间。

The cargo shall be discharged within the number of running days/hours as indicated in Box 16, weather permitting, Sundays and holidays excepted, unless used, in which event time used shall count.

如果天气许可，货物应在第16栏规定的连续天/小时数内卸完，星期日和节假日除外，除非已使用，只计算实际使用的时间。

5.2 Total Laytime for Loading and Discharging
5.2 装货和卸货合并计算时间

The cargo shall be loaded and discharged within the number of total running days/hours as indicated in Box 16, weather permitting, Sundays and holidays excepted, unless used, in which event time used shall count.

如果天气许可，货物应在第16栏规定的总的连续天/小时数内装卸完毕，星期日和节假日除外，除非已使用，只计算实际使用的时间。

5.3 Commencement of Laytime
5.3 装卸时间的起算

Laytime for loading and discharging shall commence at 1300 hours, if notice of readiness is given up to and including 1200 hours, and at 0600 hours the next working day if notice is given during office hours after 1200 hours. Notice of readiness at the loading port shall be given to the shippers named in Box 17 or if not named, to the charterers or their agents named in Box 18. Notice of readiness at the discharging port shall be given to the receivers or, if not known, to the charterers or their agents named in Box 19.

如装卸准备就绪通知书在中午12时之前（包括12时）递交，装卸时间从13时起算；如通知书在12时以后递交，装卸时间从下一个工作日的上午6时起算。在装货港，通知书应递交给第17栏中规定的托运人。如未指定，则递交给18栏中的承租人或其代理。在卸货港，通知书应递交给收货人，如未指定，则递交给19栏中的承租人或其代理。

If the loading/discharging berth is not available on the vessel's arrival at or off the port of loading/discharging, the vessel shall be entitled to give notice of readiness within ordinary office hours on arrival there, whether in free pratique or not, whether customs cleared or not. Laytime or time on demurrage shall then count as if she were in berth and in all respects ready for loading and/or discharging provided that the master warrants that she is in fact ready in all respects. Time used in moving from the place of waiting to the loading/discharging berth shall not count as laytime.

船舶到达装/卸港而无泊位，无论检疫通过与否，无论清关与否，有权在到达后在办公时间内递交通知书。装卸时间或滞期时间开始计算，犹如已靠泊并在各方面做好装/卸准备一样，但船长应保证船舶事实上在各方面均准备完毕。从等泊位置移到装/卸泊位的时间不计入装卸时间。

If after inspection, the vessel is found not to be ready in all respects to load/discharge, time lost after the discovery thereof until the vessel is again ready to load/discharge shall not count as laytime. Time used before commencement of laytime shall count.

如经检验发现船舶未准备就绪，从发现之时起至再次准备就绪的时间不得计入装卸时间。装卸时间起算前已实际使用的时间计为装卸时间。

UNIT 6　DEMURRAGE AND DISPATCH MONEY
第六单元　滞期费和速遣费

Demurrage and dispatch money are also very important in the voyage charter party. There may be considerable sums of money at stake, which will have a noticeable effect on a ship's profitability or a charterer's income. In this unit we mainly deal with this matter.

航次租船合同下，滞期费和速遣费也是非常重要的。这可能是相当大的一笔数额，直接影响船舶出租人的收益或者承租人的收入。本单元主要探讨此类问题。

1. Demurrage
1. 滞期费

According to *Laytime Definitions for Charter Parties 2013*, demurrage shall mean an agreed amount payable to the shipowner in respect of delay to the Vessel once the Laytime has expired, for which the shipowner is not responsible. Demurrage shall not be subject to exceptions that apply to Laytime unless specifically stated in the charter party.

根据《2013租船合同装卸时间定义》，滞期费是指不是由船舶出租人的责任所造成的，超过装卸时间的船舶因迟延而付给船舶出租人的约定金额。滞期不适用装卸时间的除外规定，除非租船合同中有特别规定。

1.1 Nature of Demurrage
1.1 滞期费性质

A demurrage clause is merely a clause providing for liquidated damages for a certain type of breach. It is presumably the parties' estimate of the loss of prospective freight which the shipowner is likely to suffer if his ship is detained beyond the laytime. An agreement to pay demurrage is normally treated as preventing the shipowner recovering from the charterer more than the agreed sum for the wrongful detention of his ship. Unless the demurrage period is fixed, the demurrage rate is applied not just for a reasonable time but for as long as the ship is detained under the contract. In such a case the shipowner is entitled to the demurrage rate and no more as compensation for detention.

滞期费条款本质上是针对某类违约行为约定违约金的条款。该条款通常被视为合同双方对以下损失的预估：若船舶在装卸时间之外被滞留，船舶出租人可能遭受的预期运费损失。

一般而言，约定支付滞期费的协议具有限制效力：对于船舶因不当滞留产生的损失，船舶出租人向承租人索赔的金额不得超过协议约定的滞期费总额。除非合同明确约定滞期期限，否则滞期费率的适用不受合理时间限制，而是覆盖船舶依据合同约定被滞留的全部期间。在此情况下，船舶出租人有权获得按滞期费率计算的赔偿，且该赔偿为船舶滞留损失的全部补偿（不得额外主张其他损失）。

Demurrage is intended to reflect the daily running cost of a vessel, including port bunker consumption and where applicable, a reasonable profit level. Shipping being a free market, however, and exposed to market forces and necessities, there may be occasions when shipowners accept low or negotiate high demurrage rates.

滞期费反映了船舶日常经营管理的成本，包括港口燃油消耗以及合理利润水平。然而航运业属于自由市场，受市场力量及实际需求影响，因此有时船舶出租人会接受较低的滞期费率，或通过洽谈争取较高的滞期费率。

1.2 Provision of Demurrage Clause Printed in Gencon Form 1994
1.2 1994年金康合同范本滞期费条款的规定

"Demurrage at the loading and discharging ports is payable by the charterers at the rate stated in Box 20 per day or pro rata for any part of a day. Demurrage shall fall due day by day and shall be payable upon receipt of the shipowners' invoice. In the event the demurrage is not paid as provided above, the shipowners shall give the charterers 96 running hours of written notice to rectify the failure. If the demurrage is not paid at the expiration of this time limit and if the vessel is in or at the loading port, the shipowners are entitled at any time to terminate the charter party and claim damages for any losses caused thereby."

"在装货港和卸货港产生的滞期费由承租人按第20栏中规定的每日费率支付，不足一日者按比例计算。滞期费按日并在收到船舶出租人的发票后支付。如未按上述规定支付，船舶出租人应给承租人在96小时内支付的书面通知，要求其纠正错误。如仍未在此期限内付清，且如船舶在装货港或卸货港，则船舶出租人有权在任何时候终止本租船合同并向承租人索赔由此引起的任何损失。"

To reflect current practice when making fixtures on the GENCON, the reference to ten running days on demurrage allowed to the charterers in the port of loading and discharging has been deleted. However, in the absence of a specific provision allowing the charterers to keep the vessel on demurrage for a limited period, the shipowners need to have an express right in the charter party to cancel the charter party in the event of outstanding payments of demurrage, as otherwise, they may find themselves in the position where they would have to keep the vessel waiting for cargo loading operations to start for a considerable time without being able to terminate the charter party. This would, in particular, appear to be a problem under English law when the shipowners are not able to cancel until there is a repudiation of the charter party.

在以金康合同为蓝本订立租船合同时，为了反映目前的实务做法，允许承租人在装货港和卸货港有10天滞期期限的规定已被删除。然而，在缺乏允许承租人将船舶滞期一段有限时间的具体规定的情况下，船舶出租人需要在租船合同中拥有一项明确权利，即在滞期费未支付时解除租船合同；否则，他们可能会陷入这样一种境地：不得不让船舶长时间地等待货物装载作业的开始，还无法解除租船合同。在英国法下这尤是一个问题，船舶出租人不能够取消合同，直到合同的解除情形出现。

Accordingly, to give the shipowners a legal remedy when these unfortunate situations occur, it is now expressly provided that if demurrage is not paid on the expiration of the time limit provided, i.e. 96 hours, the shipowners shall have a right to terminate the charter party and claim damages for any loss incurred thereby. It is to be noted, however, that the right to terminate the charter party applies to the loading port only and, for all practical purposes, depends on no cargo or part cargo having been loaded and no bill of lading having been issued transferring the rights to the cargo to a third party.

因此，当这些不幸的情况发生时，为了给船舶出租人法律救济，现在明确规定，如果滞期费未在限制期限到期时支付，即96小时，船舶出租人将有权终止合同，并对由此引起的任何损失要求赔偿。但是，应当指出的是，有权解除租船合同仅适用于装货港，并且就整个实务目的来说，其取决于没有任何货物或部分货物装载在船上以及未签发将货物转让第三方的提单。

1.3 Once on Demurrage, Always on Demurrage
1.3 一旦滞期，永远滞期

Once laytime has been fully used, demurrage should normally run continuously, night and day, weekends and working periods, with no interruptions until cargo work is completed unless the contract expressly provides otherwise—e.g. "shifting time from anchorage to berth not to count as laytime or as time on demurrage". Normally, however, laytime interruptions such as bad weather, weekends and holidays, will not interfere with demurrage time; it can usually be said that the much-used shipping expression "once on demurrage, always on demurrage" means what it says.

一旦装卸时间届满，滞期时间将连续计算，不论白天和黑夜、周末和工作期间，直到完成货物作业，除非合同另有明文规定，如"从锚地移泊时间不计为装卸时间或滞期时间"。通常情况下，诸如不良天气、周末和节假日等导致装卸时间中断的情形，并不会对滞期时间产生影响；常常使用的航运术语"一旦滞期，永远滞期"表述了此含义。

【Case】A vessel had been chartered under a voyage charter party, which contained a strike clause stating that the time for discharging should not count against the charterer during the continuance of a strike. The vessel began to discharge the cargo, but after the laytime had expired a strike took place which interrupted further unloading.

【案例】一艘船舶以航次租船合同方式出租，其中载有一条罢工条款，说明罢工时间不应该计入卸货时间。该船开始卸货，在装卸时间已经届满后，罢工的发生阻碍了进一步的卸货工作。

Held by the House of Lords, that the charterer could not rely on the strike clause, because it was not sufficiently clearly worded to have the effect of relieving the charterer from the payment of demurrage. Consequently, the charterer had to pay demurrage for the whole period after the laytime had expired.

英国最高法院上议院判决：承租人不能援引罢工条款，因为它没有以充分明确的措辞解除承租人支付滞期费的义务。因此，承租人必须支付装卸时间已经届满后的全部时间的滞期费。

【Case】A charter party stated: "Lightering if any, at discharging ports to be at the shipowner's risk and expense, and time used not to count as laytime. "It was held that once laytime had expired, the clause had no further application and the charterer was liable for the whole of the time used in lightening.

【案例】租船合同规定："如果在卸货港有减载的话，由船舶出租人承担风险和费用，使用时间不计算为装卸时间。"判决：一旦装卸时间已经届满，该条款不再进一步适用，承租人对减载的全部时间负责。

It should be noted that several standard charter party forms limit the time on demurrage to a certain number of days after which the shipowner will claim "damages for detention". If the time on demurrage exceeds the number of days contained in the clause the parties may agree to treat all the time as time on demurrage or claim "damages for detention".

应当指出的是，许多标准租船范本规定了一定的期限来限制滞期时间，过此期限之后，船舶出租人会要求赔偿"滞留损失"。假如滞期时间超过限制的滞期时间，当事人可以约定把所有的时间作为滞期时间，或者要求赔偿"滞留损失"。

1.4 Damages for Detention
1.4 滞留损失

If charterers fail to abide by the provisions of a contract and, as a result, permitted laytime is exceeded, shipowners are normally entitled to reimbursement for their loss, if any. One method of reimbursement could be by claiming "damages for detention", however, this could be a lengthy and costly legal exercise. Consequently, most parties to a shipping contract avoid the problem by negotiating a daily level of demurrage for the time spent more than the agreed laytime. The difference between demurrage and damages for detention is that demurrage is only paid for an agreed number of days and damages for detention are to be paid for further delay that takes place. So damages for detention become payable either: on the expiration of a reasonable time for loading or unloading when no laytimes are specified; or on the expiration of the fixed number of days for which demurrage has been stipulated.

如果承租人所用的实际装卸时间超过了合同规定的允许使用时间，承租人必须向船舶出租人支付因船舶发生滞期而遭受的损失。一种补偿的方式是提出"滞留损失赔偿请求"，但是这可能是一个耗时而成本高昂的法律程序。因此，大多数航运合同当事人通过洽谈，约定超出规定装卸时间按每天的滞期费率来支付赔偿以避免此问题。滞期费和滞留损失的区别是，滞期费按约定期限支付，而滞留损失则需支付超出规定天数的进一步的延误费用。因此，在没有规定装卸时间的情况下，滞留损失要么在超出合理的装货或卸货时间支付，要么在超过合同限定的滞期时间到期时支付。

It is rare to find a similar provision like Clause 7 in the Gencon Form 1976 limiting only to ten days on demurrage. Naturally, under such a provision, if the vessel continues to be delayed, the charterers will have to pay damages for detention beyond the ten days. It is only to be expected that this provision is no longer to be found in the new Gencon Form 1994.

很难找到与1976年金康合同范本第7条一样限制滞期时间为10天的类似规定。当然，在这样一个规定下，如果该船继续被延误，承租人要付出10天之后的对滞留损失的赔偿。新的1994年金康合同范本已没有该项规定。

1.5 Demurrage and Shipowner's Default
1.5 滞期费和船舶出租人过失

Once a vessel is on demurrage no exceptions will operate to prevent demurrage continuing to be payable unless the exceptions clause is worded to have that effect. One question is if due to the fault of the shipowner during the time of demurrage, does the charterer have an obligation to pay the demurrage for that period?

一旦船舶处于滞期，没有除外事项可以停止滞期时间的继续计算，除非除外条款清楚地规定使其有这样的效果。问题是，如果由于船舶出租人在滞期时间内有过失，承租人是否有支付该期间的滞期费的义务？

【Case】The chartered vessel duly arrived at the discharge port. Laytime expired while she was still awaiting berth and demurrage had begun to accrue under the charter party. When a berth became available and one pilot boarded in order to take the vessel into that berth. About 60 minutes later she grounded and remained aground for 5 days. The shipowner claimed that demurrage continued to accrue during this period. The charterer successfully disputed this claim in the arbitration on the ground that the grounding was due to default, consisting of negligent navigation or management of shipowners or those for whom they were responsible, and that the charterer was therefore excused the obligation to pay demurrage during the period the vessel was a ground.

【案例】船舶抵达卸货港。装卸时间届满时，它仍在等待泊位，滞期时间根据租船合同开始产生。当泊位可用时，引航员登船以便将船引航到泊位。大约引航60分钟后，船搁浅并持续5天。船舶出租人称，滞期时间在此期间继续产生。仲裁中，承租人获胜，理由是搁浅是由于疏忽，与船舶出租人航行或管理疏忽一样，船舶出租人应负责，承租人在船舶搁浅期间无义务支付滞期费。

2. Dispatch Money
2. 速遣费

"Dispatch money" or "Dispatch" shall mean an agreed amount payable by the shipowner if the vessel completes loading or discharging before the laytime has expired.

"速遣费"是指承租人在规定的装卸时间内提前完成货物装卸，由船舶出租人支付给承租人的约定的报酬。

Within the dry cargo markets it can be agreed that if a vessel completes cargo operations within the available laytime, the charterer will be rewarded by the payment of dispatch money, which is normally set at half the daily rate of demurrage. The object of dispatch is to encourage the charterer to load or discharge in less than the agreed laytime.

在干散货运市场，可以约定如果在可用的装卸时间内完成装卸货物业务，承租人有权获得速遣费，其通常是按滞期费每日费率的一半支付的。速遣费的目的是鼓励承租人在约定装卸时间内提前完成装货或卸货。

It should be borne in mind, however, that a few charterers negotiate that daily dispatch is the same as daily demurrage, while for vessels that normally might expect a fast turn-round in port, it is not at all unusual for the contract to specify "free dispatch", i.e., no dispatch at all. This is the case in the tanker market.

应该记住的是，一些承租人会洽谈将每日速遣费设定与滞期费相同；而对于那些通常在港口快速装卸的船舶，合同中明确写明"免速遣费"，即没有速遣费的情况也并不罕见。油船市场便是如此。

However, no address commissions or brokerages are payable on dispatch money. Where dispatch is payable, it can be sub divided as being payable on all time saved or on working time or laytime saved.

然而，速遣费是不支付洽租佣金或佣金的。当支付速遣费时，它可以细分为根据所有节省的时间，或节省的工作时间或装卸时间支付。

2.1 All Time Saved
2.1 节省全部时间

"Dispatch on all time saved" shall mean that dispatch money shall be payable for the time from the completion of loading or discharging to the expiry of the laytime including periods excepted from the laytime.

"节省全部时间速遣"是指承租人提前按租船合同中规定的装卸时间完成装卸任务，船舶出租人付给承租人包括除装卸时间之外的所有时间的速遣费。

It is perhaps easier to understand dispatch on "all time saved" by the use of an example.

通过例子可以更容易地理解"节省全部时间"的含义。

The AAA completes loading at 1200 hours on a Friday, her charter party being "per weather working day of 24 consecutive hours, Saturdays, Sundays and Holidays excepted, even if used". Thus laytime would be suspended in normal circumstances from Friday 2400 hours through to Monday 0001 hours.

"AAA"号船在星期五的12时完成装货，租船合同规定"连续24小时良好天气工作日，星期六、星期日及节假日除外，即使使用"。因此，装卸时间将在正常情况下从周五的24时到周一的0时暂停计算。

At 1200 hours on Friday there are 3 days of laytime remaining and, since the term "all time saved" means exactly what it says, the calculator of laytime has to base figures on the hypothetical case that "if the vessel had not completed loading on the Friday at 1200 hours but had remained in port working cargo, when would laytime have been fully used"?

在星期五的12时，尚有3天装卸时间，按照"节省全部时间"的实际含义，装卸时间的计算按下列假设的情况进行，"如果该船未在星期五的12时完成装货，但仍在港口进行货物作业，装卸时间将何时被完全地使用完"？

Dispatch would thus be calculated as shown in Table 5:

速遣费因此将按表5所示计算：

Table 5　Dispatch Calculation

Day of the Week	All time saved	Laytime
Friday	1200 hours−2400 hours	12 hours
Saturday	0000 hours−2400 hours	0 hours
Sunday	0000 hours−2400 hours	0 hours
Monday	0000 hours−2400 hours	24 hours
Tuesday	0000 hours−2400 hours	24 hours
Wednesday	0000 hours−1200 hours	12 hours
Total	5 days	3 days

表5　速遣费计算

星期	节省全部时间	装卸时间
周五	1200 点—2400 点	12小时
周六	0000 点—2400 点	0小时
周日	0000 点—2400 点	0小时
周一	0000 点—2400 点	24小时
周二	0000 点—2400 点	24小时
周三	0000 点—1200 点	12小时
合计	5天	3天

Allowing for the weekend that has been "saved" by the charterer due to finishing before the expiry of permitted laytime, the charterer has in effect "saved" the shipowner some 5 days and, under "all time saved" terms, are thus entitled to 5 days dispatch.

由于承租人准许在装卸时间届满前结束装卸作业，周末被"节省"，共节省船舶出租人5天时间；根据"节省全部时间"的条款，承租人有权请求5天的速遣费。

2.2 Working Time or Laytime Saved
2.2 节省工作时间或装卸时间

"Dispatch on (all) working time saved" or "on (all) laytime saved" shall mean that dispatch money shall be payable for the time from the completion of loading or discharging to the expiry of the laytime excluding any periods excepted from the laytime.

"节省（全部）工作时间或装卸时间"是指承租人提前按租船合同中规定的装卸时间完成装卸任务，船舶出租人付给承租人不包括装卸时间中除外时间的速遣费。

Using the same example but on the basis of "working time saved" or "laytime saved", only the 3 remaining days of laytime would apply as dispatch, despite weekends or holidays or bad weather or any other factor occurring once the ship had departed.

同样的例子，在"节省工作时间或装卸时间"术语下，一旦船舶离开港口，不管是否为周末或节假日或不良天气或有任何其他因素发生，只有3天的装卸时间可以适用速遣费。

You will readily see that "dispatch on all time saved" favors the charterers whilst "laytime saved" or "working time saved" is better for the shipowners; the "fairness" of one versus the other is a perpetual debate. The shipowners naturally say that as laytime is except for certain periods like Sundays and Holidays then dispatch should be on the same basis. The charterers counter this by arguing that a ship is earning all the time she is at sea regardless of which day of the week it is, so getting the ship to sea that much quicker should reward the charterers for every day without exception.

很容易看出，"节省全部时间速遣"有利于承租人，"节省工作时间或装卸时间"有利于船舶出租人。公平与否是一个永久的话题。船舶出租人自然主张，周日和节假日在装卸时间中除外，那么速遣费的计算也应当如此。承租人会辩称，船舶在航行期间无论周几均在产生收益（即持续为船舶出租人创造运费价值），因此，若能让船舶提前启航（因承租人提前完成装卸），则承租人应获得所有提前天数的速遣奖励，且不排除任何日期（包括周末、节假日等）。

One final word about dispatch: it should be borne in mind that some markets (e.g. bulk sugar) are based on laytime far in excess of the time actually required to perform cargo operations. It is, therefore, important for shipowners to take this into account when negotiating business and to reflect the "saved" time as a "dispatch expense" in a voyage estimate.

关于速遣费，最后需要注意一点：应该记住，一些市场（如大宗糖）在租船合同中对装卸时间的规定远远超过了实际需要进行货物装饰作业的时间。因此，船舶出租人在洽谈业务时务必将这一情况纳入考量，并在估计航次预算中，将"节省"的时间对应的成本列为一项"速遣费用"。

UNIT 7   OTHER CLAUSES

第七单元　其他条款

In this until, some other clauses that also consist of parts of the charter party will be discussed such as a bill of lading clause, lien clause, taxes and dues clause, agency clause, brokerage clause, law and arbitration clauses, etc.

在本单元中，将学习到租船合同其他条款的规定内容，如提单条款、留置权条款、税费和规费条款、代理条款、佣金条款、法律和仲裁条款等。

1. Bill of Lading under Charter Party
1. 租船合同下的提单

The issue of a bill of lading for goods on a chartered ship may create new obligations, but does not put an end to the obligation under the charter party.

租船合同下签发提单可引发新的义务问题，但不使租船合同的义务结束。

1.1 Bill of Lading in the Hands of the Charterer
1.1 提单在承租人手中

Where the charterer is himself the shipper, and receives as such shipper a bill of lading in terms differing from the charter, the proper construction of the two documents taken together is that, prima facie and in the absence of any intention to the contrary, as between the shipowner and the charterer, the bill of lading, although inconsistent with certain parts of the charter, is to be taken only as an acknowledgment of the receipt of the goods. Where the charterer becomes indorsee of a bill of lading, originally issued to a shipper other than the charterer, the bill of lading does not modify or vary the terms of the charter party.

如果承租人本人就是托运人，作为托运人收到的提单与租船合同的条款有所不同的话，对于两个单证的恰当解释是：在没有任何与此相反的意图下，就船舶出租人与承租人之间而言，尽管该提单与租船合同的某些部分存在不一致，但仅应将其视为货物收讫的确认凭证。若船舶出租人成为最初签发给非出租人以外的托运人的提单的受让人，则该提单不得修改或变更租船合同的条款。

1.2 Bill of Lading in the Hands of Indorsee from the Charterer
1.2 提单由承租人转让给受让人

Although, as between the shipowner and charterer, the bill of lading may be merely like a receipt for the goods, yet, where it is indorsed over, as between the shipowner and the indorsee, the bill of lading must be considered to contain the contract.

虽然提单在出租人与承租人之间仅作为一个收到货物的确认收据，但是，在转让情况下，提单在船舶出租人与受让人之间构成合同。

According to the provisions of CMC, "where the holder of the bill of lading is not the charterer in the case of a bill of lading issued under a voyage charter, the rights and obligations of the carrier and the holder of the bill of lading shall be governed by clauses of the bill of lading".

根据《中华人民共和国海商法》的规定，"对按照航次租船合同运输的货物签发的提单，提单持有人不是承租人的，承运人与该提单持有人之间的权利、义务关系适用提单的约定"。

1.3 Incorporation of Charter in Bill of Lading
1.3 租船合同并入提单

The bill of lading usually contains some clauses that are contradictory to the clauses contained in the voyage charter party. To make clear that the charter party, and not the bill of lading, is the governing agreement for the shipment, shipowners often insist on having a clause inserted in the bill of lading concerning some or all of the terms of the charter party.

提单通常包含一些与航次租船合同中的条款互相矛盾的条款。为了明确指出租船合同是制约货运的协议而不是提单，船舶出租人往往坚持要在提单中并入一个参照租船合同的部分或所有条款的条款。

However, if the clauses of the voyage charter party are incorporated into the bill of lading, the relevant clauses of the voyage charter party shall apply. A wide variety of incorporating provisions are in common use. The following is a summary of the decisions on various forms of clauses.

但是，如果航次租船合同的条款被并入提单，则应适用航次租船合同中的相关条款。实务中普遍使用的并入条款形式多样。以下是对各种并入形式的判决摘要。

"Freight and all other conditions as per charter." This is the narrowest form of incorporating clauses in common use. This clause covers only such conditions of the charter as are to be performed by the consignee, or are referable to the discharge and receipt of cargo. Thus the words do not incorporate charter party exception clauses into the bill of lading.

"运费及所有其他条件参照租约规定。"这是通常使用的范围最窄的并入形式。这一条款仅涵盖了租船合同所涉及的收货人履行的条件，或者与卸货和收取货物有关。这样的条款并未将租船合同的除外条款纳入提单。

"All conditions and exceptions as per charter." An express reference to the exception clause is sufficient to make the bill of lading subject to the excepted perils contained in the charter party.

"所有条件和除外情况参照租约规定。"若明确提及除外条款，该形式即足以使提单受租船合同中所含除外风险条款的约束。

"All the terms, provisions and exceptions as per charter." These are very wide words of incorporation, and are sufficient to bring into the bill of lading almost everything that is in the charter party, provided, of course, that the terms make sense in the context of the bill, and are not inconsistent with its express provisions.

"所有的术语规定和除外情况参照租约规定。"这是范围非常广的并入形式，足以将几乎所有的租船合同规定并入提单，但是术语应在提单上下条文中讲得通，并且不能与明确规定相违背。

"All terms, conditions, clauses, and exceptions as per charter." This provision is perhaps the widest of those in common use. It has been held to be effective to incorporate into a bill of lading a clause that required demurrage to be paid if a discharging berth was not immediately available.

"所有术语、条件、条款和除外情况参照租约规定。"这一规定也许是使用最广泛的。曾判决，如果没有立即可用的卸货泊位，要支付滞期费的条款被认为有效地并入了提单。

In normal cases, the arbitration clause is not incorporated into the bill of lading. Courts in England have held that unless there is a specific reference in a bill of lading to the law and arbitration clause in the governing charter party it may not necessarily be deemed part of the terms and conditions of the bill of lading.

在通常情况下，仲裁条款不会并入提单。英国法院曾判决，除非提单中明确提及管辖租船合同中的法律和仲裁条款，否则该条款未必会被视为提单条款和条件的一部分。

1.4 UCP 600 Refers to Charter Party Bill of Lading
1.4 跟单信用证600关于租船合同提单

(1) A bill of lading, however named, containing an indication that it is subject to a charter party (charter party bill of lading), must appear to be signed by:

（1）表明其受租船合同约束的提单（租船合同提单），无论名称如何，必须看似由以下人员签署：

(a) the master or a named agent for or on behalf of the master, or

（a）船长或船长指定的代理人或代表船长，或

(b) the shipowner or a named agent for or on behalf of the shipowner, or

（b）船舶出租人或船舶出租人指定的代理人或代表船舶出租人，或

(c) the charterer or a named agent for or on behalf of the charterer.

（c）承租人或承租人指定的代理人或代表承租人。

Any signature by the master, shipowner, charterer, or agent must be identified as that of the master, shipowner, charterer, or agent.

船长、船舶出租人、承租人或代理人的任何签字必须标明其船长、船舶出租人、承租人或代理人的身份。

Any signature by an agent must indicate whether the agent has signed for or on behalf of the master, shipowner, or charterer.

代理人签字必须表明其是否代表船长、船舶出租人或者承租人签字。

An agent signing for or on behalf of the shipowner or charterer must indicate the name of the shipowner or charterer.

代理人代表船舶出租人或承租人签字时必须注明船舶出租人或承租人的名称。

(2) A bill of lading, however named, containing an indication that it is subject to a charter party (charter party bill of lading), must appear to indicate that the goods have been shipped on board a named vessel at the port of loading stated in the credit by:

（2）无论名称如何，表明其受租船合同约束的提单（租船合同提单），必须看似通过以下方式表明货物已在信用证规定的装货港装上指定船舶：

(a) pre-printed wording, or

（a）预先印就的文字，或者

(b) an onboard notation indicating the date on which the goods have been shipped on board.

（b）在已装船批注上注明货物的装运日期。

The date of issuance of the charter party bill of lading will be deemed to be the date of shipment unless the charter party bill of lading contains an onboard notation indicating the date of shipment, in which case the date stated in the onboard notation will be deemed to be the date of shipment.

租船合同提单的出具日期将被视为装运日期，除非租船合同提单包含装船批注注明的装运日期，此时已装船批注上注明的日期将被视为装运日期。

(3) A bill of lading, however named, containing an indication that it is subject to a charter party (charter party bill of lading), must appear to indicate shipment from the port of loading to the port of discharge stated in the credit. The port of discharge may also be shown as a range of ports or a geographical area, as stated in the credit.

（3）无论名称如何，表明其受租船合同约束的提单（租船合同提单），必须看似表明货物从信用证规定的装货港运输至卸货港。卸货港也可显示为信用证规定的港口范围或地理区域。

(4) A bill of lading, however named, containing an indication that it is subject to a charter party (charter party bill of lading), must appear to be the sole original charter party bill of lading or, if issued in more than one original, be the full set as indicated on the charter party bill of lading.

（4）无论名称如何，表明其受租船合同约束的提单（租船合同提单），必须看似为唯一的正本租船合同提单，或如出具多份正本提单，租船合同提单应注明全套正本份数。

A bank will not examine charter party contracts, even if they are required to be presented by the terms of the credit.

银行将不审核租船合同，即使信用证要求提交租船合同。

1.5 Provision of Gencon Form 1994
1.5 1994年金康合同范本规定

The bills of lading shall be presented and signed by the master as per the "CONGENBILL" bill of lading form, Edition 1994, without prejudice to this charter party, or by the owner's agents provided that written authority has been given by owners to the agents, a copy of which is to be furnished to the charterers. The charterers shall indemnify the owners against all consequences or liabilities that may arise from the signing of bills of lading as presented to the extent that the terms or contents of such bills of lading impose or result in the imposition of more onerous liabilities upon the owners than those assumed by the owners under this charter party.

提单应按照 1994 年版 "康金提单" 格式提交并由船长签署，且不影响本租船合同；或者由船舶出租人的代理人签署，前提是船舶出租人已向该代理人出具书面授权，且授权书副本应提供给承租人。对于按所提交的提单条款签署提单而可能产生的一切后果或责任，只要此类提单的条款或内容给船舶出租人施加的责任，或导致船舶出租人承担的责任，比船舶出租人根据本租船合同所承担的责任更为繁重，承租人应就此向船舶出租人作出赔偿。

First of all, the clause now prescribes that the bill of lading to be used is the CONGENBILL. The CONGENBILL 2007 was approved by BIMCO's Documentary Committee at its meeting in Copenhagen on 16 November 2007. Secondly, the clause now provides that the shipowners' agents can sign bills of lading on the condition that a written authority has been given by the shipowners for the agent to do so, a copy of which is to be furnished to the charterers.

首先，该条款目前规定所使用的提单是康金提单。2007 年版本的康金提单是BIMCO 文件委员会于 2007 年 11 月 16 日在哥本哈根会议上通过的。其次，该条款目前规定，船舶出租人的代理人可以在船舶出租人给予书面授权的条件下签发提单，但应向承租人提供该书面授权的副本。

It will also be noticed that a provision has been included giving the shipowners an express right of indemnity from the charterers for issuing bills of lading at the charterers' request and as a result of which the shipowners may assume greater liabilities than under the charter party. It is recognized that in some cases the courts would probably deem such a right of indemnity to be implied.

还需注意的是，租船合同中通常会包含一项条款，明确赋予船舶出租人向承租人追偿的权利。该权利针对的情形是：船舶出租人应承租人的要求出具提单，且因此可能承担比航次租船合同约定更重的责任。实践中普遍认为，在某些情况下，法院大概率会将此类追偿权认定为（租船合同中）默认存在的权利（即无须条款明确约定，法律或司法实践已隐含该权利）。

2. Lien Clause
2. 留置权条款

The shipowner may have a lien on goods carried on board the vessel for charges like freight, dead freight, demurrage, expenses for the cargo, general average contribution, etc. Lien on goods can be based on the general law, on express agreement in the charter party or bill of lading.

船舶出租人因未收取的运费、亏舱费、滞期费、货物费用、共同海损分摊等而对船上装运的货物有留置权。留置权可以依据法律、合同或者提单中的明文规定产生。

In voyage chartering it is not unusual that the charter party contains a clause that relieves the charterers from liability from the moment the vessel has been loaded. The intention is that the shipowners shall turn to the cargo owners with any additional claims such as, for instance, demurrage at the discharging port. It is not unusual that this cesser clause and lien clause are combined which have the heading "lien clause".

在航次租船下，通常租船合同都有一条关于在船舶装货后承租人责任终止的条款。其意图是由船舶出租人向货主提出任何额外的索赔，如卸货港的滞期费。通常情况下，责任终止条款与留置权条款合并在一起冠之"留置权条款"。

Under such a clause, the shipowners cannot simply go to the charterers afterward, without first having claimed from the receivers by exercising a lien. The co-existence principle applies to this clause which means that it is only capable of protecting the charterers from liabilities that the shipowners can effectively resort to against the consignees by way of a lien on cargo.

在此条款下,船舶出租人在没有首先就索赔向收货人行使留置权时,不能简单地直接向承租人提出。并存原则适用于该条款意味着船舶出租人对收货人能有效行使留置权,而免除承租人履行租船合同的责任。

Before the shipowners exercise a lien on the cargo they must find out the legal and practical possibilities and difficulties in the actual country and port. In some countries, it is not at all legally possible to exercise a lien over cargo.

船舶出租人在行使留置权前必须了解具体国家和港口的法律以及实际操作的可能性和困难。有些国家可能从法律层面上完全无法对货物行使留置权。

The provision of the lien clause in Gencon Form 1994 is quite different from those in other charter forms as well as in Gencon Form 1976. It states that "the owners shall have a lien on the cargo and all sub-freight payable in respect of the cargo, for freight, dead freight, demurrage, claims for damages and for all other amounts due under this charter party including costs of recovering same". This provision only gives the shipowners' right of lien on cargo and does not relieve the charterers' liability.

1994年金康合同范本对留置权的规定与其他合同范本及1976年金康合同范本的规定完全不一致。它规定:"船舶出租人因未收取的运费、亏舱费、滞期费和损失索赔,以及所有应付费用包括为取得该笔收入所花的费用而对货物和该批货物的转租运费有留置权。"该规定仅赋予船舶出租人货物留置权而没有解除承租人的责任。

3. Taxes and Dues Clause
3. 税费和规费条款

This clause specifies which party to the contract is responsible for taxes and dues that may be levied against the vessel and/or her cargo and/or the freight.

该条款规定了哪一方合同当事人承担可能是对船舶和/或其货物和/或运费征收税费和规费的责任。

In many countries, the tax system includes special taxes on freight and other taxes connected with the loading or discharging of ships in the country. It is the recipient of the freight who is liable to pay this tax, not the party paying the same, and therefore this charge is frequently levied against the shipowner, being usually added to port disbursements incurred by the vessel concerned and thus collected via the offices of the port agent.

许多国家的税收体系中包括对运费征收的特别税种和其他与在该国装卸货物的船舶有关的税种。谁收取运费,谁负责支付这笔税项,而不是支付运费的当事人,因此通常其是对船舶出租人征收的,被添加到该船的港口使费中,通过港口代理支付。

The parties must agree on whose account such taxes shall be borne. The best way is to find out exactly what taxes will be levied for the intended voyage. Taxes known beforehand can be dealt with directly in the charter party but as new tax laws may be introduced with very short notice it is advisable also to have a clause dealing with the question in a more general way, as in Gencon Form 1994 which stipulates that: "the shipowners shall pay for all dues, charges and taxes customarily levied on the vessel, howsoever the amount thereof may be assessed. The charterers shall pay for all dues, charges, and taxes customarily levied on the cargo, howsoever the amount thereof may be assessed. Unless otherwise agreed in Box 23, taxes levied on the freight shall be for the charterers' account".

双方必须对谁应支付该项税费做出协议。最好的办法是搞清楚对预定航程要征收哪些税费。事先知道的税费可以直接在租船合同中加以规定，但由于可能在很短的时间内出台新税法，最好还是应该有一个关于税费的条款，如1994年金康合同范本规定："船舶出租人支付所有对船舶征收的税费、费用和税款。承租人支付所有对货物征收的税费、费用和税款。除非第23栏另有规定，承租人支付所有对运费征收的税款。"

4. Agency Clause
4. 代理条款

The ship's agent is the local expert who will represent the shipowner in every port the ship visits. To the owner of an international trading ship, the appointment of an agent in every foreign port is essential, ensuring that the visit to the port will go smoothly. The ship and those aboard her may never have visited that port before; they may not speak the language or even understand it, but the agent will ensure that everything need will be delivered.

船舶的代理人是当地的专家，代表挂靠各个港口的船舶出租人。对于从事国际贸易的船舶的船舶出租人，在每一个外国港口任命代理人，确保船舶挂靠港口的顺利进行是至关重要的。船舶和船上的船员可能之前从来没有到过该港口，他们可能不会说甚至不理解当地语言，代理人能确保提供给他们需要的东西。

In any charter party, reference should be made as to which of the parties is responsible for the selection of an agent. Normal practice in voyage chartering is that agents are nominated and paid by the shipowners. Shipowners shall have full liberty to select and appoint their agents at ports of loading and discharging to look after the business of their ships and assist their masters.

任何租船合同，最好应规定谁对代理人的选择负责。在航次租船下，通常的做法是，船舶出租人委托代理人并支付代理费。船舶出租人应充分自由地选择并任命自己的装卸货港的代理人，由该代理人来负责处理船舶业务及协助船长。

If, however, a ship under a charter party is consigned to agents nominated by charterers, the agents so appointed shall perform all the normal services for the ship and its master as if the agents had been appointed directly by the shipowners. The agents shall only charge the normal fee for their work, and such fees shall not exceed what would have been charged under a direct appointment by the shipowners.

但是，如果根据租船合同，船舶被委托由承租人指定代理人管理，被委托的代理人犹如船舶出租人直接委托的代理人一样执行所有正常的代理服务。代理人只收取他们正常工作的费用，这种费用不得超过船舶出租人直接任命的费用。

Agents appointed by time charterers shall perform all the normal services for the ship and its master as would have been performed if the ship called under a voyage charter and the agents were appointed by the shipowners. All normal agency fees for ordinary agency services shall be charged against the time charterers.

由定期承租人指定的代理人应执行所有正常的、对船舶和船长的服务，如同航次租船下船舶代理是由船舶出租人聘请的代理一样。所有代理服务费一般由定期承租人承担。

The agents shall inform the shipowners well in advance of the approximate amount required for the ship's disbursements and the shipowners shall remit such funds to the agents in advance of the ship's arrival. The agents shall return any unused funds without undue delay.

代理人应预先通知船舶出租人船舶挂靠港口的大约费用，船舶出租人应在船舶抵达前将备用金打入代理人的账户。代理人应毫不迟延地归还任何未使用的资金。

5. Brokerage Clause
5. 佣金条款

A chartering broker's income from voyage chartering is based on a percentage of the gross freight payable to a shipowner and this income is payable by the shipowner to all the brokers involved in the fixture. A chartering broker's income is usually termed brokerage to distinguish it from commission or address commission used to describe a charterer's negotiated entitlement to a discount on freight payment. The practice of deducting address commission from freight, dead freight and demurrage is one peculiar to the dry cargo trades, and is rarely encountered in the tanker trades.

租船经纪人的收入是基于船舶出租人运费收入总额的百分比计收的，由船舶出租人支付给所有涉及合同订立的经纪人。租船经纪人的收入通常被称为经纪人佣金，用以区分治租佣金即承租人支付运费的折扣。事实上，从运费、亏舱费和滞期费中扣减治租佣金是干散货租船的习惯做法，该做法几乎很少出现在油船运输中。

Brokerage normally amounts to 1.25% of gross freight, dead freight and demurrage and is payable by a shipowner from sums received to each broker involved in a transaction, although it frequently occurs that a charterer will deduct an appropriate amount from freight payment to the shipowner and undertake to pay the brokerage directly to his own and other brokers involved. Thus, for the involvement of two brokers, 2.5% brokerage is payable, 3.75% for three, and so on.

佣金通常为总运费、亏舱费和滞期费的1.25%，由船舶出租人支付给所有涉及合同订立的经纪人，但实务中常出现这样的情况：承租人会从应支付给船舶出租人的运费中扣除一笔相应金额，然后负责将这笔经纪费直接支付给自己的经纪人，以及其他涉及此次租船业务的经纪人。如果两个经纪人参与治租，佣金为2.5%；三人为3.75%等。

This was a dispute over fees payable to a broker by a shipowner. The charter party provided for daily demurrage which had been unpaid by the charterer. The shipowner attempted to set off the unpaid demurrage from the fees payable to the broker. Both at first instance and on appeal the court held that the shipowner was not entitled to claim a set-off.

以船舶出租人向经纪人支付佣金的争议举例。租船合同规定滞期费由承租人支付，但滞期费尚未支付。船舶出租人试图以未付的滞期费抵销应支付给经纪人的佣金。一审和上诉法院均判决，船舶出租人无权要求抵销。

Address commission also varies in amount. The total commission—address commission plus brokerage due on dry cargo business may vary from as little as 1.25% to as much as 7.5% perhaps even more. The norm for deep-sea dry cargo business is around 3.75 % to 5%.

洽租佣金数额也有所不同。在干散货运输中的佣金总额——洽租佣金加上经纪人佣金，可能低至1.25%，高至7.5%，甚至更高。远洋干散货业务标准为3.75%~5%。

When brokers have been involved they are entitled to commission. The commission is usually a certain percentage of the freight. Nevertheless, a broker may be able to gain some protection in the case of non-performance of confirmed business, as is provided, for example, in the Gencon Form 1994, which states: "A brokerage commission at the rate stated in Box 24 on the freight, dead freight and demurrage earned is due to the party mentioned in Box 24. In case of non-execution 1/3 of the brokerage on the estimated amount of freight to be paid by the party responsible for such non-execution to the brokers as indemnity for the latter's expenses and work. In case of more voyages the amount of indemnity to be agreed."

当经纪人参与了洽租时，他们有权获得佣金。佣金通常是一定比例的运费。不过，在合同订立后没有履行的情况下，经纪人可能获得一些保护，如，在1994年金康合同范本中规定："经纪人的佣金按已收取的运费、亏舱费和滞期费，以第24栏所规定的费率，支付给第24栏所指定的当事人。当合同不履行时，由责任方向经纪人至少支付按估算的运费确定的佣金的1/3，作为经纪人所花费用和工作的补偿。在多个航次的情况下，补偿的数额由双方协议决定。"

6. Law and Arbitration Clause
6. 法律和仲裁条款

To avoid discussion and disputes about what law applies to the charter party, all charter party forms should contain a clause dealing with the law applicable to and the procedure for handling disputes between the parties. The charter parties usually have reference to arbitration while the bill of lading more often refers to procedure in the courts.

为了避免何种法律适用于租船合同的纠纷，所有租船合同范本都包含了一条法律适用和双方之间纠纷处理程序的条款。租船合同纠纷通常提交仲裁，而提单纠纷更经常提交法院诉讼。

6.1 Gencon Form 1994 Provision
6.1 1994年金康合同范本的规定

(a) This charter party shall be governed by and construed in accordance with English law and any dispute arising out of this charter party shall be referred to arbitration in London in accordance with the Arbitration Acts 1950 and 1979 or any statutory modification or re-enactment thereof for the time being in force. Unless the parties agree upon a sole arbitrator, one arbitrator shall be appointed by each party and the arbitrators so appointed shall appoint a third arbitrator. The decision of the three-man tribunal thus constituted, or any two of them, shall be final. On the receipt by one party of the nomination in writing of the other party's arbitrator, that party shall appoint its arbitrator within fourteen days, failing which the decision of the single arbitrator appointed shall be final.

（a）本租船合同适用英国法，如有任何争议应提交至伦敦，根据1950年和1979年仲裁法以及随后所做的修订版进行仲裁。除非双方同意独任仲裁，适用三人仲裁庭，双方各指定一名仲裁员，第三人由该两人选择，他们或其中任何两人的决断是最终的。一方收到另一方已指定一名仲裁员的书面通知后，应在14天内指定另一名仲裁员，否则已指定的那名仲裁员的决断为最终决断。

For disputes where the total amount claimed by either party does not exceed the amount stated in Box 25 the arbitration shall be conducted in accordance with the Small Claims Procedure of the London Maritime Arbitrators Association.

如争议金额未超过第25栏规定的金额，该仲裁应按伦敦海事仲裁委员会的小额索赔程序进行。

(b) This charter party shall be governed by and construed in accordance with Title 9 of the *United States Code* and the *Maritime Law of the United States*. Should any dispute arise out of this charter party, the matter in dispute shall be referred to three persons at New York, one to be appointed by each of the parties hereto, and the third by the two so chosen; their decision or that of any two of them shall be final, and for the purpose of enforcing any award, this agreement may be made a rule of the court. The proceedings shall be conducted in accordance with the rules of the Society of Maritime Arbitrators, Inc.

（b）本租船合同适用《美国法典》第9条和《美国海运法》，如有任何争议应提交至纽约的三人仲裁庭，双方各指定一名仲裁员，第三人由该两人选择，他们或其中任何两人的裁决是最终的。为执行该裁决，应按法庭规则做出仲裁裁决。仲裁应按海事仲裁协会的规则进行。

For disputes where the total amount claimed by either party does not exceed the amount stated in Box 25, the arbitration shall be conducted in accordance with the Shortened Arbitration Procedure of the Society of Maritime Arbitrators, Inc.

如争议金额未超过第25栏规定的金额，该仲裁应按海事仲裁协会的简易仲裁程序进行。

(c) Any dispute arising out of this charter party shall be referred to arbitration at the place indicated in Box 25, subject to the procedures applicable there. The laws of the place indicated in Box 25 shall govern this charter party.

（c）本租船合同引起的任何争议应提交至第25栏指定的地方仲裁。第25栏指定地点的法律应作为本租船合同的准据法。

(d) If Box 25 in part 1 is not filled in, sub-clause (a) of this clause shall apply.

（d）如第25栏未填写，适用本条（a）款。

(a), (b) and (c) are alternatives; indicate the alternative agreed in Box 25.

（a），（b）和（c）选择其一，并填入第25栏。

6.2 China Maritime Arbitration Commission Clause
6.2 中国海事仲裁委员会条款

The following is the model arbitration clause prepared by the China Maritime Arbitration

Commission (CMAC): "Any dispute arising from or in connection with this contract shall be submitted to China Maritime Arbitration Commission for arbitration which shall be conducted in accordance with the Commission's arbitration rules in effect at the time of applying for arbitration. The arbitral award is final and binding upon both parties."

以下是中国海事仲裁委员会制定的示范仲裁条款。该条款的具体规定为："凡因本合同引起的或与本合同有关的任何争议，均应提交中国海事仲裁委员会，按照申请仲裁时该会现行有效的仲裁规则进行仲裁。仲裁裁决是终局的，对双方均有约束力。"

【ASSIGNMENT】

Ⅰ. **Answer the following questions and check your answer from the text.**

1. What is the meaning of demurrage?

2. What is the meaning of notice of readiness?

3. What does laytime mean?

4. What does dispatch money mean?

5. What does freight mean?

Ⅱ. **Choice questions.** (Choose the one you think is correct from the followings.)

1. If Sundays and holidays are not counted as laytime, the contract should be based on (   ).

    A. SHEX   B. FHEX

    C. SHINC   D. SSHEX

2. After the vessel's arrival, a notice of readiness shall be given to the (   ).

    A. master   B. shipowner

    C. charterer   D. stevedores

3. The period of time agreed for loading and discharging is called (   ).

    A. weather working days   B. laytime

    C. laycan   D. working days

4. The time spent more than the agreed laytime, the shipowner is entitled to (   ).

    A. demurrage   B. dispatch

    C. dead freight   D. disbursement

5. Suppose 2 days of demurrage at the loading port and 2 days of dispatch at the discharge port, which of the following methods mean the charterer would not pay for demurrage? (   )

    A. Reversible.   B. Average.

    C. All purposes.   D. Normal laytime.

Ⅲ. **True or false questions.**

1. FOLI means the shipowners pay for the cost of loading and the charterers pay for cost of discharging. (   )

2. "Reversible laytime" shall mean an option given to the charterer to add together the time allowed for loading and discharging. (   )

3. The vessel is unseaworthy, the shipowner can still rely on the exception clauses in the charter party, if the loss has not been caused by unseaworthiness. (   )

4. Unless otherwise agreed in the contract, taxes levied on the freight shall be for the

shipowners' account according to the Gencon Form 1994. (　　)

5. "Dispatch on working time saved" shall mean that dispatch money shall be payable for the time from the completion of loading or discharging to the expiry of the laytime excluding any periods excepted from the laytime. (　　)

Ⅳ. Calculation of Demurrage and Dispatch Money

Vessel Moon arrived at the loading port on Thursday 9th Oct. 2003, the master tendered the NOR at 1400 hours the same day. Loading began at 0800 hours on 10th Oct. and was completed at 1800 hours on 15th Oct. The charter party stated that: "3WWDSHEX, laytime for loading shall commence at 1300 hours, if NOR is given up before 1200 hours, and at 0600 hours next working day if NOR given after 1200 hours. Demurrage USD 4,000 per day or pro rata for any part of a day." Please calculate the demurrage or dispatch if any.

MODULE FOUR
TIME CHARTER PARTY

模块四　定期租船合同

◎ LEARNING OBJECTIVES

Through studying this module, students will be required to obtain a basic knowledge of the time charter party, such as the description of the vessel and cargo, the period of charter and delivery/redelivery, the hire and payment of hire, the off-hire clause, other clauses, etc.

学习目标

通过学习本模块，学生应掌握定期租船合同的基本知识，诸如船舶和货物说明，合同租期和交还船，租金和租金支付，停租条款以及其他条款等。

◎ CONTENTS

1. Description of Vessel and Cargo;
2. Period of Charter and Delivery/Redelivery;
3. Hire and Payment of Hire;
4. Off-hire Clause;
5. Other Clauses.

学习内容

1. 船舶和货物说明；
2. 合同租期和交还船；
3. 租金和租金支付；
4. 停租条款；
5. 其他条款。

KEY POINTS

Vessel Speed and Bunker Consumption; Trading Limits; Cargo Liability; Inter-club Agreement; Period of Charter; Delivery/Redelivery; Payment of Hire; Off-hire Clause; Damage to Vessel; Performance of Voyage; Allocation of Costs.

学习要点

船舶航速和燃油消耗；航区限制；货物责任；协会内部协议；合同租期；交还船；租金支付；停租条款；船舶损坏；航次履行；费用分摊。

SKILL REQUIREMENTS

1. Have obtained basic knowledge of time charter party;
2. Have the ability to calculate the amount of hire;
3. Have the ability to calculate the period of the charter;
4. Have the ability to distinguish the cargo liability;
5. Have the ability to distinguish the allocation of costs.

技能要求

1. 获得定期租船合同的基本知识；
2. 具备计算租金数额的能力；
3. 具备计算租期的能力；
4. 具备分辨货物责任的能力；
5. 具备分辨费用分摊的能力。

Study Guidance Map

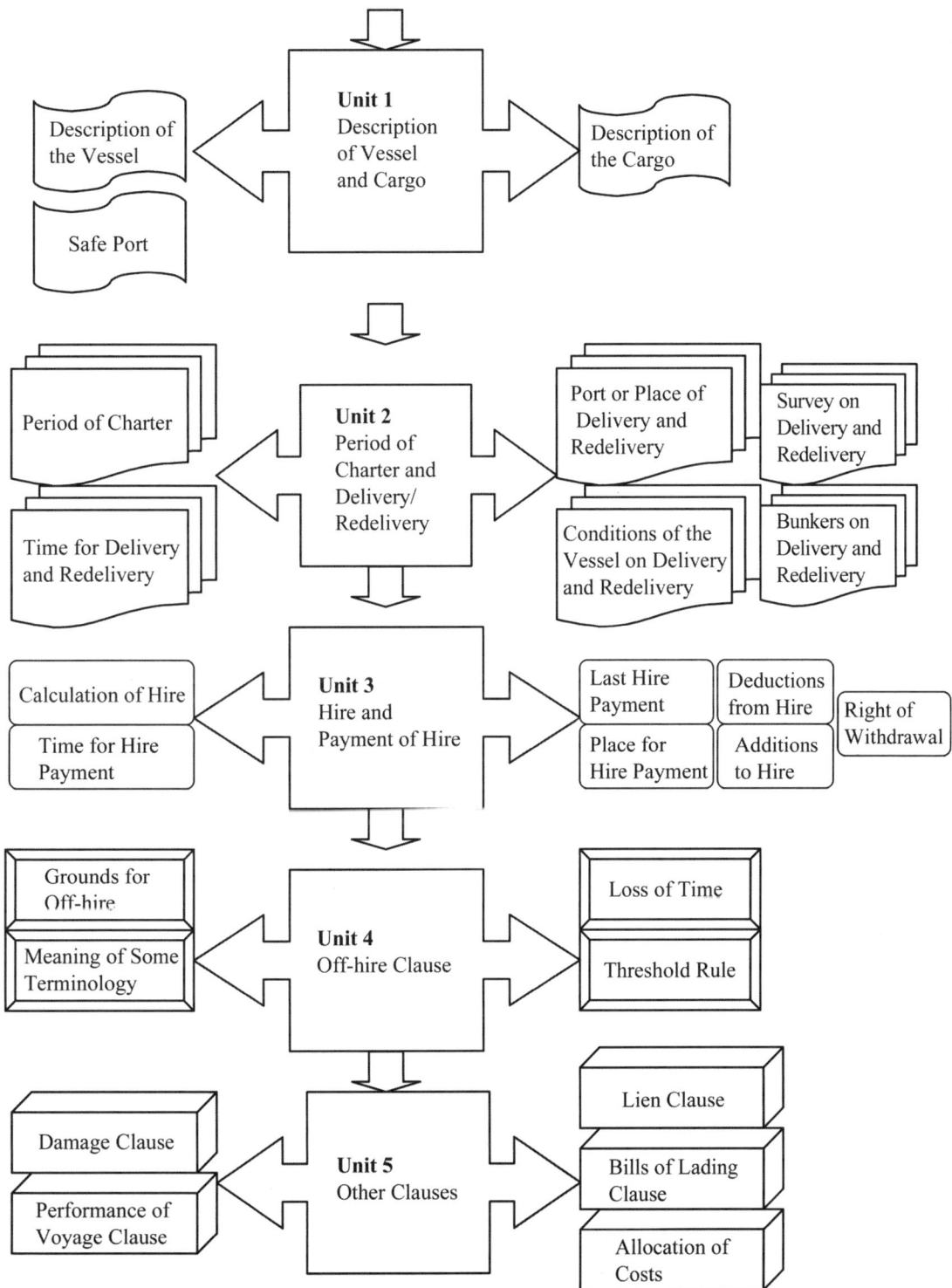

Unit 1
Description of Vessel and Cargo

Description of the Vessel

Safe Port

Description of the Cargo

Unit 2
Period of Charter and Delivery/Redelivery

Period of Charter

Time for Delivery and Redelivery

Port or Place of Delivery and Redelivery

Conditions of the Vessel on Delivery and Redelivery

Survey on Delivery and Redelivery

Bunkers on Delivery and Redelivery

Unit 3
Hire and Payment of Hire

Calculation of Hire

Time for Hire Payment

Last Hire Payment

Place for Hire Payment

Deductions from Hire

Additions to Hire

Right of Withdrawal

Unit 4
Off-hire Clause

Grounds for Off-hire

Meaning of Some Terminology

Loss of Time

Threshold Rule

Unit 5
Other Clauses

Damage Clause

Performance of Voyage Clause

Lien Clause

Bills of Lading Clause

Allocation of Costs

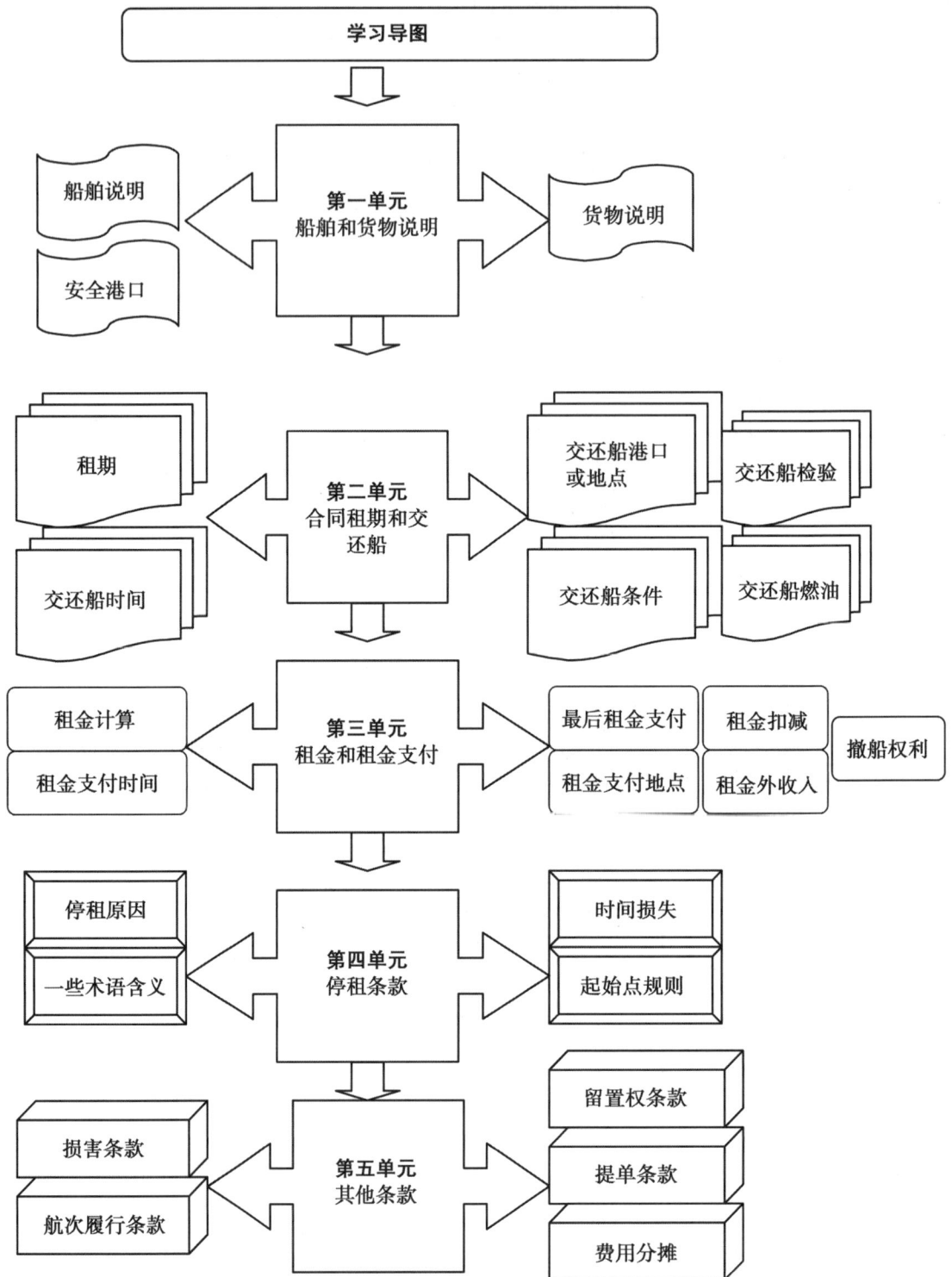

学习导图

第一单元
船舶和货物说明

船舶说明

安全港口

货物说明

第二单元
合同租期和交
还船

租期

交还船时间

交还船港口
或地点

交还船检验

交还船条件

交还船燃油

第三单元
租金和租金支付

租金计算

租金支付时间

最后租金支付

租金支付地点

租金扣减

租金外收入

撤船权利

第四单元
停租条款

停租原因

一些术语含义

时间损失

起始点规则

第五单元
其他条款

损害条款

航次履行条款

留置权条款

提单条款

费用分摊

UNIT 1　DESCRIPTION OF VESSEL AND CARGO

第一单元　船舶和货物说明

A time charter party is a contract under which the shipowner provides a designated manned ship to the charterer. The charterer employs the ship during the contractual period for the agreed service against payment of hire. The time charter party may be described as an agreement for the hire of a certain vessel.

定期租船合同，是指船舶出租人向承租人提供约定的由出租人配备船员的船舶，由承租人在约定的期间内按照约定的用途使用，并支付租金的合同。定期租船合同可以概述为租用特定船舶的协议。

A time charter party mainly contains the name of the shipowner, the name of the charterer; the name, nationality, class, tonnage, capacity, speed, and fuel consumption of the ship; the trading area; the agreed service; the contractual period; the time, place and conditions of delivery and re-delivery of the ship; the hire and the way of its payment and other relevant matters.

定期租船合同的内容，主要包括出租人和承租人的名称，船名、船籍、船级、吨位、容积、船速、燃料消耗，航区，用途，租船期间，交船和还船的时间和地点以及条件，租金及其支付，以及其他有关事项。

By far the largest number of time charter parties have been fixed on the basis of the New York Produce Exchange (NYPE) charter party form. For convenience, we will examine the elements of a time charter party based on the NYPE Form 1993 to provide some ideas of the normal clauses required in a time charter party.

直至目前为止，大多数定期租船合同使用纽约交易所制定的土产格式合同范本。为方便起见，我们将以1993年土产格式为蓝本，探讨定期租船合同的主要内容，讲解定期租船合同中所需的常规条款。

1. Description of the Vessel
1. 船舶说明

Generally, the description of the vessel is more important in the time charter party than in the voyage charter party and the description is also mostly more detailed and precise. All details about the ship such as name, flag, classification, port of registry, deadweight, capacity, year of construction, speed, fuel consumption, nationality, tonnage, etc. must be known by the charterers during the negotiation with the shipowners. Charterers should form an opinion about the commercial value of the vessel and it is therefore important for them that they have correct and sufficient information about her.

一般来说，定期租船合同关于船舶的说明比航次租船合同更重要，船舶说明也大多更加详细和精确。承租人在与船舶出租人洽谈时必须获知所有有关船舶的详细资料，如名称、船旗、船级、登记港、载重吨、舱容、建造年份、航速、燃料消耗、船籍、吨位等。承租人据此形成对船舶商业价值的意见，因此掌握正确和充分的船舶信息对他们来说是重要的。

1.1 Name of the Ship
1.1 船舶名称

There seems to be no direct English authority on the question of whether the name by which a vessel is described is a condition of a charter party. The famous book *Scrutton on Charter Parties and Bills of Lading* states: "Substantial accuracy in the name of the vessel will be a condition of the contract." The charter party is for the named ship alone and the charterers cannot be required to accept delivery under it of another, even of identical characteristics. It is open to the parties to agree that another ship may be substituted for the originally named ship or to agree to more than one substitution. The parties may also agree that the substitution be made at any time, whether before the start of the charter period, during it, or after the loss of the named or any substituted ship. But if it is intended to give a right of substitution after loss, particularly clear words must be used; for otherwise the charter party will be held to have been frustrated by the loss and the right to substitute will terminate with the termination of the charter.

租船合同中的船舶名称是不是条件条款似乎英国司法没有直接明确。著名的《斯克鲁顿论租船合同和提单》指出："船名的主要精确是合同的一个条件。"租船合同是为了单个指定的船舶，甚至不能要求承租人接受有相同特征的另一条船。双方当事人可以自由商议另一艘船是否可以取代原先指定的船舶或同意多个替代。当事人也可以在任何时候同意替换，无论是租期开始前、租期期间或在指定的或任何替代船舶灭失后。但是，如果打算在灭失后有权利替代，必须使用特别明确的文字，否则该租船合同将被认为因灭失而失效，替代的权利也将随着合同的终止而终止。

1.2 Sale of the Ship and Flag
1.2 船舶出售和船旗

It seems that it is not in itself a breach of the charter for the shipowners to sell the ship during the period of the charter. The original shipowners will however continue to be responsible to the charterers for the performance of all the obligations assumed by them under the charter party.

在租船期间船舶所有人出售船舶本身没有违反合同。原来的船舶出租人继续履行原租船合同下对承租人所有的义务。

According to CMC, where the ownership of the ship under charter has been transferred by the shipowner, the rights and obligations agreed upon under the original charter shall not be affected. However, the shipowner shall inform the charterer thereof in time. After such transfer, the transferee and the charterer shall continue to perform the original charter party.

根据《中华人民共和国海商法》，船舶所有人转让已经租出的船舶的所有权，定期租船合同约定的当事人的权利和义务不受影响，但是应当及时通知承租人。船舶所有权转让后，原租船合同由受让人和承租人继续履行。

It is submitted that the statement as to the ship's flag will usually be an intermediate term. But where the flag of the ship has a vital bearing on her safety or her trading opportunities, the statement may be treated as a condition, so that any breach will allow the charterers to treat the contract as discharged.

对船旗的表述通常被确认为是中间性条款。但是，在船旗对船舶的安全或其贸易机会具有重要影响时，船旗的表述可被视为一个条件条款，因此，任何违约将允许承租人解除合同。

1.3 Cargo Capacity
1.3 船舶载货量

The ship's cargo capacity is described in the same way as in the voyage charter party, i.e., in most cases by deadweight and/or cubic capacity. In some cases, it is necessary to have additional information about the vessel's cargo capacity, for instance, how many containers she can take on deck and under deck respectively. A vessel's cargo capacity is normally of great importance to the charterer. If a chartered vessel cannot load all the cargo the charterer wishes to ship, clearly he may miss his intended market or incur extra warehouse or transport expenses onshore as well as in arranging substitute tonnage.

船舶载货量的说明方式与航次租船合同相同，即在大多数情况下以载重吨和/或舱容表示。在某些情况下，有必要了解船舶载货量的其他信息，例如，在甲板上和舱内分别可以装载多少集装箱。船舶载货量通常对承租人是非常重要的。如果租用的船舶无法装载承租人想要的所有货物，很显然他将失去预计的市场，或在岸上产生额外的仓储或运输费用或者安排替代运力。

The time charterers dispose of all compartments which can be used for cargo. In the NYPE Form 1993 this is expressed in the following way:

定期承租人有权使用所有可用于货物的舱容。1993年土产格式的表示方式如下：

"The whole reach of the vessel's holds, decks, and other cargo spaces (not more than she can reasonably and safely stow and carry), also accommodations for supercargos, if carried, shall be at the charterers' disposal, reserving only proper and sufficient space for the vessel's officers, crew, tackle, apparel, furniture, provisions, stores, and fuel."

"船舶的所有货舱、甲板和通常装货空间（不超过其能合理安全地积载和装运的范围），以及押运员（如有的话）舱室的全部空间，除仅为高级船员、普通船员、船具、属具、家具、供应品、物料和燃料留有适当和足够的空间外，均归承租人使用。"

As information about the vessel's cargo capacity is very important for the time charterers, the shipowners must declare these details as correctly as possible. Statements of cargo capacity usually constitute intermediate terms. Incorrect information about the cargo carrying capacity may lead to a deduction of the hire or, when the difference is big, the charterers may also be entitled to cancel the contract and claim damages.

由于船舶载货量的信息对定期承租人来说非常重要，船舶出租人必须尽可能准确地提供这些细节。船舶载货量的表述通常是中间性条款。关于船舶货物的运载能力不正确的信息可能导致租金被扣除，差别较大时，承租人也有权取消合同并索赔损失。

1.4 Speed and Bunker Consumption
1.4 航速与燃油消耗

As the charterers pay hire per time unit, the vessel's speed capability and bunker consumption are essential for judging the operating potential of the vessel. The speed capability and bunker consumption statements in the time charter parties are usually connected to certain weather conditions and a certain draught. Also, the type of fuel is important.

由于承租人根据单位时间支付租金，船舶的航速能力和燃油消耗是必不可少的判断船舶经营潜力的要素。船舶的航速能力和燃油消耗在定期租船合同中通常和特定的天气条件以及一定的吃水有关联。另外，燃料型号也是重要的。

In the NYPE Form 1993, it is said that "speed about _____ knots, fully laden, in good weather conditions up to and including maximum force _____ on the Beaufort wind scale, on a consumption of about _____ long/metric tons of _____".

1993年土产格式中规定，"在良好天气条件下，风力达到包括最大风力蒲福_____级，船舶满载航行时船速大约_____节，消耗大约_____长吨/公吨的_____（燃油）"。

It seems that statements as to speed and fuel consumption will usually constitute intermediate terms by English law. The consequences of misdescription will then depend upon the nature and consequences of the breach. Usually, a lack of speed or an excess of consumption can be compensated for by damages alone. However, a serious discrepancy in either respect may be so fundamental to the charter as to entitle the charterers to treat it as being discharged.

根据英国法，船舶的航速能力和燃油消耗的表述看起来通常是中间性条款。错误说明的后果取决于违约的性质和后果。通常，航速减少或超额耗油只能要求赔偿损失。然而，若任何一方面与合同约定严重不符的话，承租人有权解除合同。

There is a divergence of view on the question of whether the ship has to comply with the description as to speed at the time the charter is entered into or at the time of delivery, or whether it is a continuing warranty. The whole purpose of the description of the vessel containing a speed warranty is that when she enters her service, she will be capable of the speed in question, subject, of course, to any protection that her owners may obtain if there has been some casualty between the date of the charter party and the date of delivery affecting her speed which, under an exceptions clause, protects them from liability for a failure to comply with the warranty. Commercial considerations require the description as to the vessel's speed to be applicable as at the date of her delivery whether or not it is applicable at the date of the charter party.

对于船舶是必须在签订租船合同时还是在交付时符合有关航速的说明，或者这一说明是否属于一项持续有效的保证条款，存在不同的观点。船舶保证航速的说明的整个目的是，当船舶开始服务时，它必将能达到该速度。当然，船舶出租人可以获得任何保护，如果在租船合同订立的日期与交船日期之间发生影响它速度的事故，根据免责条款，免除出租人未能遵守保证的责任。商业上的考虑要求航速的说明以该船在交付日期时符合为准，不论其在租船合同订立日期时是否符合。

【Case】A vessel that was chartered under a time charter party was described as capable of steaming at 14.5 knots. Due to her bottom being fouled and encrusted with mollusks, she was only capable of steaming at 10.61 knots. Held, that the shipowners were guilty of a breach of warranty, but were protected by an exceptions clause.

【案例】一艘以定期租船合同出租的船舶的航速表述为14.5节。由于船底被一些软体动物缠绕，它的航速仅达到10.61节。判决船舶出租人违反保证，但可以受到除外条款的保护。

The word "about" when qualifying the warranty as to speed allows a margin on either side of the stated speed; the extent of the margin is a matter of fact, not one of law. It was argued that there were only two possible margins that could be allowed for the word "about", half a knot or five percent. The English Court of Appeals considered that it must be tailored to the ship's configuration, size, draught and trim, etc.

"大约"一词就所规定的航速节数给予一定的浮动幅度，幅度的大小是一个事实问题，而不是法律问题。曾经有争议认为，关于"大约"，只有两个浮动幅度可以被允许，即半节或百分之五。英国上诉法院对此认为，必须考虑船舶的结构、尺寸、吃水和平衡等因素。

2. Safe Port
2. 安全港口

Under the time charter party, the primary obligation of the charterers is to order the vessel only to safe ports where the ship may safely lie always afloat. In general, the criteria applicable in the case of voyage charters apply also to time charters. But the shipowners of vessels are more in need of protection from a safe port promise when operating under a time charter, in accordance with which they may be required to go to ports worldwide, than when operating under a voyage charter with named or listed loading and discharging ports.

在定期租船合同下，承租人的主要义务仅是指示船舶到达能使其始终漂浮的安全港口。一般情况下，适用于航次租船的标准也可以适用于定期租船。但是，若根据定期租船方式运营，船舶出租人更需要得到安全港口的保障承诺，因为船舶可能被指派到世界各地的任一港口，而按照航次租船方式运营（合同中会指定或列出装卸港口）则不会有这样的保障承诺。

2.1 Definition of Safe Port
2.1 安全港的定义

The classic definition of a "safe port" is that a port will not be safe unless, in the relevant period, the particular ship can reach it, use it, and return from it without, in the absence of some abnormal occurrence, being exposed to danger which cannot be avoided by good navigation and seamanship.

安全港是指一个港口能使船舶在抵达、进港、在港停泊和离港的整个相关期内，在未出现某些非常事件的情况下，不会处于运用了良好的航海技术和船艺仍不能避免的危险中。

If the charterer sends the vessel to an unsafe port, and she is damaged as a result, the charterer will have to indemnify the shipowner. But if the master has acted unreasonably, knowing of the danger in the port and having proceeded to enter it, and damage results the charterer will not be liable.

如果承租人指示船舶到不安全的港口，船舶因此而损坏，承租人要赔偿船舶出租人。但如果船长的行为不合理，知道港口危险仍进入港口并造成损害后果，承租人将不承担责任。

【Case】The Sussex Oak was time chartered under the BALTIME Form and was ordered to proceed to Hamburg. On her passage up the Elbe, ice was encountered, but the pilot considered it safe to proceed. When the ship was nearing the approaches to Hamburg she was stopped by a large ice flow. The ship was then in a part of the river in which she could neither turn, go astern nor anchor in safety and on the advice of the pilot forced her way through the ice, sustaining damage in consequence. It was found as a fact that the master acted properly in proceeding without ice breaker assistance, and it was held that the charterer was liable for the damage on the ground that Hamburg was then an unsafe port. The charterer does not guarantee that the most direct route or any particular route to the port is safe, but the voyage he orders must be one that an ordinarily prudent and skillful master can find a way of making in safety.

【案例】"Sussex Oak"号船是以波尔的姆定期租船合同形式出租，并被命令前往汉堡。它在过易北河通道时遇到冰，但引航员认为可以安全通过。当船接近汉堡，它被一大块冰流阻滞。该船在河中既不能返航，又不能直航，也不能安全锚泊，在引航员的建议下，船舶强行破冰，结果造成损害。事实是船长在没有破冰船协助的情况下，采取行为是适当的，判决承租人承担责任，理由是汉堡当时是不安全的港口。承租人不保证大多数直接的航线或某条航线的港口是安全的，但他所指令的航程必须是一名通常谨慎和干练的船长可以采取一种方法使船舶安全的航程。

Where the charter party requires the vessel to use safe ports only, the port, at the time when the order is given, must be prospectively safe for her to get to, stay at, so far as necessary, and in due course leave it. But if some unexpected and abnormal event thereafter suddenly occurs which creates conditions of unsafety where conditions of safety had previously existed and as a result the ship is delayed, damaged, or destroyed, the charterer is not liable.

如果租船合同要求船舶只能使用安全港口，在承租人下达该命令时，该港口必须是预计安全的，即船舶抵达、停留或离开该港时应该是安全的。然而，如果因意外和异常事件的发生导致原本存在的安全条件突然变为不安全条件，使该船舶延误、损坏或遇到破坏，承租人不承担责任。

Where the time charterer has performed his primary obligation by ordering the ship to a port which at the time of the order was prospectively safe, and while she is still proceeding to that port new circumstances arise which render the port unsafe, he is under a secondary obligation to cancel his original order and order her to go to another port which at the time when the fresh order is given is prospectively safe.

如果定期承租人已履行了其主要义务，下命令使船舶驶往当时看起来是安全的港口，但在船舶驶向该港口时出现了新情况，使港口变为不安全，则承租人负有辅助性义务，即取消原先的指令，并重新指示船舶前往另一个预计安全的港口。

Where the vessel has entered the port and new circumstances arise which render the port unsafe, the charterer is under no secondary obligation to nominate another port, if the vessel can't avoid the danger by leaving the port. But if she can avoid the danger by leaving the port, the charterer must order her to leave forthwith, whether or not she has completed loading and discharge, and order her to go to another safe port.

如果船舶进入港口，新的情况出现以致港口不安全，且船舶离开港口仍不可能避免危险，承租人没有义务再指令另一个港口。但是，如果离开港口船舶有可能避免危险，则不论船舶是否已完成装货和卸货，承租人必须命令船舶立即离开，并指令船舶到另一个安全的港口。

【Case】The Evia under a time charter party which required the charterer to use safe ports only was ordered by him in March 1980 to load cargo in Cuba for discharge at Basrah. She arrived and berthed on 20 August and completed discharge on 22 September, on which day war broke out between Iran and Iraq. The ship was unable to leave because of the danger to navigation. The shipowner claimed damages from the charterer for breach of his safe port obligation.

【案例】"Evia"号船以定期租船合同出租，合同规定承租人只能使用安全港口。该船于1980年3月被指令在古巴装载货物到巴士拉卸货。"Evia"号船于8月20日抵达并靠泊且在9月22日完成卸货，在那一天伊朗和伊拉克之间爆发战争。该船因为航行危险无法离开。船舶出租人要求违反安全港义务的承租人赔偿。

It was held by the House of Lords that there would be judgment for the charterer, for Basrah was prospectively safe at the time of nomination, and the unsafety was due to an unexpected and abnormal event after her arrival. The charterer was not under a secondary obligation to make a fresh nomination because such an order would have been ineffective.

上议院做出有利于承租人的判决，巴士拉在承租人下命令时是预计安全的，在到达时由于意外和异常事件变为不安全。承租人没有一个继发性义务给予新的指令，因为这种指令将是无意义的。

2.2 Trading limits
2.2 航区限制

The time charter parties usually contain additional limits for the trading. It is the time charterers who direct the vessel. The object of this clause is not to grant liberty but to impose a limit or restriction, by cutting down the unlimited and universal liberty of the charterer and excluding him from certain areas. The trading limits usually include several kinds of limitations. The shipowners must, in the first place, see to it that those limits stipulated by the underwriters are included also in the time charter party. This is usually done by the wording "but always within hull underwriters' trading limits" or similar. Note that a reference to Institute Warranty Limits is not always sufficient as other limits are used by many underwriters.

定期租船合同通常包含额外航区限制。一般情况下，由定期承租人指挥船舶。该条款的目的是给航区自由施加限制，通过削减承租人无限制和普遍的自由，将某些地区排除在外。航区限制通常包括几种限制。船舶出租人必须首先查看保险人规定的限制是否包括在定期租船合同中。通常有"总是在船舶保险人航区限制内"的文字或类似表述。请注意，保险协会航区限制并不是很充分，许多保险人还有一些其他限制。

If the time charterers wish to direct the vessel to ports or places outside the limits of the charter party they must first get permission from the shipowners, who sometimes must get permission from the underwriters.

如果定期承租人想要船舶驶往租船合同限制外的港口或地方，他们必须首先得到船舶出租人的许可，而船舶出租人必须获得保险人的许可。

It is a breach of the contract for the charterers to employ the ship outside the limits stated; the master may properly refuse an order from the charterers to proceed outside them. Mere compliance, without more, with the charterers' order to proceed outside the trading limits will probably not amount to a waiver of shipowners' rights either to refuse further compliance subsequently or to claim damages for the breach. Nor will the master's obedience to such an order usually amount to a waiver as he is under the charterers' orders and directions as regards employment.

船舶出租人将船舶用于规定范围之外的用途构成违约。船长完全有权拒绝承租人发出的驶离该范围的指令。仅仅服从承租人发出的驶离航行范围的指令（无其他行为），很可能不构成对船舶出租人权利的放弃，船舶出租人仍有权在日后拒绝进一步的服从，或就该违约索赔损失。船长服从此类指令通常也不构成放弃（权利），因为在船舶使用方面，船长受承租人的指令和指示约束。

According to the provisions of article 134 of CMC, "the charterer shall guarantee that the ship shall be employed in the agreed maritime transport between the safe ports or places within the trading area agreed upon. If the charterer acts against the provisions of the preceding paragraph, the shipowner is entitled to cancel the charter and claim any losses resulting therefrom".

根据《中华人民共和国海商法》第134条的规定："承租人应当保证船舶在约定航区内的安全港口或者地点之间从事约定的海上运输。承租人违反前款规定的，出租人有权解除合同，并有权要求赔偿因此遭受的损失。"

3. Description of the Cargo
3. 货物说明

The time charter party differs from the voyage charter party which is rather an agreement for carriage of a certain cargo, with a certain vessel and certain ports. Instead of mentioning a certain cargo, the time charter party, mostly in general terms, states the types of cargo the time charterers are allowed to carry with the ship. Besides the trading restriction, the most important restriction as regards the time charterers' freedom to use and direct the ship is the restriction on cargo to be carried in the vessel. The general description of cargo accepted for the vessel sometimes excludes some cargoes. The printed charter party forms usually also contain a specification of cargo that is not allowed.

定期租船合同与规定特定货物、特定船舶、特定港口的航次租船合同不同。定期租船合同不规定特定货物，大多笼统地规定允许承租人装船的货物种类。除了航区限制外，对承租人自由地使用和指示船舶最重要的限制就是船上装载的货物了。允许装船的货物通常以除外货物的方式来表述。印就的租船合同范本通常还会包含不允许装运货物的详细说明。

3.1 Cargo Exclusions in NYPE Form 1993
3.1 1993年土产格式除外货物

In NYPE Form 1993 this clause has the following wording:

在1993年土产格式中，这一条款措辞如下：

"(1) The vessel shall be employed in carrying lawful merchandise excluding any goods of a dangerous, injurious, flammable or corrosive nature unless carried in accordance with the requirements or recommendations of the competent authorities of the country of the vessel's registry and ports of shipment and discharge and of any intermediate countries or ports through whose waters the vessel must pass. Without prejudice to the generality of the foregoing, in addition, the following are specifically excluded: livestock of any description, arms, ammunition, explosives, nuclear, and radioactive materials.

（1）"船舶应被用于运输合法货物，不包括任何危险性、伤害性、易燃性或者腐蚀性的货物，但根据船舶登记国、装货港、卸货港和船舶必经水域的港口或国家的主管当局的要求或者指示运输的除外。此外，在不影响上述一般原则的情况下，下列货物应明确除外：任何品名的牲畜、武器、弹药、爆炸物、核材料和放射性材料。

(2) If IMO-classified cargo is agreed to be carried, the amount of such cargo shall be limited to _____ tons and the charterers shall provide the master with any evidence he may reasonably require to show that the cargo is packaged, labeled, loaded, and stowed in accordance with IMO regulations, failing which the master is entitled to refuse such cargo or, if already loaded, to unload it at the charterers' risk and expense."

（2）如果协议运输国际海事组织所属的货物，该货物的数量不应超过_____吨，承租人应向船长提供其可能合理要求的，表明货物已经根据国际海事组织的规定进行包装、加标、装船和积载的任何证据，否则，船长有权拒绝该货物；或者，如果货物已经装船，船长有权将货物卸下，并由承租人承担风险和费用。"

Lawful merchandise may include military stores and munitions. But goods will not be lawful merchandise if their loading amounts to a breach of the local law nor if they cannot lawfully be discharged at the nominated discharge ports. Presumably, they must also be lawful under the law of the ship's flag and the proper law of the charter.

合法货物可以包括军事物资和弹药。但如果装货港或卸货港法律认为其属于非法的，则该货物即是不合法货物。其也必须是根据船旗国法和合同适用的法律认可的合法货物。

It is a breach of the contract for the charterers to ship goods excluded by the charter and the master may properly refuse an order to load such cargo. Also, according to the provisions of Article 135 of CMC, "the charterer shall guarantee that the ship shall be employed to carry the lawful merchandise agreed. Where the ship is employed by the charterer to carry live animals or dangerous goods, prior consent of the shipowners is required. The charterer shall be liable for any loss of the shipowner resulting from the charterer's violation of this article."

承租人装运租船合同除外的货物，是违反租船合同的，船长可以适当地拒绝关于装载这些货物的命令。根据《中华人民共和国海商法》第135条的规定："承租人应当保证船舶用于运输约定的合法的货物。承租人将船舶用于运输活动物或者危险货物的，应当事先征得出租人的同意。承租人违反规定致使出租人遭受损失的，应当负赔偿责任。"

The time charter parties often incorporate the *United States Carriage of Goods by Sea Act* or the *Hague Rules.* According to these rules relating to dangerous cargo carried, first, the Rules allow the shipowners to land, destroy, or render innocuous inflammable, explosive or dangerous goods to the shipment of which they have not consented with knowledge of their nature. Secondly, the shippers (charterers) are liable for all damages and expenses arising out of such shipment. Thirdly, it concerns the shipment of such cargoes to which the shipowners have consented with knowledge of their nature but which become a danger to their ship or its cargo and it gives the shipowners the rights listed in the first.

定期租船合同往往将《美国海上货物运输法》或《海牙规则》并入。根据这些规则就危险货物运输而言，第一，当他们并没有同意装运以及不知其性质时，它允许船舶出租人卸岸、销毁或使易燃、易爆或危险品无害；第二，托运人（承租人）对可能引起的所有的损失和费用负责；第三，如果船舶出租人已同意并知晓其性质，但当对于船舶或货物有危险时，船舶出租人有权按照第一种所述的情况处置。

3.2 Cargo Liability
3.2 货物责任

In time chartering, the charterers and shipowners can allocate the liability for cargo as they wish but as liability under a bill of lading is also often involved, the situation is sometimes complex from a legal standpoint. Cargo owners usually claim under the bill of lading and the first question is whether the shipowners, time charterers, or both, are liable to the cargo owners. The second question is how the liability should ultimately be allocated between the charterers and shipowners.

在定期租船中，承租人和船舶出租人可以根据意愿分配对货物的赔偿责任，但提单项下责任也经常涉及，从法律的角度看情况有时更为复杂。货主通常根据提单提出索赔，第一个问题是船舶出租人、承租人或两者对货主承担责任；第二个问题是赔偿责任如何最终在承租人与船舶出租人之间分配。

3.2.1 Transfer of Responsibility to the Charterers
3.2.1 责任转移给承租人

In the absence of express provision, the obligation to load, stow, trim, and discharge the cargo is at common law on the shipowners. The NYPE Form 1993 has the effect of shifting from the shipowners to the charterers the primary responsibility for loading, stowing and trimming the cargo. It provides that "the Charterers shall perform all cargo handling, including but not limited to loading, stowing, trimming, lashing, securing, dunnaging, unlashing, discharging, and tallying, at their risk and expense, under the supervision of the Master".

在没有明文规定的情况下，装载、积载、平舱和卸载货物的义务在普通法下归属于船舶出租人。1993年土产格式将货物装载、积载和平舱的主要责任从船舶出租人转移给承租人。它规定"承租人在船长的监督下，自负风险和费用，负责全部货物的操作，包括但不限于装载、积载、平舱、绑扎、加固、垫舱、解绑、卸载和理货"。

The master has the right to supervise the cargo operation, particularly from a ship safety point of view, irrespective of the words "under the supervision of the master". But, leaving aside considerations of safety, he has no duty to the charterers to supervise. These words only qualify the primary responsibility that the NYPE Form 1993 places on the charterers for the loading and stowing of the cargo: (a) if loss or damage is attributable to want of care in matters particularly within the province of the master, such as, the stability of the ship; (b) if the master supervises the cargo operations and loss or damage is attributable to that supervision.

特别是从船舶安全的角度看，船长有权监管货物的作业，不管是否有"在船长的监督下"的字眼。但是，撇开对安全的考虑，他对承租人没有监管的责任。这些话仅限于1993年土产格式承租人关于装卸、积载货物的基本责任：（a）如果灭失或损坏是由于缺乏照料，尤其是在船长的职责内，如船舶的稳定性；（b）如果船长实际监督货物作业，而灭失或损害归因于该监督。

Where it is intended by the parties that responsibility for the operations shall be upon the shipowners, it is usual for the words "and responsibility" to be inserted after "supervision". The addition of these words has been held to effect a prima facie transfer from the charterers back to the shipowners of liability for the entire operation of loading, stowing, trimming, and discharging of the cargo.

当双方当事人规定由船舶出租人承担货物作业的责任，通常在"监管"之后插入"和责任"一词。这些附加文字被判定为将承租人对整个货物装载、积载、平舱和卸货的作业过程的责任转移给船舶出租人的表面证据。

3.2.2 The Inter-Club Agreement
3.2.2 协会内部协议

In order to avoid endless discussions between shipowners and charterers, several P&I Clubs have made a special agreement for the apportionment of liability for cargo under the time charter party based on the NYPE Form 1993.

为了避免船舶出租人和承租人之间无休止的讨论，一些保赔协会已基于1993年土产格式就定期租船合同下货物的责任分摊达成了一项特别协议。

In NYPE Form 1993, it states that "cargo claims as between the owners and the charterers shall be settled in accordance with the Inter-Club New York Produce Exchange Agreement of February 1970, as amended May 1984, or any subsequent modification or replacement thereof".

1993年土产格式规定："出租人和承租人之间的货物索赔，应根据1970年2月纽约土产交易所协会内部协议1984年5月修正案或其以后的任何修正案或代替案解决。"

This agreement, officially named "The Inter-Club New York Produce Exchange Agreement", is usually called "The Inter-Club Agreement". The latest replacement is *the Inter-Club Agreement 1996*, which has the following allocations:

该协议正式命名为"协会内部纽约土产交易所协议"，通常称为"协会内部协议"。最新版本的1996年协会内部协议，对责任做了以下分配：

(a) Claims, in fact, arising out of unseaworthiness and/or error or fault in navigation or management of the vessel: 100% owners save where the owners prove that the unseaworthiness was caused by the loading, stowage, lashing, discharge, or other handling of the cargo, in which case the claim shall be apportioned under sub-clause (b).

（a）船舶不适航和/或航行过失或管船过失引起的货物索赔，船舶出租人负100%的责任。除非船舶出租人证明不适航是由装载、积载、绑扎、卸载或其他货物的操作造成的，在这种情况下，应按照（b）进行分摊。

(b) Claims, in fact, arising out of the loading, stowage, lashing, discharge or another handling of cargo: 100% charterers unless the words "and responsibility" are added in clause 8 or there is a similar amendment making the master responsible for cargo handling in which case: 50% charterers, 50% owners save where the charterers prove that the failure properly to load, stow, lash, discharge or handle the cargo was caused by the unseaworthiness of the vessel in which case: 100% owners.

（b）由装载、积载、绑扎、卸载或其他货物的操作造成的货物索赔，承租人负100%的责任，如果"负责"一词加在第8条中或者有类似使船长对货物的操作负责的改动，则船舶出租人和承租人各负50%的责任。若承租人证明未尽适当地装载、积载、绑扎、卸载或货物的操作是由船舶不适航引起的，在这种情况下，船舶出租人负100%的责任。

(c) Subject to (a) and (b) above, claims for shortage or overcarriage: 50% charterers, 50% owners unless there is clear and irrefutable evidence that the claim arose out of pilferage or acts or neglect by one or the other (including their servants or sub-contractors) in which case that party shall then bear 100% of the claim.

(c)除前两款规定外，短少或溢装引起的货物索赔，船舶出租人和承租人各负50%的责任。除非有清楚且无可辩驳的证据证明货物索赔是由一方当事人（包括其雇佣人员或分包商）偷窃或某行为或疏忽引起的，则该当事人承担100%的责任。

(d) All other cargo claims whatsoever (including claims for delay to cargo): 50% charterers, 50% owners unless there is clear and irrefutable evidence that the claim arose out of the act or neglect of the one or the other (including their servants or sub-contractors) in which case that party shall then bear 100% of the claim.

(d)所有任何其他货物索赔（包括迟延索赔），船舶出租人和承租人各负50%的责任。除非有清楚且无可辩驳的证据证明货物索赔是由一方当事人（包括其雇佣人员或分包商）的行为或疏忽引起的，则该当事人承担100%的责任。

UNIT 2　PERIOD OF CHARTER AND DELIVERY/REDELIVERY
第二单元　合同租期和交还船

The time charter parties regularly contain a clause stating the length of the charter period. To avoid recurring disputes on the duration of the charter, it is recommended to specify clearly the exact period of hire with any margin. The vessel must be delivered to the time charterer by the shipowner not later than a certain date and at the end of the charter period, the charterer has to redeliver the vessel.

定期租船合同常常载有一个说明该合同租期期限的条款。为了避免发生租期纠纷，建议清楚地订明租用的确切时间以及宽限期。船舶出租人必须不得迟于某一特定日期将船舶交付承租人，而承租人在租期届满时必须还船。

1. Period of Charter
1. 租期

1.1 Implied Margin or Allowance
1.1 默示宽限期

When a charter party is for a stated period—such as "three months" or "six months"—without any express margin or allowance, then the court will imply a reasonable margin or allowance. The reason is that no one can calculate exactly the day on which the last voyage will end. Where such a margin is implied, the charterer is not in breach if he sends the vessel on a final voyage which can reasonably be expected to end beyond the stated period itself but within the implied margin. It is legitimate for the charterer to send the vessel on a last voyage which may exceed the stated period by a few days. If the vessel's redelivery exceeds the stated period and the market rate has gone up, the charterer is only bound to pay the charter rate until she is redelivered.

当租船合同规定一定期间时，如"3个月"或"6个月"，是未明确约定宽限期，法院将默示适用合理的宽限期。原因是任何人都无法精确地计算出最后航行结束之日。当适用这种默示宽限期时，如果承租人安排船舶最后航程时合理地预计会超出规定的租期但没有超出默示的宽限期，则没有违反合同。承租人安排船舶最后航程可能超过规定租期几天是合法的。如果还船超过规定租期，市场租金上升，承租人仅需负责支付至还船时合同约定的租金。

1.2 No Margin or Allowance Express or Implied
1.2 没有明示或默示宽限期

But it is open to the parties to provide in the charter party by express words or by implication that there is to be no margin or allowance as between a certain "minimum" and a certain "maximum" time. In such a case, the court will not imply an additional margin beyond the stated "maximum". The charterer must ensure that the vessel is redelivered within the stated period. If he does not do so and the market rate has gone up, he will be bound to pay the extra. That is to say, he will be bound to pay the charter rate up to the end of the stated period, and the market rate thereafter.

但是，各方当事人可以通过明示或默示的方式在租船合同中自由订立没有宽限期，即规定确定的最低和最高租期。在这种情况下，法院将不给予超出最高租期的宽限期。承租人必须确保船舶在上述期间内还船。如果他没有这样做，市场租金上涨，他将必须支付额外的租金。这就是说，承租人将必须按合同规定的租金支付至租期结束，其后按市场租金支付。

【Case】The Mareva was chartered under the NYPE for a trip. By addendum No. 1 the charter period was extended to five months, twenty days more or less at the charterer's option. Subsequently, a further addendum was concluded providing "the charterer is to keep the vessel on time charter for a further period of 2 months minimum, 3 months maximum, in direct continuation from the end of the full period of 5 months and 20 days". It was held by the court that no margin beyond the further three months was to be allowed.

【案例】"Mareva" 号船以土产格式出租一个航次。在附录第1条中规定租期延长至5个月，承租人选择20天的宽限期。随后，订立另一个附录进一步规定在 "从5个月20天租期结束后，承租人可以继续租船最低2个月以上、最多3个月"。法院判决，对于其后3个月的租期没有宽限期。

1.3 Express Margin or Allowance
1.3 明示宽限期

It is also open to the parties themselves to fix expressly what the margin or allowance shall be. If this has been done, such as by adding to the basic period "20 days more or less", that leaves no room for any implied margin or allowance. The express margin is greater than any period that would normally be implied.

各方当事人可以在租船合同中自由订立明确的宽限期。如果出现这种规定，如增加的宽限期为 "或多或少20天"，则没有任何默示的宽限期。明确的宽限期优于任何通常的默示宽限期。

To avoid recurring disputes on the duration of the charter, it is recommended to specify clearly the exact period of charter with any margin, if any is agreed.

为了避免租期纠纷，建议明确规定租期以及宽限期。

1.4 Extension of the Period
1.4 租期延长

Charterers are not entitled to an extension of the period because of the off-hire period that occurred during the charter unless this is expressly stated in the charter party. If such a clause is inserted, it is advisable also to state the latest time by which the charterers must notify the shipowners that they intend to use their option to extend the charter period. Furthermore, the hire for the additional period should be determined as well as the question of whether off-hire during the extension period will give the charterer a right to an additional extension.

若租期中发生停租，承租人无权延长租期，除非在租船合同中明确规定。如果有这样的条款并入租约，最好也规定承租人打算利用其选择权延长租期的最迟通知船舶出租人的时间。此外，应明确延长租用期间的租金支付方式，以及延长期如发生停租是否给予承租人再次延长租期的权利。

2. Time for Delivery and Redelivery
2. 交还船时间

In time chartering it must be agreed when the vessel shall be ready to be delivered to the charterer not later than a certain date and redelivered to the shipowner at the end of the charter period.

在定期租船中，必须规定船不得迟于某一特定日期交付承租人并在租期届满时还船给船舶出租人。

2.1 Time for Delivery
2.1 交船时间

For the delivery, it is usually to state several days which are so-called laydays, for instance, "March 1−10". If the vessel arrives too early, the charterers are not obliged to take delivery before the layday and if she arrives too late they are entitled to cancel the charter party.

对于交船，通常表述为一段日期，即所谓的受载期，例如"3月1日至10日"。如果该船到达太早，承租人没有义务在受载期前接船；如果到达太晚，承租人有权取消租船合同。

The shipowners shall give the charterers not less than a few days' notice of the expected date of delivery, such as "7/5/3/2/1 notice of the expected date of delivery".

船舶出租人应给承租人不少于几天的预计交船日期的通知，如"7/5/3/2/1预计交船日期的通知"。

Under the NYPE Form, the charterers are given the option to cancel if the ship shall not have given notice of readiness by the stated date; and the shipowners' notice of readiness must be valid as well as timely. The exercise by the charterers of their right to cancel does not deprive them of the right to claim damages if the shipowners were in breach of any of their obligations under the charter and the charterers suffered loss as a result.

根据土产格式，如果船舶在规定日期没有给予装卸准备就绪通知书，承租人可以选择取消合同。装卸准备就绪通知书必须是有效和及时的。如果船舶出租人违反合同规定的义务并致使承租人遭受了损失，承租人有权取消合同并不剥夺其要求赔偿的权利。

According to the provisions of Article 131 of CMC, "the shipowner shall deliver the ship within the time agreed upon in the charter party. Where the shipowner acts against the provisions of the preceding paragraph, the charterer is entitled to cancel the charter. However, if the shipowner has notified the charterer of the anticipated delay in delivery and has given an estimated time on arrival of the ship at the port of delivery, the charterer shall notify the shipowner, within 48 hours of the receipt of such notice from the shipowner, of his decision whether to cancel the charter or not".

根据《中华人民共和国海商法》第131条的规定："出租人应当按照合同约定的时间交付船舶。出租人违反前款规定的，承租人有权解除合同。出租人将船舶延误情况和船舶预期抵达交船港的日期通知承租人的，承租人应当自接到通知时起四十八小时内，将解除合同或者继续租用船舶的决定通知出租人。"

According to the NYPE Form 1993, it states that "if the owners warrant that, despite the exercise of due diligence by them, the vessel will not be ready for delivery by the canceling date, and provided the owners can state with reasonable certainty the date on which the vessel will be ready, they may, at the earliest seven days before the vessel is expected to sail for the port or place of delivery, require the charterers to declare whether or not they will cancel the charter party. Should the charterers select not to cancel, or should they fail to reply within two days or by the canceling date, whichever shall first occur, then the seventh day after the expected date of readiness for delivery as notified by the owners shall replace the original canceling date. Should the vessel be further delayed, the owners shall be entitled to require further declarations of the charterers in accordance with this clause".

根据1993年土产格式的规定："如果出租人确定，尽管其尽到谨慎处理义务，船舶仍不能在解约日之前做好交船准备，只要出租人能明确一个船舶将做好交船准备的合理的确定日期，则最早在船舶预计驶往交船港口或地点的前7天，出租人可以要求承租人宣布是否解除本租船合同。如果承租人选择不解除合同，或在两天内或解约日之前（以两者中较早者为准）未作出答复，则以出租人通知的预计做好交船准备之日后的第7天代替原来的解约日。如果船舶进一步延期，出租人根据本条规定有权要求承租人再次做出声明。"

2.2 Time for Redelivery
2.2 还船时间

The charterers shall redeliver the ship on the agreed redelivery date or within the agreed redelivery period. Sometimes the vessel is redelivered before and sometimes after the agreed redelivery date or period. The shipowners cannot refuse to take the ship if the charterers redeliver her earlier than they are entitled to do so despite this being a breach of contract on the charterers' side. The shipowners must try to minimize their loss by seeking alternative employment for the vessel but if they fail or if they get lower revenue compared with the previous charter, they are entitled to compensation from the charterers. It is, however, not always clear how this compensation should be calculated.

承租人应当在约定的还船日期或期间还船。有时承租人会比约定的还船日期或期间提早还船或者滞后还船。如果承租人早于约定的还船日期还船，船舶出租人不能拒绝接收船舶，即便是承租人一方违约。船舶出租人有责任通过另外的方法尽量减少船舶损失，但如果不能避免损失或者获得收入比先前合同约定的收入低的话，他们有权从承租人处获得补偿。然而，补偿的计算方法并非总是很清楚。

【Case】The Alaskan Trader was chartered on the NYPE Form for 24 months and delivered in December 1979. In October 1980 she suffered a serious engine breakdown which it was clear would take several months to repair. The charterer indicated that he had no further use for the ship but the shipowner nevertheless proceeded with the repairs. The repairs were completed in April 1981 but the charterer declined to give the master any orders and said he regarded the charter as at an end. The shipowner did not treat the charterer's conduct as a repudiation but continued to hold the ship at the charterer's disposal, fully crewed and ready to sail until the charter expired in December 1981. She was then sold for scrap. Hire was paid throughout by the charterer on a without prejudice basis. The charterer claimed to recover the hire he had paid on the basis that the shipowner should have accepted his repudiation and claimed damages.

【案例】"The Alaskan Trader"号船以土产格式期租24个月,在1979年12月交船。1980年10月,该船主机产生了严重的故障,很明显需要几个月的时间来修复。承租人表示不再使用该船舶,而船舶出租人仍然进行维修。1981年4月维修工作完成,但承租人拒绝给船长发布任何指令,并说他们认为合同已经结束。船舶出租人没有把承租人的行为看作是合同终止,继续保持船舶在承租人处置之下,船员在船并待命开航,直到1981年12月合同期满。船舶后来被出售拆解。承租人在坚持合同已终止的基础上支付了整个租期的租金。承租人在船舶出租人已经接受终止的基础上要求收回支付的租金并要求赔偿损失。

It was held by an arbitrator that the shipowner was not obliged to accept the charterer's repudiation in October 1980, but that he should have done so in April 1981 as the finality of the charterer's refusal to accept the ship made it "clear that the charter was dead". The arbitrator held further that the shipowner had no legitimate interest in holding the charterer to his contract rather than claiming damages.

仲裁员裁定,船舶出租人没有义务在1980年10月接受承租人合同关系解除的决定,但应该在1981年4月接受,因为承租人最终拒绝接受该船舶使得合同已经终止。仲裁员进一步指出,船舶出租人与其要求承租人履行合同,不如主张损害赔偿,后者更符合其合法利益。

When the charterers are planning the last voyage for the vessel under the charter they must take into consideration that she has to be redelivered in accordance with the agreement in the charter party. As it is often difficult to determine beforehand exactly when the vessel shall be redelivered, the time charter party forms usually have a special clause about the last voyage.

当承租人根据租船合同规划最后航次时,他们必须考虑到船舶应当按照合同规定还船。由于往往很难事先确定什么时候将船舶交还,租船合同范本通常有一个关于最后航次的特别条款。

If the charterer sends the vessel on a voyage that it is reasonably expected will be completed by the end of the charter period, the shipowner must obey the directions. If she is delayed by causes for which neither party is responsible, hire is payable at the charter rate until redelivery even though the market rate may have gone up or down.

如果承租人在发布最后航次时,合理预计该航次将在租期结束前完成,则船舶出租人必须服从指示。如果船舶是由非任何一方的原因延误,租金按照合同规定支付直至还船为止,无论市场租金率可能上升或下跌。

【Case】The London Explorer was chartered under the NYPE Form for "12 months 15 days more or less in charterer's option". She was sent on a final voyage that could have allowed redelivery well within this period but which was extended by unforeseen strikes until considerably after its expiry. The freight market had fallen and the charterer sought to establish that he was in breach and, therefore, obliged to pay damages for the period of "overlap" at the then market rate instead of continuing throughout that period to pay hire at the (higher) rate stipulated in the charter. The House of Lords rejected this argument, holding that there was no breach of contract. The orders for the final voyage were good and did not cease to be so because of unexpected delays thereafter. In any event, the hire was payable at the charter rate until redelivery.

【案例】"London Explorer" 号船以土产格式期租 "12个月、15天宽限期，由承租人选择"。承租人在安排最后航次时预计能在合同期满时还船，但由于不可预见的罢工延长至期满后还船。航运市场租金下降，承租人试图证明其存在违约行为，因此有义务按照当时的市场费率支付超期损害赔偿，而不是按照整个租期规定的租金（较高）支付。英国上议院拒绝了这一说法，认为承租人没有违约。最后航程的指令是适宜的，并没有因为意外延误停止。在任何情况下，应根据合同规定的租金支付直至还船。

If the charterer sends the vessel on a voyage that she cannot reasonably be expected to complete within the charter period, the shipowner is entitled to refuse that direction and call for another one. If the charterer refuses to give it, the shipowner can accept his conduct as a breach of contract, fix a fresh charter for the vessel, and sue for damages.

如果承租人指示船舶进行其合理预期无法在租期内完成的航次，船舶出租人有权拒绝这一指令，并要求承租人发出另一项指示。如果承租人拒绝发出新指示，船舶出租人可以把承租人的行为视为违反合同，从而确定一个新的租船合同，并诉请损失赔偿。

If the shipowner agrees to the voyage originally ordered by the charterer, he is entitled to be paid hire at the current market rate for the excess period.

如果船舶出租人同意承租人发布的原航次命令，其有权要求以当前市场租金率支付超期部分的租金。

According to the provisions of Article 143 of CMC, "if, based on a reasonable calculation, a ship may be able to complete her last voyage at around the time of redelivery specified in the charter and probably thereafter, the charterer is entitled to continue to use the ship to complete that voyage even if its time of redelivery will be overdue. During the extended period, the charterer shall pay the hire at the rate fixed by the charter, and, if the current market rate of hire is higher than that specified in the charter, the charterer shall pay the hire at the current market rate."

根据《中华人民共和国海商法》第143条的规定："经合理计算，完成最后航次的日期约为合同约定的还船日期，但可能超过合同约定的还船日期的，承租人有权超期用船以完成该航次。超期期间，承租人应当按照合同约定的租金率支付租金；市场的租金率高于合同约定的租金率的，承租人应当按照市场租金率支付租金。"

3. Port or Place of Delivery and Redelivery
3. 交还船港口或地点

The port or place of delivery and redelivery can be more or less specified. Sometimes a certain port is mentioned and sometimes a certain area or range, i.e. "vessel to be delivered and redelivered in the Mediterranean". When only an area or a range is mentioned it is usually the shipowners who choose the place of delivery and the charterers who decide the port of redelivery.

交货港或交货地以及还船港或还船地的规定详细程度可能有所不同。有时指定某个确定港口，有时指定一定区域或范围，即"船舶在地中海交还船"。当只有一个地区或一个范围时，通常是船舶出租人选择交船地点，承租人决定还船港口。

Delivery and redelivery may not necessarily take place when the vessel is in port. It is not unusual that the charter parties contain a delivery or a redelivery clause of the following types: "vessel to be delivered/redelivered on Dropping Outward Pilot at one safe port" or "Taking Inward Pilot at one safe port" or "Arrival Pilot Station at one safe port".

交还船不一定发生在船舶在港时。通常，租船合同载有以下类型的交还船条款："船舶应在某一安全港引航员下船时交还船"或"船舶在某一个安全港引航员上船时交还船"或"船舶到达某一个安全港引航站时交还船"。

"Arrival Pilot Station" signifies a location on arrival at which a vessel will be delivered to a time charterer. This term has the advantage to the shipowner when compared with TIP.

"船舶到达引航站" 标志着一个到达地点，船舶出租人将船交付给定期承租人。当与"引航员上船时交还船"术语相比较时，这个术语有利于船舶出租人。

"Dropping Outward Pilot" signifies a point of delivery to a time charterer or redelivery to a shipowner, following a vessel's sailing from port.

"引航员下船时交还船"标志着船舶从港口向外航行，引航员下船时船舶交付承租人或还船给船舶出租人。

"Taking Inward Pilot" signifies a location on arrival at which, upon taking aboard the pilot, the ship is delivered to her time charterer. It has the advantage to the charterer when compared with APS as in the event of a suspension of the pilotage service, or late boarding by a pilot, the risk and expense of delay are that of the shipowner.

"引航员上船时交还船"标志着船舶到达某一地点时，搭载引航员即视为其向承租人交付船舶。与"船舶到达引航站"相比较，它有利于承租人，因为领港服务停止或引航员延迟登船的风险和费用由船舶出租人承担。

When describing delivery and redelivery points, it should be noted that these terms may not be sufficiently clear and may cause difficulties at a late stage, taking into account that pilotage, at many ports or places, may be performed in two or three stages and that the employment of compulsory and/or non-compulsory port pilots and river pilots may be necessary. The parties are accordingly recommended to describe the delivery and redelivery points as exactly as possible and to check in advance whether the contractual arrangement matches the actual conditions. Therefore the term "Dropping Last Outward Sea Pilot" may be used which indicates that all acts of pilotage must be completed at which a vessel will be delivered to a time charterer or redelivered to a shipowner.

当描述交还船地点时，应当注意：鉴于许多港口或地点的引航可能分为两到三个阶段进行，且可能需要雇用强制性和/或非强制性的港口引航员或内河引航员，这些术语可能不够明确，并可能在后期引发争议。因此，建议有关各方尽可能准确地指定交还船地点，并提前检查合同约定与实际情况是否相匹配。因此，可以使用"最后一个引航员下船时交还船"术语，该术语表明在所有引航行为完成后船舶交付承租人或还船给船舶出租人。

4. Conditions of the Vessel on Delivery and Redelivery
4. 交还船条件

There are some requirements for the state of the vessel on delivery and redelivery.

租船合同对交还船时船舶的状况有一些要求。

4.1 Conditions for Delivery of Vessel
4.1 交船时条件

The vessel shall, on delivery to the charterers, be seaworthy and conform to the requirements of the contract. This is, for example, stated in NYPE Form 1993 such as "the vessel on her delivery shall be ready to receive cargo with clean-swept holds and tight, staunch, strong and in every way fitted for ordinary cargo service, having water ballast and with sufficient power to operate all cargo handling gear simultaneously".

船舶交给承租人时应当适航并与合同要求一致。例如：1993 年土产格式规定"在交船时，船舶应做好接收货物的准备，货舱须打扫干净，船体紧密、坚实、牢固，并在各个方面适合于普通货物的运输。船舶应装备有压载水舱，同时具有启动所有装货设备的足够的动力"。

If the vessel is not in the state required by the charter, a valid notice of readiness cannot be given under the canceling clause; and upon the expiry of the time allowed in the charter, the charterers may exercise their option to cancel the charter. If the state of the vessel is due to breach of any of the shipowners' obligations under the charter, the charterers will normally be entitled to damages if they have suffered loss as a result.

如果船舶状况不符合合同要求，在解约日条款下不能递交一份有效的装卸准备就绪通知书，在合同允许的时间届满后，承租人可以行使其选择权取消合同。如果船舶的状况是由于船舶出租人违反任何合同义务，承租人如果遭受了损失，其通常有权获得损害赔偿。

The words "ready to receive cargo with clean-swept holds" are a concept much developed in cases under voyage charters, particularly in relation to the commencement of laytime. It is considered that the general propositions developed in these voyage charter cases apply also to time charter parties which require that on delivery the vessel shall be ready to load or receive cargo.

"做好接收货物的准备，货舱须打扫干净"这一概念在航次租船合同相关案例中已有诸多阐释，特别是涉及装卸时间起算的问题。通常认为，这些在航次租船中形成的一般性原则也适用于定期租船合同，即要求船舶须在交船时做好装载或接收货物的准备。

The words "tight, staunch, strong, and in every way fitted for ordinary cargo service" constitute an express obligation of seaworthiness. The express obligation of seaworthiness at the beginning of the charter period is reduced from an absolute obligation that the vessel will be seaworthy to an obligation to exercise due diligence to make the vessel seaworthy. It includes the requirement that the vessel must have certain kinds of documents, and it also includes the requirement that the vessel must be provided with a sufficient and competent crew.

"船体紧密、坚实、牢固，并在各个方面适合于普通货物的运输"构成了一项明确的适航义务。租期开始时的明确适航义务已从船舶必须绝对适航的义务，简化为履行谨慎处理使船舶适航的义务。它包括船舶必须持有特定种类的文件，还包括必须配备足够且适任的船员。

【Case】The Madeleine was chartered under the BALTIME Form for three months. The cancelling date was 10 May. On 6 May the vessel's de-ratting exemption certificate expired. On 9 May the vessel completed discharge of her inward cargo. However, after inspecting her, the port authorities refused to issue a new de-ratting exemption certificate. They ordered fumigation, with a view to issuing thereafter a de-ratting certificate. In the absence of a valid de-ratting exemption certificate, the vessel could not trade as the charter provided. Fumigation could not be completed before 12 May. At 8 a.m. on 10 May, the charterer advised the shipowner that he cancelled the charter and he gave a further notice of cancellation at 8:48 p.m. the same day. The certificate was issued on 12 May and the shipowner claimed that the charterer's cancellation was wrongful. It was held by the court that the vessel had to be delivered in the condition required by Clause 1 ("in every way fitted for ordinary cargo service", which means in a seaworthy condition) and that since the vessel was not delivered in a seaworthy condition by 6 p.m. on 10 May the charterer was entitled to cancel.

【案例】"Madeleine"号船以波尔的姆格式出租3个月。合同规定的解约日期为5月10日。5月6日该船的除鼠豁免证书过期。5月9日，该船完成进口货物的卸货。但在检查船舶后，港口当局拒绝签发一份新的除鼠豁免证书。他们命令船舶熏蒸，以便签发新的除鼠豁免证书。在缺乏一个有效的除鼠豁免证书的情况下，船舶不能在合同期间营运。熏蒸无法在5月12日前完成。5月10日早上8点，承租人通知船舶出租人取消合同，并于同日晚8时48分进一步发出取消通知。除鼠豁免证书已于5月12日签发，船舶出租人主张承租人的解约行为构成违约。法院判决：船舶必须按照第1条（在各个方面适合于普通货物的运输意味着处于适航条件）的规定交付，由于该船未能在5月10日晚6点处于适航状态交付，承租人有权解除合同。

According to the provisions of Article 132 of CMC, the shipowners shall exercise due diligence to make the vessel seaworthy at the time of delivery. The vessel delivered shall be fit for the intended service. Where the shipowners act against the provisions in the preceding paragraph, the charterers shall be entitled to cancel the charter and claim losses resulting therefrom.

根据《中华人民共和国海商法》第132条的规定，出租人交付船舶时，应当做到谨慎处理，使船舶适航。交付的船舶应当适于约定的用途。出租人违反前款规定的，承租人有权解除合同，并有权要求赔偿因此遭受的损失。

4.2 Conditions for Redelivery of Vessel
4.2 还船条件

As regards redelivery, the following or similar clauses are used:

就还船而言，通常使用下列术语：

"The vessel to be redelivered on the expiration of the charter in the same good order and condition, ordinary wear and tear excepted."

"船舶在合同期满时以交船时的同样良好状态（正常损耗除外）还船。"

The vessel should under many charter party forms be redelivered in the same good order and condition as when delivered. The charterers will be liable for damages if as a result of a breach of any of their obligations under the charter they redeliver the vessel in a worse condition than when delivered, ordinary wear and tear excepted.

根据许多租船合同范本，船舶应按照交船时相同的良好状况还船。如果承租人违反任何合同义务使得还船时的情况比交船时的情况要差，承租人将承担损害赔偿责任，但正常损耗除外。

This does not mean that the charterers are prevented from redelivering her before damages have been repaired for their account. Under normal circumstances, the shipowners cannot refuse to take redelivery of a damaged vessel. The charterers may make a valid redelivery of a damaged ship at the end of the charter period even if that damage has been caused by a breach of their obligations under the charter. They may thus bring to an end their obligation to pay the hire. The shipowners cannot refuse the redelivery and are left to a claim for damages. If the charterers are liable for the damage, and the repairs delay the ship, the shipowners can instead include the loss of time in their claim against the charterers.

这并不意味着承租人在修理船舶前不能交付船舶。在正常情况下，船舶出租人不能拒绝接受受损的船舶。承租人仍可在租期届满时对受损船舶进行有效还船，并据此终止其支付租金的义务。船舶出租人不得拒绝还船，但可以主张损害赔偿。如果承租人对船舶损坏负有责任，因维修导致船舶延误，船舶出租人可以在对承租人提出的索赔中包括时间损失。

According to the provisions of Article 142 of CMC, when the charterer redelivers the vessel to the shipowner, the vessel shall be in the same good order and condition as it was at the time of delivery, with fair wear and tear excepted. Where, upon redelivery, the vessel fails to remain in the same good order and condition as it was at the time of delivery, the charterer shall be responsible for rehabilitation or compensation.

根据《中华人民共和国海商法》第142条的规定："承租人向出租人交还船舶时，该船舶应当具有与出租人交船时相同的良好状态，但是船舶本身的自然磨损除外。船舶未能保持与交船时相同的良好状态的，承租人应当负责修复或者给予赔偿。"

5. Survey on Delivery and Redelivery
5. 交还船检验

When the vessel is delivered under the charter, liability for certain costs, for instance, the costs for bunkers, harbor dues, and agency fees, goes over from the shipowners to the charterers. In the same way liability for these costs goes back to the shipowners at redelivery.

当根据合同交船时，对某些费用的责任，例如燃油的费用、港口费用和代理费用，从船舶出租人转移到承租人。还船时，这些费用的责任同样重新归于船舶出租人。

To get a base for the allocation of costs, special survey reports, on-hire and off-hire survey reports, are usually issued in connection with the delivery and the redelivery. In these reports，the exact time for delivery and redelivery and quantities of fuel and diesel on board are stated. Usually, damage to the vessel and her general condition are also stated. Such damage reports often have an important function in discussions about liability for damages which sometimes arise during and after the charter period.

为了确定费用分配的基准，特别的检验报告即起租和停租检验报告通常是在交还船时签发。这些报告应对交还船时间、船上燃料和柴油的数量都做以记录。通常，船舶损坏情况及其整体状况也会被记录在案。这种损害报告往往对租期内还是租期外的损害责任划分起到重要作用。

The charterers and shipowners can make separate surveys but it is also common that they agree to have a joint survey by an independent surveyor. The parties must agree not only on whose account the survey is but also on whose time.

承租人及船舶出租人可以进行各自的检验，但通常他们同意由一个独立检验师开展联合检验。双方当事人不仅必须就检验费用由谁承担达成一致，还需就检验时间计入谁的时间达成一致。

The following On-Off hire survey clauses are from NYPE Form 1993:

以下是1993年土产格式关于起租和停租检验的条款：

"Prior to delivery and redelivery the parties shall, unless otherwise agreed, each appoint surveyors, for their respective accounts, who shall not later than at the first loading port/last discharging port respectively, conduct joint on-hire/off-hire surveys, for the purpose of ascertaining the quantity of bunkers on board and the condition of the vessel. A single report shall be prepared on each occasion and signed by each surveyor, without prejudice to his right to file a separate report setting forth items upon which the surveyors cannot agree. If either party fails to have a representative attend the survey and sign the joint survey report, such party shall nevertheless be bound for all purposes by the findings in any report prepared by the other party. On-hire survey shall be on charterers' time and off-hire survey on owners' time."

"除另有约定外，在交船和还船前，双方当事人应自负费用指定各自的验船师，分别在船舶到达第一个装货港/最后一个卸货港之前进行交船/还船联合检验，以确定船上所存的燃油量和船舶状态。每次检验后应做出一份联合检验报告，并由每名验船师签字，该报告并不妨碍验船师享有提交一份其上列有其不同意见的独立报告的权利。如果一方当事人未能派代表参加检验，并未能在联合检验报告上签字，该当事方应受另一当事人方做出的任何报告中的调查结果的约束。交船检验由承租人承担时间损失，还船检验由出租人承担时间损失。"

6. Bunkers on Delivery and Redelivery
6. 交还船燃油

As regards bunkers on delivery and redelivery, the charter party should state the quantity and prices of bunkers remaining on board the ship to be applied at delivery and redelivery.

交还船时应该在租船合同中说明船上尚存燃油的数量和价格。

The provision on bunkers in NYPE Form 1993 stipulates that: "The charterers on delivery, and the owners on redelivery, shall take over and pay for all fuel and diesel oil remaining on board the vessel as hereunder. The vessel shall be delivered with: _____ long/metric tons of fuel oil at the price of _____ per ton; _____ tons of diesel oil at the price of _____ per ton. The vessel shall be redelivered with: _____ long/metric ton of fuel oil at the price of _____ per ton; _____ tons of diesel oil at the price of _____ per ton."

1993年土产格式规定："承租人在交船时，出租人在还船时，应接受并支付下述船上所述的所有燃油和柴油。交船时船上所存燃油为_____长吨/公吨，油价为_____/吨；柴油为_____吨，油价为_____/吨。还船时船上所存燃油为_____长吨/公吨，油价为_____/吨；柴油为_____吨，油价为_____/吨。"

The charterers must take care that the bunkers they provide are suitable for the type of engines fitted to the particular ship. The charterers retain the property in bunkers which have been supplied and paid for by them on board the vessel during the period of charter.

承租人必须确保他们提供的燃油适宜装载在特定船舶的主机中。在合同有效期内，承租人对已供应且已支付费用并装载于船上的燃油享有所有权。

UNIT 3 HIRE AND PAYMENT OF HIRE
第三单元 租金和租金支付

The hire is the financial payment to the shipowners for leasing the manned and equipped vessel to the time charterers. The basic rule is that the hire shall be paid from the moment when the vessel is delivered to the charterers until she is again redelivered to the shipowners at the termination of the charter period. Under some circumstances the time charterers are relieved from their obligation to pay hire to the shipowners under the off-hire clauses.

租金是定期承租人支付给船舶出租人雇佣其船舶的货币支出。其基本规则是，租金支付应从该船交付承租人时起直到合同终止还给船舶出租人时止。在某些情况下，主要是停租条款下，定期承租人解除支付给船舶出租人租金的义务。

The standard forms of time charter recognize the importance to the shipowners of the regular receipt of hire by the inclusion of a provision that allows the shipowners to terminate the charter altogether should the charterers fail to pay the hire due on or before each appropriate date.

认识到船舶出租人定期收取租金的重要性，定期租船标准合同格式因此纳入一项条款，即如果承租人未能在每个相应日期或之前支付租金，船舶出租人有权终止合同。

1. Calculation of Hire
1. 租金计算

Time charter hire is commonly calculated and described in charter parties as a daily rate—e.g., USD 8,000 per day. To this is applied a pro-rata adjustment for part of a day. Thus a vessel on hire for 10 days 12 hours would be entitled to gross hire of USD 84,000.

租金在定期租船合同中一般计算和表述为日租金率，例如：每日 8 000 美元，不足一天按比例计算。因此，租船 10 天零 12 小时将有权获得 84 000 美元的总租金。

An alternative but less utilized method of calculating hire is to base it on a vessel's deadweight tonnage per calendar month. Thus for a 40,000 ton summer deadweight bulk carrier, the equivalent time charter rate to USD 8,000 daily can be calculated as follows:

另一种较少使用的计算方法是按照船舶每日历月的载重吨位计算租金。40 000 吨夏季载重吨散货船，等同于合同租金率每天 8 000 美元，计算方式如下：

USD 240,000 ÷ 40,000 SDWT = USD 6 per SDWT ton

240 000美元÷40 000夏季载重吨 = 每夏季载重吨6美元

In NYPE Form 1993, the above two alternatives are inserted for parties to choose one of them. 1993年土产格式规定了以上两种方式，供双方当事人选择其中之一。

2. Time for Hire Payment
2. 租金支付时间

The hire is payable in advance in nearly every case, i.e. monthly or semi-monthly or every fifteen days in advance. It is common practice to pay hire every fifteen days in advance, which continues to allow for subsequent equal payments irrespective of whether a calendar month comprises 28, 29, 30 or 31 days.

几乎每一个合同都规定租金预付，即每月或每半月或每隔15天预付。通常的做法是每隔15天提前支付租金，随后将继续每隔相同期间支付，不论该月是28、29、30或31天。

Hire is to be paid in advance meaning that each periodic payment must be made by the charterers on or before but not later than the due day. In the absence of express agreement or settled practice, the charterers have until midnight on the due day in which to effect each periodic payment. The obligation to pay hire in advance applies equally to the first as to subsequent installments. If the due day for a particular payment falls on a Sunday or some other non-banking day the charterers must make their payment on an earlier banking day.

租金预付意味着每个定期付款到期之前，但不得迟于到期日，承租人支付租金给船舶出租人。在没有明确的协议或结算实务的情况下，承租人应在到期日的午夜前支付。预先支付租金的义务同样适用于以后的每个付款期。如果付款到期日适逢星期日或其他非银行工作日，承租人必须在前一个银行工作日支付。

3. Last Hire Payment
3. 最后租金支付

If the charter does not expressly provide to the contrary, hire payable in advance for a month or half a month will be payable in full even if it is clear that the vessel will be redelivered before the end of the month or half a month. As the last period of hire in most cases is not as long as the full hire period and as the charterers will usually have a claim against the shipowners in connection with the redelivery for bunkers remaining on board, the time charter party forms frequently contain a last hire payment clause. The following provision is printed in NYPE Form 1993: "Should the vessel be on her voyage towards port of redelivery at the time the last and/or the penultimate payment of hire is/are due, said payment is/are to be made for such length of time as the shipowners and the charterers may agree upon as being the estimated time necessary to complete the voyage, and taking into account bunkers actually on board, to be taken over by the owners and estimated disbursements for the owners' account before redelivery. Should the same not cover the actual time hire is to be paid for the balance, day by day, as it becomes due. When the vessel has been redelivered, any difference is to be refunded by the owners or paid by the charterers, as the case may be."

如果租船合同没有相反的明文规定，应提前一个月或半个月全额预付租金，即便是船舶将在本月末或半月末之前还船。由于在大多数情况下，最后一个租金支付期并不与整个租期等长，以及承租人通常会在还船时就船上剩余燃油向船舶出租人提出索赔，因此租船合同范本常常包含最后一期租金的支付条款。下列是1993年土产格式的规定："在最后一期租金和/或倒数第二期租金应付之时，船舶在驶往还船港的航程中，对出租人和承租人可能同意的，为完成该航程所估计的必要时间应支付租金。考虑船上实际储存的燃油由出租人接收，还船前预计的港口使费由出租人负担。该租金不足以支付实际租用的时间时，差额租金应按时每天支付。还船后有余额的，由出租人退还；不足的，由承租人支付。"

4. Place for Hire Payment
4. 租金支付地点

Payments of hire are commonly made via banks and in most cases, payment is not considered effective before money reaches the shipowners' bank. The time charter hire has to be transferred in good time from the bank of a charterer to the bank account of a shipowner. If this hire does not arrive in time, then technically the charterer is in breach of the contract and the shipowner has a case for withdrawing his vessel from the charterer's employ.

租金支付通常通过银行进行，在多数情况下租金没有转到船舶出租人账户上不算有效支付。租船的租金必须从承租人的银行账户及时汇至船舶出租人的银行账户。如果租金没有及时到账，就法律层面而言，承租人即构成违约，船舶出租人可以撤船。

5. Deductions from Hire
5. 租金扣减

When the advance payment of hire is to be made the charterers often wish to make deductions for off-hire during the previous period, for cash paid by agents to the master, for disbursement for shipowners' account and for other monetary claims that the charterers may have against the shipowners. As default in payment may give the shipowners a right to cancel the charter, it is important for charterers to rely on a clause in the charter party that may give them a right to make such deductions. Normally hire is subject to deductions for: address commission and/or brokerage; port disbursements; bunkers; off-hire, etc.

当需要预付租金时，承租人通常希望从预付金额中扣除以下款项：此前停租期间的费用，代理人向船长支付的现金、需由船舶出租人承担的垫付款项，以及承租人可能对船舶出租人提出的其他金钱索赔。由于拖欠会使船舶出租人有权解除租约，因此对承租人最重要的是依据租船合同的条款使他们有权做出这种扣减。通常情况下，洽租佣金和/或经纪人佣金、港口使费、燃油费、停租费等可以用于租金扣减。

6. Additions to Hire
6. 租金外收入

Where some vessels deliver on time charter some distance from their original position, their shipowners may negotiate a positioning bonus (so-called ballast bonus) to cover time and expenses incurred between departure from the original position and the vessel's delivery under the new employment.

当交船地点离船舶原来的位置有一定距离时，船舶出租人可以就空放费（即所谓的压舱补偿费）与承租人洽谈，以弥补船舶从原来的位置到新租约下交船地点所产生的时间成本和各项费用。

Quite apart from ballast bonuses, there may be other additions to hire payments made from time to time such as the following: supercargo accommodation expense, port employee's expense, radio message expense, and hold cleaning expense.

除了空放费外，有时还可能有一些额外的费用被计入租金支付中，如押运员的费用、港口工人的膳食、电台信息费用、货舱清洁费用。

7. Right of Withdrawal
7. 撤船权利

If the charterers fail to make punctual payment of an installment of hire, that is to say payment on or before the due date, the shipowners are entitled by the withdrawal clause to withdraw the ship from their service and thus bring the charter to an end.

如果承租人未能准时支付租金，也就是说未在到期日或到期日之前付款，船舶出租人有权依据撤船条款撤回其负责服务的船舶，从而终止租船合同。

The right to withdraw is not lost merely because the charterers tender the overdue hire before the shipowners have given notice. If the charterers fail to pay in time they are in default and their tender of hire thereafter cannot alter that position. The shipowners may accept a late tender of the hire as if it had been paid punctually. If they are found to have done so they will be held to have waived their right to withdraw.

撤船权利不因为船舶出租人发出通知前承租人支付逾期租金而消灭。如果承租人未能及时支付租金即构成违约，其此后支付租金的行为亦无法改变该违约状态。船舶出租人可以将接受的逾期租金视为按时支付并予以接受，如果他们这样做，则将被认为已放弃了撤船的权利。

【Case】A vessel was chartered to the charterer under a time charter party stating that hire was to be paid in cash semi-monthly in advance, and that "failing the punctual and regular payment of the hire" the shipowner was to be at liberty to withdraw the vessel from the charterer's service. The charterer tendered payment one day late, and the shipowner withdrew the vessel. Held, by the House of Lords, that the shipowner was entitled to do so. The breach of the obligation to pay in advance could not be cured by a late tender. There was no evidence that the breach had been waived.

【案例】某船以期租形式出租给承租人，合同规定租金以现金形式每半月预付，"未能准时全额支付租金时"，船舶出租人可随意撤船。承租人支付租金晚了一天，船舶出租人撤回船舶。上议院判决：船舶出租人有权这样做。提前支付的义务一旦违约，不能以事后支付来补正。没有证据表明该违约行为已被豁免。

The shipowners' right to withdraw may operate very harshly against the charterers, who may lose a valuable charter and suffer heavy losses as a consequence of a small error on their part or that of their bankers. So there is a printed provision of the so-called "anti-technicality clause" appearing in NYPE Form 1993. There is no printed provision of this kind in the NYPE 1946 or BALTIME Forms, but the parties frequently add an anti-technicality clause in typescript.

船舶出租人的撤船权可能对承租人造成严苛影响：承租人可能仅因自身或其银行方的轻微过错，就失去一份宝贵的租船合同，并蒙受重大损失。因此，1993年土产格式中载有一项预设条款，即所谓的"反技术性条款"。1946年土产格式及波尔的姆格式中均无此类预设条款，但合同双方通常会以印刷形式额外添加一条反技术性条款。

An anti-technicality clause is a clause designed to modify the rigor of the withdrawal clause. It usually provides for a 48-hour or 72-hour notice to be given by the shipowners to the charterers, after default has occurred, before withdrawal. The following clause is printed in NYPE Form 1993:

一条反技术性条款在于缓和撤船条款的严格性。它通常规定，船舶出租人需在违约发生后、行使撤船权利前，向承租人发出48小时或72小时的通知。以下条款是1993年土产格式中印刷的相关条款：

"Where there is failure to make punctual and regular payment of hire due to oversight, negligence, errors or omissions on the part of the Charterers or their bankers, the Charterers shall be given by the Owners _____ clear banking days (as recognized at the agreed place of payment) written notice to rectify the failure, and when so rectified within those _____ days following the Owners' notice, the payment shall stand as regular and punctual.

"由于承租人或其银行一方的疏忽、过失或错误而未能准时支付租金时，出租人应向承租人发出书面通知，要求其在_____净银行工作日（为协议的支付地点所承认）补交未付的租金，当承租人根据出租人通知在_____天内予以补交时，应视为其准时支付租金。

Failure by the Charterers to pay the hire within _____ days of their receiving the Owners' notice as provided herein, shall entitle the Owners to withdraw as set forth in Sub-clause 11 (a) above."

如承租人在收到出租人通知的_____天内未能支付租金，依据第11条款（a）的规定，出租人有权撤船。"

UNIT 4　OFF-HIRE CLAUSE
第四单元　停租条款

The off-hire clause operates as an exception to the charterers' primary obligation to pay hire continuously throughout the charter period. Charterers are entitled to off-hire only if the ship is delayed for a reason which is in accordance with the off-hire clause in the charter party.

停租条款是承租人在整个租船期间不断履行支付租金的基本义务的除外规定。承租人只有在租船合同中停租条款规定的延误理由下延误才有权停付租金。

1. Grounds for Off-hire
1. 停租原因

Provision is usually made in time charter party for hire to cease in certain specified events. The following is the printed off-hire clause in NYPE Form 1993:

定期租船合同通常规定在特定事件下的停付租金。下列是1993年土产格式印刷的停租条款：

"In the event of loss of time from deficiency and/or default and/or strike of officers or crew, or deficiency of stores, fire, breakdown of, or damages to hull, machinery or equipment, grounding, detention by the arrest of the vessel (unless such arrest is caused by events for which the charterers, their servants, agents or subcontractors are responsible), or detention by average accidents to the vessel or cargo (unless resulting from inherent vice, quality or defect of the cargo), dry docking for the purpose of examination or painting bottom, or by any other similar causes preventing the full working of the vessel, the payment of hire and overtime, if any, shall cease for the time thereby lost. Should the vessel deviate or put back during a voyage, contrary to the orders or directions of her charterers, for any reason other than an accident to the cargo or where permitted in lines 257 to 258 hereunder, the hire is to be suspended from the time of her deviating or putting back until she is again in the same or equidistant position from the destination and the voyage resumed therefrom. All bunkers used by the vessel while off-hire shall be for the charterers' account.

"如果船舶由于船员不足和/或船员罢工，或物料不足，船舶发生火灾，船体、船机或设备发生故障或损害，船舶搁浅，船舶被扣押而延误（因承租人，其雇佣人员、代理人或分合同人应负责的事件被扣押时除外），或船舶或货物发生海损事故而延误（因货物的潜在瑕疵、质量或缺陷引起的除外），船舶为检验或漆底而入干船坞，或由于任何其他类似原因阻碍船舶的充分工作时，对因此所损失的时间停付租金和加班费（如有的话）。船舶在航行中，非由于货物发生事故或下述第257~258行允许情况的任何其他原因，违反承租人的指示或命令，而发生绕航或返航，则从船舶绕航或返航之时起，至船舶再次驶回相同航向或距目的港等距离的地点时止，承租人停止支付租金，并且航次从那时开始。停租期间所使用的所有燃料由承租人承担。

In the event of the vessel being driven into port or to anchorage through the stress of weather, trading to shallow harbors or to rivers or ports with bars, any detention of the vessel and/or expenses resulting from such detention shall be for charterers' account. If upon the voyage the speed be reduced by a defect in, or breakdown of, any part of hull, machinery, or equipment, the time so lost, and the cost of any extra bunkers consumed in consequence thereof, and all extra proven expenses may be deducted from the hire."

由于恶劣天气，船舶被迫驶入港口或锚泊时，驶往浅水港或带有沙滩的河流或港口，所产生的船舶的任何延误和/或由此延误所产生的费用由承租人负担。如果船舶在航行时，由于船体、船机或设备的任何部分的缺陷或故障而使船速下降，因此损失的时间，任何额外消耗的燃料费用和全部经证实的额外费用，可以从租金中扣减。"

2. Meaning of Some Terminology
2. 一些术语含义

The expression "deficiency of men" does not apply to the situation in which there is on board a full complement of officers and men able to work but some or all of them refuse to do so. Even if there is a numerical deficiency of men, the ship will not be off-hire if the numerical deficiency does not affect the efficiency of the ship and thus does not prevent the full working of the vessel.

"人员不足"的表述不适用于船上有完全胜任的船员，但部分或全部船员拒绝工作的情况。即使是人员数量不足，若其不影响船舶的效率，从而未妨碍船舶的正常运行，则船舶不得停租。

【Case】The latest London Arbitration award relating to this issue is that the vessel was delayed at the discharge port by means of a police investigation into the collision and sinking of a Korean fishing trawler by an unidentified vessel. The question is whether the vessel is off-hire or not. Held, the vessel was off-hire during the dispute period that lasted for two days. The vessel could not sail without the master and chief engineer, so there was a deficiency of men under clause 15 of NYPE Form 1993. See London Arbitration 1/2003.

【案例】最近的伦敦仲裁裁决涉及这样一个问题，一艘船舶因警方对不明船只与韩国渔船碰撞并致其沉没事件的调查而在卸货港被延误。问题是该船舶停租与否。仲裁裁决认为，在持续两天的争议期间，船舶处于停租状态。该船没有船长及轮机长无法航行，因此，根据1993年土产格式第15条，属于人员不足。见伦敦仲裁2003年第1号。

Where the loss of time results from machinery defects and the condition of the machinery becomes progressively worse, a "breakdown" occurs when it becomes reasonably necessary to make for a port of refuge for repairs.

当时间损失由机械缺陷导致且机械状况逐渐恶化时，若船舶驶往避难港进行修理是合理必要的，则构成"故障"。

【Case】A vessel that was chartered on the NYPE Form carried grain from the U.S. Gulf to Algiers. The cargo was wet-damaged owing to leakage through defective hatch covers. Because of the damage, discharge at Algiers took 15 days longer than it otherwise would have done; but at all times the vessel was fully capable of performing every service required of her and, in particular, fully capable of discharging cargo from all her holds. It was held that the vessel was not "detained" by an average accident to her cargo and was not, therefore, off-hire.

【案例】某船以土产格式出租，从美国海湾装载谷物到阿尔及尔。货物由于有缺陷的舱口盖渗漏水导致湿损。由于损害，在阿尔及尔卸货时间比平时多出15天，但在这期间，船舶能完全履行它具有的每项服务能力，特别是充分的卸货能力。判决，该船不是因为海损事故导致货物延误，因此不能停租。

The expression "preventing the full working of the vessel" qualifies not only any other similar cause but also all the mentioned causes in the charter. It takes effect if the full working of the vessel was thereby prevented and time was lost in consequence. The meaning of "full working of the vessel" has been considered in subsequent cases which follow.

"妨碍船舶全面运行"这一表述不仅适用于任何其他类似原因，也适用于租船合同中提及的所有原因。只要因此妨碍了船舶的全面运行并导致时间损失，该表述即生效。"船舶全面运行"的含义在后续相关案件中已有考量，如下所述。

【Case】The Aquacharm was time chartered for a trip on the NYPE Form. Having been ordered to load to maximum draught for a passage through the Panama Canal, the master negligently failed to take into account that in passing through a freshwater lake which forms part of the Canal the ship's forward draught would increase. The vessel was consequently refused entry to the Canal; after considerable delay, part of the cargo had to be discharged, carried through the Canal on another vessel,and then reloaded. It was argued by the charterer that the vessel was off-hire because she was prevented by her draught from performing the service immediately required. It was held that the vessel was fit to perform the service immediately required and was therefore not off-hire. This decision was upheld by the Court of Appeal.

【案例】"Aquacharm"号船按照土产格式期租一个航次。船舶被命令装载至最大吃水通过巴拿马运河，船长疏忽，没有考虑到在通过淡水湖泊（构成了运河的一部分）时船舶的船首吃水将增加。该船因此被拒绝进入运河。在经历延误后，部分货物不得不被卸下，通过另一艘船经运河运输，然后重新装载。承租人主张船舶因吃水问题无法立即履行所需的运输服务而停租。但法院认为，船舶本身适合立即履行所需的服务，因此不构成停租。这一判决得到了上诉法院的支持。

【Case】The Roachbank was chartered under the NYPE Form, Clause 15 being amended by the addition of the word "whatsoever" after "any cause". In the South China Sea the vessel sighted a boat in distress and took on board from it a large number of Vietnamese refugees. When the vessel arrived at Kaohsiung the authorities refused to allow the refugees to land and required the ship to lie outside the port. The charterer claimed that the vessel was off-hire for the time so lost. It was held by the court that neither the presence of the refugees on board nor their number prevented the vessel from performing the service immediately required of her, which was to enter the port and load cargo. Hence the full working of the vessel was not prevented and the vessel remained on hire.

【案例】"Roachbank"号船以土产格式出租，并对第15条做了修改，在"任何原因"后加了"无论如何"字样。在南海航行时，该船遇到一条遇难船，搭载了大量越南难民。当船舶抵达高雄港时，当局拒绝难民上岸并要求该船舶在港外停泊。承租人声称其受到的时间损失构成停租。法院认为，船上有难民和难民的人数都不会妨碍船舶履行进入港口和装载货物的服务。因此，该船的全面运行没有被阻止，租金应继续支付。

The weight of judicial opinion appears to be in favor of the view that the scope of the words "any other cause" should be restricted in accordance with the ejusdem generis rule, or at least that their meaning is limited by their context in the off-hire clause and the charter party. If, however, the word "whatsoever" is inserted in the off-hire clause after "any other cause", the ejusdem generis rule is excluded.

司法意见似乎支持这种观点，"任何其他原因"一词的范围应根据同类解释规则受到限制，或者至少受合同和停租条款的约束。如果停租条款中在"任何其他原因"后加了"无论如何"一词，则同类解释规则不适用。

3. Loss of Time
3. 时间损失

Charterers are not always entitled to off-hire for all time lost. The happening of one of the listed incidents, such as a breakdown of machinery, does not result in an automatic interruption of hire. It must be shown also that time was lost to the charterers in consequence.

承租人并不总是有权对所有实际的损失时间要求停租。在列出的事件中，如发生机械故障，并不自动导致租金支付的中断。它还必须能够证明其结果造成了承租人的时间损失。

Thus, a breakdown of the propulsion machinery will not usually put the ship off-hire if it happens and is cured during a period of loading or discharging cargo. Regard must be had to the particular work that is required of the ship at the relevant time and only if that is affected does the possibility of off-hire arise. It follows that a ship may be off-hire because of a breakdown of propulsion machinery while she is, or is required to be, at sea but on hire again immediately that machinery is no longer relevant to the particular service the charterers next require.

因此，如果推进器机械故障发生在装卸货物期间且已修复，通常不会导致船舶停租。此时必须考量船舶在相关时间点所承担的具体工作，只有当该工作受到影响时，停租才可能产生。因此，船舶可能因推进器机械故障而停租，但当机器不再与承租人下一个要求的特别服务有关时，可立即恢复起租。

Under the off-hire clause in the NYPE Form 1993 the hire should be deductible in case of partial inefficiency only if and to the extent that time is lost by reason of partial inefficiency.

根据1993年土产格式的停租条款，租金在部分效率低下的情况下应予以扣除，但仅限于时间损失是部分效率低下导致的。

4. Threshold Rule
4. 起始点规则

Many standard time charter party forms have thresholds where it is stated that the charterers are entitled to off-hire only if the vessel is hindered or prevented from working more than an agreed number of hours (usually 12 or 24 hours). The hindrance must continue for a certain number of consecutive hours. If the vessel has to stop for 35 hours due to engine breakdown, the off-hire deduction will be for 35 hours and not 35 less 24 hours. In NYPE Form no such favor is given to the shipowners.

许多标准定期租船合同范本有对起始点的规定，只有在船舶被妨碍或阻止超过规定的时间（通常为12或24小时）时承租人才有权停租。该障碍必须持续为若干个小时。如果船舶因主机故障已停航35小时，则停租时间是35小时，而不是35减24个小时。土产格式没有给予船舶出租人这种优惠。

According to the provisions of Article 133 of CMC, "where the vessel has not been operated normally for 24 consecutive hours due to its failure to maintain the seaworthiness or the other conditions as agreed upon, the charterer shall not pay the hire for the operating time so lost, unless such failure was caused by the charterer".

根据《中华人民共和国海商法》第133条的规定，"船舶不符合约定的适航状态或者其他状态而不能正常营运连续满二十四小时的，对因此而损失的营运时间，承租人不付租金，但是上述状态是由承租人造成的除外。"

There is another question when full hire again becomes payable. That is whether the hire becomes payable again as soon as the ship becomes once more fully efficient or whether the ship regains the position she was in when the event occurred. It depends on the circumstances in the cases. It seems therefore that under English law full hire becomes payable as soon as the ship again becomes efficient. In NYPE Form 1993, regarding the vessel's deviation, contrary to the orders or directions of the charterers, the hire is to be suspended from the time of her deviating until she is again in the same or equidistant position from the destination and the voyage resumed therefrom.

此外，另一个问题是，从何时起应恢复全额支付租金，也就是说租金从该船恢复完全效能时立即恢复支付，还是在船舶回到事件发生时的位置时才恢复支付。这取决于案件的情况。因此，根据英国法，租金从该船再次恢复效能时支付。在1993年土产格式中，关于船舶违反承租人命令或指令的绕航情形，租金从绕航之时起暂停支付，直到它再一次处于与目的港相同或等距的位置并从此继续航行时为止。

UNIT 5   OTHER CLAUSES
第五单元   其他条款

There are also other clauses written in NYPE Form 1993. In this unit, some other clauses that also consist of parts of the charter party will be discussed such as damage clause, performance of voyage clause, lien clause, bill of lading clause, etc.

1993年土产格式包括其他印就的条款。在本单元，主要学习租船合同其他条款的规定内容，如损害条款、航次履行条款、留置权条款、提单条款等。

1. Damage Clause
1. 损害条款

The vessel, during the charter period, is exposed to certain risks of damage. The damage may cause considerable maintenance and repair expenditure and it is therefore important to make the allocation of liability in this respect as clear as possible.

在租船期间，船舶面临受到一定损害的风险。这种损害可能会造成相当大的保养和维修开支，因此，尽可能清楚地订立在赔偿责任方面的分配是十分重要的。

1.1 Damage Caused by Bad Weather, Collision, and Grounding
1.1 不良天气、碰撞和搁浅造成的损害

Shipowners normally have little chance of obtaining compensation from the charterers for damage caused to the vessel by bad weather, collision, grounding, etc. Only if the shipowners can prove that the charterers' breach of contract or negligence has caused the damage may they have a chance of obtaining compensation. The most practical example is where time charterers have directed the vessel to an unsafe place or port.

通常情况下，船舶出租人因不良天气、碰撞、搁浅等导致船舶受损而从承租人处获得赔偿的机会很小。只有船舶出租人能够证明承租人违反合同或存在过失导致损害时，才可能有机会获得赔偿。最实际的例子是，定期承租人指示船舶驶往不安全的地方或港口。

1.2 Damage Caused by Cargo
1.2 货物造成的损害

If the vessel has been damaged by cargo, the shipowners can seek compensation from the charterers in two ways. Firstly, the charterers may be held responsible if they have shipped on the vessel a cargo that is not permitted under the charter party. As mentioned before, time charter parties usually have a clause that excludes several specified cargo types and all cargo likely to be injurious to the vessel. Secondly, the shipowners may seek compensation from charterers when the cargo has been loaded, stowed, or secured insufficiently and the vessel is damaged thereby. This situation is usually more complicated as the master and officers normally supervise the loading and securing of the cargo. It is difficult to find the borderline between the charterers' and shipowners' liability in this respect. The tendency seems to be for charterers to be held liable unless there is obvious negligence on the part of the master or officers.

如果船舶被货物损坏，船舶出租人可以通过两种方式要求承租人赔偿。首先，承租人对装运非合同许可的货物造成的损害承担责任。如前所述，定期租船合同通常有一项条款，排除了特定货物的种类以及可能会损害到船舶的货物。其次，当货物装载、积载或绑扎不足并由此造成船舶损害时，船舶出租人可向承租人要求赔偿。这种情况通常是比较复杂的，因为船长和高级船员通常监督货物的装载和绑扎。承租人和船舶出租人在这方面的责任是很难找到界线的。除非船长或高级船员存在明显过失，否则承租人似乎往往会被认定承担责任。

1.3 Damage Caused by Stevedore
1.3 装卸工人造成的损害

The most common type of damage to the ship is damage caused by stevedores. The extent of the charterers' liability should be defined by the charter party and the applicable law will supply additional rules. Time charter parties quite often contain special clauses stating under what circumstances the charterers are liable for damage caused by stevedores and these clauses are usually very harsh for shipowners. It is, for instance, not unusual to find clauses that say that the charterers are liable for stevedore damage only if the master informs the charterers immediately when the damage occurs, and also obtains a statement in writing from the stevedores that they accept liability for the damage.

最常见的船舶受损害的情形是由装卸工人所造成的损害。承租人的赔偿责任范围应在租船合同中予以界定并且适用的法律将提供额外的规定。定期租船合同中往往包含一个特别条款，表明在什么情况下承租人负责赔偿装卸工人造成的损害，而这些条款通常对船舶出租人非常苛刻。例如，通常条款规定，承租人仅在以下情形下对装卸工人造成的损害承担责任：损害发生时，船长立即通知承租人，且同时从装卸工人处取得书面声明，表明其承认对该损害承担责任。

The following stevedore damage clause is from NYPE Form 1993:

下面是1993年土产格式的装卸工人损害条款：

"Notwithstanding anything contained herein to the contrary, the charterers shall pay for any and all damage to the vessel caused by stevedores provided the master has notified the charterers and/or their agents in writing as soon as practicable but not later than 48 hours after any damage is discovered. Such notice to specify the damage in detail and to invite charterers to appoint a surveyor to assess the extent of such damage.

"尽管有与此相反的规定，只要船长在发现任何损坏后并不超过48小时书面通知承租人和/或其代理人，则承租人应赔偿装卸工人对船舶造成的任何和全部损害。该通知应详细说明船舶损害情况，并要求承租人指派一名验船师以确定该损害的程度。

(a) In case of any and all damages affecting the vessel's seaworthiness and/or the safety of the crew and/or affecting the trading capabilities of the vessel, the charterers shall immediately arrange for repairs of such damages at their expense and the vessel is to remain on hire until such repairs are completed and if required passed by the vessel's classification society.

（a）如果任何和全部损害影响到船舶的适航和/或船员的安全和/或影响船舶的营运能力，承租人应自负费用对该损害立即安排修理，并且，到该修理结束时和如经要求通过船级检验时为止，应照付船舶租金。

(b) Any and all damages not described under point (a) above shall be repaired at the charterers' option, before or after redelivery concurrently with the shipowners' work. In such case no hire and/or expenses will be paid to the shipowners except and insofar as the time and/or expenses required for repairs for which the charterers are responsible, exceed the time and/or expenses necessary to carry out the shipowners' work."

（b）对上述第（a）款未提及的任何和全部损害，根据承租人的选择，在还船之前或还船之后同出租人要做的修理一起进行。在此情况下，不应向出租人支付租金和/或费用，除非承租人负责修理所需的时间和/或费用，超过出租人修理所需的必要时间和/或费用，并仅以此超过时间为限。"

1.4 Stevedore Damage Clause for Time Charter Parties 2008
1.4 2008年定期租船合同装卸工人损害条款

The BIMCO Stevedore Damage Clauses have been revised and updated to reflect current commercial practice and to provide a balanced solution to this often contentious issue. The clauses were adopted by the Documentary Committee at its meeting in London in May 2008.

BIMCO装卸工人损害条款已修订和更新，以反映当前的航运习惯做法，并给经常引起争议的问题提供一个均衡的解决方法。该条款于2008年5月在伦敦由波罗的海国际航运公会单证委员会通过。

(a) The charterers shall be responsible for damage (fair wear and tear excepted) to any part of the vessel caused by stevedores. The charterers shall be liable for all costs for repairing such damage and for any time lost.

（a）承租人应当对装卸工人造成船舶任何部分的损害负责（正常损耗除外）。承租人应承担修复这种损害的费用和任何的时间损失。

(b) The master or the owners shall notify the charterers or their agents and the stevedores of any damage as soon as reasonably possible, failing which the charterers shall not be responsible.

（b）船长或船舶出租人应对船舶造成的任何损害尽快通知承租人或其代理人以及装卸工人，否则承租人不负责任。

(c) Stevedore damage affecting seaworthiness shall be repaired without any delay before the vessel sails from the port where such damage was caused or discovered. Stevedore damage affecting the vessel's trading capabilities shall be repaired prior to redelivery, failing which the charterers shall be liable for resulting losses. All other damage which is not repaired prior to redelivery shall be repaired by the owners and settled by the charterers on receipt of the owners' supported invoice.

（c）在装卸工人的损害影响适航的情况下，应于起航前在造成或发现损害的港口立即进行修复。装卸工人的损害影响了船舶的营运能力，应在离开最后卸货港前修理，否则该承租人应当对造成的损失承担责任。所有其他未修理的损害应在船舶离开最后卸货港前由船舶出租人修复，承租人按修理发票结算。

2. Performance of Voyage Clause
2. 航次履行条款

2.1 Provisions in NYPE Form 1993
2.1 1993年土产格式的规定

The master shall perform the voyage with due dispatch and shall render all customary assistance with the vessel's crew. The master shall be conversant with the English language and (although appointed by the owners) shall be under the orders and directions of the charterers as regards employment and agency; and the charterers shall perform all cargo handling, including but not limited to loading, stowing, trimming, lashing, securing, dunnaging, unlashing, discharging, and tallying, at their risk and expense, under the supervision of the master. If the charterers shall have reasonable cause to be dissatisfied with the conduct of the master or officers, the owners shall, on receiving particulars of the complaint, investigate the same, and, if necessary, make a change in the appointments.

船长应使船舶在航次中尽快速遣，并会同船员提供习惯性帮助。船长应精通英语，并且（尽管由船舶出租人任命）在有关船舶使用和代理方面应服从承租人的指示和命令；承租人在船长的监督下，自负风险和费用，负责全部货物的操作，包括但不限于装载、积载、平舱、绑扎、加固、垫舱、解绑、卸载和理货；如承租人有合理的原因对船长或者高级船员的行为表示不满，出租人在收到投诉后应调查事实，如有必要，对人员的任命予以调整。

2.2 Master's Position
2.2 船长的地位

The master has a difficult position under a time charter since he has to follow the instructions of both the shipowner and the time charterer. He represents two parties and has to look after the interests of them both. The master should keep full and correct logs of the voyage as requested by the time charterers or their agents. The master should furnish charterers when required to do so with copies of log books, port sheets, weather reports, and reports about the ship's speed and bunker consumption, etc. All these documents are important for the time charterers, both for their relationship with sub-charterers, shippers, and receivers and for their relationship with the shipowners.

在定期租船合同下船长处于困难的境地，因为他必须遵循船舶出租人和承租人的指示。他代表着双方并且要照顾双方的利益。船长应保存承租人或其代理人要求的完整和正确的航行日志。在承租人要求时，船长应提供给承租人航海日志、港口时间表、天气报告以及关于船舶航速和燃料消耗的报告等副本。所有这些文件对承租人与分租人、托运人和收货人以及他们与船舶出租人的关系都是重要的。

Most time charter parties state that the master must give the charterers customary assistance with the vessel's crew. The general definition of the customary assistance concept is that the master and the crew should give the same assistance to the time charterers as they would give the shipowners if they were trading for their account.

大多数定期租船合同规定船长与船员必须向承租人提供习惯性协助。习惯性协助的一般定义是，船长和船员应给予承租人如同给予船舶出租人那样的协助。

2.3 Employment
2.3 雇佣

Although the master basically should comply with instructions from the charterers, he should not necessarily in every situation follow the orders and instructions he gets from the time charterers. The master has a responsibility for the safety of the crew and the vessel and he usually also has responsibilities with regard to the cargo owners and other third parties. If, according to the master's well-founded opinion, the time charterers' orders and instructions jeopardize the crew, ship, cargo or other persons or property, he has not only a right but also an obligation, not to obey the orders. The master must, in such a difficult situation, contact not only the time charterers but also the shipowners and try to deal with the situation without causing too many problems for the parties involved.

虽然船长基本上应听从承租人的指示，但他并不一定在任何情况下都遵循来自承租人的命令和指示。船长对船员和船舶安全负责，并且他通常也对货主和其他第三方的安全负责。如果船长有充分的理由认为，承租人的命令和指示危及船员、船舶、货物或其他人员或财产，他不仅有权利，也有义务不服从命令。在这种困难的情况下，船长不仅必须联系定期承租人，还需联系船舶出租人，并努力在不给相关各方造成太多问题的前提下处理该局面。

"Employment" has been held by the House of Lords to mean "the employment of the ship", not employment of persons, and to include orders to proceed to certain ports for loading and discharge of cargo, but exclude orders as to how those instructions are to be executed in terms of navigation, which always remains the responsibility of the master.

"雇佣"已被上议院判决意指雇佣船舶，而不是雇佣人员，并包括命令驶往装载和卸货的某些港口，但其不包括如何航行的问题，这始终是船长的职责。

【Case】A time charter party provided that the master was to obey the orders of the charterer "as regards employment". The vessel was ordered to leave port by the charterer's representative. The master did so although the weather was very bad. As a consequence of the storm she was stranded, and sustained serious damage. Held, by the House of Lords, that the charterer was not liable. The order which had been given was not one as regards to employment.

【案例】一份定期租船合同规定，船长 "在船舶使用方面" 须服从承租人的指令。承租人的代表指示船舶离港，尽管当时天气恶劣，船长仍应照此执行。船舶因风暴搁浅并遭受严重损坏。上议院裁定，承租人无须承担责任，因为所下达的指令不属于 "在船舶使用方面" 的指令。

2.4 Implied Indemnity
2.4 默示赔偿

In the NYPE Form, there is no express indemnity given to the shipowners. However, an indemnity will normally be implied against liability incurred by the shipowners as a consequence of complying with the charterers' orders or directions.

在土产格式中，对船舶出租人没有赋予明确的追偿权。但通常会默认船舶出租人享有一项追偿权——因遵守承租人的命令或指示而产生责任时，可依据该权利向承租人追偿。

If the master is required by the charterers to sign or permit to be signed bills of lading that impose on the shipowners greater liability than that which they have assumed under the charter, the shipowners will usually be entitled to be indemnified by the charterers in respect of their additional liability.

如果船长应承租人的要求签署或被允许签署提单而加大了船舶出租人比他们在租船合同下承担的责任，船舶出租人通常有权要求承租人赔偿他们为此承担的额外责任。

3. Lien Clause
3. 留置权条款

A lien is a right in one man to retain that which is in his possession belonging to another, till certain demands of the person in possession are satisfied. This accurately describes the nature of the shipowners' lien upon cargo or charterers' lien upon the ship, which is in their possession. Maritime liens play an important role in the chartering of the vessels, as the liens provide both the shipowners and charterers with a form of security by creating rights in the maritime property engaged in the maritime venture. Maritime liens may arise by operation of the maritime law or by contract.

留置权，是指权利人在其特定债权得到清偿前，有权留置其占有的他人财产的权利。这一表述精准界定了船舶出租人对其占有的货物享有的留置权，以及承租人对其占有的船舶享有的留置权的本质。船舶优先权在船舶租船业务中发挥着重要作用：通过对参与海上营运的海事财产设定权利，船舶优先权为船舶出租人与承租人双方均提供了一种担保形式。船舶优先权可通过海事法的规定产生，也可通过合同约定产生。

3.1 Shipowners' Liens upon Cargoes
3.1 船舶出租人对货物的留置权

In NYPE Form 1993, it states that "the shipowners shall have a lien upon all cargoes and all sub-freights and/or sub-hire for any amounts due under this charter party including general average contributions".

1993年土产格式规定："出租人因根据本租船合同应得的任何款项，包括共同海损分摊，而对所有货物和所有转租运费和/或转租租金行使留置权。"

The words in the NYPE Form 1993 do not expressly limit the cargoes that may be liened to those owned by the charterers. This raised the question of whether the shipowners may detain on board their ship cargo not owned by the charterers. There are conflicting decisions on this point. It seems that where the bills of lading incorporate the charter lien clause, the shipowners then have the contractual right to lien the cargo, whether or not it is owned by the charterers. Sub-freights or sub-hires include any remuneration earned by the charterers from the employment of the ship, whether by way of voyages freight or time hire.

在1993年土产格式中没有明确限制留置承租人所拥有的货物。这就引出了质疑，船舶出租人是否可以留置船上非承租人拥有的货物。在这一点上存在相互矛盾的判决。似乎当提单并入租船合同的留置权条款时，无论货物是否属于承租人所有，船舶出租人均享有留置货物的权利。转租运费或转租租金包括承租人通过使用船舶（无论是以航次租船还是定期租船的方式）所获得的任何报酬。

According to the provision of Article 141 of CMC, the charterer fails to pay the hire or other sums of money as agreed upon in the charter, the shipowner only has a right to lien on the charterer's goods and other property on board the ship.

根据《中华人民共和国海商法》第141条，承租人未向出租人支付租金或者合同约定的其他款项的，出租人对船上属于承租人的货物和财产以及转租船舶的收入有留置权。

3.2 Charterers' Liens on the Ship
3.2 承租人对船舶的留置权

In the NYPE Form 1993, the charterers are given a lien on the ship for all monies paid in advance and not earned. Although the lien given to the charterers cannot be a true possessory lien, for the time charterers unlike the demise charterers do not obtain and so cannot retain possession of the ship, it seems that it confers a similar right, namely to prevent the shipowners at the end of the charter period from resuming control of the use of the ship for their purposes.

1993年土产格式规定，承租人因所有预付但未收取的款项而对船舶行使留置权。虽然赋予承租人的留置权不能成为一个真正的留置权，即定期承租人不同于光船承租人，不能获得且不能保留船舶的占有，但似乎赋予了类似的权利，即在租船期届满时，可阻止船舶出租人收回船舶使用权并用于船舶出租人自身的经营目的。

4. Bills of Lading Clause
4. 提单条款

The bills of lading clause in the NYPE Form 1993 has three paragraphs.

1993年土产格式提单条款有三个段落。

(a) The master shall sign the bills of lading or waybills for cargo as presented in conformity with mate's or tally clerk's receipts. However, the charterers may sign bills of lading or waybills on behalf of the master, with the owner's prior written authority, always in conformity with mates or tally clerk's receipts.

（a）船长应签发所呈递的、与大副收据或理货员收据一致的提单或运单。但是，在有出租人事先书面授权的情况下，承租人可代表船长签发与大副收据或理货员收据一致的提单或运单。

(b) All bills of lading or waybills shall be without prejudice to this charter party and the charterers shall indemnify the owners against all consequences or liabilities which may arise from any inconsistency between this charter party and any bills of lading or waybills signed by the charterers or by the master at their request.

（b）所有提单或运单不应与本租船合同有抵触，对由于承租人签发的或经其要求由船长签发的提单或海运单与本租船合同之间的任何不一致可能造成的所有后果或责任，由承租人赔偿给出租人。

(c) Bills of lading covering deck cargo shall be claused: "Shipped on deck at Charterers', Shippers' and Receivers' risk, expenses and responsibility, without liability on the part of the

Vessel, or her Owners for any loss, damage, expense or delay howsoever caused."

（c）包含有甲板货的提单应列有："货物装载于甲板，由承租人、托运人和收货人承担风险，对此装载所造成的任何灭失、损害、费用或延误，船舶或出租人一方不负责任。"

The first paragraph entitles the charterers to present bills of lading to the master for signature by him on behalf of the shipowners or charterers may sign bills of lading on behalf of the master. The second paragraph entitles the shipowners to get indemnity from the charterers against all consequences or liabilities arising from any inconsistency between the charter party and bills of lading. The third paragraph states that bills of lading covering deck cargo shall be claused: "Shipped on deck at charterers', shippers' and receivers' risk, expense and responsibility, without liability on the part of the vessel, or her owners for any loss, damage, expense or delay howsoever caused."

第一段赋予承租人以下权利：向船长提交提单以由其代表船舶出租人签署，或承租人可代表船长签署提单。第二段赋予船舶出租人向承租人索赔的权利，以补偿因租船合同与提单不一致而产生的所有后果或责任。第三段规定，涵盖甲板货的提单应批注："货物装于甲板，由承租人、托运人及收货人承担风险、费用和责任，船舶或其所有人对无论何种原因导致的任何损失、损害、费用或延误均不承担责任。"

The master of a vessel chartered on the NYPE Form must normally sign bills of lading "as presented" to him by the charterers or their agents. Thus where bills of lading are signed by the master the bill of lading contracts will usually, although not invariably, be between the holders of the bill of lading and the shipowners. Bills of lading signed by the charterers or their agents "for the master" will usually be regarded as binding by the shipowners. It may indicate so clearly that the charterers are the carriers under the contract of carriage evidenced by the bill that the charterers will be bound by the bill despite how it is signed.

以土产格式出租的船舶的船长通常必须签署由承租人或其代理人向他"所呈递"的提单。因此，船长对于提单的签署，通常（虽然并不一定）表明了提单持有人和船舶出租人之间存在提单合同。承租人或其代理人代表船长签署的提单通常被视为对船舶出租人具有约束力。这可能清楚地表明，承租人是提单证明的运输合同的承运人，不管提单的签发方式如何，承租人将受提单的约束。

【Case】The vessel was chartered for a trip on the NYPE Form. An additional clause gave the shipowners an express indemnify from the charterers in respect of liabilities arising from the charterers or their agents, including the master, signing bills of lading. The vessel loaded on deck a consignment of plywood which there suffered damage by rainwater. The bills of lading were issued by the charterer's agent and signed by them for the master; they contained the typewritten words "shipped under deck". The shipowner contended that he had no liability to the receiver of the plywood under these bills as the charterer's agent had no authority to issue or sign them in that form. Held that although the charterer's agent had no actual authority to issue and sign under-deck bills for cargo on deck, he did have ostensible authority and accordingly the shipowner was bound by the bills.

【案例】某船以土产格式出租一个航次。附加条款明确规定了承租人对船舶出租人因承租人或其代理人，包括船长签署提单引发的责任给予赔偿。船舶在甲板上装载胶合板货物并因雨水遭受损害。提单由承租人的代理人签发并代表船长签署，提单上印就文字"装于舱内"。船舶出租人主张，在这种情况下他们对货物收货人不承担责任，因为承租人的代理人没有权力签发提单。法院判决，尽管承租人的代理人没有实际权力为甲板货物签发舱内提单，但其也有表见授权，因此船舶出租人受提单的约束。

5. Allocation of Costs
5. 费用分摊

The shipowners must place the vessel at the time charterers' disposal and during the charter period provide and pay for manning, ship's insurance, and maintenance. The charterers provide and pay for fuel, harbor dues, pilotage, costs for loading and discharging, and other costs relating to the commercial use of the vessel. The time charter party normally contains clauses in which the parties' respective obligations are specified.

船舶出租人必须在合同期间将船舶处置于承租人之下并且支付人员费用、船舶保险费和维修费。承租人提供和支付燃料费、港口使费、引航费、装卸费用以及有关船舶营运的其他费用。定期租船合同通常包含了当事双方各自义务的条款。

5.1 Shipowners to Provide Clause
5.1 出租人负责的事项条款

According to the provision of NYPE Form 1993, "the owners shall provide and pay for the insurance of the vessel, except as otherwise provided, and for all provisions, cabin, deck, engine-room and other necessary stores, including boiler water; shall pay for wages, consular shipping and discharging fees of the crew and charges for port services pertaining to the crew; shall maintain the vessel's class and keep her in a thoroughly efficient state in hull, machinery and equipment for and during the service, and have a full complement of officers and crew".

根据1993年土产格式的规定："除另有约定外，出租人应负责并支付船舶保险费、全部供应品、舱室、甲板、机舱和其他必要的物料，包括锅炉用淡水；并支付船员的工资、上船和离船的领事费以及有关船员的港口服务费；维持船级并使船体、船机和设备在租期内处于充分有效状态，配备足够的胜任的高级船员和普通船员。"

The provisions in NYPE Form 1993 require the shipowners to insure against war risks as well as against hull and machinery risks. A provision that the shipowners are to pay for the insurance of their ship does not imply that they may not claim against the charterers for damage to the ship caused by the charterers or their servants. Also, according to the provision of Clause 39 in NYPE Form 1993, the charterers shall have the benefit of any return insurance premium receivable by the shipowners from their underwriters as and when received from underwriters by reason of the vessel being in port for a minimum period of 30 days if on full hire for this period or pro rata for the time actually on hire.

1993年土产格式的条款要求船舶出租人投保战争风险以及船体和机械风险。船舶出租人为其船舶支付保险费用的规定，并不意味着船舶出租人不得就承租人或其受雇人造成的船舶损害向承租人索赔。此外，根据1993年土产格式第39条的规定，若船舶在某一期间内处于在港状态，且满足以下条件，则承租人有权享有出租人从其保险人处收取的返还保险费：若船舶在该在港期间全程处于"足额付租状态"（即租船人按合同约定全额支付租金），且在港时间至少满30天；若船舶在该在港期间仅部分时间处于"付租状态"，则按实际付租时间占30天的比例享有返还保险费。

It imposes an obligation for shipowners to maintain the ship during the charter period. If the ship, her machinery, or equipment does become inefficient during the charter period the shipowners are obliged by reason of this provision to take reasonable steps within a reasonable time to put them right. The obligation of the shipowners under this provision is an intermediate obligation, not a condition, and so the charterers do not have the right to treat the charter as discharged for any breach of the obligation.

船舶出租人有义务维护租用期间的船舶。如果船舶、机器或设备在租用期间状态不好，船舶出租人根据此规定有义务在合理的时间内采取合理的步骤，尽快恢复。根据该条款，船舶出租人承担的义务属于中间义务，而非条件义务，因此承租人无权因船舶出租人违反该义务而将租船合同视为解除。

The provision of Article 133 of CMC stipulates that "during the charter period if the ship is found at variance with the seaworthiness or the other conditions agreed upon in the charter, the shipowner shall take all reasonable measures to have them restored as soon as possible".

《中华人民共和国海商法》第133条规定："船舶在租期内不符合约定的适航状态或者其他状态，出租人应当采取可能采取的合理措施，使之尽快恢复。"

5.2 Charterers to Provide Clause
5.2 承租人负责的事项条款

The charterers while the vessel is on hire, shall provide and pay for all the bunkers except as otherwise agreed; shall pay for port charges (including compulsory watchmen and cargo watchmen and compulsory garbage disposal), all communication expenses pertaining to the charterers' business at cost, pilotages, towages, agencies, commissions, consular charges (except those pertaining to individual crew members or flag of the vessel), and all other usual expenses except those stated in Clause 6, but when the vessel puts into a port for causes for which the vessel is responsible (other than by stress of weather), then all such charges incurred shall be paid by the owners. Fumigation ordered because of illness of the crew shall be for the owners' account. Fumigations ordered because of cargo carried or ports visited while the vessel is employed under this charter party shall be for the charterers' account. All other fumigations shall be for the charterers' account after the vessel has been on charter for a continuous period of six months or more.

除另有约定外，在租期内，承租人应当提供并支付所有燃油、港口使费（包括强制看管人、货物看管人和强制垃圾处理费），与承租人的经营成本有关的所有通信费用、引航费、拖带费、代理费、佣金、领事费（有关船员或船旗的领事费除外），以及第6条所述费用以外的所有其他通常费用。但是，当船舶由于其本身应承担责任的原因（并非由于恶劣天气）进港时，则所产生的所有费用由出租人支付。船舶由于船员疾病而被指令熏舱时，由出租人负担费用。在本租船合同项下使用船舶期间，因所载货物或所挂靠港口而被指令进行的熏蒸，费用由承租人承担。船舶被租用连续六个月或更长时间后，所有其他熏蒸费用由承租人承担。

The charterers shall provide and pay for necessary dunnage and also any extra fittings requisite for a special trade or unusual cargo, but the owners shall allow them the use of any dunnage already aboard the vessel. Prior to redelivery the charterers shall remove their dunnage and fittings as their cost and in their time.

承租人应提供并支付必要的垫舱物料，以及特殊运输或特殊货物所需的任何额外设备，但出租人应允许承租人使用船上已有的任何垫舱物料。还船前，承租人应自费和在规定时间内将其提供的垫舱物料和设备移走。

【ASSIGNMENT】

Ⅰ. **Answer the following questions and check the answers from the text.**

1. What does a time charter party mean?

2. What is the purpose of on-hire/off-hire surveys under the time charter party?

3. What are the requirements for the state of the ship on delivery and redelivery?

4. In which circumstances can the vessel from be placed off-hire?

5. In which circumstances can hire be deducted?

Ⅱ. **Choice questions.** (Choose the one you think is correct from the following.)

1. Where the charter party requires the vessel to use safe ports only, the port, at the time when the (　　) must be prospectively safe for her to get to, stay, and in due course leave.

    A. order is given   B. ship arrival

    C. ship departure   D. charter concluded

2. In the same good order and condition, ordinary wear and tear excepted require that (　　).

    A. the vessel to be redelivered on the expiration of the charter

    B. the vessel to be delivered on the beginning of the charter

    C. the vessel to be in service during the whole period of the charter

    D. A+B

3. An anti-technicality clause is a clause designed to modify the rigor of the (　　).

    A. withdrawal clause   B. off-hire clause

    C. lien clause   D. canceling clause

4. Which of the following certain specified events can charterer off-hire? (　　)

    A. Deficiency crew.   B. Fire.

    C. Breakdown of machinery.   D. A+B+C.

5. Under the Inter-Club Agreement, claims for handling of cargo are allocated (　　).

    A. 100% owners   B. 100% charterers

    C. 50% charterers   D. 50% owners

Ⅲ. **True or false questions.**

1. Fumigations ordered because of cargoes carried or ports visited while the vessel is employed under the time charter party shall be for the charterers' account. (　　)

2. The expression "deficiency of men" does not apply to the situation in which there is on board a full complement of officers and men able to work but some or all of them refuse to do so. (　　)

3. The speed capability and bunker consumption statements in the time charter parties are not

usually connected to certain weather conditions and a certain draught. (　　)

4. When a charter party is for a stated period—such as "three months" without any express margin or allowance, then the court will not imply a reasonable margin or allowance. (　　)

5. If the charterers fail to make punctual payment of an installment of hire, that is to say, payment on or before the due date, the shipowners are entitled by the withdrawal clause to withdraw the ship from their service and thus bring the charter to an end. (　　)

IV. Case study.

ABC Shipping Co. Ltd. let their vessel Grey Wolf to Northern XYZ Industries Ltd. Under a time charter party "for 12 months, 20 days more or less at charterers" option from January 1, 2000. The charter party states that:

(1)Hire was to be paid punctually in cash monthly in advance, otherwise the vessel would be withdrawn at the shipowners' direction.

(2)Hire was to cease in the event of deficiency of men, breakdown of machinery, or other accident hindering the working of the vessel.

(3)The master was to be under the orders of the charterers as regards employment or another arrangement, and they were to indemnify the shipowners against all consequences arising from him complying with such orders.

(4)The vessel was to be employed between good and safe ports.

(5)She was to be redelivered in good condition (fair wear and tear excepted).

On January 13, 2000, whilst off the coast of Spain on a voyage from London to Singapore via Gibraltar, the vessel's main engine broke down. She went back to Falmouth for repairs. She sailed from there on February 5, and did not regain her former position until February 12. When she arrived at Gibraltar, her steering gear was out of commission for 2 days, but her cranes were fit to discharge her cargo.

At Singapore, the charterers loaded drums of chemicals for delivery at a port in British Columbia. The master was ordered by the charterer to sail at 0930 a.m. on September 1. He did so despite the wind being of hurricane force. The radio equipment was damaged as a result. The charterer nominated Vancouver as the port of discharge. The master went there although he well knew that there was an underwater obstruction in the fairway. The vessel was damaged when she struck it. On discharge, the chemicals were found to have leaked and damaged the holds.

On November 1 the vessel was temporarily withdrawn for 14 days by the shipowner because the charterer continued to pay hire by cheque instead of in cash. On January 10, 2001, the charterer sent the vessel on a voyage from New York to New Zealand. At New York the charterer ordered the master to sign clean bills of lading in respect of goods that were in bad condition, and the shipowner had to pay damages to the indorsees of the bills. The vessel reached New Zealand on February 20. Freight rates had risen in the meanwhile. She was redelivered to her owners on February 23 with the paintwork in her holds badly damaged. Advise the shipowner as to the legal position on all the matters stated above.

APPENDIX 1 LAYTIME DEFINITIONS FOR CHARTER PARTIES 2013

PREAMBLE

Words, phrases, acronyms and abbreviations ("Words and Phrases") used in a Charter Party shall be defined, for the purposes of Laytime only, in accordance with the corresponding Words and Phrases set out below, when any or all such definitions are expressly incorporated into the Charter Party.

"Charter Party" shall include any form of contract of carriage or affreightment including contracts evidenced by bills of lading.

Singular/Plural

The singular includes the plural and vice versa as the context admits or requires.

List of Definitions

1. PORT shall mean any area where vessels load or discharge cargo and shall include, but not be limited to, berths, wharves, anchorages, buoys and offshore facilities as well as places outside the legal, fiscal or administrative area where vessels are ordered to wait for their turn no matter the distance from that area.

2. BERTH shall mean the specific place where the Vessel is to load or discharge and shall include, but not be limited to, any wharf, anchorage, offshore facility or other location used for that purpose.

3. REACHABLE ON ARRIVAL shall mean that the charterer undertakes that an available loading or discharging Berth be provided to the Vessel on arrival at the Port which the Vessel can reach safely without delay.

4. ALWAYS ACCESSIBLE shall mean that the charterer undertakes that an available loading or discharging Berth be provided to the Vessel on arrival at the Port which the Vessel can reach safely without delay. The charterer additionally undertakes that the Vessel will be able to depart safely from the Berth and without delay at any time before, during or on completion of loading or discharging.

5. LAYTIME shall mean the period of time agreed between the parties during which the owner will make and keep the Vessel available for loading or discharging without payment additional to the freight.

6. PER HATCH PER DAY shall mean that the Laytime is to be calculated by dividing the quantity of cargo by the result of multiplying the agreed daily rate per hatch by the number of the Vessel's hatches.

Thus:

$$\text{Laytime} = \frac{\text{Quantity of cargo}}{\text{Daily rate} \times \text{Number of hatches}} = \text{days}$$

Each pair of parallel twin hatches shall count as one hatch. Nevertheless, a hatch that is capable of being worked by two gangs simultaneously shall be counted as two hatches.

7. PER WORKING HATCH PER DAY or PER WORKABLE HATCH PER DAY shall mean that the Laytime is to be calculated by dividing the quantity of cargo in the hold with the largest quantity by the result of multiplying the agreed daily rate per working or workable hatch by the number of hatches serving that hold. Thus:

$$\text{Laytime} = \frac{\text{Largest quantity in one hold}}{\text{Daily rate per hatch} \times \text{Number of hatches serving that hold}} = \text{days}$$

Each pair of parallel twin hatches shall count as one hatch. Nevertheless, a hatch that is capable of being worked by two gangs simultaneously shall be counted as two hatches.

8. DAY shall mean a period of twenty-four (24) consecutive hours. Any part of a Day shall be counted pro rata.

9. CALENDAR DAY shall mean a period of twenty-four (24) consecutive hours running from 0000 hours to 2400 hours. Any part of a Calendar Day shall be counted pro rata.

10. CONVENTIONAL DAY shall mean a period of twenty-four (24) consecutive hours running from any identified time. Any part of a Conventional Day shall be counted pro rata.

11. WORKING DAY shall mean a Day when by local law or practice work is normally carried out.

12. RUNNING DAYS or CONSECUTIVE DAYS shall mean Days which follow one immediately after the other.

13. RUNNING HOURS or CONSECUTIVE HOURS shall mean hours which follow one immediately after the other.

14. HOLIDAY shall mean a Day other than the normal weekly Day(s) of rest, or part thereof, when by local law or practice work during what would otherwise be ordinary working hours is not normally carried out.

15. WEATHER WORKING DAY shall mean a Working Day or part of a Working Day during which it is or, if the Vessel is still waiting for her turn, it would be possible to load/discharge the cargo without interruption due to the weather. If such interruption occurs (or would have occurred if work had been in progress), there shall be excluded from the Laytime a period calculated by reference to the ratio which the duration of the interruption bears to the time which would have or could have been worked but for the interruption.

16. WEATHER WORKING DAY OF 24 CONSECUTIVE HOURS shall mean a Working Day or part of a Working Day of 24 consecutive hours during which it is or, if the vessel is still waiting for her turn, it would be possible to load/discharge the cargo without interruption due to the weather. If such interruption occurs (or would have occurred if work had been in progress) there shall be excluded from the Laytime the period during which the weather interrupted or would have

interrupted work.

17. WEATHER WORKING DAY OF 24 HOURS shall mean a period of 24 hours made up of one or more Working Days during which it is or, if the Vessel is still waiting for her turn, it would be possible to load/discharge the cargo without interruption due to the weather. If such interruption occurs (or would have occurred if work had been in progress), there shall be excluded from Laytime the actual period of such interruption.

18. (WORKING DAY) WEATHER PERMITTING shall have the same meaning as WEATHER WORKING DAY OF 24 CONSECUTIVE HOURS.

19. EXCEPTED or EXCLUDED shall mean that the days specified do not count as Laytime even if loading or discharging is carried out on them.

20. UNLESS SOONER COMMENCED shall mean that if turn-time has not expired but loading or discharging is carried out, Laytime shall commence.

21. UNLESS SOONER COMMENCED, IN WHICH CASE ACTUAL TIME USED TO COUNT shall mean that actual time used during turn-time shall count as Laytime.

22. UNLESS USED shall mean that if Laytime has commenced but loading or discharging is carried out during excepted periods, actual time used shall count as Laytime.

23. TO AVERAGE LAYTIME shall mean that separate calculations are to be made for loading and discharging and that any time saved in one operation is to be set off against any excess time used in the other.

24. REVERSIBLE LAYTIME shall mean an option given to the charterer to add together the time allowed for loading and discharging. Where the option is exercised the effect is the same as a total time being specified to cover both operations.

25. NOTICE OF READINESS shall mean the notice to the charterer, shipper, receiver or other person as required by the Charter Party that the Vessel has arrived at the Port or Berth, as the case may be, and is ready to load or discharge.

26. TIME LOST WAITING FOR BERTH TO COUNT AS LOADING OR DISCHARGING TIME or AS LAYTIME shall mean that if no loading or discharging Berth is available and the Vessel is unable to tender Notice of Readiness at the waiting-place then any time lost to the Vessel is counted as if Laytime were running, or as time on Demurrage if Laytime has expired. Such time ceases to count once the Berth becomes available. When the Vessel reaches a place where she is able to tender Notice of Readiness, Laytime or time on Demurrage resumes after such tender and, in respect of Laytime, on expiry of any notice time provided in the Charter Party.

27. WHETHER IN BERTH OR NOT (WIBON) or BERTH OR NO BERTH shall mean that if the designated loading or discharging Berth is not available on arrival, the Vessel on reaching any usual waiting place at the Port, shall be entitled to tender Notice of Readiness from it and Laytime shall commence in accordance with the Charter Party.

28. WHETHER IN PORT OR NOT (WIPON) shall mean that if the designated loading or discharging Berth and the usual waiting place at the Port are not available on arrival, the Vessel shall be entitled to tender Notice of Readiness from any recognised waiting place off the Port and Laytime shall commence in accordance with the Charter Party.

29. VESSEL BEING IN FREE PRATIQUE shall mean that the Vessel complies with port health requirements.

30. DEMURRAGE shall mean an agreed amount payable to the owner in respect of delay to the Vessel once the Laytime has expired, for which the owner is not responsible. Demurrage shall not be subject to exceptions which apply to Laytime unless specifically stated in the Charter Party.

31. DESPATCH MONEY or DESPATCH shall mean an agreed amount payable by the owner if the Vessel completes loading or discharging before the Laytime has expired.

32. DESPATCH ON ALL WORKING TIME SAVED or ON ALL LAYTIME SAVED shall mean that Dispatch Money shall be payable for the time from the completion of loading or discharging until the expiry of the Laytime excluding any periods excepted from the Laytime.

33. DESPATCH ON ALL TIME SAVED shall mean that Dispatch Money shall be payable for the time from the completion of loading or discharging to the expiry of the Laytime including periods excepted from the Laytime.

APPENDIX 2　GENCON CHARTER 1994

"Gencon" Charter (As revised 1922, 1976 and 1994)

1.Shipbroker	RECOMMENDE THE BALTIC AND INTERNATIONAL MARITIME COUNCIL UNIFORM GENERAL CHARTER (AS REVISED 1922,1976 AND 1994) (To be used for trades for which no specially approved form is in force) CODE NAME:"GENCON"　**Part** I	
	2.Place and date	
3.Owners/Place of business(Cl.1)	4.Charterers/Place of business(Cl.1)	
5.Vessel's name (Cl.1)	6.GT/NT (Cl.1)	
7.DWT all told on summer load line in metric ton (abt.) (Cl.1)	8.Present position (Cl.1)	
9.Expected ready to load (abt.) (Cl.1)		
10.Loading port or place (Cl.1)	11.Discharging port or place (Cl.1)	
12.Cargo also state quantity and margin in Owners' option, if agreed; if full and complete cargo not agreed state"part cargo"(Cl.1)		
13.Freight rate (also state whether freight prepaid or payable on delivery) (Cl.4)	14. Freight payment (state currency and method of payment; also beneficiary and bank account) (Cl.4)	
15.State if vessel's cargo handling gear shall not be used (Cl.5)	16. Laytime (if separate laytime for load and disch. is agreed, fill in (a) and (b). If total laytime for load and disch., fill in (c) only) (Cl.6)	
17.Shippers/Place of business (Cl.6)	(a) Laytime for loading	
18.Agents (loading) (Cl.6)	(b) Laytime for discharging	
19.Agents (discharging) (Cl.6)	(c) Total laytime for loading and discharging	
20.Demurrage rate and manner payable (loading and discharging) (Cl.7)	21.Canceling date (Cl.9)	
	22.General; Average to be adjusted at (Cl.12)	
23.Freight Tax (state if for the Owners' account) (Cl.13(c))	24.Brokerage commission and to whom payable (Cl.15)	
25. Law and Arbitration (state 19(a), 19(b) or 19(c); if 19(c) agreed also state Place of Arbitration (if not filled in 19(a) shall apply (Cl.19)) (a) State maximum amount for small claims/shortened arbitration (Cl.19)	26.Additional clauses covering special provisions, if agreed	

It is mutually agreed that this contract shall be performed subject to the conditions contained in this charter party which shall include Part 1 as well as Part 2. In the event of conflict of conditions, the provisions of Part 1 shall prevail over those of Part 2 to the extent of such conflict.

Signature (Owners)	Signature (Charterers)

PART II

"GENCON" Charter (As Revised 1922, 1976 and 1994)

1.It is agreed between the party mentioned in Box 3 as the Owners of the Vessel named in Box 5, of the GT/NT indicated in Box 6 and carrying about the number of metric tons of deadweight capacity all told on summer loadline stated in Box 7, now in position as stated in Box 8 and expected ready to load under this charter party about the date indicated in Box 9, and the party mentioned as the charterers in Box 4 that:

The said vessel shall, as soon as her prior commitments have been completed, proceed to the loading port or place stated in Box 10 or so near thereto as she may safely get and lie always afloat, and there load a full and complete cargo (if shipment of deck cargo agreed same to be at the charterers' risk and responsibility) as stated in Box 12, which the charterers bind themselves to ship, and being so loaded the vessel shall proceed to the discharging port or place stated in Box 11 as ordered on signing Bills of Lading, or so near thereto as she may safely get and lie always afloat, and there deliver the cargo.

2. Owner's Responsibility Clause

The owners are to be responsible for loss of or damage to the goods or for delay in delivery of the goods only in case the loss, damage or delay has been caused by personal want of due diligence on the part of the owners or their Manager to make the Vessel in all respects seaworthy and to secure that she is properly manned, equipped and supplied, or by the personal act or default of the Owners or their Manager.

And the Owners are not responsible for loss, damage or delay arising from any other cause whatsoever, even from the neglect or default of the Master or crew or some other person employed by the Owners on board or ashore for whose acts they would, but for this clause, be responsible, or from unseaworthiness of the Vessel on loading or commencement of the voyage or at any time whatsoever.

3. Deviation Clause

The vessel has liberty to call any port or ports in any order, for any purpose, to sail without pilots, to tow and/or assist vessels in all situations, and also to deviate for the purpose of saving life and/or property.

4. Payment of Freight

(a) The freight at the rate stated in Box 13 shall be paid in cash calculated on the intaken quantity of cargo.

(b) Prepaid. If according to Box 13 freight is to be paid on shipment, it shall be deemed earned and non-returnable, Vessel and/or cargo lost or not lost.

Neither the Owners nor their agents shall be required to sign or endorse bills of lading showing freight prepaid unless the freight due to the Owners has actually been paid.

(c) <u>On delivery</u>. If according to Box 13 freight, or part thereof, is payable at destination it shall not be deemed earned until the cargo is thus delivered. Notwithstanding the provisions under (a), if freight or part thereof is payable on delivery of the cargo the Charterers shall have the option of paying the freight on delivered weight/quantity provided such option is declared before breaking bulk and the weight/quantity can be ascertained by official weighing machine, joint draught survey or tally.

Cash for Vessel's ordinary disbursements at the port of loading to be advanced by the Charterers, if required, at highest current rate of exchange, subject to two (2) per cent to cover insurance and other expenses.

5. Loading/Discharging

(a) Costs/Risks

The cargo shall be brought into the holds, loaded, stowed and/or trimmed, tallied, lashed and/or secured and taken from the holds and discharged by the charterers, free of any risk, liability and expense whatsoever to the owners. The charterers shall provide and lay all dunnage material as required for the proper stowage and protection of the cargo on board, the owners allowing the use of dunnage available on board. The charterers shall be responsible for and pay the cost of removing their dunnage after discharge of the cargo under this charter party and time to count until dunnage has been removed.

(b) Cargo Handling Gear

Unless the vessel is gearless or unless it has been agreed between the parties that the vessel's gear shall not be used and stated as such in Box 15, the owners shall throughout the duration of loading/discharging give free use of the vessel's cargo handling gear and of sufficient motive power to operate all such cargo handling gear. All such equipment to be in good working order. Unless caused by negligence of the stevedores, time lost by breakdown of the vessel's cargo handling gear or motive _____ pro rata the total number of cranes/winches required at that time for the loading/discharging of cargo under this charter party _____ shall not count as laytime or time on demurrage.

On request the owners shall provide free of charge cranemen/winchmen from the crew to operate the vessel's cargo handling gear, unless local regulations prohibit this, in which latter event shore labourers shall be for the account of the charterers. Cranemen/winchmen shall be under the charterers' risk and responsibility and as stevedores to be deemed as their servants but shall always under the supervision of the Master.

(c) Stevedore Damage

The charterers shall be responsible for damage (beyond ordinary wear and tear) to any part of the vessel caused by stevedores. Such damage shall be notified as soon as reasonably possible by the Master to the charterers or their agents and to their stevedores, failing which the charterers shall not be held responsible. The Master shall endeavour to obtain the stevedores' written acknowledgement of liability.

The charterers are obliged to repair any stevedore damage prior to completion of the voyage, but must repair stevedore damage affecting the vessel's seaworthiness or class before the vessel sails from the port where such damage was caused or found. All additional expenses incurred shall be for the account of the charterers and time lost shall be for the account of and shall be paid to the owners by the charterers at the demurrage rate.

6. Laytime

(a) Separate laytime for loading and discharging

The cargo shall be loaded within the number of running days/hours as indicated in Box 16, weather permitting, Sundays and holidays excepted, unless used, in which event time used shall count.

The cargo shall be discharged within the number of running days/hours as indicated in Box 16, weather permitting, Sundays and holidays excepted, unless used, in which event time used shall count.

(b) Total laytime for loading and discharging

The cargo shall be loaded and discharged within the number of total running days/hours as indicated in Box 16, weather permitting, Sundays and holidays excepted, unless used, in which event time used shall count.

(c) Commencement of laytime (loading and discharging)

Laytime for loading and discharging shall commence at 1300 hours, if notice of readiness is given up to and including 1200 hours, and at 0600 hours next working day if notice given during office hours after 12.00 hours. Notice of readiness at loading port to be given to the shippers named in Box 17 or if not named, to the charterers or their agents named in Box 18. Notice of readiness at the discharging port to be given to the receivers or, if not known, to the charterers or their agents named in Box 19.

If the loading/discharging berth is not available on the vessel's arrival at or off the port of loading/discharging, the vessel shall be entitled to give notice of readiness within ordinary office hours on arrival there, whether in free pratique or not, whether customs cleared or not. Laytime or time on demurrage shall then count as if she were in berth and in all respects ready for loading/discharging provided that the master warrants that she is in fact ready in all respects. Time used in moving from the place of waiting to the loading/discharging berth shall not count as laytime.

If after inspection, the vessel is found not to be ready in all respects to load/discharge time lost after the discovery thereof until the vessel is again ready to load/discharge shall not count as laytime.

Time used before commencement of laytime shall count.

7. Demurrage Clause

Demurrage at the loading and discharging port is payable by the charterers at the rate stated in Box 20 in the manner stated in Box 20 per day or pro rata for any part of a day. Demurrage shall fall due day by day and shall be payable upon receipt of the owners' invoice.

In the event the demurrage is not paid in accordance with the above, the owners shall give the charterers 96 running hours written notice to rectify the failure. If the demurrage is not paid at the expiration of this time limit and if the vessel is in or at the loading port, the owners are entitled at any time to terminated the charter party and claim damages for any losses caused thereby.

8. Lien Clause

The Owners shall have a lien on cargo and on all sub-freights payable in respect of the cargo, for freight, deadfreight, demurrage, claims for damages and for all other amounts due under this Charter Party including costs of recovering same.

9. Canceling Clause

(a) Should the vessel not ready to load (whether in berth or not) on the cancelling date indicated in Box 21, the charterers shall have the option of canceling this charter party.

(b) Should the owners anticipate that, despite the exercise of due diligence, the vessel will not be ready to load by the canceling date, they shall notify the charterers thereof without delay stating the expected date of the vessel's readiness to load and asking whether the charterers will exercise their option of canceling the charter party, or agree to a new canceling date.

Such option must be declared by the charterers within 48 running hours after the receipt of the owners' notice. If the charterers do not exercise their option of canceling, then this charter party shall be deemed to be amended such that the seventh day after the new readiness date stated in the owners' notification to the charterers shall be the new canceling date.

The provisions of sub-clause (b) of this clause shall operate only once, and in case of the vessel's further delay, the charterers shall have the option of canceling the charter party as per sub-clause (a) of this clause.

10. Bills of Lading

The Bills of lading shall be presented and signed by the Master as per "Congenbill" Bill of Lading form, Edition 1994, without prejudice to this charter party, or by the Owners agents provided written authority has been given by Owners to the agents, a copy of which is to be furnished to the charterers. The charterers shall indemnify the owners against all consequences or liabilities that may arise from the signing of bills of lading as presented to the extent that the terms or contents of such bills of lading impose or result in the imposition of more onerous liabilities upon the owners than those assumed by the owners under this charter party.

11. Both-to-Blame Collision Clause

If the vessel comes into collision with another vessel as a result of the negligence of the other vessel and any act, neglect or default of the master, mariner, pilot or the servants of the owners in the navigation or in the management of the vessel, the owners of the cargo carried hereunder will indemnify the owners against all loss or liability to the other or non-carrying vessel or her owners in so far as such loss or liability represents loss of, or damage to, or any claim whatsoever of the owners of said cargo paid or payable by the other or non-carrying vessel or her owners to the owners of said cargo and set-off, recouped or recovered by the other or non-carrying vessel or her owners as part of their claim against the carrying vessel or the owners.

The foregoing provisions shall also apply where the owners, operators or those in charge of any vessel or vessels or objects other than, or in addition to, the colliding vessels or objects are at fault in respect of a collision or contact.

12. General Average and New Jason Clause

General Average shall be adjusted in London unless otherwise agreed in Box 22 according to York-Antwerp Rules 1994 and any subsequent modification thereof. Proprietors of cargo to pay the cargo's share in the general expenses, even if same have been necessitated through neglect or default of the Owners' servants (see clause 2).

If General Average is to be adjusted in accordance with the law and practice of the United States of America, the following clause shall apply: "In the event of accident, danger, damage or disaster before or after the commencement of the voyage, resulting from any cause whatsoever, whether due to negligence or not, for which, or for the consequence of which, the owners are not responsible, by statute, contract or otherwise, the cargo shippers, consignees or the owners of the cargo shall contribute with the owners in general average to the payment of any sacrifices, losses or expenses of a general average nature that may be made or incurred and shall pay salvage and special charges incurred in respect of the cargo. If a salving vessel is owned or operated by the owners, salvage shall be paid for as fully as if the said salving vessel belonged to strangers. Such deposit as the owners, or their agents, may deem sufficient to cover the estimated contribution of the goods and any salvage and special charges thereon shall, if required, be made by the cargo, shippers, consignees or owners of the goods to the owners before delivery."

13. Taxes and Dues Clause

(a) On Vessel—The Owners shall pay for all dues, charges and taxes customarily levied on the vessel, howsoever the amount thereof may assessed.

(b) On Cargo—The charterers shall pay for all dues, charges and taxes customarily levied on the cargo, howsoever the amount thereof may assessed.

(c) On Freight—Unless otherwise agreed in Box 23, taxes levied on the freight shall be for the charterers' amount.

14. Agency

In every case the Owners shall appoint their own Agent both at the port of loading and the port of discharge.

15. Brokerage

A brokerage commission at the rate stated in Box 24 on the freight, dead-freight and demurrage earned is due to the party mentioned in Box 24.

In case of non-execution 1/3 of the brokerage on the estimated amount of freight to be paid by the party responsible for such non-execution to the Brokers as indemnity for the latter's expenses and work. In case of more voyages the amount of indemnity to be agreed.

16. General Strike Clause

(a) If there is a strike or lock-out affecting or preventing the actual loading of the cargo, or any part of it, when the vessel is ready to proceed from her last port or at any time during the voyage to the port or ports of loading or after her arrival there, the master or the owners may ask the charterers to declare, that they agree to reckon the laydays as if there were no strike or lock-out.

Unless the charterers have given such declaration in writing (by telegram, if necessary) within 24 hours, the owners shall have the options of canceling this charter party. If part of cargo has already been loaded, the owners must proceed with same (freight payable on loaded quantity only) having liberty to complete with other cargo on the way for their own account.

(b) If there is a strike or lock-out affecting or preventing the actual discharging of the cargo on or after the vessel's arrival at or off port of discharge and same has not been settled within 48 hours, the charterers shall have the option of keeping the vessel waiting until such strike or lock-out is at an end against paying half demurrage after expiration of the time provided for discharging until the strike or lock-out terminates and thereafter full demurrage shall be payable until the completion of discharging, or of ordering the vessel to a safe port where she can safely discharge without risk of being detained by strike or lock-out. Such orders to be given within 48 hours after the master or the owners have given notice to the charterers of the strike or lock-out affecting the discharge. On delivery of the cargo at such port, all conditions of this charter party and of the bill of lading shall apply and the vessel shall receive the same freight as if she had discharged at the original port of destination, except that if the distance to the substituted port exceeds 100 nautical miles, the freight on the cargo delivered at the substituted port to be increased in proportion.

(c) Except for the obligations described above, neither the charterers nor the owners shall be responsible for the consequences of any strikes or lock-outs preventing or affecting the actual loading or discharging of the cargo.

17. War Risks ("Voywar 1993")

(1) For the purpose of this clause, the words:

(a) The "Owners" shall include the shipowners, bareboat charterers, disponent owners, managers or other operators who are charged with the management of the vessel, and the master, and

(b) "War Risks" shall include any war (whether actual or threatened), act of war, civil war, hostilities, revolution, rebellion, civil commotion, warlike operations, the laying of mines (whether actual or reported), acts of piracy, acts of terrorists, acts of hostility or malicious damage, blockades (whether imposed against all vessels or imposed selectively against vessels of certain flags or ownership, or against certain cargoes or crews or otherwise howsoever), be any person, body, terrorist or political group, or the government of any state whatsoever, which, in the reasonable judgement of the master and/or the owners, may be dangerous or are likely to be or to become dangerous to the vessel, her cargo, crew or other persons on board the vessel.

(2) If at any time before the vessel commences loading, it appears that, in the reasonable judgement of the master and/or the owners, performance of the contract of carriage, or any part of it, may expose, or is likely to expose, the vessel, her cargo, crew or other persons on board the vessel to war risks, the owners may give notice to the charterers canceling this contract of carriage, or may refuse to perform such part of it as may expose, or may likely to expose, the vessel, her cargo, crew or other persons on board the vessel to war risks; provided always that if this contract of carriage provides that loading or discharging is to take place within a range of ports, and at the port or ports nominated by the charterers the vessel, her cargo, crew, or other persons on board the vessel may be exposed, or may likely to be exposed, to war risks, the owners shall first require the charterers to nominate any other safe port which lies within the range for loading or discharging, and may only cancel this contract of carriage if the charterers shall not have nominated such safe port or ports within 48 hours of receipt of notice of such requirement.

(3) The owners shall not be required to continue to load cargo for any voyage, or to sign bills of lading for any port or place, or to proceed or continue on any voyage, or on any part thereof, or to proceed through any canal or waterway, or to proceed to or remain at any port or place whatsoever, where it appears, either after the loading of the cargo commences, or at any stage of the voyage thereafter before the discharge of the cargo is completed, that, in the reasonable judgement of the master and/or the owners, the vessel, her cargo (or any part thereof), crew or other persons on board the vessel (or any one or more of them) may be, or are likely to be, exposed to war risks. If it should so appear, the owners may by notice request the charterers to nominate a safe port for the discharge of the cargo or any part thereof, and if within 48 hours of the receipt of such notice, the charterers shall not have nominated such a port, the owners may discharge the cargo at any safe port of their choice (including the port of loading) in complete fulfilment of the contract of carriage. The owners

shall be entitled to recover from the charterers the extra expenses of such discharge and, if the discharge takes place at any port other than the loading port, to receive the full freight as though the cargo had been carried to the discharging port and if the extra distance exceeds 100 miles, to additional freight which shall be the same percentage of the freight contracted for as the percentage which the extra distance represents to the distance of the normal and customary route, the owners having a lien on cargo for such expenses and freight.

(4) If at any stage of the voyage after the loading of the cargo commences, it appear that, in the reasonable judgement of the master and/or the owners, the vessel, her cargo , crew or other persons on board the vessel may be, or are likely to be, exposed to war risks on any part of the route (including any canal or waterway) which is normally and customarily used in a voyage of the nature contracted for, and there is another longer route to the discharging port, the owners shall give notice to the charterers that this route will be taken. In this event the owners shall be entitled, if the total extra distance exceeds 100 miles, to additional freight which shall be the same percentage of the freight contracted for as the percentage which the extra distance represents to the distance of the normal and customary route.

(5) The vessel shall have liberty:

(a) to comply with all orders, directions, recommendations or advice as to departure, arrival, routes,

sailing in convoy, ports of call, stoppages, destinations, discharge of cargo, delivery or in any way whatsoever which are given by the Government of the Nation under whose flag the vessel sails, or other Government to whose laws the owners are subject, or any other Government which so requires, or any body or group acting with the power to compel compliance with their orders or directions;

(b) to comply with the orders, directions or recommendations of any war risks underwriters who have the authority to give the same under the terms of the war risks insurance;

(c) to comply with the terms of any resolution of the Security Council of the United Nations, any directives of the European Community, the effective orders of any other Supranational body which has the right to issue and give the same, and with national laws aimed at enforcing the same to which the owners are subject, and to obey the orders and directions of those who are charged with their enforcement;

(d) to discharge at any other port any cargo or part thereof which may render the vessel liable to confiscation as a contraband carrier;

(e) to call at any other port to change the crew or any part thereof or other persons on board the vessel when there is reason to believe that they may be subject to internment, imprisonment or other sanctions;

(f) where cargo has not been loaded or has been discharged by the owners under any provisions of this clause, to load other cargo for the owners' own benefit and carry it to any other port or ports whatsoever, whether backwards or forwards or in a contrary direction to the ordinary or customary route.

(6) If in compliance with any of the provisions of sub-clause (2) to (5) of this clause anything is done or not done, such shall not be deemed to be a deviation, but shall be considered as due fulfilment of the contract of carriage.

18. General Ice Clause

Port of loading

(a) In the event of the loading port being inaccessible by reason of ice when the vessel is ready to proceed from her last port or at any time during the voyage or on the vessel's arrival or in case frost sets in after the vessel's arrival, the master for fear of being frozen in is at liberty to leave without cargo, and this charter party shall be null and void.

(b) If during loading the master, for fear of the vessel being frozen in, deems it advisable to leave, he has liberty to do so with what cargo he has on board and to proceed to any other port or ports with option of completing cargo for the owners' benefit for any port or ports including port of discharge. Any part cargo thus loaded under this charter party to be forwarded to destination at the vessel's expense but against payment of freight, provided that no extra expenses be thereby caused to the charterers, freight being paid on quantity delivered(in proportion if lump sum), all other conditions as per this charter party.

(c) In case of more than one loading port, and if one or more of the ports are closed by ice, the master or the owners to be at liberty either to load the part cargo at the open port and fill up elsewhere for their own account as under section (b) or to declare the charter party null and void unless the charterers agree to load full cargo at the open port.

Port of discharge

(a) Should ice prevent the vessel from reaching port of discharge the charterers shall have the option keeping the vessel waiting until the reopening of navigation and paying demurrage or of ordering the vessel to a safe and immediately accessible port where she can safely discharge without risk of detention by ice. Such orders to be given within 48 hours after the master or the owners have given notice to the charterers of the impossibility of reaching port of destination.

(b) If during discharging the master for fear of the vessel being frozen in deems it advisable to leave, he has liberty to do so with what cargo he has on board and to proceed to the nearest accessible port where she can safely discharge.

(c) On delivery of the cargo at such port, all conditions of the bill of lading shall apply and the vessel shall receive the same freight as if she had discharged at the original port of destination, except that if the distance of the substituted port to be increased in proportion.

19. Law and Arbitration

*(a) This charter party shall be governed by and construed in accordance with English law and any dispute arising out of this charter party shall be referred to arbitration in London in accordance with the Arbitration Acts 1950 and 1979 or any statutory modification or re-enactment thereof for the time being in force. Unless the parties agree upon a sole arbitrator, one arbitrator shall be appointed by each party and the arbitrators so appointed shall appoint a third arbitrator, the decision of the three-man tribunal thus constituted or any two of them, shall be final. On the receipt by one party of the nomination in writing of the other party's arbitrator, that party shall appoint their arbitrator within fourteen days, failing which the decision of the single arbitrator appointed shall be final.

For dispute where the total amount claimed by either party does not exceed the amount stated in Box 25 the arbitration shall be conducted in accordance with the Small Claims Procedure of the London Maritime Arbitrators Association.

*(b) This charter party shall be governed by and construed in accordance with Title 9 of the United States Code and the maritime law of the United States and should any dispute arise out of this charter party, the matter in dispute shall be referred to three persons at New York, one to be appointed by each of the parties hereto, and the third by the two so chosen; their decision or that of any two of them shall be final, and for purpose of enforcing any award, this agreement may be made a rule of the Court. The proceedings shall be conducted in accordance with the rules of the Society of Maritime Arbitrators, Inc.

For dispute where the total amount claimed by either party does not exceed the amount stated in Box 25 the arbitration shall be conducted in accordance with the Shortened Arbitration Procedure of the Society of Maritime Arbitrators, Inc.

*(c) Any dispute arising out of this charter party shall be referred to arbitration at the place indicated in Box 25, subject to the procedures applicable there. The laws of the place indicated in Box 25 shall govern this charter party.

(d) If Box 25 in part 1 is not filled in, sub-clause (a) of this clause shall apply.

*(a), (b) and (c) are alternatives; indicate alternative agreed in Box 25.

APPENDIX 3   GENCON CHARTER 2022

PART I

UNIFORM GENERAL CHARTER

1. Shipbroker	2. Place and Date
3. Owners/Place of business (full style address, email)	4. Charterers/Place of business (full style address, email)
5. Vessel (i) Name: (ii) IMO Number: (iii) Class/Classification Society: (iv) P&I Club:	6. GT/NT (i) GT: (ii) NT:
	7. DWT all told on summer load line in metric tons (about)
8. Present position (Cl. 1)	9. Expected ready to load (about) (Cl. 1)
10. Loading port(s) or place(s) (Cl. 1)	11. Discharging port(s) or place(s) (Cl. 1)
12. Cargo (also state quantity and margin in Owners' option, if agreed) (Cl. 1) (i) Part cargo (yes/no): (ii) Commodity(ies): (iii) Quantity: (iv) Margin/tolerance:	
13. Cargo transfer operations (state whether Charterers are permitted to use barges/lighters) (Cl. 3(e))	
14. Freight rate (state rate or lumpsum and amount and currency) (Cl. 7(a))	15. Freight payment (state how and when payment is to be made and name of beneficiary and bank account) (Cl. 7(a))
16. Cargo handling gear (state if Vessel's cargo handling gear shall not be used) (Cl. 4(c))	

17. Laytime (if separate laytime for loading and discharging is agreed, fill in (i) and (ii). If total laytime for loading and discharging, fill in (iii) only) (Cl. 10(b))

(i) Loading (state days or rate, and if SHINC or SHEX):

(ii) Discharging (state days or rate, and if SHINC or SHEX):

(iii) Total laytime for loading and discharging (state days or rate, and if SHINC or SHEX):

18. Laydays/Canceling (Cl. 9(d), 14(a))	19. Demurrage (state rate and whether per day or pro rata) (Cl. 13(a))
20. Freight Tax (state for whose account) (Cl. 25 (c))	21. Vessel's agents (state party to nominate) (Cl. 26)
22. General Average (Cl. 29)	23. Brokerage commission and to whom payable (Cl. 35)
24. ETA Notices for loading (Cl. 8) to be given to:	25. ETA Notices for discharging (Cl. 8) to be given to:
26. Notice of Readiness for loading (state party(ies) for notices) (Cl. 9(a))	27. Notice of Readiness for discharging (state party(ies) for notices) (Cl. 9(a))
28. Owners' contact details for operational notices (Cl. 36)	29. Charterers' contact details for operational notices (Cl. 36)
30. Email address for receipt of arbitration notices and communications on behalf of Owners (Cl. 37)	31. Email address for receipt of arbitration notices and communications on behalf of Charterers (Cl. 37)

32. Law and Arbitration (choose law and arbitration venue. If alternative (g)(Other) is chosen, Clause 37 must be appropriately filled in or replaced, failing which alternative (a)(English law/London arbitration) shall apply) (Cl. 37).

33. Additional clauses (state numbers, if agreed)

It is mutually agreed that this Charter Party shall be performed in accordance with the terms and conditions contained in Part I, including additional clauses, if any agreed and stated in Box 33, as well as Part II. In the event of a conflict of terms and conditions, the provisions of Part I shall prevail over those of Part II to the extent of such conflict.

The party responsible for issuing the final execution version of this Charter Party warrants that it is an Authentic BIMCO Template procured from a properly authorised source and that all modifications to it are clearly visible. "Authentic BIMCO Template" means a BIMCO-approved standard contract in an editable electronic format.

Signature (Owners)	Signature (Charterers)

PART II

GENCON 2022 Uniform General Charter

1. Scope of Contract Voyage

It is agreed between the Owners and the Charterers that:

(a) the Vessel now at the position stated in Box 8 and expected ready to commence loading under this Charter Party on or about the date stated in Box 9 shall, unless prevented or hindered by events beyond the Owners' control, commence its approach voyage to the port or place stated in Box 10 as soon as its prior commitments have been completed, or if more than one port or place or a range of ports or places is stated, to the first port or place, or so near thereto as it may safely get and lie always afloat; and

(b) the Charterers shall ship and the Vessel shall carry the Cargo stated in Box 12; and

(c) upon completion of loading, the Vessel shall proceed to the discharging port(s) or place(s) stated in Box 11, or, if a range of ports or places is stated, to the nominated port(s) or place(s), or so near thereto as it may safely get and lie always afloat, and there deliver the Cargo.

2. Owners' Responsibilities

Subject to any risks or responsibilities that the Charterers have assumed under this Charter Party, (a) (i) the Owners shall exercise due diligence to provide a Vessel that shall:

(1) at the commencement of loading Cargo at each loading port or place under this Charter Party be properly manned, equipped and supplied for its loading and have holds, refrigerating and cool chambers and all other parts of the Vessel in which such Cargo is to be carried fit and safe for its reception,carriage and preservation; and

(2) at the commencement of each Cargo-carrying voyage be seaworthy and properly manned, equipped and supplied;

and

(ii) the Owners shall, from the time when it is loaded to the time when it is discharged, properly and carefully carry, keep and care for the Cargo.

(b) The Owners shall be entitled to rely on all rights, defences, immunities, time bars and limitations of liability that are available in any event to a "Carrier" under the Hague-Visby Rules. Furthermore, unless the loss, damage, delay or failure in performance in question has been caused by a breach of subclause (a)(i) above, the Owners shall also be entitled to rely on all other rights, defences, immunities, time bars and limitations of liability that are available to a "Carrier" under the Hague-Visby Rules.

All such rights, defences, immunities, time bars and limitations of liability are deemed to be applicable to any claim that may be made against the Owners or the ship for loss, damage, delay or failure in performance of whatsoever nature.

3.Cargo

(a) The Charterers shall ensure that at their risk, responsibility and expense:

(i) all Cargo loaded under this Charter Party will be properly and clearly described and documented, and (as appropriate) marked and/or numbered, packed, loaded, stowed, and trimmed and/or secured strictly in accordance with all applicable laws, regulations and conventions (including any relevant IMO recommendations or circulars), with any special requirements to be provided or complied with by the Charterers;

(ii) all packing, stowing, lashing and securing materials (including pallets, crates and dunnage) will be properly treated, handled and disposed of in accordance with all applicable laws and regulations, duly marked, and accompanied by all proper certification;

(iii) the shipment, export, transportation and import of the Cargo will be and will remain lawful in all respects;

(iv) the Cargo when presented for loading (including any necessary strapping, packing, internal securing and/or lifting lugs) will be in all respects fit and suitable for loading, stowage, carriage and discharge; and

(v) all necessary information will be provided to the Owners to enable the Owners to submit timely and accurate advance Cargo declarations.

(b) Bulk Cargo: Unless caused by the act, neglect or default of the Owners or their servants, agents or subcontractors:

(i) where bulk cargo is shipped and stowed other than in accordance with the Vessel's natural segregation, the Charterers shall be responsible for any resulting claim for commingling, contamination, spoiling, deterioration in quality or loss of cargo; and

(ii) where bulk cargo is to be delivered to more than one receiver or discharged at more than one berth or anchorage, other than in accordance with the Vessel's natural segregation, the Charterers shall be responsible for any resulting claim for short delivery or over-landing caused thereby, including any fines or legal costs.

(c) Part Cargo: Where the Cargo to be shipped under this Charter Party is less than a full cargo for the Vessel, the Owners shall be entitled to load additional or top-off cargo within the Vessel's natural segregation for their own account or that of other charterers, and such additional or top-off cargo may be loaded and/or discharged before or after the Charterers' Cargo, all as part of the contract voyage.

(d) Cargo Harmful to the Marine Environment: If the Cargo may be harmful to the marine environment according to the criteria of the relevant provisions of MARPOL Annex V, as amended from time to time, the removal, custody, storage and disposal of all Cargo residues (including hold washing water) shall be at the risk, responsibility and expense of the Charterers, and any resulting loss of time shall be compensated by the Charterers at the demurrage rate stated in Box 19.

(e) Lighterage: Unless stated otherwise in Box 13, the Charterers may require the Vessel to load and/or discharge Cargo from/into barges or lighters. Such transfer operations shall be at the Charterers' risk and responsibility, and the Charterers shall provide and pay for adequate fendering and any other necessary equipment, all to the reasonable satisfaction of the Master. If, at any time, in the Master's reasonable judgement the transfer operations are, or are likely to become, unsafe, the Master may order them to be suspended or discontinued in which event the Master shall have the right to order the barges or lighters away from the Vessel or to remove the Vessel. In the case of lighterage, the lighter shall be considered the relevant berth for the purposes of this Charter

Party.

4.Loading and Discharging

(a) The Charterers shall under the supervision of the Master but at their risk, responsibility and expense:

(i) load, tally, stow, trim and/or secure the Cargo, and take the Cargo from the holds and discharge it; and

(ii) ensure that the Vessel is left with Cargo properly stowed, trimmed and/or secured so as not to impair the Vessel's seaworthiness for the laden voyage and also for any shifting between loading berths, ports and places, and between discharging berths, ports and places. Any related expenses shall be for the Charterers' account and laytime or time on demurrage shall continue to count.

(b) (i) If a berth, mooring, anchorage or other location at which the Vessel is directed to load, discharge or lay by is such that the Owners may have to incur additional costs to ensure the continuing safety of the Vessel, including temporarily shifting away or hiring standby tugs, pilots or other external assistance, any such additional costs shall be for the account of the Charterers.

(ii) In the event that the Vessel has to vacate the berth during cargo operations for reasons of safety, the Charterers shall ensure that any Cargo then on board is safely stowed and secured at their risk, responsibility and expense.

(c) Cargo Handling Gear and Lighting: Unless the Vessel is gearless, or Box 16 states that the Vessel's gear shall not be used, the Owners shall provide free use of the Vessel's cargo-handling gear and sufficient power to operate the same. Unless caused or contributed to by the act or neglect of the Charterers' servants, agents or subcontractors, time actually lost by breakdown of the Vessel's cargo-handling gear or lack of sufficient power shall not count as laytime or time on demurrage. The Owners shall provide free use of lighting as on board.

(d) Stevedore Damage:

(i) The Charterers shall be responsible for stevedore damage (fair wear and tear excepted) to any part of the Vessel. The Charterers shall be liable for all costs for repairing such damage and for anytime lost thereby, which shall be paid at the demurrage rate stated in Box 19.

(ii) The Master or the Owners shall notify the Charterers or their agents and the stevedores of any damage as soon as reasonably possible, failing which the Charterers shall not be responsible for any such damage. Such notice shall describe the damage and shall invite the Charterers to appoint a surveyor to assess the extent of such damage.

(iii) Stevedore damage affecting seaworthiness shall be repaired without any delay before the Vessel sails from the port where such damage was caused or discovered or otherwise as required by the Vessel's Classification Society. Stevedore damage restricting the Vessel's trading capabilities shall be repaired before leaving the last port of discharge, failing which the Charterers shall be liable for any resulting losses. All other stevedore damage which is not repaired before leaving the last port of discharge shall be repaired by the Owners and settled by the Charterers on receipt of the Owners' supporting invoice.

5.Cargo Fumigation

(a) The Charterers shall have the option to fumigate the Cargo in the Vessel's holds in port and/or at anchorage and/or in transit. Such fumigation shall be performed always in accordance with all applicable IMO Recommendations as amended from time to time. Fumigation shall not be commenced without written confirmation from the Master that loading (including trimming and/or securing) is complete.

(b) Fumigation shall be at the Charterers' risk and responsibility. Any costs and expenses incurred in connection with or as a result of such fumigation, including but not limited to gas detection equipment, respiratory protective equipment and crew training, shall be for the Charterers' account. The Charterers shall indemnify the Owners for any liabilities, losses or costs arising out of or resulting from Cargo fumigation.

(c) If local authorities or IMO Recommendations require the crew to be accommodated ashore as a result of fumigation ordered by the Charterers, all costs and expenses reasonably incurred in connection thereto including, but not limited to, transportation, accommodation and victualling shall be for Charterers' account.

(d) At the discharging port or place all fumigant remains, residues and fumigation equipment shall be removed from the Vessel as soon as possible and disposed of by the Charterers at Charterers' risk, responsibility, cost and expense in accordance with MARPOL Annex V or any other applicable rules relating to the disposal of such materials.

(e) All time lost to the Owners in connection with or as a result of fumigation performed in accordance with subclause (a) above prior to commencement of laytime and/or after cessation of laytime or time on demurrage shall be considered as detention and shall be compensated by Charterers at the demurrage rate stated in Box 19. Any unused laytime shall be deducted from such detention, in which case any dispatch payable shall be deducted from such compensation.

(f) The exercise by the Charterers of the option to fumigate the Cargo under this Clause shall not be construed as evidence as to the condition of the Cargo at the time of shipment, and the Master or the Owners may not clause bills of lading solely by reason of fumigation.

6.Deck Cargo

(a) The Vessel shall not be required to load or carry Cargo on deck without the Owners' written agreement.

(b) If the Owners permit the Charterers to load or carry Cargo on deck, the Charterers shall:

(i) ensure, always to the reasonable satisfaction of the Master, that such carriage on deck does not exceed the permissible loads on the deck/hatch covers and will not impair the seaworthiness, stability and navigability of the Vessel;

(ii) provide and pay for any extra fittings that are required for deck or hatch cover Cargo; and

(iii) properly load, stow, dunnage, lash and secure such Cargo at their risk and expense under the supervision of the Master.

(c) Cargo that is carried on deck is carried at the Charterers' risk and the Owners are not to be responsible for loss or damage of whatsoever nature and howsoever arising irrespective of whether or not due to the Owners' negligence. The Charterers shall ensure that all bills of lading that are issued in relation to such deck Cargo shall record the fact that such Cargo has been shipped on deck.

7.Freight

(a) The freight shall be paid as stated in Boxes 14 and 15 and shall be paid in full without discount or deduction. Freight shall be paid in readily available and transferable funds and free of bank charges except as imposed by the Owners' bank.

(b) Freight other than lumpsum freight is earned progressively throughout the loading and is to be calculated in accordance with the quantity recorded in the Mate's Receipts.

(c) Lumpsum freight is earned on completion of loading.

(d) Freight is non-returnable, ship and/or Cargo lost or not lost.

(e) Neither the Owners nor the Master shall be required to sign or endorse bills of lading showing freight prepaid unless such freight has been received in full by the Owners.

8. ETA Notices

The Owners or the Master shall give notices of the Vessel's ETA to the Charterers and to the parties stated in Boxes 24 and 25, as appropriate, and shall notify them without unreasonable delay of any material change in the Vessel's position.

9. Notice of Readiness

(a) Subject to subclause (b) below, at each port or place of loading or discharge, Notice of Readiness shall be tendered in writing to the party(ies) identified in Boxes 26 and 27 respectively at any time, day or night, when the Vessel is in the loading or discharging berth, securely moored, and is in all respects ready to load or discharge. Before tendering Notice of Readiness, the Owners shall exercise due diligence to ensure that all holds in which Cargo is there to be loaded are clean, dry and in all respects suitable to receive the Cargo.

(b) If the loading or discharging berth is not designated or reachable on the Vessel's arrival at or off the port or place in question, the Vessel shall be entitled to tender Notice of Readiness from any waiting place that may be ordered by any relevant authority, or failing such order, at the customary anchorage, whether in free pratique or not, whether customs cleared or not. Laytime and time on demurrage shall then count, even if the holds were subsequently to fail the initial inspection under subclause (c) below, as if the Vessel were in berth and in all respects ready for loading or discharging, but time used in actually moving from such waiting place or customary anchorage to the loading or discharging berth shall not count as laytime or time on demurrage.

(c) If, after the commencement of laytime such holds are found on initial inspection not to be ready in all respects to load, only such time as is actually lost until the Vessel is found after a subsequent joint re-inspection to be ready to load shall not count as laytime or time on demurrage. However, if after a subsequent joint re-inspection the holds are found not to be ready upon the expiry of ninety-six (96) hours or by 23.59 hours local time on the cancellation date, whichever is the later, the Charterers shall have the option of terminating this Charter Party in writing within twelve (12) hours thereafter, provided the Vessel remains Cargo-free at the time the option is exercised. If the Charterers exercise their right of termination under this subclause, they shall compensate the Owners at the demurrage rate for all time spent waiting for a berth after tendering Notice of Readiness pursuant to subclause (b) above.

The provisions of this subclause and the exercise or non-exercise by the Charterers of their rights under this subclause shall not prejudice any claims which the Owners or the Charterers may have against each other.

(d) Notice of Readiness at the first or sole port or place of loading may be tendered prior to 00.01 hours local time at the loading port(s) or place(s) on the date stated in Box 18. However, laytime shall not begin before that time unless Cargo operations are sooner commenced.

(e) In the event that at any port or place of loading or discharge more than one Notice of Readiness is tendered, each such Notice of Readiness shall be deemed to have been tendered without prejudice to the validity of any preceding or subsequent Notice of Readiness.

10. Laytime

(a) The BIMCO Laytime Definitions for Charter Parties 2013 shall be deemed incorporated and form part of this Charter Party, except where inconsistent with its terms.

The expression "SHINC" shall mean that laytime is to run continuously and without interruption for public holidays or customary days of rest at the port or place in question, whether or not work is done at overtime rates.

The expression "SHEX" shall mean that there shall be excluded from laytime public holidays and customary days of rest at the port or place in question unless used.

(b) (i)* Separate laytime for loading and discharging:

The Cargo shall be loaded either within the number of running days or at the rate stated in Box 17(i), except to the extent that the actual loading is delayed or prevented by weather.

The Cargo shall be discharged either within the number of running days or at the rate stated in Box 17(ii), except to the extent that the actual discharging is delayed or prevented by weather.

Laytime for loading and discharging shall be non-reversible. (ii)* Total laytime for loading and discharging:

The cargo shall be loaded and discharged either within the total number of running days or at the rate stated in Box 17(iii), except to the extent that the actual loading and/or discharging is delayed or prevented by weather.

*Alternative (i) or (ii) shall apply as agreed in Box 17.

(c) Short-loading: Where laytime is to be calculated on the basis of the quantity of Cargo shipped and the Charterers have agreed to pay full freight in respect of any short-shipment, the laytime shall be calculated on the basis of the bill of lading quantity plus the quantity of such short-shipment.

11. Commencement of Laytime

Subject to subclause 9(d), laytime at each port or place of loading and discharging shall commence at the earlier of:

(a) commencement of Cargo operations; and

(b) (i) where SHINC terms apply, 14.00 hours local time if Notice of Readiness is tendered up to and including noon, and 08.00 hours local time on the next day if Notice of Readiness is tendered after noon but during office hours; or

(ii) where SHEX terms apply, 14.00 hours local time if Notice of Readiness is tendered up to and including noon on a working day, and 08.00 hours local time on the next working day if Notice of Readiness is tendered after noon, or, if Notice of Readiness is tendered on a non-working day, 14.00 hours local time on the next working day.

12. The Running of Laytime

(a) Shifting: In the event that the Vessel is required to load or discharge at a second or subsequent berth at the same port or place, or to shift out of and back to the same berth, other than for the Owners' purposes, shifting time between the berths shall count as laytime or time on demurrage and any related tug and pilot expenses shall be for the account of the Charterers.

(b) Environmental: Any delay in loading or discharging arising out of environmental or public health concerns relating to the Cargo shall count as laytime or time on demurrage, and all related expenses, including measures for dust suppression, shall be for the account of the Charterers.

(c) Completion of Cargo Operations: Laytime or time on demurrage shall run continuously until completion of Cargo operations, which includes the removal of any stevedores' equipment from the Vessel. The Charterers shall be permitted three hours after completion of cargo operations at each loading port or place in which to provide a full set of accurate Cargo documents. If the Vessel is prevented from sailing upon the expiry of that period as a result of awaiting a full set of accurate Cargo documents, laytime or time on demurrage shall recommence and run until such documents are received.

13. Demurrage and Dispatch

(a) Demurrage shall be payable by the Charterers at the rate stated in Box 19 and dispatch shall be payable by the Owners at half the demurrage rate on all laytime saved.

(b) Except as provided otherwise, demurrage shall accrue continuously and without interruption save where, and then only to the extent that, time is actually lost to the Charterers by the Vessel not being available to perform the service immediately required unless caused by the act or omission of the Charterers or their servants, agents or subcontractors.

(c) Demurrage shall fall due day by day and shall be payable upon receipt of the Owners' invoice.

14. Canceling

(a) Without prejudice to subclause (b) below, should the Vessel not have tendered Notice of Readiness at the first or sole port of loading in accordance with Clause 9 (Notice of Readiness) by 23.59 hours local time on the cancellation date stated in Box 18, the Charterers shall have the option of cancelling this Charter Party within forty-eight (48) hours after 23.59 hours local time on the cancellation date.

(b) Should the Owners anticipate that, despite the exercise of due diligence, the Vessel will not be able to tender such Notice of Readiness at the first or sole port or place of loading by 23.59 hours local time on the cancellation date, they shall notify the Charterers accordingly without delay, stating when the Vessel is expected to be able to tender Notice of Readiness and asking whether the Charterers will exercise their option of cancelling the Charter Party, or agree to a new cancellation date on 23.59 hours local time on the date notified by the Owners. Such option must be declared by the Charterers within forty-eight (48) hours after the receipt of the Owners' notice or by 23.59 hours local time on the cancellation date, whichever is the earlier. If the Charterers do not exercise their option of cancelling, then the proposed new cancellation date shall replace the cancellation date stated in Box 18. The provisions of this subclause (b) shall operate only once, and if the Vessel shall not have tendered Notice of Readiness in accordance with Clause 9 (Notice of Readiness) by 23.59 hours local time on such new cancellation date, the Charterers shall have the option of cancelling this Charter Party within forty-eight (48) hours after 23.59 hours local time on the new cancellation date.

(c) The provisions of this Clause and the exercise or non-exercise by the Charterers of their rights under this Clause shall not prejudice any claims which the Owners or the Charterers may have against each other.

15. Lien

The Owners shall have a lien on the Cargo and on all sub-freights payable in respect of the Cargo for freight, deadfreight, demurrage, general average contributions, salvage, claims for compensation or damages and for all other amounts due under or pursuant to this Charter Party and all costs of recovering same, including legal costs.

16. Suspension and Termination

(a) Without prejudice to Clause 15 or to any other rights or claims whatsoever that the Owners may have, should the Charterers fail to pay freight, deadfreight, demurrage or other compensation in accordance with the requirements of this Charter Party, the Owners shall be entitled at any time thereafter to suspend the performance of any and all of their obligations hereunder.

(b) If the Charterers fail either to rectify their failure to pay in full or to provide security for such sums in terms acceptable to the Owners within ninety six (96) hours of their receiving a notice from Owners to do so, the Owners shall be entitled to terminate this Charter Party at any time thereafter while such sums remain outstanding and/or to discharge the Cargo at any port or place, and such action shall not be considered to be a breach or deviation under any relevant bills of lading.

(c) The Charterers shall indemnify the Owners for all damages, losses, expenses or liabilities that they may incur as a result of the Owners exercising their rights under this Charter Party including any liability that the Owners may incur to third parties by doing so. The Charterers shall promptly provide appropriate security or substitute security to avoid any delays to the Vessel in the event of its actual or threatened arrest or detention. Compensation for time lost to the Owners shall be paid by the Charterers at the demurrage rate.

17. Strikes

(a) If at any time before commencement of loading the Cargo at the first or sole port or place of loading, there exists a strike or lockout that is likely to delay or prevent the actual loading or any part of it at any port or place of loading, the Owners may request the Charterers to affirm that laytime and time on demurrage shall count as if there were no strike or lockout. Unless the Charterers have made such affirmation in writing within twenty-four (24) hours, the Owners shall have the option of cancelling this Charter Party and any Notice of Readiness given during such period of twenty-four (24) hours shall not prejudice such right of cancellation. Where the Charterers have made such affirmation, subclause (b) below shall not apply to such strike or lockout.

(b) If at any time after commencement of loading the Cargo, strike(s) or lockout(s) delay or prevent the actual loading at any port or place of loading, any demurrage caused thereby shall be incurred at half rate for the first ten (10) cumulative days and thereafter (subject to subclause (c) below) at full rate.

(c) In any case, where strike(s) or lockout(s) delay or prevent the actual loading, at any port or place of loading, for a cumulative total delay of twenty-five (25) days, the Owners shall be entitled thereafter to be compensated at the higher of (i) a daily rate equivalent to the demurrage rate, and

(ii) the prevailing market hire rate plus bunkers consumed until completion of loading.

(d) If strike(s) or lockout(s) delay or prevent the actual discharging of the Cargo or any part of it, at any discharge port or place, any demurrage caused thereby shall be incurred at half rate for the first ten (10) cumulative days and thereafter at full rate until the end of the twenty fifth (25) cumulative day. Should discharge continue beyond the twenty fifth (25) cumulative day of delay, the Owners shall be entitled thereafter to be compensated at the higher of (i) a daily rate equivalent to the demurrage rate, and (ii) the prevailing market hire rate plus bunkers consumed until completion of discharge.

(e) All amounts due under this Clause shall be paid every seven (7) days unless otherwise agreed.

(f) Except as provided in this Clause, neither party shall be responsible for the consequences of strike(s) or lockout(s) which prevent or affect the actual loading or discharging of the Cargo.

18. General Exceptions Clause

Neither the Vessel nor the Owners nor the Charterers, nor their respective servants, agents or subcontractors, shall, unless otherwise expressly provided in this Charter Party, be responsible for loss of or damage or delay to or failure to supply, load, discharge or deliver the Cargo as a result of the following events unless they can reasonably be avoided or guarded against: Act of God; act of war; act of public enemies, act of pirates or assailing thieves; arrest or restraint of princes, rulers or people; seizure under legal process (other than when caused by breach of obligations relating to this Charter Party), provided that reasonable steps are taken to furnish adequate security promptly to release the Vessel or Cargo; floods; fires; blockades; riots; insurrections; civil commotions; earthquakes; explosions; infectious or contagious disease; or any other similar event. However, nothing in this Clause shall interrupt the running of laytime or time on demurrage nor relieve the Charterers of, nor diminish their obligation for, payment of any sum that is due to the Owners under this Charter Party.

19. Bills of Lading

The Master or the Vessel's agents, provided written authority (a copy of which is to be furnished to the Charterers) has been given by the Owners to the agents, shall, without prejudice to this Charter Party, sign bills of lading as presented in terms no less favourable to the carrier than those of CONGENBILL 2022 and always in conformity with the mate's receipts. The Charterers shall indemnify the Owners against all consequences or liabilities that may arise as a result of signing bills of lading to the extent that the provisions or contents of such bills of lading impose or result in the imposition on the carrier and/or the Owners of any exposure, liability or responsibility that is more onerous than those to which the Owners would have been subject had the claim been made against them under this Charter Party.

20. BIMCO Electronic Bills of Lading Clause 2014

(a) At the Charterers' option, bills of lading, waybills and delivery orders referred to in this Charter Party shall be issued, signed and transmitted in electronic form with the same effect as their paper equivalent.

(b) For the purpose of subclause (a) above the Owners shall subscribe to and use Electronic

(Paperless) Trading Systems as directed by the Charterers, provided such systems are approved by the International Group of P&I Clubs. Any fees incurred in subscribing to or for using such systems shall be for the Charterers' account.

(c) The Charterers agree to hold the Owners harmless in respect of any additional liability arising from the use of the systems referred to in subclause (b) above, to the extent that such liability does not arise from the Owners' negligence.

21. Classification and Insurance

The Owners shall ensure that:

(a) the Vessel is classed with the Classification Society stated in Box 5(iii); and

(b) the Vessel is insured for third party liabilities with the P&I Club or liability underwriter stated in Box 5(iv);

and that it will be so maintained throughout the term of this Charter Party unless agreed otherwise by the Charterers, such agreement not to be unreasonably withheld.

22. Liberty and Deviation

(a) The Vessel shall have liberty to sail with or without pilots, to tow or go to the assistance of vessels in distress, to deviate for the purpose of saving life or property and for any other purpose reasonably necessary for the safe continuation of the voyage, including calling at any place for bunkers, taking on board spares, stores or supplies, repairs to the Vessel, crew changes, landing of stowaways or persons rescued at sea, medical emergencies and ballast water exchange, and the Owners shall not be liable for any loss or damage (including delay) arising or resulting therefrom.

(b) This Clause shall be incorporated into any sub-charter and any bill of lading issued pursuant hereto.

23. Substitution

With the prior written consent of the Charterers, which shall not be unreasonably withheld, the Owners may nominate and provide a substitute vessel of materially similar characteristics within the laydays/cancelling spread stated in Box 18, provided that the Owners shall always remain responsible for the due performance of this Charter Party. Such substitute vessel shall become the Vessel for the purposes of this Charter Party.

24. Sub-let and Assignment

With the prior written consent of the Owners, which shall not be unreasonably withheld, the Charterers may sub-let or assign this Charter Party, provided that the Charterers shall always remain responsible for the due performance of this Charter Party.

25. Taxes and Dues

(a) On the Vessel: The Owners shall pay all dues, charges, duties and taxes customarily levied on the Vessel, howsoever the amount thereof may be assessed.

(b) On the Cargo: The Charterers shall pay all dues, charges, duties and taxes customarily levied on the Cargo, howsoever the amount thereof may be assessed.

(c) On freight: Unless otherwise agreed in Box 20, taxes levied or calculated on the freight shall be for the Charterers' account.

26. Agency

(a) Unless stated otherwise in Box 21, the Vessel will be consigned to agents to be nominated by the Charterers. Such agents will be appointed and paid by the Owners at the ports or places of loading and discharge, but shall in any and all matters relating to or arising out of or in connection with the cargo and its loading, discharge and delivery (including the preparation and presentation of bills of lading), be deemed to be the agents of the Charterers.

(b) Always subject to the terms of this Charter Party, the parties shall each be responsible for the act, neglect or default of their respective servants, agents and sub-contractors. Shippers and receivers shall be deemed to be the agents of the Charterers in the performance of any function which is the responsibility of the Charterers under this Charter Party.

(c) Unless otherwise agreed, the agents shall comply with the minimum quality standards that are prescribed by FONASBA (The Federation of National Associations of Ship Brokers and Agents), ISO (The International Organisation for Standardisation) or other equivalent quality standards.

27. Limitation of Liability

(a) Nothing contained in, or done or not done, under this Charter Party shall constitute a surrender or waiver of any right of limitation which might otherwise be available as a matter of law to the Owners, the Charterers, the Vessel, its registered or disponent owners, or the managers, operators, charterers, any person or party for whose act, neglect or default such parties may be liable, or the liability insurers of such parties.

(b) The Charterers shall ensure that the terms and conditions of access and use at any berth or place to which they may require the Vessel to proceed (unless expressly named in this Charter Party) shall not prejudice any such right of limitation and shall indemnify the Owners against any loss, damage or liability arising or resulting from failure to do so.

28. Protective Clauses

The New Jason Clause, Both-to-Blame Collision Clause and International Group of P&I Clubs/ BIMCO Himalaya Clause for Bills of Lading and Other Contracts 2014 as contained in CONGENBILL 2022 shall be deemed incorporated and form part of this Charter Party and shall be expressly incorporated in any bill of lading issued under this Charter Party.

29. General Average

General Average shall be adjusted, stated and settled in London, unless otherwise stated in Box 22, according to York-Antwerp Rules 2016.

Cargo's contribution to General Average shall be paid to the carrier even when such average is the result of a fault, neglect or error of the Master, Pilot or Crew.

30. BIMCO Ice Clause for Voyage Charter Parties 2005

The Vessel shall not be obliged to force ice but, subject to the Owners' approval having due regard to its size, construction and class, may follow icebreakers.

(a) Port of Loading:

(i) If at any time after setting out on the approach voyage the Vessel's passage is impeded by ice, or if on arrival the loading port is inaccessible by reason of ice, the Master or Owners shall notify the Charterers thereof and request them to nominate a safe and accessible alternative port.

If the Charterers fail within 48 hours, Sundays and holidays included, to make such nomination or agree to reckon laytime as if the port named in the contract were accessible or declare that they cancel the Charter Party, the Owners shall have the option of cancelling the Charter Party. In the event of cancellation by either party, the Charterers shall compensate the Owners for all proven loss of earnings under this Charter Party.

(ii) If at any loading port the Master considers that there is a danger of the Vessel being frozen in, and provided that the Master or Owners immediately notify the Charterers thereof, the Vessel may leave with Cargo loaded on board and proceed to the nearest safe and ice free place and there await the Charterers' nomination of a safe and accessible alternative port within 24 hours, Sundays and holidays excluded, of the Master's or Owners' notification. If the Charterers fail to nominate such alternative port, the vessel may proceed to any port(s), whether or not on the customary route for the chartered voyage, to complete with Cargo for the Owners' account.

(b) Port of Discharge:

(i) If the voyage to the discharging port is impeded by ice, or if on arrival the discharging port is inaccessible by reason of ice, the Master or Owners shall notify the Charterers thereof. In such case, the Charterers shall have the option of keeping the Vessel waiting until the port is accessible against paying compensation at the demurrage rate stated in Box 19 or of ordering the Vessel to a safe and accessible alternative port.

If the Charterers fail to make such declaration within 48 hours, Sundays and holidays included, of the Master or Owners having given notice to the Charterers, the Master may proceed without further notice to the nearest safe and accessible port and there discharge the Cargo.

(ii) If at any discharging port the Master considers that there is a danger of the Vessel being frozen in, and provided that the Master or Owners immediately notify the Charterers thereof, the Vessel may leave with Cargo remaining on board and proceed to the nearest safe and ice free place and there await the Charterers' nomination of a safe and accessible alternative port within 24 hours, Sundays and holidays excluded, of the Master's or Owners' notification. If the Charterers fail to nominate such alternative port, the vessel may proceed to the nearest safe and accessible port and there discharge the remaining Cargo.

(iii) On delivery of the Cargo other than at the port(s) named in the contract, all conditions of the bills of lading shall apply and the Vessel shall receive the same freight as if discharge had been at the original port(s) of destination, except that if the distance of the substituted port(s) exceeds 100 nautical miles, the freight on the Cargo delivered at the substituted port(s) shall be increased proportionately.

31. BIMCO ISPS/MTSA Clause for Voyage Charter Parties 2005

(a) (i) The Owners shall comply with the requirements of the International Code for the Security of Ships and of Port Facilities and the relevant amendments to Chapter XI of SOLAS (ISPS Code) relating to the Vessel and "the Company" (as defined by the ISPS Code). If trading to or from the United States or passing through United States waters, the Owners shall also comply with the requirements of the US Maritime Transportation Security Act 2002 (MTSA) relating to the Vessel and the "Owner" (as defined by the MTSA).

(ii) Upon request the Owners shall provide the Charterers with a copy of the relevant

International Ship Security Certificate (or the Interim International Ship Security Certificate) and the full style contact details of the Company Security Officer (CSO).

(iii) Loss, damages, expense or delay (excluding consequential loss, damages, expense or delay) caused by failure on the part of the Owners or "the Company"/"Owner" to comply with the requirements of the ISPS Code/MTSA or this Clause shall be for the Owners' account, except as otherwise provided in this Charter Party.

(b) (i) The Charterers shall provide the Owners and the Master with their full style contact details and, upon request, any other information the Owners require to comply with the ISPS Code/MTSA.

(ii) Loss, damages or expense (excluding consequential loss, damages or expense) caused by failure on the part of the Charterers to comply with this Clause shall be for the Charterers' account, except as otherwise provided in this Charter Party, and any delay caused by such failure shall count as laytime or time on demurrage.

(c) Provided that the delay is not caused by the Owners' failure to comply with their obligations under the ISPS Code/MTSA, the following shall apply:

(i) Notwithstanding anything to the contrary provided in this Charter Party, the Vesselshall be entitled to tender Notice of Readiness even if not cleared due to applicable security regulations or measures imposed by a port facility or any relevant authority under the ISPS Code/MTSA.

(ii) Any delay resulting from measures imposed by a port facility or by any relevant authority under the ISPS Code/MTSA shall count as laytime or time on demurrage, unless such measures result solely from the negligence of the Owners, Master or crew or the previous trading of the Vessel, the nationality of the crew or the identity of the Owners' managers.

(d) Notwithstanding anything to the contrary provided in this Charter Party, any costs or expenses whatsoever solely arising out of or related to security regulations or measures required by the port facility or any relevant authority in accordance with the ISPS Code/MTSA including, but not limited to, security guards, launch services, vessel escorts, security fees or taxes and inspections, shall be for the Charterers' account, unless such costs or expenses result solely from the negligence of the Owners, Master or crew or the previous trading of the Vessel, the nationality of the crew or the identity of the Owners' managers. All measures required by the Owners to comply with the Ship Security Plan shall be for the Owners' account.

(e) If either party makes any payment which is for the other party's account according to this Clause, the other party shall indemnify the paying party.

32. BIMCO Sanctions Clause for Voyage Charter Parties 2020

(a) For the purposes of this Clause:

"Sanctioned Activity" means any activity, service, carriage, trade or voyage subject to sanctions imposed by a Sanctioning Authority.

"Sanctioning Authority" means the United Nations, European Union, United Kingdom, United States of America or any other applicable competent authority or government.

"Sanctioned Party" means any persons, entities, bodies, or vessels designated by a Sanctioning Authority.

(b) Owners warrant that at the date of this Charter Party and throughout its duration they, the registered owners, bareboat charterers, intermediate disponent owners, managers, the Vessel and any substitute are not a Sanctioned Party.

(c) Charterers warrant that at the date of this Charter Party and throughout its duration they and any subcharterers, shippers, receivers and cargo interests are not a Sanctioned Party.

(d) If at any time either party is in breach of subclause (b) or (c) above then the party not in breach may terminate and/or claim damages resulting from the breach.

(e) If performance of this Charter Party involves a Sanctioned Party or a Sanctioned Activity, without prejudice to any other rights that may be available in subclause (d) above:

(i) if loading has not commenced, Owners may cancel this Charter Party; or

(ii) if the voyage or the loading has commenced, Owners may refuse to proceed and discharge any cargo already loaded at any safe port or place of their choice (including the port or place of loading) in complete fulfilment of this Charter Party,

provided always that if this Charter Party provides that loading and/or discharging is to take place within a range of ports or places that do not involve a Sanctioned Party or a Sanctioned Activity, Owners must first request Charterers to nominate an alternative port or place and may cancel the Charter Party or refuse to proceed on the voyage only if such nomination is not made within forty-eight (48) hours after the request.

(f) If in compliance with subclause (e) above anything is done or not done, such shall not be deemed a deviation, but shall be considered due fulfilment of this Charter Party.

(g) Charterers shall indemnify Owners against any and all claims brought by the owners of the cargo and/or the holders of bills of lading, waybills or other documents evidencing contracts of carriage and/or subcharterers against Owners by reason of Owners' compliance with such alternative voyage orders or delivery of the cargo in accordance with subclause (e) above.

(h) Charterers shall procure that this Clause shall be incorporated into all sub-charters and bills of lading, waybills or other documents evidencing contracts of carriage issued pursuant to this Charter Party.

33. BIMCO War Risks Clause for Voyage Chartering (VOYWAR 2013)

(a) For the purpose of this Clause, the words:

(i) "Owners" shall include the shipowners, bareboat charterers, disponent owners, managers or other operators who are charged with the management of the Vessel, and the Master; and (ii) "War Risks" shall include any actual, threatened or reported: War, act of war, civil war or hostilities; revolution; rebellion; civil commotion; warlike operations; laying of mines; acts of piracy and/or violent robbery and/or capture/seizure (hereinafter "Piracy"); acts of terrorists; acts of hostility or malicious damage; blockades (whether imposed against all vessels or imposed selectively against vessels of certain flags or ownership, or against certain cargoes or crews or otherwise howsoever), by any person, body, terrorist or political group, or the government of any state or territory whether recognised or not, which, in the reasonable judgement of the Master and/or the Owners, may be dangerous or may become dangerous to the Vessel, cargo, crew or other persons on board the Vessel.

(b) If at any time before the Vessel commences loading, it appears that, in the reasonable judgement of the Master and/or the Owners, performance of the Contract of Carriage, or any part of it, may expose the Vessel, cargo, crew or other persons on board the Vessel to War Risks, the Owners may give notice to the Charterers cancelling this Contract of Carriage, or may refuse to perform such part of it as may expose the Vessel, cargo, crew or other persons on board the Vessel to War Risks; provided always that if this Contract of Carriage provides that loading or discharging is to take place within a range of ports, and at the port or ports nominated by the Charterers the Vessel, cargo, crew, or other persons on board the Vessel may be exposed to War Risks, the Owners shall first require the Charterers to nominate any other safe port which lies within the range for loading or discharging, and may only cancel this Contract of Carriage if the Charterers shall not have nominated such safe port or ports within 48 hours of receipt of notice of such requirement.

(c) The Owners shall not be required to continue to load cargo for any voyage, or to sign bills of lading, waybills or other documents evidencing contracts of carriage for any port or place, or to proceed or continue on any voyage, or on any part thereof, or to proceed through any canal or waterway, or to proceed to or remain at any port or place whatsoever, where it appears, either after the loading of the cargo commences, or at any stage of the voyage thereafter before the discharge of the cargo is completed, that, in the reasonable judgement of the Master and/or the Owners, the Vessel, cargo, crew or other persons on board the Vessel may be exposed to War Risks. If it should so appear, the Owners may by notice request the Charterers to nominate a safe port for the discharge of the cargo or any part thereof, and if within 48 hours of the receipt of such notice, the Charterers shall not have nominated such a port, the Owners may discharge the cargo at any safe port of their choice (including the port of loading) in complete fulfilment of the Contract of Carriage. The Owners shall be entitled to recover from the Charterers the extra expenses of such discharge and, if the discharge takes place at any port other than the loading port, to receive the full freight as though the cargo had been carried to the discharging port and if the extra distance exceeds 100 miles, to additional freight which shall be the same percentage of the freight contracted for as the percentage which the extra distance represents to the distance of the normal and customary route, the Owners having a lien on the cargo for such expenses and freight.

(d) If at any stage of the voyage after the loading of the cargo commences, it appears that, in the reasonable judgement of the Master and/or the Owners, the Vessel, cargo, crew or other persons on board the Vessel may be exposed to War Risks on any part of the route (including any canal or waterway) which is normally and customarily used in a voyage of the nature contracted for, and there is another longer route to the discharging port, the Owners shall give notice to the Charterers that this route will be taken. In this event the Owners shall be entitled, if the total extra distance exceeds 100 miles, to additional freight which shall be the same percentage of the freight contracted for as the percentage which the extra distance represents to the distance of the normal and customary route.

(e) (i) The Owners may effect War Risks insurance in respect of the Vessel and any additional insurances that Owners reasonably require in connection with War Risks and the premiums therefor shall be for their account.

(ii) If, pursuant to the Charterers' orders, or in order to fulfil the Owners' obligation under this Charter Party, the Vessel proceeds to or through any area or areas exposed to War Risks, the Charterers shall reimburse to the Owners any additional premiums required by the Owners' insurers. If the Vessel discharges all of her cargo within an area subject to additional premiums as herein set forth, the Charterers shall further reimburse the Owners for the actual additional premiums paid from completion of discharge until the Vessel leaves such area or areas. The Owners shall leave the area or areas as soon as possible after completion of discharge.

(iii) All payments arising under this Sub-clause (e) shall be settled within fifteen (15) days of receipt of Owners' supported invoices.

(f) The Vessel shall have liberty:

(i) to comply with all orders, directions, recommendations or advice as to departure, arrival, routes, sailing in convoy, ports of call, stoppages, destinations, discharge of cargo, delivery, or in any other way whatsoever, which are given by the government of the nation under whose flag the Vessel sails, or other government to whose laws the Owners are subject, or any other government of any state or territory whether recognised or not, body or group whatsoever acting with the power to compel compliance with their orders or directions;

(ii) to comply with the requirements of the Owners' insurers under the terms of the Vessel's insurance(s);

(iii) to comply with the terms of any resolution of the Security Council of the United Nations, the effective orders of any other Supranational body which has the right to issue and give the same, and with national laws aimed at enforcing the same to which the Owners are subject, and to obey the orders and directions of those who are charged with their enforcement;

(iv) to discharge at any alternative port any cargo or part thereof which may expose the Vessel to being held liable as a contraband carrier;

(v) to call at any alternative port to change the crew or any part thereof or other persons on board the Vessel when there is reason to believe that they may be subject to internment, imprisonment, detention or similar measures;

(vi) where cargo has not been loaded or has been discharged by the Owners under any provisions of this Clause, to load other cargo for the Owners' own benefit and carry it to any other port or ports whatsoever, whether backwards or forwards or in a contrary direction to the ordinary or customary route.

(g) The Charterers shall indemnify the Owners for claims arising out of the Vessel proceeding in accordance with any of the provisions of subclauses (b) to (f) above which are made under any bills of lading, waybills or other documents evidencing contracts of carriage.

(h) When acting in accordance with any of the provisions of subclauses (b) to (f) of this Clause anything is done or not done, such shall not be deemed to be a deviation, but shall be considered as due fulfilment of the Contract of Carriage.

34. BIMCO Piracy Clause for Single Voyage Charter Parties 2013

(a) If, after entering into this Charter Party, in the reasonable judgement of the Master and/or the Owners, any port, place, area or zone, or any waterway or canal (hereinafter "Area") on any part of the route which is normally and customarily used on a voyage of the nature contracted for becomes dangerous, or the level of danger increases, to the Vessel, cargo, crew or other persons on board the Vessel due to any actual, threatened or reported acts of piracy and/or violent robbery and/or capture/seizure (hereinafter "Piracy"), the Owners shall be entitled to take a reasonable alternative route to the discharging port and, if they so decide, immediately give notice to the Charterers that such route will be taken. Should the Vessel be within any such place as aforesaid which only becomes dangerous, after entry, it shall be at liberty to leave it.

(b) In any event, if the Vessel proceeds to or through an Area exposed to the risk of Piracy the Owners shall have the liberty:

(i) to take reasonable preventative measures to protect the Vessel, crew and cargo including but not limited to re-routeing within the Area, proceeding in convoy, using escorts, avoiding day or night navigation, adjusting speed or course, or engaging security personnel and/or deploying equipment on or about the Vessel (including embarkation/disembarkation);

(ii) to comply with the requirements of the Owners' insurers under the terms of the Vessel's insurance(s);

(iii) to comply with all orders, directions, recommendations or advice given by the Government of the Nation under whose flag the Vessel sails, or other Government to whose laws the Owners are subject, or any other Government, body or group (including military authorities) whatsoever acting with the power to compel compliance with their orders or directions; and

(iv) to comply with the terms of any resolution of the Security Council of the United Nations, the effective orders of any other Supranational body which has the right to issue and give the same, and with national laws aimed at enforcing the same to which the Owners are subject, and to obey the orders and directions of those who are charged with their enforcement.

(c) This Clause shall be incorporated into any bills of lading, waybills or other documents evidencing contracts of carriage (hereinafter "Contracts of Carriage") issued pursuant to this Charter Party. The Charterers shall indemnify the Owners against all consequences or liabilities that may arise from the Master signing Contracts of Carriage as presented to the extent that the terms of such Contracts of Carriage impose or result in the imposition of more onerous liabilities upon the Owners than those assumed by the Owners under this Clause.

(d) If in compliance with this Clause anything is done or not done, such shall not be deemed a deviation, but shall be considered as due fulfilment of this Charter Party. In the event of a conflict between the provisions of this Clause and any implied or express provision of the Charter Party, this Clause shall prevail.

35. Brokerage

A brokerage commission at the rate(s) stated in Box 23 on the freight, deadfreight and demurrage received by the Owners under this Charter Party shall be paid by the Owners to the party (ies) stated in Box 23.

36. Notices

For the purpose of giving notices, except for notices given under the BIMCO Law and Arbitration Clause 2020, the Owners' contact details are stated in Box 28 and the Charterers' contact details are stated in Box 29. Any notice or approval to be given under this Charter Party shall be in writing.

37. BIMCO Law and Arbitration Clause 2020

The Parties have been given a choice of law and arbitration alternatives in Box 32 and this is the clause that shall apply.

(a) This contract shall be governed by and construed in accordance with English law and any dispute arising out of or in connection with this contract shall be referred exclusively to arbitration in London in accordance with the Arbitration Act 1996 or any statutory modification or re-enactment thereof save to the extent necessary to give effect to the provisions of this clause. The seat of arbitration shall be London even where any hearing takes place in another jurisdiction.

(b) The reference shall be to three (3) arbitrators unless the Parties agree otherwise.

(c) The arbitration shall be conducted in accordance with the London Maritime Arbitrators Association (LMAA) Terms.

(d) In cases where neither the claim nor any counterclaim exceeds the sum of USD 100,000 (or such other sum as the Parties may agree) the arbitration shall be conducted in accordance with the LMAA Small Claims Procedure.

In cases where the claim or any counterclaim exceeds the sum agreed for the LMAA Small Claims Procedure and neither the claim nor any counterclaim exceeds the sum of USD 400,000 (or such other sum as the Parties may agree) the Parties may agree that the arbitration shall be conducted in accordance with the LMAA Intermediate Claims Procedure.

(e) The terms and procedures referred to in subclauses (c) and (d) above shall be those current at the time when the arbitration proceedings are commenced.

(f) Any and all notices and communications in relation to any arbitration proceedings under this clause, including commencement notices and appointment of arbitrators, shall be treated as effectively served from the date and time the e-mail was sent if sent by e-mail to the e-mail addresses below:

Owners

E-mail address(es) for receipt of notices and communications on behalf of the Owners:

Charterers

E-mail address(es) for receipt of notices and communications on behalf of the Charterers:

Either party shall be entitled to change and/or add to the e-mail addresses above by sending notice of change to the other party at the above address (or, if previously amended by notice, the relevant amended addresses).

Nothing in this Clause shall prevent any notice and communication in relation to any arbitration proceedings in connection with this contract being served by other effective means.

38. Original Charter Party

Upon demand, each party shall promptly provide to the other a duly executed original of this Charter Party with each page initialled by the signatory(ies) thereto.